Blackball, the Black Sox, and the Babe

# Blackball, the Black Sox, and the Babe

## Baseball's Crucial 1920 Season

### ROBERT C. COTTRELL

McFarland & Company, Inc., Publishers
*Jefferson, North Carolina, and London*

**Library of Congress Cataloguing-in-Publication Data**

Cottrell, Robert C., 1950–
    Blackball, the Black Sox, and the Babe: baseball's crucial 1920
season / Robert C. Cottrell.
      p.     cm.
    Includes bibliographical references and index.
    ISBN 0-7864-1164-3 (softcover : 50# alkaline paper) ∞
    1. Ruth, Babe, 1895–1948.   2. Foster, Rube, 1879–1930.
3. Landis, Kenesaw Mountain, 1866–1944.   4. Weaver, Buck,
1890–1956.   5. Baseball players — United States–Biography.
I. Title.
GV865.A1C66   2002
796.357'092'2 — dc21             2001044774
[B]

British Library cataloguing data are available

Manufactured in the United States of America

*On the cover:* Buck Weaver *(National Baseball Hall of Fame Library)*

*McFarland & Company, Inc., Publishers*
  *Box 611, Jefferson, North Carolina 28640*
  *www.mcfarlandpub.com*

WEST END

To my sisters:
Edie Kreisler,
Sharon Gerson,
and Ruth Schneider

# Acknowledgments

Having completed a series of works that dealt with committed and controversial figures who were associated with heated political and social issues, I cast about for a book idea that involved another longtime passion of mine: baseball. The national pastime, after all, had piqued my initial love of both history and statistics. At home and in dusty libraries, I had scoured through all sorts of magazines and newspapers and learned, well before my classmates, how to compute batting averages and earned run averages. Thus, crafting *Blackball, the Black Sox, and the Babe* was a labor of love for me and a return to my roots as well.

Fortunately and somewhat surprisingly, a host of friends and colleagues in the academic realm proved wonderfully supportive of this enterprise. I even received a bit of funding from my workplace, California State University, Chico, along with a sabbatical leave to complete the book. I'm particularly appreciative of the support afforded to me by Randy Wonsong and Dale Steiner. Dale was enthusiastic about this project when I first broached it with him; he continued to champion it all along.

Other professionals helped out, in their own fashion. The archival staffs at the Chicago Historical Society, the *Sporting News* Archives in St. Louis, and, most all, the National Baseball Hall of Fame Library were a delight to work with. At CSUC, the interlibrary loan folk, George Thompson and Jo Ann Bradley, were characteristically generous, good-humored, and efficient, all at the same time.

As I took off for my east coast ventures, my wife Sue cheered me on, while my daughter Jordan was there to greet her daddy when he returned. Writing is a solitary enterprise, but it seldom seems that way in my household.

Finally, I've dedicated this book to my sisters — three in all!— because of who they are and what they mean to me. They probably still remember their disheveled brother playing catch as he hurled his baseball at the front porch on Hermosa Street; they also undoubtedly recall the thousands of baseball cards he wishes he still had.

# Contents

# Introduction

The year 1920 proved momentous for four of the most important figures ever to grace American baseball diamonds.

In early January, news reports indicated that southpaw pitching ace turned slugger George Herman "Babe" Ruth had been traded from the Boston Red Sox to the New York Yankees. Thus was the stage set for the emergence of organized sports' most storied franchise. During his first year in pinstripes, Ruth shattered his own home run record, established just the previous season, ushering in a long-ball revolution that transformed the national game. His trade also set in motion — or so many who frequented Fenway Park would later charge — the "curse of the Bambino." The Red Sox, who had won four World Series championships in the 1910s alone, three with Ruth as an integral part of their regular season line-ups, ended the twentieth century with no additional title.

In February, former great blackball pitcher Andrew "Rube" Foster, manager of the Chicago American Giants, helped to establish the Negro National League. Long envisioned by African American owners, field bosses, and journalists, the new circuit provided a league for black players who were denied the right to compete in organized baseball. It was a venue for some of America's greatest ballplayers who were not allowed to play against Ruth, Ty Cobb, Walter Johnson, Pete Alexander, Rogers Hornsby, and other stars of the era, simply because of the color of their skin. Performing for teams like the American Giants, the Detroit Stars, and the Kansas City Monarchs, players like

Oscar Charleston, Cristobal Torriente, John Henry Lloyd, Smokey Joe Williams, and Bullet Joe Rogan set the stage for future baseball giants. The next wave of black superstars, which included Satchel Paige, Josh Gibson, and Buck Leonard, in turn enabled younger players like Jackie Robinson, Willie Mays, and Hank Aaron to display their athletic prowess in front of scouts who steered them into organized baseball.

In November 1920, the man who had done as much as any individual to ensure that racial barriers remained in place, Federal Judge Kenesaw Mountain Landis, had been appointed commissioner of major league baseball. Baseball magnates and reporters alike were determined to refurbish the game's image, after word unfolded that the previous year's World Series had been fixed. They turned to Judge Landis, who had established a reputation as both a foe of John D. Rockefeller's Standard Oil, anarcho-syndicalist Wobblies, and anti-war proponents, and the man who had effectively quashed the Federal League's anti-trust suit against major league ball. To his credit, Landis strove to clean up his beloved game, but he administered justice as commissioner the same way he had presided over his Chicago courtroom: passionately and erratically. Furthermore, Landis, until his death in 1944, presided over the game with an iron hand, working to curb barnstorming affairs between white and black competitors and dashing Foster's hopes that his blackball dynasty could become Chicago's third major league squad.

Landis also squashed the dreams of George "Buck" Weaver, the American League's finest third baseman and one of eight Chicago White Sox who, in 1920, were accused of having conspired to fix the 1919 World Series. Suspended from the game at the tail end of the 1920 campaign, Weaver, along with such stars as pitcher Eddie Cicotte and outfielder "Shoeless" Joe Jackson, eventually was declared innocent of criminal charges in a Chicago courthouse but was banished from organized baseball by its new boss. This was true despite the fact that Weaver, in contrast to the other so-called Black Sox, played superbly throughout the championship fare against the Cincinnati Reds. Weaver, however, in Landis's eyes, was culpable of "guilty knowledge" of the fix that his teammates carried out.

Thus 1920 changed forever the lives of the four men examined in this volume: Babe Ruth, Rube Foster, Kenesaw Mountain Landis, and Buck Weaver. Through their stories, the book provides a prism to view the transformations that both baseball and America experienced. The nation had recently welcomed its men home from trench warfare in Europe, only to be confronted with social, economic, and political alterations of all sorts. The threat of change, as represented by political, labor, and cultural radicals; by proud, even defiant blacks; and by working, somewhat emancipated women, frightened many and led to heavyhanded repression and Americanization campaigns. Not surprisingly, baseball, which many viewed as sacrosanct, was seen as a repository of time-honored American values and a respite from the cares of a society that was undergoing urbanization, industrialization, and massive immigration. When news broke of the scandal involving America's greatest sporting event, many responded with dismay and anger.

The furor that threatened to unfold was muted somewhat because of Babe Ruth's record-shattering performance. It also was tempered by the decision to place Judge Landis, with his carefully honed image of moral rectitude, at the helm of organized baseball. Merely an afterthought for most was Rube Foster's own historic undertaking and the often exquisite athleticism exhibited by black baseball players. Not so was the tale of Buck Weaver, who had been viewed as the embodiment of competitiveness and team play but whose image was irreparably tarnished by his involvement with the Black Sox scandal. So it is that Weaver, in contrast to the other three subjects of this collective biography — who have all been ushered into baseball's Hall of Fame in Cooperstown — has never received a single vote for entrance into the game's Valhalla.

# CHAPTER ONE

# *America's Greatest Game*

As early as the 1850s, Henry Chadwick, a transplanted Englishman, referred to baseball as America's "national pastime." In a public address three decades later, Mark Twain, the nation's greatest writer, asserted that "baseball is the very symbol, the outward and visible expression of the drive and push and rush and struggle of the raging, tearing, booming nineteenth century." Increasingly taken for granted was the widespread belief that baseball was indeed "the American national game." So too, surprisingly — given its early, checkered past — was the sense that baseball was largely immune to the corruption that had crippled other sports. In the pages of the recently established *Baseball Magazine*, editorialists in early 1909 highlighted the twin themes of the game's epochal importance and wholesome essence:

> We are striving to unite honesty and manliness with the great gospel of being a man of the pure, free out-doors. Our motto is: Go out into the God-given air and then be a manly, manful man. We are devoted to all healthy, wholesome forms of exercise. Baseball, football, running, jumping and the rest of them are all grand, good things and help to make our men strong and hearty — the kingly representatives of a glorious country. And we are proud to be able to say that it is our privilege to promote these health-giving pastimes, and to further the noble, cause of Clean, Honest Athletics.

However, it was baseball that purportedly stood as "the Greatest of All Games ... the grand national game."[1]

5

In that same issue, the Reverend George Landor Perin explained why he liked baseball. While only the athlete could play the game well, Perin declared, "anyone ... can enjoy it and enjoy it fully." Major league ball, he pointed out, was "played honestly. ... Among the intelligent and the fair-minded there is no suspicion that games are being 'fixed' or 'thrown.'" Rather, professional baseball was genuinely competitive, its outcome uncertain, requiring "strength and skill and wit." Like no other sport, it melded "athletic strength ... skill ... intelligence;" it also involved team play, which all Americans supposedly strove for. One month later, New York Giant pitching ace Christy Mathewson christened baseball "the greatest sport in the world," and indicated that its stature was growing yearly. Baseball, he contended, was increasingly becoming "a thinking game" and "a worthy profession" supported by "the best men and the keenest minds in all the country." Moreover, baseball afforded "unlimited opportunities to a young man of ability who is willing to work hard and conscientiously." Happiest of all, Mathewson exclaimed, "a still better and brighter era is yet to come."[2]

A similar sentiment was expressed by none other than Walter Camp, who was deemed "the Father of Football" and devised many of its initial rules, thereby ensuring its unique American quality. Writing in *The Century Magazine* in April 1910, Camp termed baseball "typical and characteristic of its people — rapid, exciting, with no long-drawn-out delays." Camp did underscore a problem that was hardly unique to baseball: how to balance offense and defense. Calling for an expansion of fair territory, Camp insisted that "the public likes to see the ball hit." Concluding his ode to baseball, the man who first selected All-American teams in college football declared,

> There is no sport that gives an opportunity for so many of our younger boys to enjoy exciting, skilful, and developing exercise. In fact, to put it concisely, there is no game so well adapted to the American boy and man, player and spectator, as the one which had its small beginnings seventy years ago, and which has come through time and stress up to its present standing in the hearts of an American people.[3]

In the October 1910 issue of *Baseball Magazine*, W. A. Phelon suggested heading for the ballpark if one wanted to partake of "the greatest display of pure democracy that can be found in any nation, any city, any gathering." There, he said, the poor and the rich mingled "on even footing," while the laborer spoke easily with his stern boss. A baseball stadium was "the one spot where the nations meet and mix on equal terms, where pride of race and birth and ancestry are laid aside and the brotherhood of man holds full, untrammeled sway." Indeed, "the ball field is the real crucible, the melting-pot wherein the rival races are being mixed, combined and molded to the standard of real citizenship and the requirements of the true American." Thus, baseball "can be regarded as the greatest of all agents for the promotion of a pure democracy."[4]

* * *

During the midst of the general celebratory treatment of "our national sport," a small number of sportswriters began to highlight issues that tainted both the game and the American landscape. Pointing to the series in the spring of 1911 that pitted major leaguers against Cuban ballplayers, A. D. Roberds and David L. Belding recognized that the islanders often had more than held their own against top American teams and stars. The poor showings of many American competitors, including the 1910 world champion Philadelphia Athletics, induced Roberds to suggest that overconfidence—which he stated was "perhaps a racial fault"—might have played a factor. Belding understood the rationale behind American League President Ban Johnson's recent announcement that similar series would not be allowed in the future. The shellacking of the A's "by some hitherto unknown teams on an alien soil" hardly served the commercial interests of "the National Game."[5]

Roberds acknowledged the sportsmanship of the Cuban players and the graciousness of the fans, as exemplified by the outpouring of appreciation for Detroit Tiger outfielder Ty Cobb, reputed to be—and correctly so—a notorious racist. Having noted that American teams had suffered defeat after defeat on the island during the past several years, Roberds then pointed to white Cubans who were currently flourishing in the minor leagues. This fact, and the play of so many others, had led to suggestions that "only ... color" had prevented many Cubans from attaining big league tryouts. Various Cuban ballplayers, Roberds asserted, "would shine with equal brilliancy" on American playing fields "were it not for that color line." No doubt, "there are four or five pitchers in the Cuban League who would be quickly snapped up by astute managers, were it not for their smoky skin." Pitchers like Jose Mendez and Bombin Pedroso, among others, possessed "whips that have puzzled some of the best hitters the United States could send to Cuba." However, Roberds reflected, "all have too dark a skin to be allowed across that color line—but they can play ball, all of them, and a club that beats them generally realizes that it has been in real ball game."[6]

In February 1912, William A. Phelon revisited the issue of interracial baseball following more successful encounters by the 1911 world champion Athletics and the National League pennant winning New York Giants. After the A's had taken five out of nine contests and the Giants eight of twelve, Phelon exulted: "This shows that great as the dark athletes may be, a big league team that goes down there with anything like its full strength, and pays attention to business, can defeat them." To Phelon, "the charm of the Cubans" did not reside in their athletic prowess but rather "their glorious hospitality, the splendid fashion in which they treat any stranger who comes to them franked with the credentials of good fellowship. They have the art of hospitality down to a fine point, and the way they entertain you can find few parallels." Phelon called the Cuban ballplayers "a great lot of fellows, even the black ones being the most polite and courteous athletes anyone could wish to see."[7]

Three months later, Phelon again discussed baseball in Cuba, or, as *Baseball Magazine* put it, the emergence of "baseball as the International world game." Phelon waxed eloquent about Mendez, terming him "a big league pitcher, there is no doubt about it. He has the goods, and cinches his class by exhibitions of fielding and batting such as few American pitchers ever dream of giving." This "remarkable" hurler who was "a little blacker than two aces of spade," Phelon stated, was "every bit as classy as Walter Johnson, good people, believe me." Phelon admitted that "the racial problem ... is a hard thing to deal with in regard to the Cuban ball players." Most were "black, jet black," with their "star battery performers ... nearly all Africans of the darkest shade." The white Cubans, including Armando Marsans and Rafael Almeida, who were playing in the United States, were top-flight but not better than many of their black countrymen. It was clear, Phelon now acknowledged, that the Cuban squads "rank right up with the best, despite the talk about 'joy trips' and 'short-handed' clubs." Unfortunately, however, the black players prevented Cuban teams from attaining "full recognition and proper welcome in the States," and thus a move was apparently underfoot to produce top white athletes to supplant "the sable warriors." Still, the blacks kept triumphing on the playing field, Phelon reported, while remaining "an exceptionally well-behaved and courteous set of colored men." Thus, "it is hard to see how they can be elbowed off the diamond."[8]

* * *

The long-time editor of *Baseball Magazine*, F. C. Lane — who seldom mentioned anything about black players during this era — proclaimed that "baseball is the King of Sports." Referring to the most recent World Series, Lane asserted that baseball had "grown by leaps and bounds," even attaining considerable popularity overseas. Comparing the national pastime with football — "its greatest rival" — Lane praised the gridiron sport but claimed "it cannot wholly equal baseball in the affections of the community." Baseball had thrived to a considerable extent, Lane pointed out, because "it is a poor man's game. Its democracy, where all classes meet on an equal footing in grandstand and bleachers, has endeared it to a nation which is founded and reared on democratic sentiment." While professionals played organized baseball, Lane contended, spectators could enjoy it for "a nominal sum" only.[9]

Nevertheless, Lane and a few other writers were beginning to examine another issue that threatened the professional game's very essence. Professional ballplayers and promoters, *The Chicago Tribune*'s I. B. Sanborn acknowledged in early 1912, were "not better and not worse than any other similar group of men." Nevertheless, baseball was "honest," Sanborn insisted, "because it cannot be fixed or made dishonest as long as there are honest men identified with it in any way. In that it differs from practically every other professional sport, and in that respect it differs from almost any line of business." No one could be certain when or if a ball would be rapped to a particular infielder or outfielder. No pitcher could intentionally lose a game, Sanborn wrote, unless his manager were also involved in the fix. And nothing of that sort would be possible without teammates getting wind of what was transpiring. Furthermore, within "an hour or a day afterward everybody would know it, for it is impossible to keep those things hidden away from the searchlight to which baseball is constantly subjected." That scrutiny helped to ensure that the game remained true, Sanborn declared, "but the greater credit is due to the glorious uncertainty of the game itself, and to the fact that it cannot be played otherwise than on the level until every one in it turns crook."[10]

An editorial in the August 1912 issue of *Baseball Magazine*, evidently shaped by Lane, again roundly praised the sport, but contained a cogent warning:

> Baseball is a great, a stable, a permanent institution. It has within itself elements of enduring strength, elements which appeal to all true lovers of sport. It is a game fast, brilliant, spectacular, fascinating. It gives the spectator physical thrills and mental exhilaration. It is a national tonic. It is fair, honest, sportsmanlike. It is a healthful sport and its popularity rests firmly on the unswerving loyalty of 90,000,000 people in this country and of the fast-growing army of enthusiastic friends in other nations who bid fair to some time embrace the whole civilized world.

That same editorial, however, pointed to baseball's potential Achilles' heel. "The only danger which could ever threaten its existence now is a danger that may arise within. This danger, and it is genuine, is the reckless spirit of gambling which has ruined so many worthy games and now seems to be seeking a firm hold on the greatest of all games, baseball."[11]

Horse racing, *Baseball Magazine* noted, had been termed "the sport of kings" and was "a wonderful sport." Eventually, it was destroyed "by that same gambling spirit which now threatens the national game." Baseball's continued success reportedly "depends upon the faith of the community." Fan loyalty would remain constant if the game were "conducted with absolute honesty." If "any widespread demonstration of the gambling spirit casts a suspicion of doubt over baseball's integrity, it will languish to a corresponding degree." A possibility existed "that the gambling spirit might grow to such proportions as to endanger its very existence." Therefore, "all true lovers of our national game" should

> unite in the crusade that is now being conducted against this evil. They should see clearly that this is the great danger, the only danger which threatens the game they love. Every participation in this evil, however slight, is a blow at the stability of the game. Any concession to the forces of gambling, however obscure, is an invitation to disaster. Gambling is an evil which threatens the very life of the game. It is an evil for whose complete suppression baseball must depend upon the loyalty and co-operation of its many million followers.[12]

In September, F. C. Lane offered another look at "baseball's greatest danger." Lane bemoaned "the rapid spread of gambling in baseball," as the sport threatened to sweep across the globe. The magnates, he insisted, were fully cognizant of "the reckless spirit of those unprincipled men who exploit the greatest and best game in the world for their own mercenary interests." The moguls, Lane indicated, "well understand the importance of keeping the game they represent free from any possible taint of dishonesty and are bending every energy toward the suppression of the evil." Gambling, he noted, "has been a destroying power in the history of the sport world." Yet he contended that "the game is much too strong" to be imperiled by that "well-nigh universal evil."[13]

Baseball, in Lane's estimation, could never succumb to gambling. "It is impossible to fix a baseball game," he wrote. After all, "to work such a scheme in baseball it would be necessary to fix several men at least and they the most important players of a club in order to be certain to affect the result." Additionally, bribing umpires, who were "all men of strict integrity" scrupulously chosen, was "practically impossible." Given the game's uncertainty, even doing so would hardly guarantee the desired outcome. It would also be difficult, Lane offered, for a pitcher to throw a game, as a particularly poor performance would lead to his ouster. Thus, it would be necessary "to tamper with the main members of a pitching staff." This, Lane declared,

> is practically impossible. Furthermore, just as in the case of the umpire, there is no pitcher in the major leagues who would stoop to such a course. The baseball players are coming more and more to be citizens with high standards and lofty ideals of sportsmanship and it is easy enough to imagine the manner in which such a dishonorable proposition would be received. If the representative of any gambling interest approached some of these husky athletes with any such scheme, it is more than an even bet that he would get his just share of physical punishment before he was through ... it would be absolutely impossible to get any number of men to combine, and without such a combination and a resulting certainty in predicting a victory no gambling interest would make the attempt.

Therefore, Lane continued, "gambling cannot destroy baseball."[14]

However, he conjectured, it could damage the game. After all, "baseball's highest recommendation has always been its honesty. To attain to its greatest development it must be above suspicion." Gambling influences of any sort could "greatly impair its reputation for strict honesty." An increase of the same would undoubtedly result in a loss of the "better class" of people, "from the President down," who were now attracted to baseball. Additionally, rumors of gambling would prove financially crippling as "the game has grown solely on its public faith."[15]

Perhaps due to that very fact and because baseball's appeal was so rooted in myth-making, the paeans to the game far outnumbered the relatively small number of critical perspectives. In the midst of the 1912 World Series featuring the Giants and the Boston Red Sox, *The Outlook* magazine defended professional baseball, terming its general influence "thoroughly wholesome." The essay pointed to the "rigorous fairness" demanded by management and the professionalism exuded by the competitors who served as models for American youngsters. The public, *The Outlook* suggested, should support "clean baseball," the kind in which "fair and skillful sportsmanship" remained "free from brutality, trickery, and organized betting." The following spring, the publication contained an article, "Baseball and the National Life," which again discussed the sport's importance in the American pantheon. H. Addington Bruce deemed baseball "something more than the great American game;" he termed it "an American institution having a significant place in the life of the people" and thus deserving of study. Players were schooled, Bruce remarked, in the "habits of sobriety and self-control," courage was required by batters, and "team spirit" was nurtured, as baseball served as "a splendid mind-builder." For spectators, the game provided a "safety-valve," thereby alleviating stress, and proved "democratizing" with all transformed into "plain, every-day" folk.[16]

Writing in *The Atlantic Monthly* in August 1914, Simeon Strunsky analyzed "the religion of democracy," which featured "a great democratic rite" solemnly participated in by great numbers of American men from April through October on a virtually daily basis. Sunshine, open air, and a crowd comprised of "all conditions, ages, races, temperaments, and states of mind" could be found. Strunsky asked, "If a true religion is that for which a man will give up wife and children and forget the call of meat and drink, what shall we say of baseball?" In the United States, "this national faith," Strunsky continued, "has created its own architecture, as all great religions have done." New ballparks like the Polo Grounds had recently sprung up, as iron-and-steel stadiums replaced fire-prone wooden ones.[17]

The potential threat posed by corruption continued to crop up, however, with *Sporting Life* arguing that the World Series particularly afforded opportunities for wholesale graft. The games, the paper declared, were "an evil which ought to be either extirpated or made financially innocuous." The struggle to make the World Series, the editorial claimed, had diminished the value of the league contests, "made magnates and players money-mad," and served as "the medium of exploitation and self-aggrandizement of a non-supporting element of the public." Most ominous of all, the World Series had "become a standing temptation to idle capital, and a constant danger to the good repute of the game by reason of the possibility of dubious happenings."[18]

In a similar vein, on June 5, 1915, *Sporting Life* indicated that a new campaign had been undertaken against baseball pools. National League President John Tener was quoted as attacking pool gambling altogether: "It should be wiped out, for it is a fast-growing menace to the community as well as to base ball itself." While condemning the pool, *Sporting Life* asserted its "high regard for base ball players as a class."[19]

* * *

While rumors of fixes proved troubling in the midst of the prewar celebration involving the national pastime, another issue threatened to transform major league baseball. Beginning in 1879, National League teams compiled reserve lists of selected players, who were deemed off-limits to their competitors. Ultimately, entire squads were saddled with the reserve clause, which was intended to restrict salaries and player movement. A short-lived Players' National League sprang up in 1890, but its demise allowed for a slashing of wages. A decade later, Ban Johnson's creation of the American League resulted in players bolting from the more established National League and a temporary jump in salaries. A peace accord under a new National Agreement melding the National and American leagues ensured that players again possessed only restricted markets for their services.

Millions of fans and mercenary owners alike, *Baseball Magazine* contended in June 1912, imperiled the game in their own way. Those who avidly followed baseball distorted "the greatest of all games" and conferred "a halo of glory" on athletes who suffered from "hero-worship." By contrast, the moguls viewed "the player as a mere business proposition." Seldom did sentiment come into play, with "the most rudimentary and merciless of business principles" generally prevailing. The owner "gets as much as he can and usually pays as little as he is obliged to."[20]

An article in the December 7, 1912 issue of *The Literary Digest* discussed the reality of the baseball "trust." It quoted an anonymous writer who contended that organized baseball was "the only trust which lives because it has been able to secure an absolute monopoly of flesh and blood." That power resided in the absolute hold the game's moguls possessed over the players, thanks to the reserve clause. Recognizing that the athletes provided baseball's allure, management "sat down together in peaceful conclave and hog-tied the hired man." Those who opposed such operations encountered a blacklist: "It was a case of submit or be put out of business, and the National Agreement was intended to end the open shop in baseball."[21]

The appearance of the new Fraternity of Professional Base Ball Players was greeted, not surprisingly, with hostility by baseball management. Writing in *Baseball Magazine*, F. C. Lane declared that the publication's sympathies resided mainly with the players: "We understand fully the difficulties under which they labor, and how mythical are many of the exaggerated conceptions of their prosperity." While admitting that baseball was "a great business," Lane insisted it was "the national sport." Consequently, he decried the appearance of "a spirit, almost mercenary in tone, guided by a cold, calculating policy to squeeze as many dollars as possible from the profits of the game."[22]

*The Sporting News* viewed the Fraternity still more warily, while waiting to see how it responded to the new Federal League, which effectively began as a minor league enterprise in 1913. "The popularity of the national game," *The Sporting News* proclaimed on January 15, 1914, "depends upon such strength as can only be given it through organization." The Fraternity, the paper continued, "owes a debt to organized ball, if it really has the best interests of its members at heart."[23]

In 1914, the Federal League opened its second year of operation, with some players bolting from their old clubs and the major leagues compelled to increase substantially the salaries garnered by top stars like Washington fireballer Walter Johnson and Detroit outfielder Ty Cobb. Not surprisingly, the Federal League, which now strove for major league status, provided support for the Players' Fraternity while threatening "a thorough airing of the reserve clause." In a lengthy article, Lane questioned whether a third big league could survive. Major league ball, he pointed out, was located in the North and East alone, with St. Louis the furthest point westward. No big league team resided south of the Mason-Dixon line. Leading northern and midwestern cities like Baltimore, Buffalo, and Milwaukee, larger than Washington, D. C. or Cincinnati, lacked major league teams, as did Kansas City and Indianapolis. Financial resources and interest existed, Lane admitted, to allow for baseball expansion. Enough quality ballplayers could be found, he contended, to stock a third big league.[24]

Notwithstanding a promising beginning, the Federal League boasted several weaknesses too. The owners of its franchises, including Robert Ward and Albert Sinclair, generally lacked baseball experience. Although they had attracted nearly 100 current or former big leaguers, many, like Mordecai "Three Finger" Brown and Eddie Plank, were fading stars, while others—particularly Bennie Kauff—had yet to demonstrate their mettle. Relying on the 10 day clause in standard player contracts, Hal Chase, the stellar but controversial first sacker, jumped from Charles Comiskey's White Sox to the Federal League's Buffalo franchise. Still, scheduling proved problematic and the Federals, in Lane's estimation, were hardly deserving of "major league standing."[25]

American League president Ban Johnson reluctantly recognized the Players' Fraternity; he also agreed to induce owners to both pay for uniforms and paint their outfield fences dark green to ward off injuries and bolster batting averages. Such major league stars as Detroit's Cobb, Washington's Johnson, New York Giant Christy Mathewson, the Chicago White Sox's Eddie Collins, and Philadelphia Phillie Pete Alexander, with Federal League monies dangled before them, received considerable financial inducements to remain with their major league squads. So did Shoeless Joe Jackson of the Cleveland Indians and Chicago White Sox infielder Buck Weaver, who inked a three year contract that raised his annual salary from $2,500 to $6,000.

CHAPTER TWO

# The People's Judge

Major league teams initiated legal action against the Federals, charging violations of player contracts, while the executives who headed the new league responded in kind with suits of their own. The Federals deliberately sought out the jurisdiction of the United States District Court for the Northern District of Illinois, presided over by Judge Kenesaw Mountain Landis. In 1907, Landis first came to national attention as a reputed trust-buster. During that year, publications like *Appleton's Magazine* sang his praises for having delivered a $29,240,000 fine against the Standard Oil Company. Judge Landis's sentence, handed down against John D. Rockefeller, author John T. McCutcheon wrote, enabled him to become "a household world, except in a few mansions where it is not safe to utter it." Indeed, McCutcheon remarked, "zealous patriots hastened to mention him for President and a "Landis" cigar is only a question of time." Landis's decree reportedly produced "the largest" smile to be found, which "rested like a sunburst on faces unaccustomed to merriment and wreathed with a pleasant glow the visage of everyone who wasn't carrying stocks on a margin." The *New York World* termed Landis's decree "a great event in American political and financial history." The subsequent ruling by the appellate court, which severely chastised Landis and overturned the Standard Oil penalty, in no way dented his reputation as a people's judge.[1]

As the article in *Appleton's* indicated, Landis's early years hardly had been auspicious ones. His peculiar first and middle names were derived from the

Battle of Kennesaw Mountain, where his father, an assistant surgeon in the Union army, had his left leg shattered by a cannonball. Born on November 20, 1866, in Millville, Ohio, Kenesaw moved with his family to Indiana in 1874. He attended school in Logansport, where he played amateur baseball and acquired a reputation as a bicyclist. A high school dropout, Kenesaw taught himself shorthand and served as a county court reporter. He determined to enroll at the Y.M.C.A. Law School in Cincinnati and graduated in 1891 from Union Law School of Chicago. Befriended by Judge Walter Q. Gresham, Landis accompanied him to Washington in 1893, following the elder gentleman's appointment as Grover Cleveland's Secretary of State. Having excelled as Gresham's personal secretary, Landis returned to Chicago, after his mentor's death in 1895. That year, he married Winifred Reed; subsequently, two children were born to the Landises. With his corporate law practice thriving, Landis became deeply enmeshed in Republican Party politics. In March 1905, President Theodore Roosevelt appointed the 39-year-old Landis to the federal bench, where his star soon rose.

Landis's theatrical bent and sometimes contorted judicial renderings led him to be viewed as a controversial, even quixotic jurist. Boasting a full head of wavy, frequently disheveled graying hair, and exhibiting a dramatic courtroom demeanor, the 5'6", 130 pound Landis delivered rulings that often were overturned on appeal. No matter, he acquired a reputation as a people's judge, thanks to his involvement in the Standard Oil and other sensational cases. Landis appeared to be a progressive magistrate, cut from something of the Republican cloth that Teddy Roosevelt exemplified during the era. In reality, Landis was a reactionary progressive, much as Teddy proved to be on occasion, particularly when his patriotic ire was aroused. The thin, wiry Landis was also an startlingly careless adjudicator, clearly guided by strong emotions. Still, his legendary courtroom "battle" with the nation's richest man made Landis's reputation. So did the sense, conveyed in the *Appleton's* article, that Landis's rulings were both highly popular and capable of engendering "corporation wrath." Landis's creed, McCutcheon suggested, was simple: "It is the duty of the Court to carry out the will of people as expressed in their laws." It was also very much in keeping with the era's increasingly ascendant progressive credo, which indicated that majoritarian perspectives necessarily resulted in advances for society as a whole. Typically, when asked about his well-connected siblings who included two congressmen and the Postmaster-General of Puerto Rico, Landis replied, "Yes, they are officeholders. I am a public servant."[2]

Landis's dispensing of "justice" was, nevertheless, curious, to say the least. Journalist Jack Lait of the *Chicago Herald* later referred to him as "an irascible, short-temperament, tyrannical despot. His manner of handling witnesses, lawyers — and reporters — was more arbitrary than the behavior of any jurist I have ever seen before or since. He resented what we wrote; he resented what we did, and probably what we wore. He regarded his courtroom as his private preserve and even extended his autocracy to the corridors."[3]

Ed Fitzgerald's reading of Landis was only somewhat more tempered:

> He made his courtroom a stage and there never was any question about who was playing the leading role. Lawyers, witnesses, plaintiffs, defendants, all were subordinated to the flamboyant Landis personality.
>
> The Judge was the kind of man who could strut sitting down. He loved to argue, loved to show off his knowledge, loved the wielding of power. A consummate showman all his life, he had the lamp on his bench so placed that when he thrust his white head forward to hear a witness or exchange words with a lawyer, his striking face was silhouetted dramatically by the cleverly-aimed beam of light. The lamp served the same purpose for this Barrymore of the courtroom that footlights do for an actor on the stage.
>
> Men stopped whatever they were and listened intently as the cocky tyrant, his back-country voice seeming to cast off its normal drawl, variously assumed the role of prosecutor, defense attorney or even technical expert.[4]

His reputation as a people's judge and as an opponent of trusts led to the Federal League's decision to try its major litigation in Landis's courtroom; the setting was natural because the headquarters of both the Federals and the American League were located in Chicago. On January 5, 1915, the Federal League presented a complaint calling for an end to the National Agreement and the rules of the National Commission. The defendants were said to have violated anti-trust provisions and participated in a monopoly. They were accused of conspiring to destroy the Federal League through such tactics as the blacklisting of ballplayers who departed from the majors. Joe Vila in *The Sporting News* insisted that the Federals had displayed their impotence in seeking "to destroy the very fabric out of which the success of the game has been woven." Rather than strive to compete "on their merits" in a battle of the turnstiles, Vila declared, the Feds were attempting to "have Organized Base Ball stigmatized in the eyes of the world as a body doing business unlawfully." An editorial in *The Sporting News* asserted that the plaintiffs desired "that Organized Base Ball be wiped off the map." National Commission chairman Gary Herrmann dismissed the Federal suit as "the dying squeal of a beaten crowd." But an editorial in *Sporting Life* on January 23 warned about possible repercussions if the general public concluded "that this national game is not a sport at all, but a mere business enterprise exploited for private profit and buttressed in illegal or immoral position for private use and protection."[5]

The next issue of *Sporting Life* highlighted other seminal issues raised by the plaintiffs, including the "restriction of player liberty," the drafting and farming out of ballplayers, the waiver rule, the reserve clause, salaries, and the "excessive" power held by the National Commission. The craft honed by major leaguers was unique, the defendants countered, more akin to that characteristic of entertainers rather than commerce as defined by anti-trust measures.[6]

As for Landis, *The Sporting News* warmly praised his handling of the case. A caption accompanying a picture of the judge indicated that all parties in the suit "unite in praising the way Judge Landis has conducted the case." The Federals' bill of complaint, the paper charged, had been "a chaotic mess" but was reshaped by the good judge. Landis had also praised the game, *The Sporting News* pointed out, "by proclaiming from the bench that it is a public institution that no one shall think of harming." Landis was referred to as "a dyed-in-the-wool fan," who had played ball himself. Thus, "the game is safe in his hands."[7]

In his courtroom, Landis demanded of a Federal League attorney, "What are you really asking of this court? If the court should see fit to issue a restraining order, on what grounds do you expect him to do so?" Landis also queried about the scope of the injunction that was being sought. Did the Federals expect the restraining order to compel organized baseball to stop operations altogether, because of illegal restraints on trade and commerce as precluded by the Sherman Anti-Trust Act? Was organized baseball to be held responsible "for holding laborers in a state of peonage?" Should the court rule on the legality of baseball's reserve clause?[8]

In a telling moment, George Wharton Pepper, one of the defendants's attorneys, declared, "Their grievance is not that we prevent them from finding the young ball players on the 'lot' and developing them through training in the various minor leagues as we do; they want to attain in one bound the advantage we have gained through ten years of labor; they want to profit from the skill developed by our money." Responding to Pepper's argument, Landis cried, "As a result of 30 years of observation, I am shocked because you call base ball 'labor.'"

The plantiffs' top litigator, Edward E. Gates, responded that an injunction should be delivered preventing the major leagues from tampering with the Federals' players and operations. Landis responded by affording defense counsel 20 days to respond to the claims. This delighted *The Sporting News*, which declared that "Judge Landis stands out as the only one who seemed to have a mind clear enough to get into the meat of the suit and divine its real purpose." As an attorney for organized baseball attempted to pique concerns about the Federal suit damaging the national pastime, Landis indicated "that he had little sympathy with the trust busting phase of it." Bluntly, Landis — displaying his prickly personality — stated, "you may leave the love and affection out of this law suit. Both sides may understand that any blow made at the thing called base ball would be regarded by this court as a blow at a national institution." To *The Sporting News*, "that sounded the death knell of the effort to dissolve organized Ball right there. Judge Landis had echoed the sentiment of millions of base ball fans. The Federals scarcely needed to learn his stand to tell them which way the wind was blowing. Public sentiment toward their anti-trust suit had already been well indicated."[9]

While the plaintiffs hoped for a rapid resolution of the case, Landis, as author David Pietrusza astutely notes, deliberately stalled, worrying that organized baseball could be grievously injured by an adverse court ruling; Landis evidently feared that such a decree might be required.[10]

In the March 1915 issue of *Baseball Magazine*, F. C. Lane discussed the case and a recent interview he had conducted with Federal League president James Gilmore. Apparently justifying Landis's fears, Gilmore had reportedly declared, "We're going to break up organized baseball. ... We'll break up the baseball trust and the National Commission. We'll free every ball player in the United States. We'll have the courts declare them free agents. ..." The game, Lane contended, would somehow survive this latest squabble among baseball titans. "Baseball as a business," he wrote, "is the people's property. They made the game." Furthermore, "the sport is too big, too broad, too popular to ever suffer material damage from transient hostilities."[11]

That fall, an editorial in *Baseball Magazine* contended that Judge Landis had been remiss in not adjudicating the Federal League suit. The case was an important one, the editorial acknowledged, that "strove to establish the legal status of baseball contracts, to define both the rights of the player and the rights of the owner." Once he had allowed the case to move forward, the editorial continued, Landis "assumed the responsibility of rendering a decision." The failure to do so had injured both parties, causing "unusual inconvenience." It also made more likely "another disastrous war" involving player raids, which the Federals had avoided at present.[12]

Landis's inaction spelled the Federal League's demise and underscored the primacy of organized ball and "baseball law," to *The Sporting News'* delight. A meeting in Chicago resulted in an agreement to terminate the Federal League suit, pending a $600,000 payment to its owners, the issuance of stock in various major league clubs, the sale of the St. Louis Browns franchise to Phil Ball, the purchase of the Chicago Cubs by Charles Weeghman, and permission to sell back several ballplayers who had bolted from the majors. As Landis quickly dismissed the case, the Federal League closed shop, which eventually proved fatal to the Players' Fraternity. The preeminence of baseball law, *The Sporting News* argued, must be acknowledged "if the game is to survive as the national institution Judge Landis has proclaimed it."[13]

The Federals' suit against the National Commission was officially dismissed in the United District Court in Chicago on February 8. In directing that the case be terminated, Landis proclaimed that because of it, organized baseball's very existence was endangered:

> The court's expert knowledge of baseball obtained by more than 30 years of observation of the game as a spectator, convinced me that if an order had been entered it would have been, if not destructive, at least vitally injurious to the game of baseball. No matter what decision had been made, neither side would have emerged from court victorious. After taking counsel with my own judgment, I decided that the court had the right, or at least the discretion, to postpone decision in the case, and this was done.[14]

Following dismissal of the suit, *Sporting Life* saluted the man it called "this learned judge" as "the best friend of base ball." Other judges, the newspaper also warned, might not prove "as understandingly friendly to Organized Ball in future suits." In the meantime, *Sporting Life* applauded Landis's acknowledgement that the professional game "had been conducted with absolute integrity by both magnates and players for 30 years." Such a declaration, *The Sporting News* claimed, made for "perhaps the greatest tribute ever paid to professional baseball."[15]

* * *

Both the owners of the Federal League franchise in Baltimore and ballplayers were troubled by the agreement calling off the latest baseball war. In 1916, Baltimore owners, who had hoped to purchase the St. Louis Cardinal club and relocate it in their city, initiated an anti-trust suit in the U.S. district court in the District of Columbia. Claiming losses of $300,000, the Baltimore officials sought triple damages. Major league owners now proceeded to slice salaries, pushing them back, in certain instances, to prewar levels. In the late winter of 1916-17, the Players' Fraternity, headed by David L. Fultz, threatened to strike if its demands were not met by the National Commission and the minor leagues' National Board. The Players' Fraternity demanded that full salaries be paid injured players, travel expenses incurred by minor leaguers during spring training be covered by owners, the unveiling of management briefs when grievance cases went against the player, and five days' notice before Class AA or A ballplayers could be released. When its proposals were rejected out of hand, talk of possible strike action loomed.[16]

That very possibility deeply troubled the editors of *Baseball Magazine*, who had previously proven sympathetic to the Players' Fraternity. "A baseball war," F. C. Lane charged, "would be more destructive and unjust than any grievance which the players have ever endured." A strike "would be as unwelcome as frost in May." In Lane's estimation, "organized baseball is an extremely delicate framework. ... A wholesale strike in baseball circles would be, in our opinion, that thing which Talleyrand called 'worse than a crime, a blunder.'"[17]

Not surprisingly, *The Sporting News* proved still less sympathetic to the possibility of a player walkout. Returning from a vacation in Cuba, Joe Vila had discovered that strike talk was in the air. "The baseball public," he warned, would hardly prove enamored "with this foolhardy movement." Furthermore,

> Organized baseball cannot afford to bend the knee. The game must be controlled by the magnates. If the Fraternity should win this fight there'd be another next year and in fact, every year. Baseball has received a rough deal in the past three years and the public is heartily sick of these quarrels, which are sure to kill interest if they are not suppressed.

Consequently, "sensible players must realize by this time that the game that gives them a livelihood cannot stand much more unpopularity."[18]

On February 20, Fultz called off the threatened strike and released players from their promises not to ink contracts. More than 600 players had initially agreed to support Fultz's stance, while at least half continued to back him until the very end. Organized baseball, *Sporting Life* declared, was "once more in the saddle, and henceforth things will be run pretty much as they were before the Federal League incursion." Thanks to the Federal League's demise, the crushing of the Fraternity, the restoration of the ten-day clause, and the termination of long-term deals, organized baseball now encountered only one threat: the anti-trust suit undertaken by Baltimore Federal League representatives.[19]

The holdout, *Sporting Life* did acknowledge, was the only weapon the ballplayer possessed in his quest to obtain a pay increase. Indeed, "from the time he first signs a professional contract, he works for one man only, and his financial improvement is at the mercy of that man." There existed "no freedom of contract" for the baseball player, that leading sports publication declared, and "it is doubtful if there ever will be." His very salary was determined by baseball management, which could cut it "at will," leaving him "no recourse," other than an appeal to the National Commission, a generally futile endeavor.[20]

The April 1917 issue of *Baseball Magazine* praised Fultz — whom it referred to as honest but "an impractical dreamer" — for having "met defeat like a man." The Players' strike, Lane concluded, amounted to an "ill-starred campaign." His publication had proved to be "the first and strongest friend of the Fraternity" and served as "the Fraternity organ." It possessed a great interest in the well-being of the player, "but our chief aim is and will be, to promote baseball. The game is greater than the player."[21]

Two months later, *Sporting Life* urged that organized baseball strive to avoid a judicial determination regarding "the legality of its system." Major league baseball, the editors of that publication admitted, "has some trust features." The question arose whether any judge beside Landis would view that operation benevolently. No other method had been devised, *Sporting Life* contended, "to keep the professional game clean and honest; to assure its adequate presentation to the public as a high-class and innocent amusement; and to make possible the financial success of the game." Thus, without organized baseball as presently concocted, so went the argument, "there will be no honest professional base ball."[22]

* * *

While the aborted strike was now terminated and the Players' Fraternity fatally wounded, organized baseball was about to confront yet another peril, one that potentially could prove far more troubling. In the same issue where F. C. Lane discussed the end of the Players' strike, he also wondered how baseball would be affected if the United States officially entered the European conflict that had torn apart that continent for the past three years. "Baseball, a sport catering to the same course of training which produces good soldiers, athletic, clean, wholesome," Lane wrote, "would furnish the moral tonic so much needed in a national calamity. In time of war a sport so deservedly popular as baseball would be a national benefit." Indeed, the war, Lane suggested, might convert baseball into an international game. During the Civil War,

Liberty Bond rally at Clark and Madison, circa 1917. Chicago Historical Society (ICHi-24364).

soldiers had helped to spread the gospel of baseball; perhaps, their counterparts, in the midst of the present conflagration, would do the same on a more global basis.[23]

One of baseball's greatest fans, Judge Kenesaw Mountain Landis, soon was involved in a series of cases that demonstrated his super-patriotism and proved all too characteristic of the temper of the times. Once the United States became a belligerent in April 1917 but continuing after the Armistice, a wave of repression swept over the land. Particularly targeted were those viewed as suspect or "un-American," including any number of conscientious objectors, socialists, radical unionists, or soon-to-be self-proclaimed communists. Landis was seen as something of a progressive Republican, due to his appointment to the federal bench by Roosevelt and his jousting with Standard Oil. In the manner of both reactionary proponents of "100 percent Americanism" and Woodrow Wilson — the second great progressive president of the early 20th Century — however, Landis considered any critic of U.S. wartime policies outside the pale.

Even as he presided over cases involving political dissidents, Landis delivered a series of charged addresses around the midwest questioning anyone's right to contest governmental policies. Just before Congress issued a declaration of war, Landis, in a talk before the Chicago real estate board, exclaimed, "What a nation of cowards we are, that we stand back and let the good fellow volunteer to fight our battles." In early June, after receiving an anonymous threatening letter, Landis attacked those he deemed "Copperheads."[24]

In July, Landis dealt with a group of draft resisters, whose incarceration resulted in a riot. The resisters were foreign-born members of the Socialist Party or the Industrial Workers of the World, a militant labor organization that propounded anarcho-syndicalist tenets. Landis characteristically referred to these defendants as "whining and belly-aching puppies." In the trial at Rockford, Illinois, Landis personally questioned the defendants regarding their national origin, date of entry into the United States, naturalization status, involvement with anti-draft organizations, reasons for opposing conscription, and whether they would now join the American military expedition. Landis delivered year-and-a-day prison sentences in a Chicago House of Correction to 117 defendants. Three others obtained lighter sentences, but all 120 were ordered to register for the draft. An additional 37 defendants, accused by Landis of "moral turpitude," were slated to be deported after completion of their sentences.[25]

Some 1,100 gathered to hear Landis talk at Decatur's high school in late November, when he urged a rallying round President Woodrow Wilson and condemned pacifists, "slackers," and others he considered "disloyal." Among those he accused of being unpatriotic were certain "German-Americans, Swedes and Irish." Landis — whose son Reed was a member of the air service stationed in England — regretted that a physically-fit 51-year-old man "cannot even jimmy himself into a uniform." On December 4, speaking in Princeton, Illinois, Landis condemned those who were garnering "exorbitant profits from the sale of necessities during the war." Such individuals, he declared, "should be publicly branded and shunned by decent people."[26]

The following spring, national attention turned to Landis' courtroom when 113 Wobblies or members of the I.W.W., including Big Bill Haywood, were charged with conspiring to damage the American war effort. Over a hundred guards were relied on to maintain order, various defendants shackled, and the atmosphere apparently reeked of "the age-old struggle of the classes." At various points, radical luminaries attended the proceedings. John Reed, who had recently completed his classic work on the Bolshevik Revolution, cuttingly referred to Landis: "Small on the huge bench sits a wasted man with untidy white hair, an emaciated face in which two burning eyes are set like jewels, parchment-like skin split by a crack for a mouth; the face of Andrew Jackson three years dead." After presiding in an apparently judicially restrained manner, Landis meted out prison sentences as severe as 20 years in a federal penitentiary, coupled with $30,000 fines. In his autobiography, the IWW chieftain bristled that "Pontius Pilate or Bloody Jeffreys never enjoyed themselves better than Landis when he was imposing those terrible sentences upon a group of working men for whom he had no feeling of humanity, no sense of justice."[27]

Congressman Victor L. Berger of Wisconsin, a German-born member of the Socialist Party of America, would undoubtedly have seconded Haywood's evaluation of Landis. The judge's nativist side had been revealed recently when, in an impassioned speech before enlisted soldiers at Camp Grant, he had declared, "Damn the hyphen." Indicted for having purportedly violated the Espionage Act, Berger and four other socialist leaders were compelled to come before Federal Judge Landis. In October 1918, Landis refused to dismiss charges, while the following month the judge denied a request for a change of venue sought on the grounds that he was prejudiced against defendants of German ancestry. Just days earlier, Landis had asserted, "If anybody has said anything about the Germans that is worse than I have said, I would like to hear it so I could use it myself."[28]

\* \* \*

The 19 month period of direct American engagement in the Great War, which aroused Judge Landis's patriotic ire, imperiled the game he so dearly loved. The previous spring, National League president John K. Tener had proclaimed,

> In case of war, I wouldn't give five cents for the base ball chances of 1916. War — a plunge into the great world struggle now going on, would smash base

ball as flat as a pancake. The American public would forget base ball, theaters, every form of diversion, and think of nothing but the fighting. The Spanish War hurt the game severely in 1898, and the Spanish War was only a flea-bite when compared to this terrific convulsion.

On February 10, 1917, *Sporting Life* seconded that notion, asserting that American participation in the war "will have a pernicious, if not fatal, effect on all sport, but particularly base ball." For "the spectacle of a lot of husky fellows engaging in base ball, or other athletic endeavor, particularly for hire, at a time when the nation required just their type of physical manhood, would be wholly intolerable." By the beginning of April, Tener declared less dramatically that should the United States enter the war, "base ball will be a second consideration with magnates and players." Captain T. L. Huston, who co-owned the New York Yankees along with Jacob Ruppert, urged that military training be undertaken by ballplayers working out in the South with their big league teams.[29]

The war, *Sporting Life* now offered, would prove fatal for all sports except for major league baseball. A *Sporting Life* editorial, dated April 7, 1917, indicated that baseball, along with intramural collegiate sports and non-competitive contests elsewhere, would probably be allowed "as a distraction from the depressing effects of war." A subsequent editorial, two weeks later, which followed the U.S. declaration of war against the Central Powers, argued that the present baseball season promised, in fact, to be "a banner one." Both the Players' strike and "the rival outlaw league" were now ended, that piece indicated, while "the national pastime will furnish interest and recreation at a critical period in our national life, when such diversion will be needed." Tener now reportedly believed "that base ball is in for a great season. He does not think that the war will affect the game, unless there is some great calamity on land or sea."[30]

White Sox owner Charles Comiskey conveyed the thoughts of army officers that military drills being conducted by American League squads had "done more to inspire a patriotic feeling among young Americans than any other influence." Purportedly, they had "aided the recruiting of soldiers immensely." Comiskey's players were the first to drill and were viewed as "the best conditioned and prepared soldiers in the circuit." *The Sporting News* declared that "it was an inspiring sight to see Eddie Collins, world's greatest second baseman, tutoring his mates in advanced evolutions learned from Sergeant Smiley, U.S.A., and from a book of military tactics which Eddie had been studying." Chick Gandil was said to have "entered the military drill and the baseball preparedness scheme with enthusiasm and spirit."[31]

In wartime, *Baseball Magazine* insisted, baseball was "not frivolous. It is not even superfluous, a needless luxury. It is a mental and physical tonic." As

National League President Tener affirmed, "This is a war of democracy against bureaucracy. And I tell you that baseball is the very watchword of democracy. There is no other sport or business or anything under heaven which exerts the leveling influence that baseball does. Neither the public school nor the church can approach it. Baseball is unique." Tener continued, "The very essence of true democracy finds its highest expression in baseball."[32]

By late June, the editors of *Sporting Life* were condemning as "slackers" their fellow practitioners who insisted that athletic competition be halted for the war's duration. America's future victories "in the cause of democracy and humanity," the editorialists claimed, could be chalked up "to the base ball diamond" and other athletic enterprises, for having early trained the nation's soldiers. As a consequence, they possessed "physical fitness, alertness of mind, keenness of eye and courage." All this was owing to American youth's love of sports. The *Baseball Monthly* went a step further, contending, as did Washington Senators owner Clark Griffith, that the national pastime was "a soldiers' game, a war game." August "Gary" Herrmann, chairman of the National Commission, typically insisted that baseball was "peculiarly dear to the American people." It also encouraged athletic accomplishments and love for the same, Herrmann wrote, which were "the foundations of a strong military organization."[33]

Baseball, insisted Reverend William A. "Billy" Sunday — himself a former ballplayer and a friend of Judge Landis — was "just as useful" to the Americans who were toiling at home as for soldiers abroad. The American people, he wrote, "need it as a mental and physical tonic." Their fighting men, he continued, could rely on it to ward off "the evils which always lurk about big concentration camps." Arguing that "baseball *is a war game,*" Sunday deemed it more necessary than ever. He also proclaimed it "the grandest sport that was ever invented. It is the squarest, the cleanest, the best. You can't say anything good about the old game that it won't stand up under. And it grows better all the time." Significantly, "baseball exerts a wholesome influence wherever it is played."[34]

The war, in turn, *The Sporting News* was indicating by late August, had proven to be a boon to baseball. George Robbins declared, "War is not killing interest in baseball. Rather it makes the hunger for it greater." White Sox mogul Charles Comiskey decided to send copies of *The Sporting News* to American soldiers stationed in Europe so that they might keep abreast of the game. Commy also determined that a "Military Day" would be featured during every American League season. After the first was held at Comiskey Park, with 28,000 in attendance, the White Sox boss declared,

*Opposite:* **White Sox drilling in outfield in military uniforms, 1917. Chicago Historical Society (ICHi-22720, detail of SDN-61132; photograph by *Chicago Daily News*).**

It was a grand spectacle. I could not stand there and watch those boys marching without choking up. After watching such drill by organizations of fine American manhood, one is bound to be a better citizen. He is bound to be impressed with the thought that these boys are a means of boosting world peace as well as participants in the world war.[35]

In early December, Comiskey insisted, "There will be no war measures to check baseball and the game will go next year just as it did last season. Some of our players may be taken in the next draft, but their places will be filled and the game will go on. The country needs baseball." In the *Sporting News'* estimation, "there isn't a more patriotic man in the United States than Charles A. Comiskey. That is one reason why he is opposed to giving up baseball, the national game." The American people, Comiskey reasoned, needed amusement to stave off depression after participating in war. The "nation's fighting men," *The Sporting News*, heartily agreed.[36]

CHAPTER THREE

# The Old Roman's Club

The joint decision in April 1917 by President Wilson and the United States Congress to enter the Great War — the European bloodbath that began three years earlier — dramatically influenced the national game. At first, baseball appeared somewhat immune to the horrors of warfare, as the 1917 season unfolded with a full slate of games. True, many ballgames began with renditions of "The Star Spangled Banner," but President Wilson himself saw fit to toss out the first ball at the Washington Senators' home opener. Attendance at major league contests was little affected, but fewer and fewer fans showed up for minor league affairs, as players began entering the armed forces. Boston Braves' catcher Hank Gowdy, batting a mere .214, became the first big leaguer to enlist; few, at that point, followed his lead.

Charles A. Comiskey's Chicago White Sox, spearheaded by slugging outfielders Happy Felsch and Joe Jackson, third baseman Buck Weaver, and 28-game winner Eddie Cicotte, captured the 1917 American League crown by nine games. Coming up short this time around were the two-time defending World Series champion Boston Red Sox, now without skipper Bill Carrigan. Even the heroics of the game's top southpaw, twenty-two year-old Babe Ruth, who won 24 games and boasted a .325 mark at the plate, failed to steer the Red Sox back into the fall classic. Relying on a hard-hitting outfield of its own, which included Federal League sensation Benny Kauff and co-home run champ, Dave Robertson, who belted twelve round-trippers, and a fine pitching staff, featuring 21-game winner Ferdie Schupp, New York took the

National League title. John McGraw's team finished 10 games in front of Pat Moran's Philadelphia Phillies, whose Pete Alexander won at least 30 games for the third straight season. Each time, Alexander captured a pitching triple crown, leading the National League in victories, strikeouts, and earned run average. Relying on the batting prowess of Jackson, Felsch, first sacker Chick Gandil, second baseman Eddie Collins, and Buck Weaver, Chicago's pitching stars Red Faber and Cicotte bested the Giants in six games during the 1917 World Series.

Sports scribes, who were clearly enamored with White Sox owner Comiskey, sang the praises of his ball club. Yet seeds of discord were apparent even in the midst of the pennant revelry. F. C. Lane, discussing the impending Series, declared that "the White Sox have more individual merit and less team cohesion, if we may use the word." Nevertheless, the World Series triumph was team owner Comiskey's first since his hitless wonders had stunned the heavily favored cross-town Cubs in 1906.[1]

Comiskey's reputation as a baseball icon was certainly well-deserved, in contrast to the accolades he received as a players' owner. Born in Chicago in 1859, Comiskey attended St. Mary's College in Kansas, before becoming a professional ballplayer. As player-manager, first baseman Comiskey led the St. Louis Browns to four straight American Association titles from 1885-88. In 1890, Comiskey bolted to the Chicago Pirates' franchise of the Players League. Following the collapse of that league, he rejoined the Browns, then served as player-manager of the Cincinnati Reds. Comiskey retired following the 1894 season, leaving behind a 838-541 managerial record, the third best win-loss percentage in major league history. He subsequently bought the Sioux City franchise in the Western League, headed by his friend Ban Johnson. Comiskey moved his squad first to St. Paul and then to Chicago's South Side; in October 1899, he renamed the team the White Stockings. In 1900, his Chicago club was one of the cornerstones of Johnson's newly christened American League; the following season, it captured the pennant. By 1902, Comiskey's players were called the White Sox and they shocked the powerful Cubs, who had won a record 116 games during the regular season, in the 1906 World Series. By the close of the following season, talk of a major squabble with Johnson was bandied about, with rumors of a third major league in the offing. In 1910, the White Sox began playing in Comiskey Park, a cement and steel edifice that seated 32,000 fans. The dimensions of the symmetrical stadium were 360 feet down the foul lines and 420 feet to dead center.[2]

No baseball executive ever received more favorable press than Comiskey. The second issue of *Baseball Magazine*, which appeared in June 1908, contained a tribute to the White Sox owner. Comiskey, George C. Rice declared, was known to virtually all baseball fans and stood as "the most popular man" in Chicago. "A brainy ball player" in his day, Comiskey had become "a shrewd and thinking business man." Rice credited the mogul's "advice and experience" with helping to keep the American League afloat. Now, there was reportedly no one in the majors "whose word carried more weight than does the 'Old Roman's.'" The following April, Frank B. Hutchinson Jr. offered an analysis of "Charles Albert Comiskey — The Man." Comiskey, Hutchinson stated, was "the most interesting man in baseball" and "probably the most influential." To the author, Comiskey was "the incarnation of Success." In seconding Rice's belief that Comiskey was his city's most beloved figure, Hutchinson argued that such popularity helped to explain "the great financial success of the White Sox." Their fans appeared the most loyal, while the recent World Series triumph over their cross-town rivals was undoubtedly "the most popular victory baseball has known in many years."[3]

Said to possess "few, if any, of the petty traits of the ordinary man," Comiskey was called "charitable to a marked degree." Frequently, Hutchinson reported, Comiskey retained a ballplayer who had "outlived his usefulness in the major league," but had helped the team win in days' past. Significantly, "Comiskey never forgets a friend and seldom an enemy." Thus, "he is a good man to have a friend, but a dangerous enemy." To Hutchinson, "truly, Charles Albert Comiskey is a wonderful man."[4]

The August 1910 issue of *Baseball Magazine* contained a extended piece on Comiskey by Hugh S. Fullerton, who was called "the greatest living authority on baseball." As Fullerton saw matters, Comiskey should be considered "THE MAN WHO MADE BASEBALL," whose "indomitable courage and steady resistance" had prevented the game's rulers from destroying it. In Chicago, Comiskey's name stood for "sportsman ... the best friend or the most open enemy ever man had, and it means squareness, gameness and honesty." Most notably, Fullerton claimed, Comiskey had served "to preserve baseball, to keep it clean and sportsmanlike, not only in his own league but throughout the country."[5]

Other writers praised Comiskey just as highly. *Baseball Magazine* in mid-1911 crafted "a lasting tribute," in the form of a literary Hall of Fame for baseball immortals. A mere dozen figures were selected, including Cap Anson, former catcher Michael "King" Kelly, powerful hitter Edward Delahanty, pitcher-labor activist John Ward, pitcher-sports entrepreneur Albert Spalding, slugger Dan Brouthers, and Charles Comiskey. Called "the brains of the American League," Comiskey was also termed "hero of the invasion of Chicago" and, simply, "one of the best ever."[6]

In January 1913, William A. Phelon discussed how the baseball magnate invariably stood as "a real and indisputable goat ... He's always and invariably the Patsy. He is the one person who is never given love, admiration, or even semi-justice." One baseball owner, Phelon reported, was viewed differently. "This towering, gray-topped figure stands for all that is sportsmanlike, all that is lovable, in the Only Game." Comiskey, he continued, grew up on the Chicago prairies, served as player, captain, and manager, established a small fortune, and then "put it where it would do the most good." Once he purchased the White Sox, "instead of growing AWAY from the people, he grew INTO their affections!" Indeed, the more prosperous he became, "the more he mixed with the fans. He held court under the rickety old stand for years, and all the baseball world came there to shake his hand." As a consequence, the rich and successful Comiskey was now "better liked than ever."[7]

In the winter of 1913-14, Comiskey and the New York Giants' John McGraw conducted a journey through Asia and Europe, to publicize the game and amass profits; the two reaped considerable praise for their adventures. "Pride in the sport," it was said, "inspired the conception of the tour." Only organized ball, *Sporting Life* claimed, made possible "such a stupendous undertaking." Organization had supposedly "made and kept the game clean and honest ... placed the game on (sic) stable and permanent basis ... made of the sport a real National Game, of which this Nation is so proud that it is willing and anxious to exhibit it to, and share it with, all the world."[8]

Few front line players from the Giants or White Sox, other than Buck Weaver, went overseas, although Boston Red Sox center fielder Tris Speaker and Detroit Tiger left fielder Sam Crawford joined the expedition, which proved quite lucrative, resulting in profits of almost $100,000. Following the venture, Hugh C. Weir completed another lengthy article on Comiskey, referring to him in the manner, popular at the time, as the "Old Roman." Comiskey was concerned about bleacher fans, Weir remarked, who purchased tickets for twenty-five cents and could move into pricier areas when it rained. His fondness for patrons, Weir suggested, possibly explained why Comiskey was "almost a popular idol in Chicago," in contrast to other owners who were castigated for their greedy ways. Comiskey's solicitude for his customers also helped the White Sox stand "as the most loyally supported baseball club in the country." Yes, some charged that Comiskey was "the greatest publicity getter in the baseball business." Weir also noted that the White Sox playing field was in shoddy shape; Comiskey deflected that charge by asking what could he do when friends or charities sought to use his ballpark.[9]

In a curious analysis, given what soon unfolded, Weir praised Comiskey's dealing with his ballplayers. While "adamant" once his mind was made up about a player's worth, Comiskey reportedly often surprised his employers "by offering more than was expected." Additionally, if a player were given too little in the spring, "there is sure to be a bonus check in the fall." An article in the *New York Evening Journal*, written during this same period, was headlined "Best Liked Magnate in Game." Comiskey, the piece declared, "has done as much to raise baseball to its present high plane as any man in the country."[10]

Like other major league owners, Comiskey had to contend with the Federal League threat. His first baseman, Hal Chase, a man with a highly checkered baseball career, was grabbed by the Federals, to the dismay of William Phelon. The reporter suggested that Comiskey was "the one man whom all warring factions should have let alone. He is the idol of the players, the public, and the scribes." Consequently, "raiding Commy's club is the one unpardonable offense, the one thing that cannot be condoned or tolerated." Indeed, "attacking Comiskey was the most suicidal thing the outlaws ever did" and would undoubtedly result in thousands of fans turning away from the Federals' Chicago franchise.[11]

As matter turned out, however, the threat posed by the Federal League had helped Comiskey craft his 1917 pennant-winning team. The Philadelphia Athletics' Connie Mack was compelled to break up his $100,000 infield, selling second sacker Eddie Collins to Comiskey for a reported $50,000; Collins inked a five year deal with Chicago for $15,000 annually. Cleveland Indian outfielder Joe Jackson subsequently was traded to the White Sox for some $65,000 and three players. His purpose, Comiskey explained, was "to give the people of Chicago, who have supported me so loyally all these years, the best club I can gather together." Thus, "I am trying as hard as I can and sparing no expense to give them a winner." Comiskey, Damon Runyon acknowledged in the summer of 1915, "has probably spent more money on his Chicago White Sox than has been spent by any other base ball magnate in the country." Yet Comiskey could not, Runyon cogently warned, "buy a very essential ingredient to baseball success ... the spirit of the pennant-winner." *The Indianapolis Freeman* also suggested that "you can't buy (a) pennant winner," as attested by the White Sox' third-place finish in 1915, despite 93 victories, which left them 9½ games behind the Boston Red Sox. The following year, the Red Sox repeated as American League champs, two games ahead of Chicago.[12]

In the midst of the 1916 season, *The Sporting News* produced an editorial entitled, "There Is But One Joe Jackson." Noting Jackson's stellar season — he ended up batting .341 — the paper stated that "Joe has grown in grace not only as a ball player but as a man." In closing, the piece declared, "So here's to Joe Jackson, a gentleman, a ball player and one of Nature's noblemen."[13]

Prior to the start of the next regular season, the White Sox were termed "formidable." Ty Cobb asserted, "If the White Sox ever wake up to a realization of their own strength, they will win the pennant sure." John J. Ward spoke of "the tremendous machine" Comiskey had put together, thanks to "the lavish investment" he had made in purchasing Collins, Jackson, and center fielder Happy Felsch, among others. In an article in *Baseball Magazine*, Comiskey was called "the genial owner of the White Sox" and "the most truly successful man ever associated with the great game he so ably typifies." *The*

*Sporting News* proclaimed that "never have hopes of Chicago fans landing a pennant been stronger than this year;" Comiskey's latest move, the acquisition of first baseman Chick Gandil — who had been dismissed by three major league managers as "a trouble-maker"— made the White Sox more potent still. Then, as the season got underway, *Sporting Life* referred to Comiskey as "universally loved."[14]

Ironically, in late May, talk of Rowland's firing unfolded as a crucial series with Red Sox began. Boston gamblers, who bet heavily on their home town team, reportedly were seeking to "disconcert the White Sox and throw them off their guard." Word of the gamblers' antics, George Robbins indicated, "made the Sox fighting mad." Consequently, "out with blood in their eyes," the White Sox blasted Boston starters Babe Ruth and Dutch Leonard in consecutive games.[15]

Prior to the start of the 1917 World Series, *The Sporting News* indicated that "real grief" awaited Comiskey. How, it asked, "can Old Roman take care of a million friends and admirers when he has but 32,000 seats?" The White Sox' defeat of McGraw's Giants led to more accolades for Comiskey, who was again deemed "the most popular man in baseball." None, it was said, begrudged him his success, as "literally millions of fans unite in congratulating him upon his personal triumph." American League umpire William Evans joined in the celebration, declaring that he had witnessed a hundred testimonials to "the self-made man of baseball." Comiskey was singular, Evans asserted, "because he always tried to figure out what the public wanted, and then gave it to them. Mr. Comiskey is unique among magnates because baseball is his business, not his hobby." Therefore, "he will live as one of the greatest characters connected with the game. His name and baseball will always be synonymous."[16]

* * *

Not all agreed with such analyses, including certain members of Comiskey's championship team. While Comiskey spent freely to acquire key components of his 1917 World Series squad and his private trains transported it to spring training in style, he remained tight-fisted in negotiating with many ballplayers. George "Buck" Weaver was one of those who seemed continually troubled by contractual dealings with White Sox management. By 1917, Weaver was acclaimed the top third sacker in the American League, but his salary remained at the $6,000 level he had agreed to in 1915, when the Federals had competed for his services.[17]

Born on August 18, 1890 in Pottstown, Pennsylvania, Weaver performed at St. Mary's College of Phoenixville, before playing semi-pro ball in Pottstown. Appearing on a series of minor league teams, Weaver starred with the San Francisco Seals in the Pacific Coast League. He became the regular

White Sox shortstop during the 1912 season. Remaining at that key infield spot throughout his first four years in the majors, Weaver's play in the field was sometimes erratic, occasionally brilliant. Not surprisingly, he committed a large number of errors, befitting his range and the small gloves infielders wielded during that period. As the plate, Weaver was equally inconsistent, compiling batting averages of .224, .272, .246, and .268. He displayed good speed, twice swiping more than 20 stolen bases, and scoring as many as 83 runs in 1915, in the midst of the dead ball era.

Second baseman Eddie Collins — purchased by Comiskey before the 1915 season began — *The Sporting News* asserted, was "bringing out the varied talents of Buck Weaver, Sox shortstop, better than any other second baseman could do. He had made Weaver a greater shortstop for the club," as Johnny Evers had aided Rabbit Maranville on the 1914 world champion Boston Braves. Shortly after the 1915 season began, Weaver had asked why the White Sox could not capture the pennant? As the "cheerful cuss" reasoned, "The Sox have the greatest infield in the American League, the best catcher in the world, the best pitching staff in the game, a great outfield and a good hitting combination from top to bottom of the batting order." The Chicago lineup — which now included catcher Ray Schalk, first baseman Jack Fournier, third baseman-outfielder Bobby "Braggo" Roth, Collins, and Weaver — was indeed formidable, Edwards contended. "There is a list of batters, eight in a row, any one of whom is likely to break up a game with a resounding wallop."[18]

Prior to the start of the 1916 season, *The Sporting News* proclaimed that White Sox manager Pants Rowland had no worries regarding the third base position. Weaver stood ready to play either shortstop or third. Another candidate was Fred McMullin, and the two, George Robbins declared, could offer new leadership for Comiskey's ball club. Robbins then defended Weaver against criticisms he had received.

> Just why some scribes persist in underrating Weaver the writer can't fathom. ... Weaver has everything to make a great third baseman for the Sox — everything that his predecessors lacked. He has the nerve to ride and tag runners coming into the bag. He isn't afraid of hot liners. He can come in good on a ball, is a dead shot on a fly and has a great throwing arm. ...
>
> The anvil chorus is after Buck though, and he'll have to lead the world at his post, it seems to avoid the knockers.[19]

While acknowledging that Weaver had not just experienced his finest year, Robbins declared nevertheless that "his work for the most part was brilliant and helpful to the pitchers." In Robbins's estimation, there isn't a shortstop in baseball, taken him year in and year out, who will field much tighter than this same Weaver when a pitcher is in a hole and needs help. It certainly is a great injustice to a player to knock him when he is cutting off more base hits and courting more errors than most of the shortstops in the major leagues.

Moreover, the loss of Weaver, Robbins insisted, would "wreck" Chicago's pennant chances.[20]

As the season unfolded, *The Sporting News* claimed that Weaver's work at third base demonstrated "class at his new station" and made him a rival for the Giants' Heinie Zimmerman. On May 25, Robbins asserted that "Weaver is a great ball player and will show well anywhere he is placed." Two weeks later, the sportswriter indicated that Buck "has no superior in the American League at short when he has his head up and plays at the top of his game." In September, Robbins stated that "there is no better infielder in the world" than Weaver. At season's end, the sportswriter pointed out that Rowland had "made Buck Weaver play the greatest ball of his career as a major leaguer." Splitting his time almost equally between shortstop and third base, Weaver's fielding percentage rose markedly; he also scored 78 runs and belted 27 doubles. The one negative note involved his batting average, which plummeted to .227, the lowest mark since his rookie year.[21]

* * *

During the off-season, as strike action loomed, most of the White Sox, *The Sporting News* reported, were "not in sympathy with the Fraternity." Collins and Weaver, in contrast to player representative Shano Collins, were not even members of the players' organization. On February 5, George Robbins noted that the White Sox were "much opposed to war. They are flocking into the fold of their good shepherd in large numbers." Robbins continued,

> Eddie Collins and Buck Weaver and other captains of high finance have figured it all out and there is nothing doing in the Fraternity business with them — not on your photograph. Living is too high even to think of such a ridiculous thing. With potatoes $3 a bushel, eggs, butter, meat and other commodities sky high, to say nothing of the cost of prunes, such financiers as these are not going to dabble in such business. Money is too scarce and rent too high to let go of the salary coin unless these players can see a reasonable return on their investment. This they fail to see. Going in or out with the Fraternity doesn't help lay in the winter's coal or fill the flour bin, the way Buck, Eddie, et al. size up things.

The following week, Robbins indicated that "White Sox players have refused to sever relations" with Comiskey. Three ballplayers, at most, had failed to come to terms with the Chicago owner.[22]

Buck Weaver warming up, 1917. National Baseball Hall of Fame Library, Cooperstown, N.Y.

* * *

Weaver's mediocre batting performance in 1916 failed to dissuade Pants Rowland from viewing him as "one of the game's greatest players." Yet it conceivably cost the White Sox the pennant, as they finished a mere two games behind the Boston Red Sox. An injury that temporarily knocked Weaver out of action in August 1917 led *The Sporting News* to proclaim such a blow a "near knockout to White Sox chances." Weaver, after all, "was about the best all around third sacker in the business this season." Toward the end of the month, with Buck still sidelined, the paper declared that he "plays far and away the best all around game of ball of any third sacker in the league, a game of the Heinie Zimmerman-Hains Groh class."[23]

But in 1917, Chicago was not to be denied, exchanging places in the league standings with Boston, while winning 100 games for the first time in franchise history. White Sox players were sprinkled throughout the list of league leaders, with Jackson and Collins tying for fourth place with 91 runs scored apiece, Jackson finishing second to Cobb with 17 triples, fifth in RBIs with 75 runs plated, and fifth in slugging percentage with a .429 average. Collins finished second in the league with 89 walks and stolen bases with 53, and fifth with an on-base percentage of .389, while Happy Felsch was second with 102 RBIs and batted a team-leading .308. Ed Cicotte led the league with 28 victories and a 1.53 ERA, and was second in strikeouts with 150, third with a .700 won-loss percentage and 29 complete games pitched, and fourth with seven shutouts. Chicago's Dave Danforth was the league's top reliever, Red Faber had a 1.92 ERA, and Reb Russell led the league with a .750 winning percentage, while Lefty Williams finished at .680.

With Eddie Collins batting only .289 and Joe Jackson a mere .301, far below their career percentages, twenty-six year-old Buck Weaver's contribution at the plate was noteworthy. He topped his previous lifetime best with a .284 batting average, while contributing 64 runs scored and 19 stolen bases, despite appearing in only 118 games. Now playing mostly third base — rookie Swede Risberg was the regular shortstop — Weaver also led the league in fielding with a .949 mark. When manager Clarence "Pants" Rowland mulled over the third base spot as the season began, Weaver offered to play there full-time. Even prior to the close of the 1917 season, Rowland was referring to Weaver as "the best third basemen in the league." When asked why he rated Weaver so highly, Rowland exclaimed,

It's the old pepper. 'Buck' is so full of it that it just naturally oozes out. No, he doesn't hit .300. But he hits 'em where they count and you will notice that he generally comes near leading the league in sacrifice hits. And he's a flash around that third bag. It's Buck's position. I thought he was a bear of a shortstop but, gosh, he's gonna make the rest of the third basemen look like a bunch of Oslerized cripples before long. And it's the old tabasco that does it. Buck is so full of it that he's just gotta exhale a coupla wild throws once in a while to settle down.

Rowland went on to add, "You can't figure a guy like Weaver out on paper. 'Pep' doesn't get into the averages, and that's why Weaver is lots better than the figures show."[24]

**Buck Weaver, 1917. Chicago Historical Society (ICHi-20697).**

Weaver, *Baseball Magazine* reported, "puts everything he has into his playing. He has a cut to his jaw that means 'scrap' and doesn't know that Webster stuck a word like 'quit' in his dictionary." While White Sox fans had believed Weaver was "going to snatch that old pennant for them," the baseball publication also claimed that the third baseman would "get a lot of the blame" if his team ended up on top.[25]

McGraw was said to have put together "the most powerful" National League squad since the Cubs' championship units of the previous decade that had featured first baseman-manager Frank Chance, the middle infield combination of Joe Tinker and Johnny Evers, and Mordecai "Three Finger" Brown's stellar pitching. However, the White Sox were also viewed as a strong club, perhaps the equal of Connie Mack's best. As the Series approached, F. C. Lane called Weaver a "star" and "a brilliant player." Weaver was termed "a beautiful fielder, a good hitter and an aggressive, snappy player whose spirit is a valuable addition to the Club Morale." Joe Vila rated Buck "the leading third baseman in the American League and a first-class hitter, also a winning fielder," although he considered the Giants' Heinie Zimmerman better in the field.[26]

In the midst of the Comiskey-McGraw led world tour that the White Sox and Giants had conducted four years earlier, Weaver, still a relative newcomer in the majors, had ridden the National Leaguers and their manager. He hollered at the famed Giants' leader, "Go-wan. You got a power-puff ball club. You're yellow. You ain't got the guts of a canary bird. I only hope we get you guys in a World Series. Then we'll show you what a real fightin' ball club is — you and your yellowbellies." As the 1917 Series opened, however, the White Sox opted not to banter with their competitors, who chortled, "Thought you were a fightin' ball club. Who're the yellowbellies now? Fightin' ball club? Hell!!!"[27]

The White Sox took the first two games in Comiskey Park, while the Giants shut them out in the third and fourth contests at the Polo Grounds. Prior to game five, the White Sox decided to "let loose." Their spikes were honed until sharpened like razors. During batting practice before the fifth game, Weaver — who played shortstop during the Series — deliberately sought to stir things up. Weaver signaled to teammate Dave Danforth to toss the ball low and outside so he could belt it down the line where the Giants were warming up. As Weaver put it, "I wanted to knock a couple of 'em cold," and no warning was issued to the Giants that the ball was going down the right field line. After the ball came their way, the Giants stopped and watched Weaver knock another one in their direction. When the Giants hollered at Weaver, he yelled back that he "was goin' to flatten a couple of 'em; that they thought they were a fightin' ball club; well, we'd show 'em a REAL fightin' team." Weaver proceeded to stroke seven or eight line drives in the direction of the Giants, who, by the third smash, left the field and sat down.[28]

His teammates followed Weaver's lead, selecting individual players to target. Weaver's choice was Giant shortstop Art Fletcher, and, as the White Sox third sacker put it, "I had him crazy." As the game progressed, the White Sox flew around the base-paths with their threatening spikes prominently displayed. The Giants, in the hard-nosed ball typical of the era, returned the favor, tagging the White Sox by slamming the ball down on them. New York led 4-1 in the bottom of the sixth inning when a controversial play involving Weaver appeared to arouse Chicago from its stupor. With one out, Weaver was perched on first when Schalk hit a single into right center. As Weaver headed for second base, he encountered interference from Giant middle infielders Buck Herzog and Art Fletcher. Weaver, *The Sporting News* indicated, was compelled "to push Herzog out of his way and he managed to side-step Fletcher." Weaver subsequently scored on Risberg's single to right. The Giants went ahead 5-2 in the seventh, but the White Sox scored three runs in the bottom of the inning and three more in the eighth to win 8-5. Two days later, they won again to take the Series four games to two. Weaver batted .333 for the Series, with seven hits and three runs scored. The star of the 1917 World Series was Red Faber, who won three games, matching the feat of Bill Dinneen, Deacon Phillippe, Christy Mathewson, Babe Adams, Jack Coombs, and Joe Wood. After the last out was recorded, McGraw tore across the field in Weaver's direction. "I wanta shake your hand, kid," the Giants' manager declared. "You're the best, and I wanta take my hat off to you."[29]

More plaudits soon came Buck Weaver's way. F. C. Lane, editor of *Baseball Magazine*, selected the White Sox third sacker for his American League All Star Team, where he joined teammates Collins, Felsch, Cicotte, and catcher Ray Schalk on the squad. In Lane's words, Weaver "was an active and dangerous element in the Sox offense, and fielded with all the snap and energy of a dynamo." Earlier feared to be the team's weak spot, third base, thanks to Weaver's performance, proved to be "one of the foundations of its strength."[30]

* * *

Predictions abounded that the White Sox would remain baseball's finest. Only the military draft, *The Sporting News* stated, could halt Chicago. However, the possibility that Charles Comiskey's club might become a dynasty was soon aborted by an unhappy combination of events. Comiskey's miserly treatment of many of his players and coaches, coupled with his seeming pampering of others, ensured that team discord was not far beneath the surface. Well before the infamous 1919 World Series, his players were referred to as the Black Sox because of their soiled uniforms, the byproduct of Comiskey's determination that his employees cover their own cleaning expenses. In the midst of the 1917 season, Comiskey promised a team bonus if the White Sox won the pennant. The actual payoff was a case of poor-quality champagne, which enraged his entire squad. Even following the World Series triumph, Comiskey proved no more generous. Weaver, for example, was forced to accept the same $6,000 salary he had first secured three years earlier, when he was a far less skilled batter and fielder. The great Joe Jackson received the same pay, Schalk a mere $1,000 more and Cicotte $1,000 less. Felsch was paid but $3,750, first baseman Chick Gandil got only $4,000, and Williams signed a contract for the 1918 season that set his salary at $3,000. Meanwhile, Eddie Collins, whom Weaver despised for refusing to sharpen his spikes during the World Series like the other White Sox, was paid $15,000 a year. Comiskey's stinginess was hardly due to financial circumstances; his team's attendance figures had topped the majors for the past two seasons. Articles reported how he had profited from his baseball investment alone; several referred to him as one of the wealthiest baseball magnates.[31]

Comiskey continued all the while to garner favorable publicity from sportswriters. *The Sporting News* applauded "the old Roman" for having "spent thousands of dollars to give the Windy City a winner." George S. Robbins cheered Comiskey for urging establishment of a fund to deliver partial salaries to players serving in the American military. *Baseball Magazine* reported Comiskey's offer, delivered in anticipation that the impending season would be a precarious one financially for many clubs, that receipts be pooled and equally divided. If such a proposition were adopted, then the White Sox, as the game's "best money-getters of them all," would suffer accordingly. To W. A. Phelon, this exemplified the Comiskey's "sportsmanship and his love for the game." More plaudits came Comiskey's way, when he contributed 10% of his reported earnings, some $17,113, to the allied war cause, and after he subscribed for $25,000 in war bonds.[32]

The now greater impact of American involvement in the war ensured that the supposedly "invincible" White Sox — predicted during the off-season to repeat as champions — failed to duplicate their 1917 success. Many more ballplayers entered the United States military during the ensuing season, a far more uncertain one for the major leagues. Criticisms were hurled regarding the frivolousness of playing such a sport in the midst of a national emergency. Attendance plummeted, and owners agreed to shorten the season to 128 games. While slashing ballplayer salaries, they also sought government imprimatur of baseball as an "essential industry." Instead, Secretary of War Newton D. Baker declared that "players in the draft age must obtain employment calculated to aid in the successful prosecution of the war or shoulder guns and fight." George S. Robbins, writing in *The Sporting News*, continued to assert that "baseball is the great summer means of entertainment for millions of Americans. ... Baseball is the national game of this country. It's a national institution — declared so by that eminent jurist, Judge

Kenesaw M. Landis in the famous suit of the Federal League against Organized Ball."[33]

Nevertheless, the work-or-fight edict, W. A. Phelon suggested, "was a numbing, shattering blow" to major league clubs. Over 200 players now enlisted or were conscripted, while others worked in defense plants. Joe Jackson was among those to follow the second course of action, and was denounced as a slacker. By contrast, former Giants' infielder Eddie Grant, a Harvard graduate, was killed overseas. Pete Alexander experienced trench warfare, resulting in hearing loss and migraines. Captain Christy Mathewson, in the midst of a drill in France that killed eight of his fellow soldiers, found his lungs filled with poison gas.[34]

Troubles began during pre-season for the defending World Series champs and never slackened. To Weaver's obvious chagrin, his mentor, coach William "Kid" Gleason, refused Comiskey's contract offer and quit the team. Military service or industrial employment took away many others, including Collins, Risberg, infielder Fred McMullin, Lefty Williams, and Red Faber. Twenty White Sox entered the American armed forces, along with many of the game's top stars, including Ty Cobb, Mathewson, and Alexander. When Williams and backup catcher Byrd Lynn headed for munitions plants, an enraged Comiskey ripped up their contracts and demanded their uniforms back. "There is no room on my ball club for players who wish to evade the Army draft by entering the employ of ship concerns," complained Comiskey. "Players like (Jim) Scott and Faber, who have enlisted in the Army and Navy have my well wishes. I wish them Godspeed and we'll be pulling for these boys wherever they go." By mid-season, Comiskey's club, *The Sporting News* claimed, was "decimated by the draft, desertions to the ship yards and voluntary enlistments."[35]

Late in the abbreviated season, W. A. Phelon reported that "Comiskey's gallant team of world's champions seems to be just about wrecked." Both "draft and desertion," he declared, had crippled the Chicago franchise. "Sundry alleged heroes joined the Safe Shelter Leagues, to the Old Roman's intense disgust," Phelon continued, "and others went, like men, to army service." A month later, the story was grimmer still. "The world's champion, a shadow of their former glory and a skeleton of the 1917 club," Phelon indicated, continued to founder. Saddest of all, he charged, was the fact that "Comiskey's heart was almost broken when Joe Jackson and Oscar Felsch deserted the club—two players whom he had treated royally at all times." The *Reach Official American League Guide* indicated that the White Sox were "riddled by draft and desertion." By season's end, "Commy" was left with "only the ghost of a ballclub."[36]

The White Sox finished in sixth place, with only a 57-67 record, 17 games behind the pennant-winning Red Sox and a mere seven games out of the cellar. Thirty-four year-old Eddie Cicotte struggled to a 12-19 record, leading the league in losses. Only Weaver, among the White Sox regulars who completed most of the season, ended up with a .300 batting average, his best mark yet. The league's top third baseman had been forced to spend most of the season at shortstop. In his wrap-up of the 1918 season, Phelon proclaimed that Chicago was "reduced to a mere wreck, a pitiable phantom of its former power."[37]

In attacking ballplayers who headed for the shipyards, Comiskey had hardly added to his ball club's morale. "I don't consider them fit to play on my ball club," he cried. "I would gladly lose my whole team if the players wished to do their duty to their country ... but I hate to see any ballplayers, particularly my own, go (to) the shipyards to escape military service."[38]

CHAPTER FOUR

# The Biggest Man in Baseball

Following an edict from the War Department, the 1918 major league season officially ended on September 2. Duplicating their 1915 and 1916 triumphs, the now Ed Barrow-led Boston Red Sox won the pennant by 2½ games over Cleveland. The defending champion White Sox, with Eddie Collins, Red Faber, and Swede Risberg called into military service, and Happy Felsch, Joe Jackson, and Lefty Williams choosing to work in defense plants, dropped to sixth place, well back of the Red Sox. Fred Mitchell's Chicago Cubs, featuring a strong pitching staff, took the National League pennant, besting McGraw's Giants by 10½ games. The 1918 World Series — which Secretary of War Baker allowed to take place — was captured in six games by the Red Sox, relying on the strong arms of Carl Mays and George Herman "Babe" Ruth, who each took a pair.

The 1918 season proved to be, in many regards, both a terribly troubled year and an historic one for the national pastime. The previous November, American League President Ban Johnson had proposed that the federal government be asked to exempt from conscription 18 players on each major league squad. His National League counterpart, John K. Tenor, termed such a suggestion "preposterous" and "unpatriotic." In December, major league bosses determined to offer a full slate of games during the upcoming season. The public relations fallout was considerable, with the *New York Times* delivering a stinging attack. "With an astonishing disregard for the new proprieties and new decencies," the *Times* charged, "the so-called 'magnates' of baseball have proclaimed in both 'leagues' their unswerving adherence to the wretched fallacy of 'business as usual.'" That decision, the *Times* claimed, "is not calculated to make us proud of baseball as an American institution."

The major league moguls soon adopted a different tack: they announced that the 1918 season would be reduced to 140 games, curtailed spring training, and cut player salaries. Secretary of War Baker's work-or-fight decree of May 23, nevertheless, was disruptive and eventually led to a further abridgment of the regular season. Having learned his lesson perhaps too well, Johnson now declared that he supported moves to "close every theatre, ball park, and place of recreation in the country and make people realize that they were in the most terrible war in the history of the world." He soon retreated from that stance, however, insisting baseball was a productive industry that contributed $300,000 in war taxes. Claiming that "the great American pastime" was "a most useful adjunct of ... war preparation," the editors of *Baseball Magazine* termed it "a gigantic industry" as well. They then remarked, "We cannot believe that the administration would wreck the national game, the peculiar institution beloved by the masses in order to supply a few hundred ill equipped young men, for industries of which they know little where their work would be on a par with the most unskilled laborer in the land."[1]

The war, Harry R. Stringer noted, was "regenerating baseball," while "a new and overwhelming enthusiasm for the grand old game is sweeping the country." It was in the military training camp, Stringer declared, that "the national pastime" was being transformed. Happily then, he wrote,

> Baseball is doing its 'bit' effectively and convincingly. It is a constructive moral and military force. It is welding and fusing the conglomerate mass and spirit of the training into a tangible and concrete body engendered with one purpose, for where does such a camaraderie thrive as on the ball field. In doing this the game perhaps is making its greatest single contribution to the cause of democracy for the esprit de corps is the soul of the army, and an army torn by internal strife, discontented and spiritless, cannot hope to win.[2]

Adopting a different approach, George S. Robbins, in an essay for *The Sporting News*, charged that Baker's decision was "a blow" that could prove crippling to the United States in "these dire times." For baseball was, as Robbins saw it, "the greatest developer of sport in the Army ... and the soul of baseball is the major league races, culminating in the national sporting classic — the World's Series." Washington officialdom, Robbins offered, appeared not to recognize "that the game of baseball is the national sport, that it is the greatest means of fanning the flame of athletic endeavor and building up the greatest army of fighters the world has ever seen." The boys in the U.S. camps, Robbins continued, "eagerly await the scores of the games." Moreover, "the national game as a means of spreading the leavening influence of sport does incalculable good. It's the biggest boost the Army gets."[3]

Notwithstanding such analyses, major league ball remained imperiled by war time developments. Any number of star players, including the White Sox's Joe Jackson, left their teams to join the ranks of ship building and steel company squads. To F. C. Lane, this "new danger" threatened the financial makeup of "the national game," as it "grossly outrages the spirit of military service." Because of a few players, Lane stated, ballplayers might become stereotyped as "slackers." Continuing to worry about the war's impact on "the greatest and best of sports," Lane wondered if baseball were "to be doomed as a sacrifice on the grim altar of war."[4]

As the abbreviated 1918 season ended, many remained troubled about organized baseball's future prospects. On October 3, George S. Robbins of *The Sporting News* called for the national game to "become an essential occupation"; big league owners, he said, should contribute to an athletic fund to construct gymnasiums for the soldiers. Such an approach would enable ballplayers to stay at their "proper place ... on the field." A week later, Paul W. Eaton charged that baseball was "going down in the United States," while "going up everywhere else." Pointing to the fact that Washington wanted the game continued, Eaton also contended, "All well informed persons agree that amusements are necessary in war time." Believing that the war's end was approaching, Charles Comiskey urged that ball park gates be opened up the following spring.[5]

Professional baseball should be played the following year, F. C. Lane agreed, even if the war dragged on. Athletic competition, Lane contended, was hardly "non-essential in war time," but rather had proven "a necessity." Changes were called for, he admitted, including a redrawing of "Eastern" and "Western" clubs to reduce costs, which also demanded that players be paid a fixed sum per game. But the game itself, Lane believed, was above reproach. Indeed, it was "the cleanest, most honest, most wholesome sport the sun ever shown upon."[6]

Others wholeheartedly agreed that baseball's merits demanded its continuance. As he called for the game to go on, former Cubs' owner Charles W. Murphy insisted, "I have constantly in mind the winning of the war." Baseball, not food or fuel, Frederick E. Parmly related, would lead to success. Through this game, American lads acquired "quickness of thought, self reliance, judgment and confidence," along with the physical dexterity demanded to put such qualities into practice. Baseball, more than any other sport, Parmly declared, encouraged "quick thinking, co-operative action, and other important characteristics." Germany would learn this, Parmly insisted, "to her chagrin." America's "National game well deserved its popularity" for contributing to the war effort.[7]

\* \* \*

In spite of such good cheer, developments both on and off the field threatened the game's very viability. Attendance plummeted precipitously downward, falling under 3,100,000, barely half the previous season's total. Most ominous of all, perhaps, were the circumstances surrounding the decision by Cincinnati Reds' manager Christy Mathewson to suspend first baseman Hal Chase for "indifferent playing." An exceptionally gifted fielder and a former batting champ, Chase had long been suspected of questionable antics. Easily forgotten was how effusively sportswriters had praised Prince Hal; at the same time, they had often discussed a darker side of the majors' top first baseman. In an early article in *Baseball Magazine*, Frederick G. Lieb had termed Chase "the premier first sacker of the present, past or any other generation since the time of Adam." Yet Lieb had also indicated that Chase "has on frequent occasions been the naughtiest lad performing" for the New York Highlanders. Refusing to play alongside those he didn't care for, Chase departed from his team in 1908 and went off to the California Outlaw League. Lieb indicated that although "this was one of the greatest offenses in organized baseball, Harold was whitewashed by the National Commission." In 1910 and 1911, *Baseball Magazine* placed Chase — whom it said was "almost unanimously credited with being the best first baseman that ever handled a ball" — on its All-American Base Ball Team. In other years, it felt compelled to explain why Chase had been left off.[8]

To be denounced by the legendary Mathewson, whose ouster of Chase was upheld by Cincinnati owner and National Commission chairman Gary Herrmann, was damning indeed. Four decades had passed, *The Sporting News* pointed out, since this kind of scandal had afflicted big league ball. But unfortunately, for some time now, "the bars against gambling in the stands have been let down a little by the clubs." Furthermore, "gambling cliques, operating in Boston and New York, have been trying to corrupt big league players all season." Reportedly, "fifty major league stars could tell of the offers made them." In the pages of *Baseball Magazine*, W. A. Phelon warned that "an ugly cloud darkened the National League horizon — the first big gambling scandal" the game had faced in four decades. Cincinnati, Francis C. Richter, editor of *The Reach Official American League Guide*, asserted, was "a heavy sufferer from the season-long insubordination of first baseman Chase."[9]

*The Reach Official American League Guide* proclaimed the 1918 season as "the most unsatisfactory, harassing and unprofitable campaign in the 47 years' history of Organized Ball." Francis C. Richter, editor of the *Reach Guide*, pointed to Provost Marshall General Crowder's "work-or-fight" as the reason why baseball suffered so. But he blamed baseball management for having failed to make the case that the national pastime, like theater, opera, and cinema, required special-exemption status. Instead, the Crowder decree adjudged baseball as non-essential, producing "general demoralization in the ranks of magnates and players, alienated for the time being a great many fans, and caused a great furor among the exponents of the game." To their credit, Richter wrote, some 60% of major league ballplayers opted for military service. Only a few, he declared, "deserted their teams for the shelter of the shipyards and munition plants to escape the draft." Thus, "base ball went out with clean hands, with honor unstained and with patriotism aflame, as becomes the greatest, cleanest and most intensely national sport this nation — or, for that matter, any nation — ever possessed or will possess."[10]

Fortunately, baseball fans also had something to cheer about even in the midst of the subdued 1918 season. The Chicago Cubs played ball at a stellar clip, easily outdistancing the Giants. Brooklyn's Zach Wheat and Cincinnati's Edd Roush waged a spirited contest for the batting title, with the Dodger prevailing by two points. The Cubs' strong-armed staff topped the league, guided by Hippo Vaughn, Claude Hendrix, and Lefty Tyler. In the American League, the race was considerably tighter, as the Red Sox just edged out Tris Speaker and the Indians, with Walter Johnson and the Senators coming in third. Ty Cobb clinched yet another batting crown — his eleventh — with a .382 mark, while Johnson completed one more pitching triple crown, winning 23 games, striking out 162 batters, and compiling a stellar 1.27 ERA.

The story of the year, however, proved to be the man-child — still only 23-years-old, but already a seasoned veteran — with the world champion Red Sox: Babe Ruth. In the decade ahead, Ruth, of course, would become major league baseball's greatest icon and the most celebrated individual performer in the American sports pantheon. In 1918, the Babe was converted into a pitcher-outfielder, thereby accomplishing a feat like Frank Merriwell's less wholesome cousin might. Amassing a 13-7 won-loss record with a 2.22 ERA, Ruth batted an even .300, while belting 11 homers, which tied him for the league lead, the first of a dozen such crowns. During that season's World Series, Ruth continued a scoreless inning streak that eventually reached 29 ⅔, bettering Christy Mathewson's old standard. Thus, it was during both the regular season and the fall classic of 1918 that the legend began of Babe Ruth as American sports' most brilliant performer.

Born in Baltimore, Maryland, on February 6, 1895, Ruth possessed a troubled childhood, little attended to by his overwrought parents, who operated a grocery store-saloon. As a consequence, Ruth became street-wise and a truant, which eventually led his little-educated German-American parents to place their seemingly incorrigible son in St. Mary's Industrial School for Boys when he was but seven. Run by the Xaverian Brothers, a lay offshoot of the Jesuits, St. Mary's served as something of an orphanage, boarding school, and way station for troubled youth. Spending most of the next twelve years there, Ruth received a general education, acquired a fine penmanship, learned how to sew expertly, and was introduced to the art of baseball by Brother Matthias. As Ruth later acknowledged, "Once I had been introduced to school athletics, I was satisfied and happy. ... All I wanted was to play. I didn't care much where." In the meantime, Ruth's mother passed away, he adopted the Roman Catholic faith, and he looked to his mentor Brother Matthias as a surrogate father. By 1913, the now 6'2", 150 pound Ruth was an exceptionally gifted ballplayer, serving as the school's leading catcher and pitcher and batting .537 in interscholastic contests.

The following year, Jack Dunn, manager-owner of the Baltimore Orioles of the International League, following the advice of Brother Gilbert, the Mount St. Joseph's School's athletic director, signed Ruth to a $600 contract. Dunn's coach took one look at Ruth and exclaimed, "Well, here's Jack newest babe now!" Ruth, early displaying remarkable prowess on the mound and at the plate, acquired the nickname for good. His very first intra-squad game led a Baltimore sportswriter to assert, "The newt batter made a hit that will live in the memory of all who saw it. That clouter was George Ruth, the southpaw from St. Mary's school. The ball carried so far to right field that he walked around the bases." The April 23, 1914 issue of *The Sporting News* first referred to Ruth as "a sterling southpaw;" it mistakenly indicated that he had been selected from a college squad in Baltimore. As Ruth began putting together an 11-7 won-loss record with the Orioles, the *Baltimore Sun* declared, "He is a wonder ... . During the past few months, his shoots have made the whole baseball world sit up and pay attention." In the meantime, Dunn faced economic ruin thanks to competition from the Federal League's Baltimore franchise. Consequently, Dunn sought to sell Ruth to the Philadelphia Athletics' Connie Mack, but the world champions' manager declined, saying, "He's a great pitcher, but he's worth more than I can afford." Subsequently, Dunn delivered his star protege, pitcher Ernie Shore, and catcher Ben Egan to the Red Sox for a figure ranging from $8,500–$25,000, along with cancellation of a $3,000 debt. The amount paid for the trio, *The Sporting News* suggested on July 16, was "perhaps a little more than the average ... as Ruth is considered a real star."[11]

Remaining with the big league club for five weeks, Ruth won two of three decisions; after his second outing, *The Sporting News* declared that "Baby Ruth continued to look and act like a cool-headed and crafty youngster." However, he was soon sent down to the Red Sox' International League team, the Providence Grays. *The Sporting News* predicted, "No one in this burg doubts he will be a big winner for the Grays. Ruth is a physical Giant and although Dunn used him frequently early in the campaign, he seems to be endowed with a frame sufficient to stand the strain."[12]

After crafting an 11-2 mark, Ruth returned to Boston for the last few days of the major league season. His first season in organized ball had proved a resounding success, resulting in a 22-9 minor league won-loss record, his first home run — belted for Providence — and his initial pair of big-league hits, one a double. The next three seasons were better still, as Ruth became the American League's foremost left-handed pitcher. In 1915, the World Champion Red Sox, who won the pennant by only 2½ games over the Tigers, benefited from Ruth's 18-8 won-loss total and 2.44 ERA. Ruth, in only 92 times at bat, led the Red Sox with four home runs, while batting .315 and posting a then remarkable .576 slugging average. The Babe's lone appearance in the World Series involved an unsuccessful pinch-hitting appearance. Proclaiming Ruth both a "sensational young southpaw" and "a terrific batter," *Sporting Life*'s issue of October 9, 1915, declared his rise "meteoric."[13]

Even before the 1916 season unfolded, Ruth — now working on a two-year contract that paid $3,500 annually — began to receive considerable ink as both a top-notch pitcher and hitter. He appeared on the cover of *Sporting Life*. The July issue of *Baseball Magazine* contained a feature that termed him "one of the greatest natural pitchers" ever to play in the big leagues. It referred to him as "a pitcher of marvelous gifts," who, until he took his place in the Red Sox rotation, "had been the Cinderella of the greatest pitching staff in the game." Highlighting Ruth's rise from "a life of neglect and poverty," author John J. Ward declared his story to be Dickensian in nature. Now packing nearly 200 pounds, "the great left-hander" was also viewed by Ward as "a dreaded batter" who was feared almost as much "for his tremendous wallops" as for his pitching acumen. The previous year, "he seemed to have a natural batting eye, and was as likely to make a home run drive as an ordinary pitcher was to scratch out a freak single." Thus, "Ruth seemed to be one of those all-around players such as pitchers of the old days used to be," more striking still because of the game's increased specialization. Later that summer, F. C. Lane noted that "so great are Ruth's gifts as a batter that there has been some talk of making an outfielder of him. But so far his marked abilities as a pitcher have prevented such a plan." Near season's end, *The Sporting News* indicated that "it will be the good arm of Babe Ruth on whom Boston's fate depends — and it is some arm."[14]

The extolling of Ruth as a slugger was even more noteworthy as it occurred in the midst of the dead ball era. Lane, who did as much as anyone to publicize Ruth's batting feats, had recently posed the question, "Is batting doomed?," while conjecturing that the age "of the fence-shattering slugger" had disappeared, "perhaps never to return." Indeed, Lane was troubled over "the general decline of batting" that the majors had experienced. The 1914 and 1915 seasons concluded with overall batting averages of .249 and .248, respectively, a drop of 20 points in only four years. The introduction of "a livelier ball," Lane suggested, might make a difference.[15]

All the while, pitcher-slugger Ruth had joined Walter Johnson in the ranks of the junior circuit's top moundsmen. The Red Sox barely edged out the White Sox for the league's title; the second place White Sox were crippled by shortstop Buck Weaver's .227 batting average and catcher Ray Schalk's .232 mark. Even Eddie Collins batted only — for him, anyway — .308. The Red Sox had few heavy hitters of their own, producing but 14 home runs for the second year in a row, with pitcher Ruth tying for the team lead with three. While Ruth's batting average dropped to .272, his slugging percentage of .419 also topped the squad. But it was on the mound where Ruth shone most brightly in 1916, as he finished third in the league with 23 wins, second with a .657 won-loss percentage, and first with nine shutouts, a 1.75 ERA, and a .201 opponents' batting average. In 323 innings pitched, he gave up only 230 hits, the fewest per game in the league, 6.40, and struck out 170, finishing third in that race. Ruth helped guide Boston to a second consecutive World Series championship, throwing a 14 inning masterpiece in game two, when he shut out the Brooklyn Dodgers after the first inning.

At the close of the 1916 season, the American League All-America Baseball Club, selected by F. C. Lane of *Baseball Magazine*, contained such familiar choices as second baseman Eddie Collins, outfielders Ty Cobb, Tris Speaker, and Joe Jackson, and pitcher Walter Johnson. Honorable mention nods went to the likes of Cleveland first baseman Chick Gandil, White Sox outfielder Happy Felsch, and Chicago's shortstop Buck Weaver, who in spite of his abysmal batting average, was said to play "a great all-around game." New additions to the starting lineup included catcher Ray Schalk of the runner-up White Sox and pitching ace Babe Ruth of the champion Red Sox. Ruth was termed "a very glutton for work," who was vying for the title of "the best left-hander in the league." He was also deemed to be, in contrast to so many pitchers, "a dangerous slugger and all-around player of great ability." Furthermore, his World Series performance was called "a classic of its kind"; as Lane put it, "the work of Ruth in that historic contest will long be remembered." Irving Sanborn's All-Star Baseball Team included a quartet of pitchers: Walter Johnson, Grover Cleveland Alexander, Pittsburgh's Albert Mamaux, and Ruth. Grantland Rice's featured the same group, along with the Yankees' Bob Shawkey. Henry P. Edwards, *The Sporting News'* Cleveland correspondent, included Johnson, Ruth, Philadelphia's Joe Bush, and Detroit's Harry Coveleski, on his American League all-star team.[16]

Ruth subsequently got off to fast start in 1917, leading *The Sporting News* to proclaim that "the giant southpaw pitcher-slugger of the Red Sox is due for a wonderful year." Burt Whitman referred to "the big gent" as "one of the most picturesque figures in the game." The fans, Whitman wrote, would never forget how he "knocked that ball over those Sportsmen's Park barriers, and the same goes for Philadelphia and for New York, where he has several times violated Shibe Park and the Polo Grounds with tremendous clouts." His pitching success, the sportswriter indicated, was attributable to his fast ball. For "when he is right he just whizzes them by the batters and that's all there is to it." Whitman believed Ruth would become the "most talked of pitcher in whole world of baseball," while Bostonians saw him as the game's greatest attraction, indeed the biggest since Christy Mathewson's heyday. Some saw his popularity as approaching that of Rube Waddell's.[17]

During the 1917 season, Ruth more than equaled his previous year's performance, producing a 24-13 won-loss record, a 2.02 ERA, six shutouts, 128 strikeouts, and a league-leading 35 complete games, an amount surpassed only once since in the junior circuit. His 326⅓ innings pitched were third in the American League, his win total second to the White Sox' Eddie Cicotte, his .649 winning percentage, shutouts, and strikeout total, fifth best. He was the American League's third stingiest pitcher according to hits allowed per game, 6.73, and opponents' batting average, .211. Smacking two more home runs, Ruth batted .325 with a .472 slugging percentage; only outfielder Duffy Lewis of the Red Sox regulars topped the .300 mark. Despite Ruth's performance and the 22 win season of Carl Mays, however, Boston finished nine full games behind Charles Comiskey's White Sox, who upheld the American League's honor during that year's World Series. Ruth continued to be singled out for his "all 'round playing ability," including his "tremendous slugging power." Termed "a man of gigantic strength," Ruth was deemed to be "one of the greatest pitchers in the American League," who had "nearly as much stuff as Walter Johnson."[18]

* * *

In early 1918, Ernest J. Lanigan, writing in *The Sporting News*, had referred to the American Association's recent outlawing of the spitball, and suggested that the major leagues would probably soon follow suit. Banning the spitball, it was believed, would "increase batting averages and put more life and pep into the game." Lanigan predicted that "long distance hitting and lots of it will be emphasized, rather than airtight pitching and marvelous defense work."[19]

By March it was clear that no major rules changes would take place immediately. Baseball management, I. E. Sanborn of the *Chicago Tribune* noted, was "notoriously superstitious." Recognizing that the game had prospered mightily under the tutelage of the present National Agreement, baseball moguls were "unwilling to risk any sort of a change." Sanborn, for his part, opposed banning the spitball as the pitch was already "dying a natural death," with fewer pitchers relying on it, and because its abolition would prove onerous for umpires. Another approach to bolster batting, Sanborn conjectured, should be resorted to, such as a four strike count or eliminating

Ruth, pitcher

BOSTON RED SOX READY FOR WORLD'S-SERIES BATTLE

**Babe Ruth preparing for the World Series, circa 1916. National Baseball Hall of Fame Library, Cooperstown, N.Y.**

foul outs. However, only another troubled financial year, Sanborn recognized, would lead to any significant rule changes.[20]

In the meantime, the legend of Babe Ruth really began to unfold during the 1918 season. He remained one of the top pitchers on the Red Sox staff, twirling complete games in 18 of his 19 starts. But more striking to sportswriters were Ruth's prowess with the bat and the allure he possessed for fans. Burt Whitman, writing in *The Sporting News*, reported that

> Boston fans regard Ruth as the biggest man in baseball, and they have not his physical proportions in mind in so thinking. He is applauded every time he steps to the plate, and the simple snare of a spent fly out there in left also draws the plaudits of the enthusiasts. They are all wild about the big fellow; they want him in every game... .

Cheered was "the all-around activity of Babe Ruth," who was proving to be a good outfielder as well as a tremendous batsman. As for Ruth himself, he was clearly fascinated by the long ball. "I'd rather make one home run than six singles, because I think it's a circus to watch the other fellows chasing the ball around the park. I guess it's just a case of the old saying that what a man likes to do, he does best." In June, he smacked home runs in four successive games, an unprecedented feat, and had rapped 11 by the close of the month. Curiously, he hit no more that season, but still tied the Athletics' Tilly Walker for the major league home run title; no other player in the league hit more than six.[21]

    As the Red Sox headed for another pennant, F. C. Lane drew a portrait of "one of the greatest all round stars of the diamond," whose market value had been set at $150,000 by Harry Frazee earlier in the season. Lane wrote, "The sensation of the closing baseball season is George (Babe) Ruth.... The fact remains that the Boston slugger bulks large as the dominating baseball figure of 1918." Almost immediately, Ruth had been recognized "as a pitcher of almost limitless possibilities." It was during the present season, with its transformed rosters and curtailed schedules, that Ruth obtained "his full measure of opportunity. And the way he has seized that opportunity and improved it to its utmost limits, is already baseball history." Lane called Ruth "a man of huge bulk, tremendous strength, iron endurance, and quenchless enthusiasm." The Boston star, Lane continued, "loves baseball, revels in it, finds on the diamond ample expression for his youth and energy and ambition." Still "one of the greatest pitchers in the American League," Ruth's performance at the plate resulted in "his laurels as the true prodigy of the present season."[22]

    Considering that Ruth was "an unusually good fielder," "a pitcher second to none," and "the most direful slugger of the horsehide in captivity," Lane exclaimed, "we begin to have some just conception of what a truly phenominal (sic) player the Red Sox champion really is." Lane related manager Ed Barrow's call to play Ruth in the field; what Lane and most observers failed to recognize was outfielder Harry Hooper's role in that decision. Hooper evidently informed Barrow, "Ed, we need outfielders not pitchers. Babe wants to play every day, the crowd is always larger when he pitches and we think that is because the fans like to see him hit, so why not put him in the outfield every day?" Initially, Barrow refused, exclaiming, "I would be the laughing-stock of the league if I took the best pitcher in the league and put him in the outfield." However, Hooper kept pressuring him: "Ed, you've got fifty thousand of your own money invested in the club. Your chief interest ought to be in the turnstiles. People are coming to the games to see Babe hit. Why not have him in there every day?" Barrow, for his part, purportedly worried, "I must have his pitching." At the same time, Barrow admitted, "I would like to play him oftener for hitting. I wish I had the nerve to play him in every game. He is big and strong enough to stand it. And I believe he would make a wonderful clean up hitter." With Ruth more than willing, Barrow took the step that many "experts" considered impossible in the "complex modern game": to convert a pitcher into a position player. More striking still, Barrow placed Ruth fourth in the lineup, helping to create "the greatest pitcher-batter the game has ever known."[23]

Ruth's batting performance was even more remarkable as he appeared in only 95 of the 126 games the 1918 Red Sox played. Nevertheless, in addition to his home run title, he easily led the league in slugging with a .555 average; Ty Cobb was the only other player to top the .500 mark. Ruth also finished second in doubles with 26, fourth in RBIs with 66, and fifth in triples with 11, while tying Buck Weaver for seventh in the batting race. *The Sporting News* also estimated that Ruth had been intentionally passed "at least 50 times." Still a top-flight hurler, the Babe ended up fourth in the league with 6.76 hits allowed per game and a .214 opponents' batting average.[24]

The Red Sox as a team batted a tepid .249, surpassing only the last-place Athletics. No other player on the team hit more than a single home run and only four belted any. Pitching, along with Ruth's slugging, carried Boston to the pennant, as Carl Mays's 21-13 record, 30 complete games, and eight shutouts headed the squad; the latter two marks were the league's best as well. Sad Sam Jones concluded a 16-5 campaign that garnered the top winning percentage, .762, in the American League. The Red Sox put together a composite 2.31 earned run average, only slightly higher than that of Washington, which was guided by Walter Johnson.

With their somewhat lackluster 75-51 record, the Red Sox were viewed by many scribes as underdogs to Fred Mitchell's National League champion Chicago Cubs. The boys of Wrigley Field posted an 84-45 mark, had the league's second highest batting average, .265, and added what was easily the top team ERA, 2.18. Shortstop Charlie Hollocher batted .316, fourth best in the National League, and led in hits and total bases. Hippo Vaughn, a 22-game winner, also led the league with a 1.74 ERA and 148 strikeouts, while Claude Hendrix had the best won-loss percentage, thanks to a 20-7 record. Lefty Tyler contributed 19 victories, along with the league's second best ERA, 2.00.[25]

In contrast to many of his colleagues, F. C. Lane made the Red Sox slight favorites to continue their undefeated World Series skein. "If any champion is capable of winning a world's series single handed," he suggested, "that man is Ruth." The Babe, along with Carl Mays, did carry Boston to another World Series championship. In the first game, Ruth tossed a six-hit shutout, besting Vaughn who gave up a lone run and only five hits; *The Sporting News* reported that "no World Series ever saw a prettier pitchers' battle." The second game was taken by the Cubs, 3-1, with Tyler hurling a six-hitter. Game three went to the Red Sox, 2-1, as Carl Mays bettered Vaughn's performance. In game four, Ruth made history, breaking Mathewson's World Series scoreless inning streak, while belting a two-run triple in the fourth. After the Cubs finally broke through to tie the game in the eighth, the Red Sox came back to score in the bottom of that frame and Joe Bush mopped up in relief. The Cubs took the next game, 3-0, with Vaughn throwing the shutout, but Mays, with a three-hitter, out-pitched Tyler, 2-1, in the finale. Ruth concluded with a 3-0 World Series lifetime pitching mark and an 0.87 ERA, having allowed but 19 hits in 31 innings.[26]

In December, Ruth joined the likes of the St. Louis Browns' first baseman George Sisler, Chicago White Sox second sacker Eddie Collins, Ty Cobb, Tris Speaker, and Walter Johnson, on *Baseball Magazine*'s All America Baseball Team. Declaring Ruth to be one of the top hurlers in the American League, F. C. Lane also referred to him as "a combination pitcher-fielder, and above all batter," who "certainly has no superior if indeed he has an equal." Terming Ruth "the greatest slugger in the game," Lane called him "the sensation of the American League in 1918." Consequently, "it would be little short of criminal," Lane wrote, "to keep him from his rightful place on an all-star team." A short while later, Lane argued that Ruth's "tremendous batting" feats, which included having over half his hits go for extra-bases, had "never been equalled at least not in the modern history of the sport." Spalding likewise included Ruth in its "Baseball Hall of Fame" for 1918.[27]

* * *

While the 1918 baseball season proved noteworthy, in large part thanks to the virtually mythical performance of Babe Ruth, problems abounded, as evidenced by uncertainties caused by the war, declining attendance figures, and the whiff of scandal that afflicted the Cincinnati Reds. With the close of the regular season, baseball's magnates terminated all contracts held by players and managers. Relying on the ten-days' notice clause contained in virtually all baseball contracts, the owners thereby avoided some $200,000 in expenses. At the same time, they agreed not to compete for the services of any players whose contracts had just been abrogated. Brooklyn first baseman Jake Daubert eventually sued for the balance of his salary, received a substantial out-of-court settlement, but then was traded to the Reds.[28]

Perhaps as a harbinger of what would lie ahead, disgruntlement abounded even among the pennant winners and right in the midst of the World Series. In January, the National Commission had determined to reduce the perceived windfalls that World Series competitors received, targeting figures of $2,000 for the winning players and $600 less for the defeated parties. The other funds were to be apportioned among the second, third, and fourth place teams in each league. As the 1918 World Series proceeded, it became clear that paltry attendance figures would result in sharply reduced payments to the pennant-winning Red Sox and Cubs. With the teams threatening not to take the field for game four in Boston, the members of the National Commission — Ban Johnson, Gary Herrmann, and John Heydler — agreed to meet with player representatives before the next contest. Herrman and Heydler got together with the Red Sox' Harry Hooper and Dave Shean, along with the Cubs' Leslie Mann and Bill Killefer, who reminded the commissioners of the earlier promised sums. Recognizing the poor fan turnout, Hopper offered to accept $1,500 and $1,000 payments respectively for members of the winning and losing ball clubs. When Hermann and Heydler refused to decide without consulting Johnson, who had stopped off at a bar, Hooper threatened, "Then we will not play today."[29]

As game time arrived and the players refused to come out of the dugouts, former Boston Mayor Honey Fitzgerald called for additional policemen in case of a riot. According to J. G. Taylor Spink, editor of *The Sporting News*, the now inebriated Johnson finally arrived and told Hooper, "Harry, do you realize you are a member of one of the greatest organizations in the world — the American League? And do you realize what you will do to its good name if you don't play?" Throwing his arm around Hooper's shoulder, Johnson exhorted him, "Harry, go out there and play. The crowd is waiting for you!" By another account, Johnson more ominously warned Hooper, "If you don't want to play, don't. But, Harry, you fellows are putting yourselves in a very bad light with the fans. There are going to be wounded soldiers and sailors at the game again today. With a war going on, and fellows fighting in France, what do you think the public will think of you ballplayers striking for more money?"[30]

The players backed down, while insisting that two conditions be met. The players were to be allowed to deliver a public statement before the game began and no punitive treatment would be accorded any ballplayer. The triumphant Red Sox eventually received a mere $1,102.51 per man, the smallest total in World Series annals, while the Cubs got only $671 apiece. To make matters worse, the National Commission withheld the granting of championship medallions to the winning players.

*The Sporting News* delivered a blistering critique of the threatened strike:

That near-strike of the World Series teams when they arrived in Boston for the second half of the Series was the most pitiful exhibition of demoralizing selfishness in all the annals of sport. Optimism is our middle name most of the time, but this time we can not see how the professional ball players will be able to live down for many years the thoroughly reprehensible and disgraceful action of the Red Sox and Cubs in trying to deprive the second, third and fourth place teams of the major leagues of their just share of the World's Series receipts, as agreed upon by the National Commission last winter. ...

We have seen many a last-minute shakedown attempted, frequently with success by low class puss and crooked wrestlers, but never did we expect to see the day when major league baseballers, fretful about money lost to them because their fellow Americans were fighting a regular he-war in France, would descend to such a trick.[31]

# CHAPTER FIVE

# *Jim Crow Baseball*

Equally grave an issue as gambling or labor strife, but seldom acknowledged by major league moguls, was the national pastime's color barrier. That was in keeping, sadly enough, with the Jim Crow practices that soiled the American landscape. The institution of slavery had been terminated due to the emancipation proclamations of 1862 and 1863 delivered by President Abraham Lincoln and the ratification of the 13th Amendment to the United States Constitution. Slavery henceforth was not allowable on American soil. Additional Reconstruction-era amendments, the 14th and 15th, were intended to protect the rights of newly freed African American citizens. The 14th defined federal citizenship, while calling for the safeguarding of privileges and immunities, due process of law, and equal protection of the law, against possible encroachments by state agents. The 15th served as a suffrage amendment for African Americans, affirming that the right to vote could not be circumscribed because of race, color, or previous condition of servitude. Additionally, congressional enactments, particularly the 1875 Civil Rights Act, were designed to shield black Americans against discrimination in public accommodations, hotels, restaurants, theaters, and the like.

While the law of the land had changed markedly, social practices, racial attitudes, and white reliance on violence to keep blacks in their place, unfortunately, had not. Coupled with the judicial activism of a decidedly conservative U.S. Supreme Court, the promises of the Civil War and Reconstruction dramatically dissipated. Federal court rulings, as exemplified by the

Slaughterhouse (1873), Civil Rights (1883), and Plessy (1896) decisions, eventually provided a judicial imprimatur for the system of segregation that was unfolding in the South and in various pockets of the country.

The national pastime was hardly immune to such developments and was, in fact, at the cutting edge when it came to supporting segregation practices. After being integrated all too briefly and only sporadically during the late 19th century, organized baseball rigidly adhered to its own Jim Crow strictures. As American baseball emerged during the mid-1840s, Walter Brown had established the short-lived National Colored League. Black ballplayers played on integrated independent squads or for "colored" independent units. By the outbreak of the Civil War, a crop of black ball clubs had appeared in the north. In 1867, the National Association of Base Ball Players denied admission to teams "composed of one or more colored persons," supposedly to ward off racial antagonisms. That year, black teams battled one another, with contests held for the "colored championship." In 1878, pitcher John "Bud" Fowler performed for the Lynn Live Oaks of the International Association, thereby shattering the minor league color barrier. When Fowler signed in 1881 with the Maple Leafs of Guelph, Ontario, his would-be white teammates refused to accept him; consequently, Fowler's odyssey through the minor leagues continued.

The year the National Agreement was devised, 1883, witnessed two black ballplayers, Fowler, now an infielder, and catcher Moses Fleetwood "Fleet" Walker, appear in the Northwestern League. The following season, when Walker's Toledo team entered the American Association, the catcher became the first black major leaguer. Walker's brother Welday joined the team for its final games. American Association owners apparently then agreed to draw a color line, but several black players performed in the minor leagues over the course of the next few years. Among those who starred at that level were Buffalo's second baseman Frank Grant and George Stovey, who pitched for Jersey City and Newark.

Unfortunately, racial antagonisms were readily apparent. In a contest against Toronto, cries rang out at Grant, "Kill that darkie!" Color barriers soon hardened, with the International League agreeing "to approve no more contracts with colored men." Manager–first baseman Adrian "Cap" Anson of the Chicago White Stockings helped to solidify baseball segregation by refusing to allow his team to face Stovey in an exhibition contest. By the mid-1890s, the segregation lines had been redrawn, precluding blacks and whites from playing ball against one another in official contests. Even then, however, barnstorming tours and special events sometimes resulted in top major leaguers squaring off against those who often played blackball year round.[1]

* * *

Shortly after the new century opened, blackball's single most important figure began to make his mark. By the advent of World War I, Andrew "Rube"

Foster had been celebrated throughout the game as blackball's greatest pitcher, manager, and administrator; indeed he was viewed as "the greatest Colored athlete of his day." Born in Calvert, Texas, on September 17, 1879, Foster was the son of the Reverend Andrew Foster, head of the African Methodist Episcopal churches throughout the southern part of the state. Starting in the spring of 1897, he played for a series of teams in Austin, Waco, and Fort Worth, before moving on to Hot Springs, Arkansas, in 1902. An Austin sportswriter, acknowledging that Foster "had him intoxicated with his playing," damned racial prejudices that prevented black players from competing against whites. Nevertheless, class as well as racial prejudices were encountered frequently, with players often denied access to various homes as "baseball and those who played it ... (were) considered by Colored as low and ungentlemanly."[2]

Attracting attention because of his pitching prowess, the 6'4", 200 pound Foster was invited in the spring of 1902 to join the Chicago Unions. When no travel expenses were forthcoming, Foster declined the opportunity but accepted a subsequent one from Frank C. Leland, who was putting together the Chicago Union Giants. Apprised that the Union Giants would be pitted against top white teams, Foster told Leland, "If you play the best clubs in the land, white clubs, as you say, it will be a case of Greek meeting Greek. I fear nobody." After three months, with Leland unable to meet his salary, Rube shifted the Ostego, Michigan ball club, with its white lineup. Later that year he became a member of the New York-based Cuban X-Giants.[3]

Foster became a topflight blackball hurler, relying on masterful control, blazing speed, a tough change up, and a devastating screwball smoothly offered in underhand fashion. The New York Giants' John McGraw — who had desperately wanted to sign the blackball pitcher himself — relied on Foster to teach Christy Mathewson how to throw the screwball. Calling the pitch the "fadeaway," Mathewson soon became the major league's greatest pitcher. In 1903, Foster, now terming himself "the best pitcher in the country," won four games as the Cuban X-Giants defeated the Philadelphia Giants in the first black World Series. A year later, Foster was pitching for the triumphant Philadelphia team against his former team, winning two complete games — one, an 18 strikeout performance, the other a three-hitter, the byproduct of bunts. In those two contests, Foster allowed but nine hits while striking out 23. In 1905, Foster reportedly compiled a 51-4 record, which included bouts against major league opponents. Along the way, he also acquired the nickname "Rube." That followed his 5-2 defeat of star southpaw Rube Waddell and his Philadelphia Athletics teammates, including power-hitters Frank Baker and Harry Davis, in an exhibition match in New York City.[4]

John L. Footslug, sports columnist of the *Indianapolis Freeman*, repeated a laudatory evaluation from the *Philadelphia Telegraph*:

If Andrew Foster had not been born with a dark skin, the great pitcher would wear an American or National League uniform. Rube Waddell, Cy Young, Matthewson (sic), McGennity (sic) and others are great twirlers in the big leagues and their praises have been sung from Maine to Texas. Foster has never been equaled in a pitcher's box. ... Aside from his twirling ability, he is a heavy hitter and a fine fielder and ranks among the foremost of the country.[5]

By 1906, Pittsburgh shortstop Honus Wagner was calling Foster "the smartest pitcher I've ever seen." Chicago Cub manager-first baseman Frank Chance adjudged him "the most finished product I've ever seen in the pitcher's box." The *Cleveland Post* asserted, "There have been but two real pitchers who have put their feet in the Cleveland ball yard. They are Addie Joss and Rube Foster." Walter Schlichter, the white owner of the Philadelphia Giants, who compiled a 108-31 record in 1906, challenged the champions of the World Series to "thus decide who can play baseball the best, the white or the black American." Charles Comiskey, who spearheaded the Chicago White Sox, surprise conquerors of their cross-town rivals, the Cubs, in that year's World Series, declined the offer.[6]

Foster's legend continued to grow, as attested by the inclusion of his essay, "How to Pitch," in the 1907 soon-to-be classic work, *Sol White's Official Base Ball Guide.*[7] That year, he returned to the Leland Giants as player-manager and was all but universally acclaimed as blackball's greatest moundsman. At the time, Foster was purportedly fielding salary offers "higher than had ever been heard of in Negro baseball." Leland's selling point was the promise of sufficient capital to put together a powerhouse ball club, provided Foster could bring along a cadre of players from the east. Some eight members of the Philadelphia Giants joined Foster on his trek out west. The 1907 Leland Giants captured 90 out of 114 games and became "the most-talked-of colored club during that time."[8]

The Foster-guided Leland Giants continued to dominate blackball, and stood as "the only straight salaried club in existence," with a weekly payroll of $250. In mid-1908, *The Indianapolis Freeman* referred to the club as

> the best organized semi-pro team in the world today. ... Each man in his position is a star, from the organizer, team manager, field captain, down to the bat carrier. Everybody works like a piece of machinery. These gentlemen's main forte is "gentlemen on and off the ball field," and have the respect of every citizen at home or wherever they may appear.

F. C. Leland, the club's general manager, termed his squad "the world's colored champion" and noted that Foster, "the world's greatest," had lost but once in the 20 games he had pitched to date. That version of the Leland

**Rube Foster batting, 1909. Chicago Historical Society (SDN-055361).**

Giants compiled a 86-20 record and captured the Park Owners' Championship.[9]

The following February, Foster — who was now called "the black McGraw" — reported that the Leland Giants were heading south for spring training. This was reportedly "the first time in the history of national game, a semi-professional team, black or white," had undertaken such an excursion. Altogether, the team covered almost 4,500 miles, while easily defeating potent Southern nines. The Lelands played in Memphis, Birmingham, Fort Worth, Austin, San Antonio, and Houston, among other spots. The receptions throughout Texas were spirited, with both white and black fans welcoming Foster back to his home state. "When he came in sight," *The Indianapolis Freeman* related, "he was given a welcome that would have done honor to the President of the United States. The people had carriages, automobiles and an opera coach for the club." Packed crowds gathered at the playing fields to watch the renowned Leland Giants. Foster, the newspaper asserted, was "without doubt the most popular ball player in the country." While naysayers had warned the trip would prove a financial disaster, Foster had given lie to that argument.[10]

\* \* \*

The 1909 season was another successful one for the Leland Giants, who again won the City League Championship. However, in October, a power struggle resulted in the resignation of the team's namesake as owner. That same month, following a challenge delivered by Foster, the Chicago Cubs — world champions for the past two years and league runner-ups in 1909, despite winning 104 games — battled his Giants in a closely fought three games series. Foster, who had broken his legs three months earlier and not pitched since, hurled the second contest against 20-game winner Orval Overall. Foster held a 5-1 lead through seven innings, gave up a run in the eighth, and then tired in the final frame. After three Cub runs had come across, Foster, believing that time had been called, walked off the mound to bring in a reliever. Outfielder Frank "Wildfire" Schulte, perched on third base, dashed home and the run was allowed to stand in the face of Foster's heated protests.[11]

In the April 16, 1910 issue of *The Indianapolis Freeman*, Foster returned to a theme long dear to him. "The time is now at hand," he wrote, "when the formation of colored leagues should receive much consideration. In fact, I believe it is absolutely necessary." The distance between organized ball and blackball was increasing, Foster argued, thus necessitating greater financial backing and organization:

> The business end of the game has lagged along to such an extent that we now find ourselves in a dangerous predicament. We have a country full of colored ball players, well developed as to playing; but the places for giving employment to them are being promoted with such an eel-like pace and the majority are founded upon such an uncertain business principle, that it is having a tendency to throw a dense cloud over the Negro as a promoter of baseball. The players have, through all sorts of adverse conditions, been able to bring our race to the notice of thousands who are interested in the game. Now will our business men and friends of the profession make an effort to help us to reach the coveted goal of complete success, or will they stand by and see us fall? Which shall it be?[12]

Foster's 1910 squad, which he considered his finest, won all but six of 129 games and became the first western team to travel to New York, where it took 21 straight contests. It included shortstop John Henry Lloyd, second baseman Grant "Home Run" Johnson, center fielder Pete Hill, and catcher Bruce Petway. Following that season, the great pitcher-manager formed a new partnership with white saloon keeper John C. Schorling, Charles Comiskey's son-in-law. With the major league team now playing at the new Comiskey Park, Schorling arranged for Foster's squad to appear at the site of the White Sox' old stadium at 39th and Wentworth. There, Schorling built a new ballpark that originally seated 9,000 spectators. Comiskey warned Foster that the new blackball team would suffer financially if it played games when the White Sox were in town, but Rube ignored the advice. Admission to soon-to-be-renamed Schorling Park cost 50 cents, with free ice water offered, and fans flocked to see blackball's best team. Indeed, one Sunday afternoon in 1911 witnessed a greater-than-capacity crowd of 11,000 gather to watch Foster's ball club, while nearby, the White Sox attracted only 9,000 fans; across town, the Cubs pulled in but 6,000 paying customers.[13]

Soon calling his team the Chicago American Giants, Foster created something of a blackball dynasty as his squad regularly won the Chicago semi-pro championship and traveled extensively. The 1911 version of the team took the city championship with 78 victories against only 27 defeats. Like Rube's earlier teams, the American Giants toured regularly, acquiring a considerable following, particularly in the south. There, tales of Foster and the American Giants were spun by *The Chicago Defender;* copies of that leading black newspaper were passed throughout the region by porters on the Illinois Central Railroad. The famous ballclub's actual arrival in one town after another was greatly anticipated. Foster used his southern ventures and subsequent ones out west to spread the gospel of blackball. In the process, the American Giants became America's most celebrated black baseball team and Foster its best known representative. Those same tours enabled Foster to scout out the best talent, either little heralded ballplayers in the cities or smaller communities the American Giants traveled through or blackball stars on other top teams.[14]

The American Giants were involved in epic battles, such as the one in late August 1912 that saw the stellar Cuban hurler, Jose Mendez, and Foster duel to a 2-2, 12-inning draw. The legend of Foster's team continued to take hold thanks to its hugely popular tours; by 1912, his team — which Rube referred to as the "undisputed colored champions of the world" — played all along the west coast, beating up on a host of major league stars and top-flight minor leaguers. Subsequently, Foster's unit won the California winter league championship and bested state league squads in Michigan and Wisconsin.[15]

\* \* \*

Billy Lewis, writing in *The Indianapolis Freeman* on February 15, 1913, declared that "the colored brother has been rather slow to take advantage of what is offered by way of baseball opportunity. He could have his league also, just like the white people, if he would." The finest blackballers, Lewis suggested, could compete with their white counterparts. After all, California scribes had sung the praises of the American Giants, "comparing them to the top-notchers in the big games ... saying that those dusky knights of the diamond stood right in their class, and near about the head." Yet such testimonials, Lewis contended, mattered little so long as black players were excluded from the majors and lacked a league of their own.[16]

As the 1913 season unfolded, Foster returned to the mound less frequently than in past years. Nevertheless, after his first outing, which resulted in a five-hit victory, the *Indianapolis Freeman* saluted the old time vigor and craftiness that has made him the "world's wonder on the mound." In August, The American Giants lost a best of 12 series to the Lincoln Giants, a rare occurrence; the team still ended up with a semi-official 90-23 mark, although *The Indianapolis Ledger* credited Foster's team with having played 200 games. At the close of the month, the *Freeman* declared that "'Rube' Foster must be given credit for having brains and being the best ... manager in the country," even surpassing Charles Comiskey for baseball genius.[17]

The following year, the American Giants, who included pitcher Smokey Joe Williams, Hill, Petway, and Lloyd, conducted another successful tour out west. They were favorably termed "colored demons" and "a great team." Lloyd was referred to as "undoubtedly one of the greatest players ever seen on a ball field. ... He gets over the ground like a whirlwind. ..." Foster made that very argument in an interview conducted with a Seattle newspaper, calling Lloyd "the greatest player in the world." Lloyd was but one of several blackball performers, Foster argued, who would soon enter the big league ranks. "Before another baseball season rolls around," Foster predicted, "colored ball players, a score of whom are equal to the brightest stars in the big league teams, will be holding down jobs in organized baseball." Boasting a handful of competitors acknowledged to be the equal of any major leaguer, Foster reasoned that the Federal League had diluted the pool of first-rate players. Soon, Foster believed, "the colored ranks will be invaded, and the best talent picked to fill the breach." After all, Cubans were now being admitted into the majors. "When they let the black men in," Foster prophesied, "just watch how many present-day stars lose their positions."[18]

Racial barriers alone kept a host of black baseball players, then in their prime, out of the big leagues. Among those who were considered to be the equal of the very best major leaguers included pitchers John Donaldson, Frank Wickware, Jose Mendez, Smokey Joe Williams, Dick "Cannonball" Redding, shortstop John Henry Lloyd, and catcher Bruce Petway. Donaldson had recently thrown 30 consecutive hitless innings and had struck out 25 batters in a 12 inning contest. John McGraw had reputedly indicated, "If Donaldson were a white man, or if the unwritten law of baseball didn't bar negroes from the major leagues, I would give $50,000 for him — and think I was getting a bargain."[19]

* * *

After a controversial series in the early summer of 1915 between his Indianapolis ABCs and Foster's American Giants, C. I. Taylor spoke of the need for blackball to become organized. He wrote, "Baseball is in its infancy among

Rube Foster with Cap Anson, circa 1915. National Baseball Hall of Fame Library, Cooperstown, N.Y.

Colored people and with the nourishment of organization it will grow to be a giant organization such as the entire race will be proud of." Baseball could thereby provide hundreds of talent young men the means to attain a college education. To usher in these developments, Taylor asserted, he had corresponded with Foster for several years.

> I write many letter to Mr. Andrew Rube Foster every winter and every summer making suggestions as to how and when the time is ripe for the launching of the Negro baseball league. ... And he has agreed that I am right in every statement that I have made in all this matter. I have told him that he is the rightful leader of us in the organization of the league. I have told him that I only wanted to act a lieutenant in helping him accomplish the thing has been uppermost in my mind and his, too, I suppose, for these many years.

Unfortunately, Taylor exclaimed, Foster appeared determined to convince all baseball fans "that he is the only man in the whole country who is trying to build while others of us are tearing down."[20]

\* \* \*

Beginning in mid–October 1915, the American Giants kicked off a six-and-a-half month tour that covered more than 20,000,000 miles, and took them along the east coast, down to Cuba, and then throughout the western United States. Foster's club won the championship of the California Winter League, which boasted a number of major leaguers. *The Chicago Defender* insisted that the American Giants "would make the White Sox look like a bunch of bush leaguers." The "colored cracks" certainly accomplished that feat in thrashing top-notch minor league teams like the Seattle Giants.[21]

In February 1916, a headline in *The Indianapolis Freeman* read, "A Big League of Negro Players." The companion story reported that Foster, acting on behalf of "a wealthy syndicate," was seeking to purchase Federal league parks in St. Louis, Pittsburgh, and Chicago. Foster was said to own a playing field in Philadelphia, so the acquisition of the other parks would allow for the formation of a four-team league.[22]

\* \* \*

The 1916 season again witnessed Foster's American Giants engage in a spirited jaunt around the country and beyond. Having departed from Hawaii, Foster now intended to take his team to Havana, New Orleans, Mississippi, and Alabama, before heading for another west coast excursion. There, the American Giants would appear in Oregon, northern California, Washington, Vancouver, South Dakota, and Montana. Foster's squad was "playing brilliant ball," exclaimed newspaper accounts that provided generous coverage of the games pitting the American Giants against local white clubs.[23]

After Chicago defeated New York's Lincoln Giants 17-7 on August 20, *The Indianapolis Freeman* proclaimed that Foster's team had won "the baseball championship of the world." *The Chicago Defender* referred to Foster as the "brainest (sic) man in baseball," who had done "more to put Chicago on the baseball map than the big league teams." Subsequently, in early October, the American Giants were slated to meet the multi-racial All-Nations team from Horton, Kansas. The American Giants bested the All-Nations twice in a three-game series, then easily defeated the Magnets, with Chicago White Sox stars Ray Schalk, Joe Jackson, and Buck Weaver in attendance.[24]

Although the *Freeman* and the *Defender* had both recently proclaimed the American Giants world champions, another series, which was intended to settle who was entitled to that claim, was held featuring Foster's squad and C. I. Taylor's Indianapolis ABCs. The teams split the first two games and the ABCs grabbed a 1-0 lead in the third. At the end of the sixth inning, Foster, who was coaching at first base, put on a glove, an action that was protested by Ben Taylor, the ABCs' first sacker. The umpire ordered Foster to remove the glove and, when he refused to do so, booted him from the game. At that point, Rube ordered his team from the playing field and victory was awarded the ABCs.[25]

Just before the series began, the *Freeman* had termed Foster "peer of Colored baseball managers." However, its sportswriter, Young Knox, bemoaned the controversy that had developed:

> We are very sorry this happened, as it will in the end hurt the men who are trying to build the game up. We can not see how it is that a team like this comes down here and tries to destroy the peace we have been having all season by a lot of bulldozing actions. Mr. Taylor has built the game up here, as it has been built up in no other place in the country, and he should not be humiliated like this. When the umpire told Mr. Foster to leave the field, he should have left without a word.

The series concluded after nine games, with the ABCs taking five, including the disputed contest.[26]

On December 2, *The Indianapolis Freeman* contained a cartoon featuring "The Rube" replete with a bandit's mask and a pistol emblazoned with "BLUFF," directed at C. I. Taylor. Foster was demanding, "Hand me that grip," while Taylor responded, "I will not, it's mine," referring to a bag with "World's Colored Championship" lettering. The title of the cartoon was "AN ATTEMPTED HOLD-UP."[27]

Throughout this period, the Cubs, White Sox, and Chicago's Federal League contingent declined challenges to play Foster's blackball champions, who captured the 1914, 1915 (shared with the New York Lincoln Stars), 1916 (contested), and 1917 Negro League titles. The appeal of the American Giants remained far-flung, as not only west coast and southern teams but leading Cuban squads clamored to battle Foster's lads.[28]

The 1917 season was yet another fruitful one for the American Giants, who won the spring championship in Palm Beach, before returning to Chicago. The American Giants, a sportswriter in *The Chicago Defender* reported, had "been royally entertained in every town they have played." After completing another championship season in blackball, sportswriter Dave Wyatt asserted that "baseball would have practically sunk away to nothing only for Andrew 'Rube' Foster, the past season. We know it to be a fact that he was the meal ticket of practically every colored club making a bid for recognition for the season of 1917. All the players, no matter to what club attached, openly displayed an attitude which pointed to Foster as their benefactor." Even C. I. Taylor of the Indianapolis ABCs admitted that in 1917 "Rube Foster has the greatest Colored aggregation in the business."[29]

As the 1917 season wound to a close, Foster deemed it a highly successful one. Various minor leagues were compelled to suspend operations, while others had to slice salaries, reduce player rosters, or fire umpires. By contrast, Foster noted, "all the Colored clubs carried more men, and paid higher salaries than any previous year." Enormously helpful in that regard were *The Chicago Defender*, *The Indianapolis Ledger*, *The Indianapolis Freeman*, and *The Pittsburgh Courier*, which helped to spread the gospel of blackball. On the playing field, the American Giants, Foster decreed, had compiled "the greatest record in their history, meeting and defeating all the big Colored clubs that had the nerve to play them — decisively." Foster's team excelled against "the crack clubs"— the Indianapolis ABCs, the Cuban Giants, the Bacharach Giants, the Chicago Giants, and the Philadelphia All-Stars, comprised of top eastern players. After being shutout by the ABCs, the American Giants won 11 in a row from their arch-rivals, taking 17 out of 21 during the course of the season, with two ties.[30]

* * *

U.S. involvement in World War I affected blackball every bit as much as it did organized baseball. By the summer of 1917, Wyatt was hoping that some black soldier-ballplayers would remain in Europe after the conflict "to play in the French National League," which he believed might someday be established. In September, Scholoring's Park featured "music, military drills and maneuvers ... patriotic songs, well sung by the soldier boys and a bevy of young maids soliciting funds to insure the boys the smoke."[31]

Foster anticipated that 1918 would be "the greatest year in Colored baseball," despite the United States' involvement in the war. As the nation was presently "flooded with money," any number of individuals were seeking Foster's assistance in establishing ball clubs of their own and stood ready "to place money in the game, something "they have always before hesitated to do." Already, Foster was slated to visit Cincinnati, Pittsburgh, Atlantic City, New York, and Detroit, to "try to complete the plans."[32]

With eight of his players exposed to the draft, Foster was compelled to reshape his championship team. His great friend John Henry Lloyd was allowed to depart, replaced by a 5'4" shortstop, Bobby Williams, from New Orleans. Also leaving were Hill, Barber, Redding, and outfielder Frank Duncan, among others. Sportswriter C. D. Marshall predicted that C. I. Taylor's Indianapolis ABCs would end up on top of the American Giants. Nevertheless, Foster reportedly saw the latest version of the American Giants playing "a better brand of the great American pastime than he has ever seen them play." This was hardly surprising to a columnist for *The Chicago Defender*, who reflected:

> There is not a manager in the country that has anything on him or that can come anywhere near him. The owners of the big league clubs used to come to him and do yet to find how such and such a white player worked against his club. If Foster thought he was O.K. against such a strong club as the American Giants, that was enough. There is many a player in the big leagues today who owes his existence there to Andrew Rube Foster, and there are a bunch of them from the coast.

Foster would be able to reconstruct his team, the columnist continued, as "there is no task in baseball that is too great for him to accomplish, once he sets his head and makes up his mind to do so." The public had demonstrated its appreciation for Foster's craftsmanship, with the American Giants attracting more fans at home than any other semi-pro team and serving as "the biggest drawing card" on the road. Thus, "the Big Roman" had retained "the foundation ... of the best ball club in the country."[33]

As the season progressed, more ballplayers were lost to military service, which Foster refused to complain about. Eventually, headlines read that Foster's crew was "shipwrecked" or "draft-wrecked." On July 20, *The Chicago Defender* indicated that the American Giants were confronting "the hardest and most crucial series in their career," to be waged against the Camp Grant ball club, comprised entirely of major league players. Foster, the article stated, "is conceded to be the brainiest man in modern baseball. His color alone keeps him from piloting any of the big league teams." While the possibility of White Sox–American Giants contests had long been discussed, "the color prejudice that exists in the big league" was said to make that "impossible." The war, however, had steered many major leaguers into shipyards and steel plants, which enabled them to compete on weekend against semi-pro teams, like the American Giants.[34]

The American Giants were proclaimed blackball's champions for 1918, while producing a 77-27 record. The Indianapolis ABCs had been selected by many sportswriters to take the title, but won only three of 12 games against Chicago. *The Chicago Defender* again sang Foster's praises, declaring that he "has wonderful business ability, a great leader of men; as to baseball brains he has no superior."[35]

Nevertheless, 1918 proved to be a particularly trying year for the American Giants on at least three counts. The team was decimated by the early decision to release shortstop John Henry Lloyd and the subsequent departure of his replacement Bobby Williams, first baseman Grant, outfielder Judy Gans, and starting pitchers Frank Wickware, College Boy Tom Williams, Dick "Cannonball" Redding, and Tom Johnson. The schedule was sometimes brutal, with the American Giants battling the best semi-pro teams around the country, many featuring major or minor league stars. The third obstacle was long-standing in nature: the notion that black baseball players, except for a select few, were simply not good enough to compete with their counterparts from organized ball.[36]

The loss of key players due to contract disputes, violations of team rules, and conscription taxed even Foster's legendary business and managerial expertise. Yet somehow he carried on as stars departed, finding replacement players, including former pitching great Jose Mendez, who now took over at shortstop. Foster — who turned 40 at season's end — took to the mound himself on occasion, as when "the Big Chief" threw eight scoreless innings against the Atlantic City squad. Tough sessions with Beloit and Joliet led to critical, even scathing analyses — however temporarily drawn — by long-time supporters of the American Giants. Yet at the year's close, the American Giants had reportedly prevailed in a series with an all-star unit made up of some of the game's finest players. That led to a reevaluation, once again, concerning the relative merits of blackball and the game played by major and minor leaguers.[37]

The Fairbanks-Morse team from Beloit, Wisconsin, was a particularly difficult foe for the American Giants. The Beloits took yet another double-header from Foster's squad in late September, in contests featuring the Chicago White Sox' Buck Weaver. *The Chicago Defender* lauded "the peppery infielder," who played "the hot corner ... where he shines with more luster than any player in the big leagues." In the twin-bill against the American Giants, Weaver and Boston Brave outfielder Al Wickland reportedly

> released one of the grandest exhibitions of fielding, throwing and batting that has been seen for some time on semi-pro grounds. Buck's performances just about caused the wise ones to scoff at the idea that the little fellows compared favorably with the top-notchers of the pastime. ... Wickland ...pulled an exhibition of fielding, hitting and base running that was an eye-opener. At any rate, the two genuine big leaguers knocked the lid completely off of our advance dope on how we compare with the best. ...

In all fairness, Wyatt concluded, the American Giants "were out-gamed and outclassed this time." After another shellacking at the hands of an all-star unit, the *Defender* acknowledged that Foster's lads "have never been badly outclassed or, until the present time, even equalled (sic)." Still, the American Giants managed to conclude the season by winning the series against that same all-star squad.[38]

The American Giants had planned to wrap-up their 1918 season against Kenosha, which featured Chicago Cub pitching ace Hippo Vaughn, but the health director ordered the ballparks shut down because of an influenza epidemic. The *Defender* praised the accomplishments of the American Giants, who, despite enormous obstacles, had again been the top blackball team and had managed a respectable showing against white semi-pro units. While the 1918 version of the American Giants was clearly weaker than earlier and later versions, its accomplishments demonstrated the success of "Rube Foster's system." The *Defender* lauded both that system, which included the booking by Foster of all Giants games, and its architect, calling him "without doubt one of the greatest leaders in baseball." If Foster "had twenty-five men, as the big leagues, all trained with experience before they come to him," the paper claimed, "there is no league pennant he would not have a monopoly on."[39]

CHAPTER SIX

# Postwar America and the National Pastime

Before the signing of the Armistice ending the war, which had greatly impacted both blackball and organized baseball, discussion loomed large regarding the major leagues' immediate future. In September 1918, F. C. Lane, in the pages of *Baseball Magazine*, asked if "baseball, the greatest and best of sports, which we have all known so intimately and loved for so many years," were "to be doomed as a sacrifice on the grim altar of war?" Two months later, Lane indicated that professional baseball had experienced "a mauling which would kill any ordinary institution." Various critics, who had striven mightily "to kill the old sport," he contended, now demanded that it be terminated until the fighting ended. Certain friends sadly commented "that the sport seems about done for, for the time being." The game, Lane declared, could and should go on, whether the conflagration continued or not. Charles W. Murphy, former owner of the Chicago Cubs, insisted that if the American people were polled, baseball would still be played. Was it necessary, Murphy wondered, "to put a stop to ... the greatest game ever invented by man and Uncle Sam's national game?" At war's end, he predicted, baseball would prove "more important than ever. It is going to cement a friendship among the liberty-loving people of all civilized nations. ... it is going to be the world game instead of only our national sport." In the meantime, Murphy explained, "When I urge a continuance of baseball I have constantly in mind the winning of the war." Undoubtedly, as he saw matters, baseball helped to sustain the soldiers' morale and elevate "the *esprit de corps*."[1]

Baseball, Frederick E. Parmly asserted, would prove the difference in the battle against Germany. It taught "the two essential factors that go to make up Americanism, individuality, combined with team-work, and no stronger combination can be found," which the Central European state was unhappily discovering. Unquestionably, Parmly stated, baseball served to bring about cooperative action among "the entire American people," unlike any other game. Some said wheat or meat or fuel would enable the U.S. to prevail, Parmly acknowledged. But in his estimation, "BASEBALL will win the war, and for the future of America baseball is absolutely essential." In fact, "it should become part of the training of every American boy in every American school, for as long as Americans are trained in the qualities developed by the game, our country can face any crisis with confidence."[2]

As the war drew to a close, columnists again extolled baseball as the national pastime. No longer trumpeting its supposed martial characteristics, their headlines now indicated that "thoughts turn to baseball as (the) natural corollary of peace." The two million soldiers returning from overseas, along with their compatriots at home, *Baseball Magazine* suggested, would soon

The return of the 33rd Division, Chicago, Illinois, 1919. Chicago Historical Society (DN 071268).

exhibit "a new zest" for sporting events of all sorts. "Who can overestimate the tremendous stimulus to the game when millions of young men imbued with a greater appreciation of athletic sport than ever before, bring that youthful enthusiasm home with them again?," its editorialists asked. In addition, many more folk could now "turn again to their accustomed interests." Thus, "There's a boom in the sport field and baseball occupies the highest seat on the band wagon." The game would flourish, W. A. Phelon agreed, with the return of veteran stars and the elevating of the standard of play.[3]

\* \* \*

Organized baseball itself, however, was about to encounter a highly tumultuous period, with grave concerns expressed about the National Commission, the threat of free agency, and the ongoing anti-trust suit. Contentious battles were about to unfold, which eventually threatened the game's supposedly pristine integrity. In the midst of such turmoil, ironically enough, major league baseball appeared more capable than ever of striking a cord that resonated with many Americans.

Various baseball moguls had been angered by National Commission decisions awarding players claimed by more than one ball club. Pittsburgh owner Barney Dreyfuss still resented the loss of first baseman George Sisler, who, in 1916, had been proclaimed a free agent by chairman Gary Herrmann; that enabled Sisler to become a St. Louis Brown, where he was reunited with his college coach, Branch Rickey. In the summer of 1918, another dispute arose over pitcher Scott Perry, sought by both the Philadelphia Athletics and Boston Braves. The National Commission ruled that Perry should end up a Brave, but Connie Mack, apparently with Ban Johnson's approval, obtained an injunction in federal court preventing him from doing so. An unsatisfactory compromise was carved out, with the A's paying Boston $2,500 for Perry's services.[4]

Increasingly, disillusionment with the workings of the National Commission led to calls for a baseball dictator. G. W. Axelson, on November 3, urged the appointment of Judge Kenesaw Mountain Landis as National Commission chairman. Axelson wrote, "None would be better fitted for the job than the man who probably saved baseball from wreck and ruin" by forcing magnates to devise "a peace agreement." Several owners, Axelson reported, favored Landis's selection. Some had ever since Landis presided over the Federal League lawsuit. At that point, Axelson heard one baseball mogul declare, "What a great man he would be for baseball!" Another had proclaimed, "He (Judge Landis) would make an ideal chairman and should appeal to all interested in the game of baseball." Still one more baseball figure had asked, "Judge Landis would make the best chairman the national commission could get, but would he resign to accept the position? ... He is the fairest man I know,

JUDGE KENESAW MOUNTAIN LANDIS *His Son* CAPTAIN REED LANDIS
*And* MRS. LANDIS. © I.f.s

**Kenesaw Mountain Landis and Mrs. Landis, with son Reed Landis, 1919. National Baseball Hall of Fame Library, Cooperstown, N.Y.**

and besides he is thoroughly familiar with the game, more so than any man I know of, who could qualify as a neutral chairman."[5]

On November 28, H. Andrew, in an article for *The Sporting News*, noted that former President William Howard Taft had been offered a job as head of major league baseball. Owners urging the change acknowledged that they were desirous of "curbing the dictatorship of Ban Johnson." *Baseball Magazine*, for its part, declared that Taft's selection "as dictator of professional baseball ... would lend unquestioned lustre (sic) to the great American Game." As controversy brewed concerning the attempt to oust Johnson from the National Commission, Taft declined the post; some accounts indicated that the former president did so because of a lack of unanimous support. Reportedly, National League owners, other the National Commissioner Herrmann, had favored the idea of one-man rule, but only two American League magnates did.[6]

Brooklyn sportswriter Thomas Rice questioned whether a one-man Commission was viable. After all, support of the American League, the National League, and the minors would be necessary. Rice proposed instead a reconstituted National Commission, to include the presidents of the two major leagues and a third appointee, "a high-class lawyer fan not connected with any club or league;" all would be compensated adequately enough for full-time employment. Kenesaw Mountain Landis, Rice suggested, was just such a "neutral" figure. After all, Landis had supposedly demonstrated "an exact knowledge of baseball conditions and baseball needs when he purposely held back his decision" in the Federal League's law suit against the major leagues. Thus, "the game will ever owe him a debt of gratitude for his action on that occasion." Significantly, Rice pointed out, "It is not likely that any other judge in the whole country would have handled the case with such a practical and common sense regard for the law as well as for the facts. His treatment of the situation was masterful." If Landis refused to accept such as appointment, Rice continued, then baseball magnates needed to select "some one who will approximate to Judge Landis in dignity, force, reputation, knowledge of law and intimate acquaintance with the ins and outs of baseball.["][7]

**Kenesaw Mountain Landis with daughter Susan, 1919. Chicago Historical Society (DN 070536).**

As the new year unfolded, the makeup of the National Commission remained a source of contention. F. C. Lane of *Baseball Magazine* supported the owners in declaring "that the game should be controlled by the magnate and not by the player." Nevertheless, he urged that consideration be given to the appointment of "a new member who would represent the players." Another possibility, Lane wrote, involved the selection of a member to represent the press and propose needed reforms.[8]

Most of the talk revolved around the status of National Commission chairman Gary Herrmann — a close ally of American League President Ban Johnson — who was evidently prepared to relinquish his post. On January 2, 1919, *The New York Times* reported that two names had been presented as possible replacements. One was John Conway Toole, who had served as counsel for organized baseball and devised the agreement to shut down the Federal League. The other was Judge Landis, although it was suggested that the Chairman's salary would have to be larger than ever as befitting "a man of his calibre." National League President John A. Heydler indicated both his opposition to Herrmann's reappointment and support for the establishment of a one-man commission. Due to his disapproval of Heydler's plan, Herrmann, by the middle of the month, no longer seemed desirous of stepping down. When the joint meeting of the two leagues was held at the Hotel Biltmore in New York on January 16, Herrmann's position appeared more secure. Both leagues were said to prefer "a neutral Chairman," but only if "a suitable candidate can be found," the *Times* stated.[9]

Talk of free agency and the ongoing suit by the owners of Baltimore's Federal League franchise also put a damper on the search for the new National Commission head. The reserve clause, *Baseball Magazine* noted in March, was "the storm centre" of the professional game. "Around this vortex revolve all the sullen currents of managerial bickering, of player resentment, or public criticism." The journal's editorialists then admitted, "Legally the reserve rule is as full of holes as porous plaster." Yet while "it doesn't follow the prescribed course of contractual obligations ... it does enable Major League teams to conduct their business. It is as vital to the welfare of professional baseball as the playing field or the grandstand." Moreover, if players were allowed to negotiate openly with any club, big cities like New York and Chicago would monopolize all the best talent. The reserve clause might engender "slavery," the editorialists acknowledged, but "it is essential to the welfare of baseball."[10]

On April 12, a jury called for the payment of $80,000 in damages by major league baseball. If the jury determination stood, then the damages would be trebled, as mandated by the Sherman Anti-Trust Act. Such a result, league presidents Johnson and Heydler warned, would demand "sweeping changes in the methods of conducting the business of organized baseball." They predicted the dissolving of the National Commission, the breaking of relations between their leagues, and the severing of existing ties between the minors and majors. Johnson also reasoned that player contracts would have to be restructured, with the dropping of the ten-day and reserve provisions. "The verdict, of course is a blow to baseball," but hardly unexpected, Johnson said. An appeal was undertaken.[11]

In an editorial dated April 15, *The New York Times* noted that two or three years would pass before the courts decided whether organized baseball, as presently constructed, was "a conspiracy in restraint of trade." The public, the *Times* declared, was little concerned with baseball's legal intricacies and was "pretty well satisfied with it as it is." Perhaps, organized baseball, the editorial admitted, did violate anti-trust laws, "for it operates quite successfully against outside competition, and it puts the players very much at the mercy of the men who own the clubs." Nevertheless, the paper concluded, "experience has shown that both of these arrangements are in the public interest, so long as the public wants professional baseball." If teams were allowed to bid freely for players, the *Times* warned, then the great metropolises of New York and Chicago would clearly attract the major's finest. Regarding the players' accusation that slavery confronted them, the newspaper insisted "they are slaves only because they prefer to play ball instead of going to work." Instances of "unfair treatment" of ballplayers, the *Times* claimed, were "not ... numerous." However, "the economic value of professional baseball," the editorial concluded, "is something of an artificial creation, and too much litigation would kill it as quickly as suspicion of the crookedness from which more than any other professional sport it has been free." *Baseball Magazine* acknowledged that "organized baseball may be a trust," but deemed it "a necessary and desirable" one.[12]

\* \* \*

Increasingly, the name of Judge Kenesaw Mountain Landis cropped up whenever talk of prospective leadership for organized baseball unfolded. Landis had made many friends among baseball officialdom in deliberately drawing out the Federal League suit against the major leagues. Landis's emotions in that case, as in so many others, guided his judicial decision-making. There, his love of baseball and concern for its well-being resulted in the delays that doomed the insurgent Federals and, as a consequence, the Players' Fraternity. Earlier, his hostility to bad big trusts had produced the multi-million dollar fine of John D. Rockefeller and Standard Oil. Later, Landis's fixation regarding 100% Americanism had shaped his harsh sentencing of Wobblies, socialists, and other opponents of the United States' involvement in World War I.

In early 1919, Landis continued to preside over the case involving the federal government's prosecution of Congressman Victor Berger and four other socialists. Throughout the trial, Landis appeared to be at his dramatic

Kenesaw Mountain Landis at 53 years of age, Chicago, Illinois, 1919. Chicago Historical Society (DN071316), photograph by *Chicago Daily News*.

best. David Karsner, writing in the *New York Call*, a socialist newspaper, indicated as much: "Landis would have been a great tragedian. He has a natural sense of the dramatic, a splendid sense of humor, a severity that has been called brutal, and a sense of right and justice and morality splendidly and consistently in keeping with the conventions of the time." On February 20, Landis meted out 20-year prison sentences at Leavenworth to all the defendants.[13]

Landis's decidedly anti-radical jurisprudence made him a target for those displeased with existing socio-economic institutions; indicating as much, the

*Chicago Herald-Examiner* deemed him the "conspicuous enemy of anarchy and Bolshevism." On May 1, 1919, 36 bombs were mailed to a series of prominent American political and industrial leaders, including John D. Rockefeller, banker J. Pierpont Morgan, Attorney General A. Mitchell Palmer, Postmaster General Albert S. Burleson, and Federal Judge Kenesaw Mountain Landis. A package delivered to the home of ex-Senator Thomas W. Hardwick of Georgia exploded, injuring his wife and their African American maid. As word of the bombing conspiracy unfolded, the press room at the Federal Building in Chicago was filled with anticipation that the metropolis would be struck. Moreover, one sage predicted, "If they do, it'll be Judge Landis who'll get the first bomb." Leading other reporters to Landis's chambers, he asked, "Did the Judge get a bomb in the mail this morning?" The secretary responded, "The judge is liable to get anything." One package arrived, containing, as others had, a Gimbel Brothers address. When Landis showed up, he sought to examine it. "It was sent to me in the mail, so it's my property," he demanded. After turning it over the police, however, Landis remained present as a bomb was discovered inside. That same month, another bomb was shipped to Chicago from Boston, with Landis once again the apparent target.[14]

Chicago area newspapers praised Landis's fearless nature. One story began, "Bombs, even real ones, hold no terrors for Judge Kenesaw Mountain Landis, the lean, keen whip of the government, the scourge of the disloyal and the vicious." Landis, the report indicated, "laughs at danger." After all, "he's a rip-snorting, wiry, fighting, tobacco chewing American. There's a punch in both his fists and a punch in his tongue. He's a human rasp. He wears the truth out of liars; he bites assets out of bankrupt frauds; and files loan sharks into human beings."[15]

\* \* \*

Much of the early speculation pertaining to the 1919 regular season also revolved around the city of Chicago, with most of the attention centered around the White Sox. The troubled times of the previous year were not easily put to rest, as indicated by a series of reports concerning managerial decision-making, contractual disputes, and the possible return of Comiskey's renegade lads. On January 2, *The Sporting News* indicated that "Commy" remained undecided whether to bring back manager Pants Rowland, a World Series winner a year earlier but a disappointing sixth-place finisher in 1918. George S. Robbins suggested that Comiskey's uncertainty was explained in part by his anger over the previous season's departure of several key players from his club. Nevertheless, Comiskey had recently announced that Joe Jackson would be welcomed back. *The Sporting News* found this interesting, given the Old Roman's declaration the previous summer that those who bolted the club "never even should be allowed in his ball park again." However, "times and sentiments change," the publication continued, and "our war madness of six months ago has subsided to a great degree."[16]

In an editorial entitled "The Return of the Prodigals," *The Sporting News* highlighted Comiskey's readiness to reunite Jackson, Lefty Williams, Oscar "Happy" Felsch, and reserve catcher Byrd Lynn with their White Sox teammates. Now, the paper insisted that Comiskey should do nothing else. After all, ballplayers who opted to work in the shipping yards rather than fight overseas "were entirely within their rights legally." Moreover, the editorial admitted, "it is not for the rest of us who didn't fight to question their consciences in the decision they made."[17]

Comiskey's call, delivered a week later, to appoint former coach William "Kid" Gleason to replace Rowland as White Sox manager, was generally well-received; *Baseball Magazine* noted that Gleason, a "picturesque character," had received "a rousing welcome." Comiskey evidently believed that Rowland "had lost his hold over the players" and justified the move on the grounds that "the loyal patrons of the White Sox" demanded it. Gleason refused to discuss past differences with his boss — evidently concerning a promised bonus — declaring, "Forget it. Commy is the best man in the world personally and as a baseball man he is second to none."[18]

While Gleason had now returned to the White Sox organization, news stories continued to be spun whether the "prodigal" ballplayers would so as well. In the *Chicago Herald and Examiner*, Sam P. Hall contended that Felsch would not play for Comiskey again until another dispute over a bonus was resolved. While Felsch had signed a contract in 1917 for $3,500, he had also been promised an $1,100 bonus that had not been paid. The previous season, Felsch, concerned about his brother who had been seriously injured in a military training camp, had left the squad. After visiting his ailing brother, Felsch had reportedly delayed returning to the White Sox. After finally doing so, Felsch's performance was not up to par — he batted only .252 during an abbreviated schedule — before he departed for good, supposedly because the bonus had not been received. In the meantime, Felsch was purportedly fined for the period he was away from the team.[19]

The bonus, Comiskey indicated, had actually been paid, even though it involved Felsch's agreement not to drink, which he had violated. Felsch, *The Sporting News* claimed, was making "his situation more embarrassing by his now setting up as another alibi that he left the team because he had a row with Eddie Collins."[20]

Kid Gleason, for his part, desired the return of his whole ball club, even "the members of the paint and putty league," as *The Sporting News* referred to them on January 23. Hoping to mediate matters between Comiskey and his still disgruntled players, Gleason sought to field the same contingent that had won the 1917 World Series. Lefty Williams had informed Gleason that he wanted Comiskey "to adjust a little salary dispute" so he might return to his old ball club. His paycheck had been withheld, Williams complained, after "he deserted the team without giving the usual notice that he was going to depart." White Sox Secretary Harry Grabiner reported that Gleason would strive mightily to win back the star players "who deserted the team last year." Felsch, it now appeared, was certain to rejoin the south-side franchise. Chicago fans, it seemed, exhibited no animosity regarding the star center fielder. As for Jackson, sportswriter George S. Robbins warned that the great slugger's "spirit is needed on the team. It must be encouraged, not broken." Through all the contractual battles, Comiskey's reputation remained untarnished as exemplified by W. A. Phelon's referring to him as "the One Magnate of the game — the one man whom the people love."[21]

However, on February 20, Robbins reported that Gleason was still concerned about Buck Weaver, who remained a holdout, in addition to the "ship yard jumpers." Gleason, the writer indicated, had to "appease Weaver, who says he must get more money in his pay check before signing a new contract." Jackson, it was suggested, might seek to be dealt off to another club. The great outfielder, Robbins suggested, "undoubtedly would play his best ball in some other city than Chicago seeing the manner in which he has been panned, roasted and lambasted here." Comiskey, Robbins offered, was largely responsible for the abuse heaped on Jackson, as the owner had never backtracked concerning the criticisms he had hurled the star's way.[22]

The following week, both Jackson and first baseman Chick Gandil agreed to terms, leaving only Weaver and Lefty Williams as holdouts. Weaver was said to be playing ball with the Fairbanks-Morse squad of the Chicago League, located in Beloit, Wisconsin. Buck, *The Sporting News* indicated, "says he must receive a substantial boost in his monthly stipend or he will quit the White Sox and play with the semi-pros." On March 13, the baseball newspaper noted that White Sox fans wondered who would yield first: Comiskey or Weaver; Williams had recently signed. The Chicago owner had declared his unwillingness to renegotiate Weaver's contract. At present, the publication noted, "there is just one cloud on the White Sox horizon, no bigger than a man's hand at present, but still a cloud and it is beginning to worry officials of the club." That involved Weaver's continued unwillingness to sign the contract tendered him; additionally, infielders Fred McMullin and Swede Risberg were also not in the fold. Weaver had informed Robbins that "he is going clear on through with his threat and that he has played his last game with the White Sox if his salary demands are not met." To demonstrate his determination to stand fast, Weaver prepared to work "in an industrial occupation."[23]

Comiskey remained a hard-liner where holdouts were concerned. Even the masterful spitballer, Ed Walsh, who once won 40 games in a season, had been compelled to deal with Comiskey "as a supplicant." Commy, Robbins wrote, "has repeatedly refused to come to terms with recalcitrant players." Moreover, "the longer those athletes have held out, the harder they have found the return road to the club." Still, Weaver appeared to have an advantage over someone like Walsh, for he was associated with an institution that exalted athletics both to entertain its employees and provide them recreation. The firm, Robbins continued, "wants Buck as an employe (sic), also as an entertainer, and the lucrative employment he is receiving at Beloit makes his holdout case assume an entirely different aspect from what it would otherwise appear."[24]

Asked about the situation, Weaver responded:

> I am absolutely through with the club if Comiskey doesn't come to terms with me by the time the team leaves Chicago on the spring training jaunt. Perhaps the owner of the Sox imagines that I'm bluffing and that I will come around to his terms if he holds out too, but this time I'm in earnest and I've made full arrangements to play ball in Beloit and continue to study mechanics if Comiskey fails to talk turkey with me.
>
> It was in the spring of 1918 that I talked with President Comiskey about a contract for that year. He told me about the bad war conditions. He said his club would do well to make money owing to unsettled conditions. I signed a contract calling for the same amount of money I was receiving the previous season, when I helped win the world's championship, although I felt I deserved a boost. 'There will be a time when I'll ask you for the benefit of the doubt,' I said to Comiskey as I signed that contract. Last year I had the best season of my life, beating my record of 1917, when we copped the flag. I outbatted and outplayed Eddie Collins. I did Comiskey a good turn when conditions were bad and now that the game is coming back, I'm simply asking him to return the favor.[25]

Weaver, Robbins suspected, might be the lone White Sox player who would refuse to give in to Comiskey. Nevertheless, both McMullin and Risberg also sought substantial salary increases. Gleason's team hardly appeared competitive without at least a pair of those infielders. Most significantly, "the club couldn't afford to lose Weaver at any hazard." Because of that fact, Robbins offered, the Chicago mogul should agree to a compromise involving his third baseman. On the other hand, Commy could treat Weaver as he had Walsh or allow him to "to remain without the fold."[26]

On March 17, Weaver met with Gleason and Grabiner at Comiskey Park. The negotiations lasted but thirty minutes, with Weaver backing off from his demand for a $2,000 annual raise. He signed a new three year deal, pegged at $7,250 a year. Weaver was evidently won over by the argument that the White Sox, unlike the Beloit nine, played ball virtually every day throughout the regular season. Additionally, Chicago once again had an excellent shot at making the World Series.[27]

As the season opener approached, only McMullin and Risberg had failed to sign up. *The Sporting News* expressed concerns about the thinness of Gleason's pitching staff and the strength of Red Faber's arm. The rest of the team, however, appeared "lovely." Buck Weaver, it was suggested, "may have the best season of his career;" *The Chicago Tribune* sportswriter Hugh S. Fullerton would soon rate Weaver the top third baseman in the American League. Swede Risberg seemed ready to serve as the regular shortstop. This was fortunate, George S. Robbins noted, because "there is no man more loyal to his club's interests, either, and that counts for much." Happy Felsch, for his part, "seems in his element this season, as does Joe Jackson." Significantly, "these great hitters seem to have caught the Gleason spirit and are working hard, even when they don't realize it." Pitcher Dick Kerr was one of the rookies who stood the best chance of becoming a regular.[28]

\* \* \*

White Sox management was hardly alone in facing contractual disputes, although the number of Comiskey's ballplayers who were disgruntled about salary negotiations was striking; so too were the strained relations between the owner and some of the American League's finest. Perhaps the two greatest stars in the game, Ty Cobb and Babe Ruth, both threatened to walk away from their teams; the longtime batting champion proclaimed himself a free agent, while the phenom of the 1918 season simply demanded more money. Cobb's five-year contract, inked in the midst of the Federal League turmoil, had ended, and rumors floated that the Yankees were willing to pay him $20,000 a year. Claims of free agency, *The Sporting News* offered, were not to be taken lightly. Furthermore, an editorial dated January 2, 1919, admitted, "We dread to think of what the civil courts would say were one of the players to press his claim to freedom." At the same time, the paper praised major leaguers as a group for not pursuing the issue. "Their recognition of the fact that it would inaugurate a state of anarchy in organized baseball were the principle admitted that all players are free to dicker without regard to previous reservations claims, belies the charge that the athletes know little and care less for the structure in which they are an important part of the framework."[29]

As the new year began, Ruth was threatening to head for the Delaware County League unless he received a considerable salary increase. Such a possibility, however remote, had to be disturbing to Boston Red Sox owner Harry Frazee and manager Ed Barrow. Ruth's lifetime totals to date included 678 at bats, 203 hits, a .299 batting average, with 48 doubles, 18 triples, 20 home runs, 347 total bases, 99 runs scored, and 115 RBIs. These were hardly numbers in keeping with ragtime baseball's dead ball era, although the homer count would soon amount to a couple of months' work for Ruth. *The Sporting News* edition of January 30 acclaimed Ruth "unquestionably ... the greatest slugger of all time. He hits the ball harder than any other man that ever lived." On top of that, Ruth remained a fine fielder and "a pitcher so remarkable" that prior to the past season's batting feats, "he was ranked among the twirling phenoms." Still, the paper acknowledged, "it's his home run hitting that has endeared him to the public."[30]

During early spring training, Ruth continued to proclaim himself "a bona fide holdout." Reports indicated that Ruth was demanding $15,000 a year, while Frazee was offering half that amount. Several other Red Sox players had yet to come to terms, as they apparently were awaiting word on what salaries Ruth and Harry Hooper would agree to. Frazee indicated his willingness to "play the 'waiting game." As of mid–March, *The New York Times* reported that Ruth, Cobb, and Cleveland star Tris Speaker were not accompanying their teams to southern training camp sites. Cobb was heard to say,

> When I got back from France I said that I probably would not play ball again, and my sentiments haven't changed any since. It isn't a question of money with me exactly. Naturally, I feel that my services are worth a certain sum and I wouldn't play for less. But I am not a holdout in the sense of demanding more money. I am a holdout mostly because I have felt the last few months that I wanted to retire from the game. If I decide to return to baseball, I do not plan to do any Spring training work this season. The training I had in the army did me a world of good and I can really say that I have been in strict training since the opening of last season.

Ruth soon altered his salary demands, now requesting a three-year annual contract of $10,000; after initially refusing, Frazee agreed to those terms.[31]

With the contract dispute behind him, Ruth now battled with manager Barrow regarding his role with the Red Sox. Ruth preferred to be assigned to the outfield so that he could play every day. Long-time outfielder Duffy Lewis, who had starred on the 1912, 1915, and 1916 world championship units but had missed the previous season due to military service, had been traded to the Yankees. Thus, a full-time outfield spot was open, but Barrow wanted Ruth to pitch and serve as a pinch-hitter. In an article crafted for *The Sporting News* on April 7, James O'Leary indicated that Barrow recognized that Ruth "is a great pitcher, but he is not so certain that he could be used to advantage regularly as an outfielder." Thus, while Ruth had done "some wonderful hitting" the previous year, it was likely that pitchers would be searching "for his weaknesses." Although "Babe is a natural, free hitter," O'Leary continued, "they are sure to get to his weakness sooner or later." Obviously relying on information received from the Boston manager, Leary affirmed that Barrow "had considered the possibilities" and thus preferred for Ruth to return to the mound. The sportswriter predicted, "It is a cinch that Babe could not be used to any considerable extent in two positions, and show at his best in either one of them, and the chances are that he would not be able to keep up his terrific hitting, if he were so used."[32]

In Tampa, in a pre-season contest against the Giants, Ruth crushed a ball that reputedly traveled over 600 feet. On April 18, performing before his home town in Baltimore, Ruth should have put to rest any notion that he not become a full-time, everyday ballplayer. In an exhibition game against Jack Dunn's Orioles, his old team, Ruth came to bat six times, was intentionally walked twice, and belted four home runs. Ruth was heard to say "that no one can teach a player to hit the way he hits." Smiling, Ruth exclaimed before an appreciative crowd, "It's a gift." In 18 spring training games, he produced 11 round-trippers.[33]

Sports pundits predicted that the 1919 season would be a great one, with the game promising to be more popular than ever. Lineups were obviously strengthened, thanks to the return of players from the army or the shipping yards. The previous year had been soiled, *The New York Times* suggested, by "indifference and shirking ... lax methods, and other unfortunate features. ..." *The Sporting News* contended that four teams — the New York Yankees, the Cleveland Indians, the Chicago White Sox, and the Red Sox — would vie for the American League crown. With the addition of outfielder Duffy Lewis and the return of third sacker Frank Baker, the Yankees possessed an offense that would "raise havoc with the opposing pitchers," while its own starters were among the best in the majors. The Indians appeared balanced, with "powerful" pitching, "heavy hitting," "excellent catching," and "the greatest fielder in the game," Tris Speaker.[34]

"The pennant bee" was said to be "again buzzing in the bonnets of the ... White Sox." With the hiring of Kid Gleason as manager, *The Sporting News* continued, "there is sure to be harmony among the players." This Chicago unit appeared as potent as the 1917 world champions, with Joe Jackson and Happy Felsch roaming the outfield once again. As for pitching, it now seemed "so rich" that Gleason "is at a loss to make a choice;" the Kid assumed he could put together a staff second to none. The infield, with Chick Gandil and Buck Weaver at the corners, Eddie Collins playing second, and Swede Risberg positioned at shortstop, and catching, with Ray Schalk behind the plate, were Chicago strong suits.[35]

Although many looked to the White Sox to return to the glory of their recent past, the defending world champion Red Sox appeared "even stronger" than the previous year's version. The addition of third baseman Oscar Vitt made Boston "strong in every department." Apparently lacking any weaknesses, the Red Sox boasted a "remarkable defense," with shortstop Everett Scott proving "more marvelous each season." The pitching staff was first-rate, although manager Barrow remained torn about how to use Babe Ruth.[36]

As the major league season began — Ruth homered on opening day against New York pitcher George Mogridge at the Polo Grounds — Babe expressed an ambition to become the American League's all-time home run king. In 1902, Philadelphia Athletic outfielder Socks Seybold had hit 16 homers, while Cub third baseman Ned Williamson smacked 27 back in 1884, playing in a band-box ballpark. *The Sporting News* worried about Ruth's homer fixation, warning that his average could plummet dramatically; it again contended that Ruth "should first and foremost be held as a pitcher, and used a pinch hitter." After all, "great pitchers"—and Ruth was clearly one—were "harder to replace than outfielders." Both Boston owner Frazee and manager Barrow agreed with this analysis, as they sought to acquire a hard-hitting outfielder.[37]

After a quick 4-1 getaway, Boston dropped a pair to the Yankees, which led to the decision to start Ruth in the next game. In delivering that announcement, Frazee declared that Ruth would serve as the Red Sox's regular left-handed starter, playing the outfield "only when they decided to use him there." Ruth was reported to have accepted management's decree. Calling Ruth "a good sport," *The Sporting News* acknowledged that

> he is a great ball player, and would be a strong drawing card if he played every game. He is unquestionably a great pitcher, but there is some doubt, considerable doubt, in fact, as to his being a world-compeller (sic) as an outfielder. There is also, the danger of his not being able to come back as a pitcher if he should be kept for any length of time as a regular in the outfield, and, eventually, fail to make good.[38]

A week into the season, Grantland Rice, in his *New York Tribune* sports column, coined the following verse:

> When you can lean upon the ball
> And lay the seasoned ash against it,
> The bally park's a trifle small,
> No matter how far out they've fenced it;
> Past master of the four-base clout,
> You stand and take your wallop proudly;
> A pretty hand bloke about —
> I'll say you are — and say it loudly.
>
> I've seen a few I thought could hit,
> Who fed the crowd on four-base rations;
> But you, Babe, are the Only It —
> The rest are merely imitations;
> I've seen them swing with all they've got
> And tear into it for a mop-up;

But what they deem a lusty swat
To you is but a futile pop-up.

Somewhere's amid another throng,
Where Fate at times became unruly,
I've heard Big Bertha sing her song
Without an encore from Yours Truly;
Yes, she had something — so to speak —
A range you couldn't get away with;
But when you nail one on the beak
They need another ball to play with.[39]

In a piece filed for *The Sporting News*, James O'Leary discussed another quandary concerning Ruth. The young pitcher-slugger was a great asset to his ball club, O'Leary suggested, due to "the confusion he injects into the camps of the opposition." Always viewing him "as a menace and a threat," they were uncertain whether to allow Boston's star to swing away or walk him. In the meantime, both the free passes and homers continued to mount at a record or near-record clip.[40]

* * *

As summer approached, it was clear that "enormous crowds" were amassing at ballparks throughout the major leagues. "King Baseball IS really back," chortled W. A. Phelon. A two-team race seemed to be unfolding in the National League, with John McGraw's Giants battling Pat Moran's surprising Cincinnati Reds. The Yankees, Indians, and White Sox were all jousting for the top spot in the American League. The White Sox, offering basically the same lineup as the 1917 World Series squad, appeared back in championship form. The 34-year-old Ed Cicotte, Phelon suggested, was "putting himself in the Young-Mathewson class for endurance." With the title-holding Red Sox struggling mightily, Babe Ruth was virtually the only Red Sox player hitting. Compounding Boston's problems, pitcher Carl Mays was foundering terribly; he would eventually win but a handful of 16 decisions for his old club.[41]

Mays was a highly skilled pitcher, as attested by both regular season and World Series performances. Known for both his ungracious demeanor and nasty, submarine delivery, coupled with a willingness to brush back players from the plate, Mays had just completed back-to-back 20-win seasons. Like Babe Ruth, he had won two games against the Cubs in the 1918 fall classic, including the clincher, a hard-fought three-hitter in which he bested Lefty Tyler, 2-1. Like fellow staff members Sad Sam Jones and Bullet Joe Bush, Mays appeared to have lost some of his effectiveness early in the 1919 season, despite managing to throw a pair of shutouts in only 16 starts. On July 13, a disgusted Mays, in the midst of a game against the White Sox, declined to continue pitching. When manager Ed Barrow telegraphed Mays to return to the team, the latter refused, effectively stating, "I could pitch with my arm, but I could not pitch with heart and soul, which every person has got to do if he pitches winning games in baseball."[42]

Red Sox owner Harry Frazee and Yankee moguls Jacob Ruppert and T. L. Huston agreed to swap Mays — whom Charles Comiskey had sought to purchase for $30,000 — for pitchers Bob McGraw and Allen Russell and $40,000. Johnson then voided the deal, stating, "Baseball cannot tolerate such a breach of discipline. It was up to the owners of the Boston Club to suspend Carl Mays for breaking his contract, and when they failed to do so it was my duty as head of the American League to act. Mays will not play with any club until the suspension is raised. He should have reported to the Boston Club before they made any trades or sale." Ruppert telegrammed Johnson that his action would work "such a terrible hardship on our club that we respectfully ask that you raise this suspension. We make this request in the friendliest spirit, without, however, waiving our legal rights." The Yankee management proceeded to obtain a temporary injunction restraining American League officials from interfering with Mays's contract.[43]

On August 10, *The New York Times* warned that "a serious baseball war" threatened to break out in the American League concerning the Mays affair. The New York, Chicago, and Boston franchises were linked in an effort to curb Johnson's power, while the other five clubs remained loyal to the league president. Colonel Huston insisted that the "snap-judgment rule" had to be discarded, due process standards adhered to, and Johnson's "arbitrary power" diminished. Within a month, during a hearing before New York State Supreme Court Justice Robert F. Wagner, the Yankees' attorney, Joseph Auerbach, termed Johnson an "unmolested despot." New York's co-counsel Charles H. Tuttle emphasized that Johnson's large stockholding interests in the Cleveland Indians prejudiced his official pronouncements. Tuttle was said to have "indulged in quite a lengthy harangue about Americanism and the necessity of making baseball a typical American sport instead of a sort of Russian pastime with an all powerful czar in charge." He warned that "syndicate baseball" could corrode the sport's foundation. Eventually, Wagner issued a permanent injunction, allowing the Yankees to keep the star pitcher.[44]

The Mays controversy, coupled with the ongoing anti-trust suit by the Baltimore Federal Leaguers, resulted in additional calls for new leadership to head organized baseball. Former Cub owner Charles Webb Murphy proposed William Howard Taft, former U.S. Supreme Court Justice and 1916 Republican Party presidential candidate Charles Evans Hughes and Elihu Root, Secretary of State under Wilson, as possible members of the defense's legal team.

Murphy said "it would be useless to add the name of Kenesaw Mountain Landis, who loves our national game and regards it as an institution, because he can't well be spared from the bench of justice."[45]

* * *

In the meantime, the 1919 regular season had continued to unfold with Ruth and Comiskey's White Sox amassing headline after headline. In early June, George S. Robbins roundly sang the praises of Chicago's American League franchise. Manager Gleason's "aggressive" style appeared to have energized Chicago, whose "fighting spirit" had proved "unparalleled" in team history. Moreover, "wonderful fielding back of superb pitching" explained Chicago's success; outfielders Joe Jackson and Happy Felsch, along with infielders Chick Gandil, Eddie Collins, Swede Risberg, and Buck Weaver, had "robbed the opposition of base wallops" and prevented the pitching staff from slumping badly. Additionally, Buck Weaver and Joe Jackson were batting leaders in a potent lineup. Importantly, the White Sox "never know when they're licked." Jackson's all around performance, Robbins declared, "stamped him as about the leading outfielder of the major league this far this year." Cicotte, rebounding from a poor 1918 season, "was the big surprise," while batterymate Ray Schalk was "playing at the top of his career."[46]

Two months later, Robbins now proclaimed that the team's "heavy and consistent clouters" were carrying a "wobbly pitching staff." With an ailing Red Faber largely on the sideline, Cicotte and Lefty Williams were Chicago's "pitching aces." It was Gleason, Robbins argued, who was leading the White Sox charge, exuding marked optimism and ably handling the squad. Gleason was ready to listen to advice from sportswriters and veterans ballplayers alike, letting Collins and Weaver "run almost as wild as Ty Cobb."[47]

While the White Sox headed for the title, the defending World Champion Red Sox continued their season-long debacle leading to an eventual sixth place finish. Unable to purchase a heavy hitting outfielder, Boston manager Ed Barrow had agreed to let Babe Ruth return to the outfield on a regular basis. History was made that summer as Ruth began shattering major league slugging records. Just after mid-season, *The New York Times* was already predicting that Ruth would break all single season home run marks. As "the home run stands out as the big happening on the ball field," the *Times* claimed, it made sense to highlight "the record-breaking performances of Babe Ruth, the Boston slugger." After Ruth equaled the American League mark of 16 round-trippers, the *Times* predicted that he would shoot for the major league mark. For now, the paper reflected, "American League pitchers appear at a loss to stop him."[48]

*The Sporting News* analyzed Ruth's slugging prowess, while the *Times* tracked his home run quest. As Boston stumbled out of the pennant race, Red

Sox fans continued to follow the team to discover how many long balls Ruth would hit. All the while, Ruth's base-clearing march continued despite more intentional walks coming his way than any player in the game. Ruth sought to reach the hitherto unattainable total of 30 home runs, *The Sporting News* reported. Should he do so, the paper declared, "there is no one now playing the game who will ever disturb it and the record should stand until a new star appears." Bostonians were undoubtedly pleased to have Ruth's home run jaunt take their minds away from the police strike that crippled the city in early September; the mayor fired the striking policemen, Massachusetts Governor Calvin Coolidge sent the National Guard into Boston, and President Wilson deemed the strike "a crime against civilization." On another front, Ruth maintained his record-setting home run pace. Moreover, four of Ruth's homers were grand slams, establishing an American League record that stood for decades. One Ruth smash was the longest homer ever struck at Comiskey Park. His 28th homer, which bettered Ned Williamson's 35 year-old total, was the longest ever hit at the Polo Grounds, surpassing one belted by Joe Jackson years earlier. "Ruth stood firmly on his sturdy legs like the Colossus of Rhodes," the *Times* exclaimed, "and, taking a mighty swing at the second ball pitched to him, catapulted the pill for a new altitude and distance record."[49]

By crushing his final homer of the season in cavernous Griffith Stadium, Ruth had managed to hit one in every American League park. In noting that Ruth had established a new major league mark, James O'Leary predicted "it will be a superman indeed who will improve on it, under similar conditions." Furthermore, "Ruth has proved himself to be the mightiest swatter that ever went to bat."[50]

With 432 official at bats in 130 games, Ruth led the league with 103 runs scored, 114 RBIs, a .456 on base percentage, an American League record .657 slugging average, and 29 homers. He batted .322, with 34 doubles and 12 triples, walked 101 times, while striking out on only 58 occasions. He even led outfielders with a .996 fielding mark. Ruth also compiled a 9-5 won-loss record, while completing 12 of 15 games started and producing a 2.97 ERA. Ruth's slugging totals soared past his closest competitors. Philadelphia's Gavvy Cravath led the National League with 12 homers, while Brooklyn's Hy Myers topped the senior circuit with 73 RBIs and a .436 slugging average. In the American League, the second highest homer total was barely a third of Ruth's, 10. Ten teams totaled fewer homers than Ruth, who was only one of three Red Sox players to smack even one. Harry Hooper contributed three, first baseman Stuffy McInnis, only one. Other heavy hitters did no or little better. Ty Cobb hit but one homer; Cincinnati's Edd Roush, four; Joe Jackson, seven; and Rogers Hornsby, eight.

At season's close, *The New York Times* analyzed Ruth's 1919 batting performance. Ruth was referred to as "the mastodonic mauler of the Boston Red

Sox, whose feats with the willow have discounted everything that went before it, batting annals since the game was introduced." The American League now boasted, the *Times* declared, "the greatest batsman the game has ever known," as well as "the hardest hitter in the history of the game." His record drives in stadium after stadium — the Polo Grounds, Detroit's Navin field, St. Louis's Sportsman's Park, Comiskey Park, and Fenway — demonstrated that Ruth's feats were still more noteworthy. With the trend toward larger ballparks, the *Times* suggested, his record was unlikely to be broken.[51]

Spalding sang Ruth's praises loudly:

> Something big and new was done in Base Ball in 1919. It was the greatest achievement of any individual ball player in a generation. It placed George H. Ruth, known to the "boys" as "Babe" Ruth, at the head of the Base Ball parade directly behind the band. It scored for the American League a point not to be denied, but more than that it demonstrated that we have not yet come to the point in Base Ball where we can say "there is nothing bigger that can be done."
>
> Ruth made twenty-nine home runs in 1919. That is a record with a vengeance. It is a regular mastodon of a record. It surpasses all the feats of the present generation of ball players and is superior to all the great performances of the ball players of the past.[52]

Ruth, not surprisingly, headed *Baseball Magazine*'s annual All American team. The American League infield was comprised of first baseman George Sisler, second sacker Eddie Collins, shortstop Roger Peckinpaugh, and Buck Weaver at the hot corner. The outfield was made up of Ty Cobb, Joe Jackson, and Babe Ruth, while Steve O'Neill was the star catcher. The pitchers were Walter Johnson and Eddie Cicotte. The National Leaguers included first baseman Jake Daubert, third baseman Heinie Groh, outfielder Edd Roush, and catcher Ivy Wingo from the first-place Cincinnati Reds, Cardinal shortstop Rogers Hornsby, and hurlers Hippo Vaughn and Jesse Barnes, from the Cubs and Giants, respectively. Babe Ruth, with "the most formidable bat that baseball has ever known," F. C. Lane wrote, "simply cannot be kept off an all star team." After all, "he smashed the ancient home run record into a thousand pieces. He broke the long distance hitting mark on almost every field of the circuit. He literally slugged his way to the topmost round of baseball fame."[53]

At year's end, Grantland Rice analyzed "the world's greatest slugger." First, Rice noted that Ruth was "also the game's greatest showman." The eccentric Rube Waddell, thanks to his "mingled genius," had once entertained the baseball public for over a decade. Babe's "greatness as showman," Rice declared, "comes from his ability to deliver his choicest wares before the largest crowds." Second, Ruth had compiled "a remarkable record." During the 1919 season, Babe, combining "terrific power and ... perfect timing," had

Babe Ruth with fans, 1919. National Baseball Hall of Fame Library, Cooperstown, N.Y.

produced time after time, surpassing the slugging accomplishments of "Ed Delehanty [sic], Dan Brouthers, Nap Lajoie, Hans Wagner, Harry Davis, Sam Crawford, Cactus Cravath, Frank Schulte," among others. Third, Ruth crafted his home run mark despite any number of obstacles, including a shortened season and repeated intentional walks.[54]

In the process, he placed the record "out of reach — out of reach of any one except himself." With a fuller season in 1920, Rice predicted, Ruth should shatter his own home run mark. "For he is without any doubt the game's greatest slugger. He has an exceptionally keen eye, his swing with all its power is well controlled; and in addition to being a home run wonder there is no reason why he shouldn't bat around .400." He had also become "the greatest card in baseball," transcending Ty Cobb in that regard. Even with the Red Sox mired in the second division, over 30,000 spectators showed up on more than one occasion at the ballpark to watch Ruth. This hardly surprised Rice who declared,

> The fan leans toward the slugger. He would rather watch a great home run hitter than a .400 hitter who depended more on science than on the wallop. And the fanatic began to understand that Ruth was an obliging man, and that once the park was filled he was almost certain to lift one out of the yard and drop it on some neighboring flat.

CHAPTER SEVEN

# In the Eye of the Storm

As events unfolded, the 1919 major league season ultimately proved to be far more significant than simply one in which Babe Ruth became the game's greatest slugger and the Cincinnati Reds and Chicago White Sox captured pennants. It brought to the forefront the issue that threatened the very existence of professional ball, at least the segregated brand played in the major and minor leagues. Intermittently, sportswriters had discussed moves by organized baseball to prevent a cancer — one that was potentially fatal, no less — in its midst. Baseball, the national pastime, was presented as a particularly wholesome sport but one that could be crippled or worse by the spectre of gambling; the National Commission appeared incapable of wrestling with that disease. In June 1917, a game between the White Sox and Red Sox was disrupted at mid-point, before it became official, to prevent bets from having to be paid. Along with hoodlums, gamblers, who had counted heavily on Boston to prevail, piqued a riot on the field that resulted in attacks on Chicago players.[1]

Before the 1918 season, discussion was had regarding moves by American President Ban Johnson "to rid ball parks of professional gamblers." *The Sporting News* referred to "a certain player of the Boston Red Sox," who had been sued for reneging on a bet regarding how the league standings would wind up. That player was ace pitcher Carl Mays, who had been charged with a breach of contract in a Boston Superior Court room the previous fall. Mays was accused of refusing to repay several hundred dollars the plaintiff had delivered to Sport Sullivan to cover a debt the pitcher owed the well-known Boston gambler. The case was eventually dismissed on a legal technicality; unresolved was the question of Mays's involvement with Boston "sportsmen."[2]

In December 1918, *Baseball Magazine* adopted the usual line, claiming that the sport was "the cleanest, most honest, most wholesome ... the sun ever shown upon." Yet in the months ahead, the unholy trinity of gambling, crooked ballplayers, and fixes repeatedly resurfaced. Little helping matters was the decision on February 8 by National League President John A. Heydler to exonerate Hal Chase of all charges leveled against him by his former manager, Christy Mathewson, and Cincinnati owner Gary Herrmann. "Chase has been acquitted," declared Heydler, "because there is no evidence to prove that he ever bet against his own team or played baseball dishonestly. He is deserving of a square deal from the public and press, inasmuch as he has established his innocence without the slightest trouble."[3]

Sports columnist Joe Vila applauded the decision, terming the charges against Chase "so flimsy that it wasn't hard to see clear through them with the naked eye." The testimony involved "nothing but hearsay, rumor, innuendo and ugly gossip. There wasn't a particle of alleged evidence that was corroborated." Chase, by contrast, in Vila's estimation, "made a fine impression" when he took the stand in his own defense. "He was straight-forward and enthusiastic in his replies. He admitted that he had made bets on ball games, but not in more than two or three instances."[4]

*The Sporting News*, in the same issue that featured Vila's apologetics, included Heydler's observation that Chase had "acted in a foolish and careless manner, both on the field and among the players." Thus, Cincinnati "was justified in bringing the charges, in view of the many rumors which arose from the loose talk of its first baseman." John E. Wray, also writing in the newspaper's February 13 edition, pulled even fewer punches regarding Chase.

> It may be observed that he is the most whitewashed entity that ever annoyed a National Baseball Commission. ... Hal, through indiscretions of various kinds, has been an in-and-outer of the rankest sort. By this we mean that he has been in and out of the major leagues — both of them — several times. But though palpably at fault on occasions, he has always won forgiveness because of a wonderful ability to cover first base and to swat them out where the enemy "ain't."

Shortly thereafter, Chase signed a contract to play under John McGraw, who, ironically enough, had added Christy Mathewson as a coach and type of assistant manager.[5]

In March, Arthur Irwin, manager of a minor league team in Rochester, discussed "the most insidious poison which blights baseball's prospects ... The gambling evil." Baseball was, at present, he admitted, "freer from this evil than any other professional sport." Nevertheless, "the taint, though slight," he warned, was related to "the world's series ... the biggest single event in all athletic sport." Dangers arose when two teams met with one club hopelessly out of the race and the other striving to enter post-season competition. Irwin asked, "How could you conceive of a greater temptation to yield a point, to concede a bit to that dishonesty," which had crippled boxing, horse racing, and wrestling? "To the everlasting credit of baseball," he wrote, "no matter how great the temptation, the scrupulous honesty of the game, save in the case of a very few individuals who have been punished for their misdeeds, is absolutely above reproach."[6]

The April issue of *Baseball Magazine* contained an editorial discussing the Chase affair, "the gambling spirit" that had wounded other sports, and the national pastime's continued reputation as "the cleanest of sports." That same issue included an analysis by F. C. Lane on the role performed by chance in the game, along with his observation that "Baseball has maintained an admirable stand on the gambling evil. Professional baseball is as free from this withering taint as it is possible to preserve a game. It is the cleanest big sport in the world."[7]

Boston was hardly the only city where betting on major league games flourished. On July 13, *The New York Times* reported that "four baseball enthusiasts" had been arrested at Comiskey Park and charged with betting on a series between the White Sox and Athletics. Still the tone of the *Times*' account hardly suggested that anything grave had occurred.[8]

A more serious note, albeit one colored by ethnic stereotypes, cropped up in Joe Vila's account of gambling incidents at the Polo Grounds. On July 17, Vila discussed a recent incident involving "the betting gang" that led to the ejection by private detectives, who had been hired by the Giants and Yankees, of "many of the ring leaders who wagered conspicuously" during a contest with the St. Louis Cardinals. Seated directly behind the Cardinal bench, "the pikers" lustily cheered the visiting squad, to the amazement of other onlookers. These "Bolsheviki," Vila declared, "continued to rant and rave" until St. Louis grabbed the lead, thus making "it possible to cash the bets placed by the gents from the Ghetto." The Giant management determined that something had to be done, with John McGraw warning, "We are going to drive out these gamblers, no matter what may happen. ... This gambling evil must be nipped in the bud else it will kill baseball.[9]

Vila likewise saw the danger as potentially grave. He wrote:

> Every club owner and manager in organized baseball should line up in a finish fight against betting on the game. The baseball pools have grown in enormous proportions. They are sold every where and thousands of dollars are invested daily. But this form of gambling is carried on outside of the ball parks and can only be suppressed by the federal, state and municipal authorities. The betting inside the parks, however, is something different. The magnates can stop it by employing the methods of the Giants and Yankees.[10]

\* \* \*

The summer of 1919 was a trying season in many other ways. A series of bombs — attributed to radicals of an anarchist or a Bolshevist stripe — exploded in urban centers around the country. One target was the home in Washington, D.C., of Attorney General A. Mitchell Palmer. While the front of his house was blown up, so was the bomber. Shortly thereafter, Congress voted to award the Justice Department's anti-radical division $500,000 to target suspect individuals and groups. Helping to coordinate that activity was a young government attorney by the name of J. Edgar Hoover.[11]

Just as telling in a very different manner, racial conflagrations began to break out. The first and deadliest of such incidents occurred in Chicago, the home station of Rube Foster's American Giants, the White Sox, the Cubs, and Federal Judge Kenesaw Mountain Landis. Viewed at the time as America's second city, Chicago had long been afflicted by political corruption, inadequate public services, and racial tension. The racial difficulties besetting Chicago were hardly unique during this era for the great urban, industrial centers of the northeast and midwest, which had experienced massive migration out of the American South since the end of the 19th Century. Driven by the intensifying of Jim Crow practices in the region and by the ready resort on the part of whites to violence, including numerous lynchings, many blacks underwent an odyssey to Philadelphia, Boston, New York, Detroit, and Chicago, among other locales. They also came because of the promise of a better life supposedly characterized by improved living conditions, well-paying jobs, and political freedoms denied

Rube Foster, circa 1919. National Baseball Hall of Fame Library, Cooperstown, N.Y.

them down south. For some, those promises bore fruit and, along with their kin in the south, they began comprising a black bourgeoisie that would lead an assault against segregation practices. For many others, however, those promises proved woefully barren, as only ghetto slums, menial employment, if any at all, and Jim Crow liberty awaited them.

Following the end of the United States' involvement in World War I — an experience shared by many African American soldiers and industrial laborers — segregation remained the norm, whether inside or beyond the cotton belt. Organized baseball, like America itself, determinedly maintained racial boundaries, although some were pushing at the gates, symbolically and apparently otherwise. Blackball continued to provide a means for some of the nation's finest athletes to ply their trade, albeit in highly circumscribed fashion. Like major league baseball, blackball suffered during the 19 months the United States was a belligerent, leading some to conjecture "where, or where, have the colored ball clubs gone?"[12]

Nevertheless, change seemed to be in the offing. In Rube Foster's adopted city of Chicago, proud African American veterans of the Great War had just returned to a warm welcome among the South Side's black community. Foster continued to war in his own fashion against racially discriminatory barriers. Indeed, no one more determinedly sought to sustain blackball and, in the process, to demonstrate that African American players could hold their own against the finest white performers than Rube Foster. Howard A. Phelps,

Rube Foster, circa 1919. National Baseball Hall of Fame Library, Cooperstown, N.Y.

in the March 1, 1919 issue of *The Half-Century Magazine*, saluted Foster as the most dominant blackball contributor of the early 20th Century and as the man who purportedly had "won more games than any pitcher who ever pitched." Foster, Phelps insisted, "harbors no envy. He beats the best of the Colored teams and then coaches them as to their mistakes."[13]

Once again as a new season approached, expectations abounded that Foster's team would be his finest. "No one in the world," declared *The Chicago Defender*, "knows better how to pick a player than 'Rube.'" Included on his squad were captain and second baseman Bingo

DeMoss, left fielder Oscar Charleston, center fielder Cristobal Torriente, right fielder Jess Barber, and pitchers Dave Brown and Richard Whitworth. Anticipating larger crowds, Foster decided to expand Schorling park to accommodate 15,000 fans. The *Defender* foresaw the American Giants establishing a new attendance record. By early June, as many as 20,000 spectators could be seen at the American Giants' park. Such a turnout led the *Defender* to assert, "Chicago has proved to the world that it is the best baseball city in the world." In a letter written July 2, Foster indicated that attendance had doubled from that of previous years. Yet despite adding 2,300 boxes, the American Giants were unable to accommodate all potential patrons. Later that summer, 25,000 turned out in New York City to watch Foster's lads sweep a twin-bill from Treat 'em Rough.[14]

\* \* \*

The twin-fold unwillingness of blacks to continue suffering the abuse long received and the contrary determination of many whites to maintain existing racial practices offered a volatile mix by the summer of 1919. Nowhere was that combination deadlier than in Rube Foster's adopted town. Racial friction had been intensifying there ever since the massive migration of blacks from the American South had unfolded in the middle of the decade. As historian William M. Tuttle Jr. notes, the previous year's summer had been a violent one, with a series of attacks on blacks in public places. During the past few months, white mobs had deliberately murdered and beaten a number of African Americans, but justice had been altogether lacking. Gangs battled one another in mid–June, with talk of a final showdown.[15]

July, with its searing heat and stifling humidity, proved more troubling still. On the evening of July 27, a massive racial conflagration began alongside Lake Michigan. Roving bands, spearheaded by white gangs, began targeting blacks who sometimes responded in kind. The explosion of pent-up hatred and rage lasted five days, resulting in 38 fatalities, more than 500 injured, and hundreds left homeless.[16]

In the aftermath of the Chicago riot, one eyewitness contended that blacks in that city had demonstrated "their readiness, willingness, and eagerness to fight the thing through." In his estimation, the riot would "decidedly" improve relations between blacks and whites: "It will bring about 'a meeting of the minds' to the effect that the colored man must not be kicked about like a dumb brute." Moreover, "our white friends, seeing the danger that besets the nation, will become more active in our cause, and the other whites will at least have a decent respect for us based on fear."[17]

Walter F. White of the NAACP offered his own analysis of the racial tinderbox that was Chicago. Strikingly, he charged that "no city in America," other than perhaps Philadelphia, was so riddled by "political trickery, chicanery and exploitation." Little helping matters was a police force that was

**"The Kill." Victim stoned and bludgeoned in the 1919 Chicago race riot. Chicago Historical Society (ICHi-30046); photograph by Jun Fujita.**

terribly ineffective and criminally negligent. "All of this," White charged, "tended to contribute to open disregard for law and almost contempt for it." At the same time, "the new spirit aroused in Negroes by their war experiences" came into play. White noted, "One of the greatest surprises to many of those who came down to 'clean out the niggers' is that these same 'niggers' fought back. Colored men saw their own kind being killed, heard of many more and believed that their lives and liberty were at stake. In such a spirit most of the fighting was done."[18]

\* \* \*

In the fall and early winter of 1919, Rube Foster strengthened his own efforts to contest Jim Crow realities. Foster urged, as he long had, the creation of a Negro league to be comprised of the top blackball performers. On October 4, Carey B. Lewis, a sports columnist with *The Chicago Defender*, indicated that "a circuit of western clubs ... owned and controlled by Race men" would likely appear the following season. Such a possibility was enhanced by both the era's prosperity and the fan loyalty that teams like the

Chicago American Giants had just experienced. Rube Foster, Lewis asserted, was "the man responsible for the proposed circuit. It has been his dream for years to see men of his Race have a circuit of their own." One rumor called for Foster to transfer his American Giants to New York where a $100,000 stadium would be constructed for the team. Foster, however, "wanted to be where he could do the most good to develop a permanent baseball circuit, and that was in the West ... where he is loved and admired and where he put baseball on the map." Painstakingly planning for the upcoming baseball year, Foster was backed by Chicago businessmen, the press, and fans. Indeed, Lewis wrote, "no man in baseball has more influence than 'Rube' Foster."[19]

Starting on November 29, Foster contributed a series of editorials to the *Defender* in which he insisted that reorganization of blackball was essential. He contended that only one "Colored Club"—obviously referring to his own American Giants—had averaged as much as $1,000 profit. He wondered how much longer teams could withstand the kinds of losses they had long experienced. At the same time, ballplayers, thanks to the mushrooming attendance figures, were due large salary increases. However, not a single black team had even ten games lined up for the upcoming season. In fact, Foster charged, "they have never known, nor will they until they are organized."[20]

In his next column, dated December 13, Foster contended that "baseball as it exists at present among our people needs a very strong leader," who in

Rube Foster, the manager, circa 1919. National Baseball Hall of Fame Library, Cooperstown, N.Y.

turn, required "able lieutenants." All of these men, for their part, needed "the confidence of the people." Despite propaganda to the contrary, his own salary structure, Foster declared, had been inflated. "No Colored baseball club has ever approached the salaries of the American Giants, and these salaries have been paid to men who are not worth any more, if ability is the standard that one must draw monthly stipend on." His American Giants had never been paid less than $1,500 monthly. The past season's bill amounted to $450 weekly and Foster was expecting the impending one to be more expensive still.[21]

In a more embittered tone in his next editorial, Foster asserted that "baseball as it exists at present among our owners is a disgrace to the name of good, honest sportsmanship." He referred to the long-standing practice of pilfering players from other owners, a phenomenon that had "wrecked" even the greatest teams. As for himself, Foster revealed, "my resourcefulness in rebuilding ball clubs has stood me well. That same cunning will be useful to me in the days to come. I have nothing to fear." Notwithstanding such a declaration, Foster worried about player raiding and soaring expenses. Thus, he argued, "What is needed is a foundation that we can build on, something that can merit the wonderful attendance and pride our followers have in us." Players and owners, he stated, had to help out. One owner after another had offered "more than they could earn" and had paid the price.[22]

Foster's final editorial for 1919 again urged that past practices be discarded and unity attained. He challenged the commonly held perception that "Colored people will not stand for organizations outside the church and secret societies." He saw no reason "that we could not as a people have things among us and pattern after the ways others have wrote (sic) success in history. It can be done if we would only stop to consider what is best. Nothing is impossible if all parties are allowed to air their differences." Foster was willing to make that effort, setting aside old grievances and calling all owners from the West and East to meet together. He urged that an arbitration board be established and "a working agreement" carved out. Players would be retained by their present clubs, which would enter into "a partnership in working for the organized good of baseball." The blackball owners, he believed, should adopt "the same identical plan" as organized baseball, with a season-ending championship series between pennant winners from the West and East. This scenario, Foster hoped, "will pave the way for such champion team eventually to play the winner among the whites." He insisted, "This is more than possible." But "only in uniform strength is there permanent success."[23]

* * *

While blackball leaders strove to acquire greater respectability and support for their version of the national game, organized baseball experienced its own resurgence of popularity. No figure associated with major league baseball remained more popular than Charles Comiskey and 1919 promised to be a very good year for him, with his full complement of stars returning from military services or the shipping yards. In *"Commy": The Life Story of Charles A. Comiskey,* G. W. Axelson saluted "the 'Grand Old Roman' of Baseball." Gary Herrmann, president of the Cincinnati Reds and president of the National Commission, declared that "Comiskey's performances as a player, record as a manager, achievements as a club executive and unblemished reputation as a sportsman, have justly earned for him merited pre-eminence in the annals of the game to which he has devoted his life." Detroit magnate Frank J. Navin acclaimed Commy as "a true sportsman. He is in baseball because he loves the game and for no other consideration." Sporting goods manufacturer A. J. Reach of Philadelphia asserted that "no man ever in baseball, with the possible exception of Al Spalding, has done more for the game in all of its branches."[24]

As for Comiskey himself, he proclaimed baseball "as honorable as any other business." Moreover, Commy considered it "the most honest pastime in the world. It has to be or it could not last a season out. Crookedness and baseball do not mix. " The game was now "immeasurably more popular" than before, he declared, and "it will be greater yet. This year, 1919, is the greatest season of them all."[25]

As the regular season unfolded, Comiskey's optimism appeared to be well-founded. To the delight of club owners, the 1919 regular season proved remarkably successful, with attendance figures surpassing six million, almost double the previous year. Babe Ruth's heroics helped to boost attendance figures throughout the league, although his Boston Red Sox foundered badly, ending up with a 66-71 record, some 20½ games behind Chicago in the American League race. Comiskey's White Sox completed an 88-52 season, 3 ½ games better than Cleveland, 7½ on top of New York, and eight better than Detroit. Chicago featured the circuit's best team batting average, a robust .287, the top mark in the league since 1902, other than the .297 total chalked up by the 1911 Philadelphia Athletics. The White Sox' prowess at the plate, in fact, led *The Sporting News* to question whether Ban Johnson truly needed to restrict trick pitches in order to increase offensive production.[26]

Chicago was led by Joe Jackson's .351 batting average, Eddie Collin's .319 total, and outfielder Nemo Leibold's .302 mark. Buck Weaver hit .296, Chick Gandil, .290, and Ray Schalk, .282. Reserve infielder Fred McMullin batted .294, while Happy Felsch hit .275 and even light-hitting shortstop Swede Risberg managed to bat .256. Jackson came in third in the league in RBIs with 96, hits with 181, and on-base percentage, .422; fourth in batting, triples, 14, and total bases, 261; and fifth in slugging average, .506. Eddie Collins won the stolen base title with 33 thefts and was fifth in the league in on-base percentage, .400, just behind Leibold. Weaver made more official appearances at the plate, 571, than any player in the league, came in fourth in runs scored, 89, got 169 hits, knocked in 75 runs, hit 33 doubles, nine triples, and three homers, and stole 22 bases. The top of the White Sox pitching staff was very good indeed, with Eddie Cicotte returning to 1917 form, leading the league in wins, 29, winning percentage, .806, complete games, 29, fewest base on balls per game, 1.44, and innings pitched, 307. Cicotte finished runner-up to Walter Johnson in ERA with a fine 1.82 mark, ended up third in hits allowed per game, 7.51, and tossed five shutouts. Lefty Williams, a 23-game winner, led the league with 40 starts, came in third in innings pitched, 297, winning percentage, .676, and strikeouts, 125, and was fourth in fewest base on balls per game, 1.76. Rookie Dickie Kerr added a 13-8 record with a 2.89 ERA, while veteran Red Faber compiled a 11-9 mark, but was saddled with arm trouble throughout much of the season.

The Sporting News analyzed the reasons for Chicago's resurgence. Cicotte had never cracked despite the pressure of carrying the staff, while little Dickie Kerr had proved to be a useful addition. Risberg's "wonderful all-around play" had been a factor, as he'd become "one of the fielding marvels of the day." Eddie Collins had "never played better ball in his life." Important too had been "the effective stick work of Leibold and Weaver," the contributions of Jackson and Felsch, Gandil's "running true to form at first," and Schalk's direction behind the plate. Significant too was manager Kid Gleason's ability to induce "his men into playing their best ball," while establishing "a team harmony that exists on few clubs in the game."[27]

Guided by Pat Moran, the Cincinnati Reds skated to the National League pennant, producing the major's best record, 96-44, nine games better than John McGraw's Giants and 21 ahead of the defending champion Chicago Cubs. With the league's second best team batting average, .263, and ERA, 2.23, the Reds were a formidable, well-balanced squad. Outfielder Edd Roush won his second batting title in three years with a .321 mark, finished second in RBIs, 71, third in hits, 162, and slugging average, .431, and fourth in total bases. Third baseman Heinie Groh — who matched Roush's slugging percentage — and first sacker Jake Daubert tied for second in runs scored, 79. Groh also finished third in walks received, 56, fourth in batting average, .310, and fifth in RBIs, 63. The Reds' deep pitching staff was spearheaded by 20-game winners Slim Sallee and Hod Eller. Dutch Ruether contributed 19 victories, Ray Fisher, 14, Jimmy Ring 10, and Dolf Luque, nine. Ruether's .760 winning percentage was the league's finest, nosing out teammates Sallee and Eller. Ruether produced a 1.82 ERA, the National League's third best, while Eller was the runner-up in strikeouts, 137, and shutouts, seven. Fisher, who started only 20 games, tossed five shutouts, fourth best in the league.

Both teams looked formidable heading into the 1919 World Series, which, thanks to a decree by the National Commission, featured a five out of nine game format for the first time since 1903. White Sox owner Charles Comiskey, Yankee president Jacob Ruppert, and Red Sox president Harry Frazee had opposed the decision, which ensured rich purses for the combatants, unlike the previous year's affair.[28]

On the surface, Chicago, *The New York Times* reported, appeared strong in all areas, evidenced by solid hitting, fine fielding, and skilled base running. In fact, Comiskey's club was considered by observers to be equal to the great Athletic and Red Sox squads earlier in the decade. Expertly guiding a veteran club, Kid Gleason could rely on "the greatest pitcher of the year," Eddie Cicotte, and the player called by John McGraw the greatest he had ever witnessed, Eddie Collins. Still, the *Times* indicated that Chicago possessed only a "slight edge" over the Reds, with their far deeper pitching staff. The competition between third basemen Heinie Groh and Buck Weaver demonstrated how closely matched the two squads were. Both were said to "rank with the best third basemen now playing the position," with Weaver "a shade more clever in the field"; stories abounded that Buck was the only third sacker that Ty Cobb would not drop down bunts against, even though Weaver sometimes played back, defying him to.[29]

*The Sporting News* also applauded Weaver, possibly the most popular of the White Sox, and his teammates. "Looking backward, we can never recall a period in which Buck Weaver has played the kind of ball he has shown the fans this year. Buck has been a wizard around third and has batted in keeping with his play on the field. Perhaps his batting has helped his fielding, and vice versa."[30]

As for Weaver's team, George S. Robbins declared that White Sox comprised "the greatest money team assembled under the National Agreement. They are after the winners' end of the classic and they have it in mind in every play. It has made them play a grade of ball that has simply taken the heart out of their opponents." Having played together for three years, the White Sox reportedly possessed "much advantage in ... team play that must not be overlooked." Joe Vila agreed with Robbins's assessment, picking the White Sox to prevail. He pointed to "their greater experience, steadiness and team play, coupled with extraordinary batting strength and the presence of such stars as Eddie Collins, Joe Jackson, Buck Weaver, Ray Schalk, Eddie Cicotte and Claude Williams in their lineup."[31]

With the Series about to begin in Cincinnati, *The Sporting News* indicated that sentiment resided with the Reds, but "judgment" called for Chicago to prevail. Robbins selected the White Sox to triumph in seven games, for "they outclass the Reds in every department of the game essential to effectiveness in a World's Series." He predicted that Dick Kerr, "the midget pitching wonder of the Sox," along with Cicotte, Williams, and Bill James, would fulfill the team's mound duties, while expert fielding, and the bats of "Jackson, Feslch, Gandil, Collins, Weaver et al. will do the rest."[32]

Buck Weaver, batting. National Baseball Hall of Fame Library, Cooperstown, N.Y.

Harry H. Fry of the *Washington Evening Star* saw the White Sox as "comparatively easy victors," making "the Reds look like selling platers alongside a big handicap thoroughbred" at every position other than third base. There, even Cincinnati star Heinie Groh had nothing "on the aggressive third sacker of the Sox." Fry called himself "a great admirer of ... Weaver."[33]

Declaring that "each is a great club," American League umpire Billy Evans also indicated that the Reds' pitching staff appeared strongest. Both teams were potent at the plate, with Cincinnati featuring the likes of Daubert, Roush, and Groh. The White Sox star hitters included "the wrecking trio, Jackson, Felsch, and Gandil," along with Collins and Weaver, among "the greatest money players in the game." Weaver, Evans indicated,

> has the nerve of a burglar. Nothing worries him. He faces the toughest situation with a smile. Weaver has an unusual yet logical theory about the art of batting. Buck doesn't go in much for place hitting. He believes the important thing is to hit the ball, and then take your chances on it going safe. Weaver has no preference, he hits them whether they are high or low, inside or outside."

In an ironic twist, Christy Mathewson suggested that the Reds could fool the so-called experts and warned that Chicago should not "rely too much on one man," such as Eddie Cicotte.[34]

Their "magnificent defense," Evans reflected, characterized the White Sox' play and was "mighty hard to break through." Catcher Schalk was first-rate, while the Chicago infield was "noted for its ability to pull the seemingly impossible." Gandil was "a remarkable fielder" and Collins "the greatest second baseman in the game," while "nothing is too difficult for" Risberg, with his "rifle-like" throwing arm, to attempt. Because Weaver had switched back and forth between shortstop and the hot corner for several years, "his great ability as a third-sacker," Evans continued, "has been overlooked by a great many of the critics." However, "not only is Weaver brilliant on defense, but he is a player who never quits, and his fighting spirit is an inspiration to the rest of his team." Groh and Weaver, Evans declared, "are the two greatest third-sackers. They should be mentioned in the same breath." The Chicago outfield included the sure-handed Shano Collins and Nemo Leibold, Joe Jackson, who was "very fast, a good judge of fly balls, and has a marvelous throwing arm," and Happy Felsch, a "great" ball player like Cincinnati center fielder Roush. "From a fielding standpoint, no outfielder in the game," Evans insisted, "has a thing on Felsch, not excepting Tris Speaker."[35]

W. A. Phelon, writing in *Baseball Magazine*, declared that "the two clubs are really the best in their respective leagues." He termed the Reds "a rattling good outfit," but called the White Sox "a great team," although not one as strong as Connie Mack's Athletics early in the decade. Phelon praised Weaver as "a wonder" who "gets them in all directions, and he is probably the best of the American Leaguers."[36]

*The New York Tribune*'s W. O. McGeehan favored Chicago in fewer than nine games, declaring that the Reds had "a few weak sisters" while "the White Sox are all battlers and under the command of a little gent whose middle name is battle." W. J. Macbeth, in another *Tribune* column, argued that Chicago possessed "every advantage" over its competition. Having suffered "one grilling series" after another, the White Sox, Macbeth predicted, "will stand up under fire." Indeed, he considered the 1919 White Sox "a more powerful aggregation" than Mack's old championship Athletic squads. "It has almost as terrific a hitting machine. It has balance. And it has more speed. Certainly it has more color and fight." While lacking only a balanced pitching staff, it possessed "two stars of the first water" in right-hander Cicotte and southpaw Williams. Macbeth was unable to "conceive of any team" beating the pair in consecutive contests. Chicago, he predicted, would take no more than seven games to prevail. Ray McCarthy, by contrast, reasoning that 1919 had been the year of the upset, saw Cincinnati winning. The Reds, he believed, were "cooperating and playing together as a unit, with plenty of confidence and speed."[37]

Grantland Rice agreed with his colleague Macbeth, favoring Chicago as it had prevailed in a stronger league, one that had largely dominated the World Series throughout the decade. The White Sox possessed the "lustiest offensive" in the major, relying heavily on Weaver, Eddie Collins, Jackson, and Felsch, plus three fine pitchers in Cicotte, Williams, and Kerr. Rice was particularly impressed with the run-producing combination of Collins and Jackson and Cicotte's terrific mound work. Cicotte, Rice predicted, "isn't going to yield more than one or two runs."[38]

* * *

In a lengthy article in *Baseball Magazine*, written as the regular season ended but before the World Series unfolded, F. C. Lane discussed the man he referred to as "The Star of American League Third Basemen." Opening the piece, St. Louis Brown manager Jimmy Burke was quoted in the following fashion:

> When you say Buck Weaver is the best third baseman on the circuit, you don't do him justice. He is the best third baseman in the league, of course. But he is more. He is one of the best infielders in the league, one of the very best. In fact off hand I know of but two or three men at any position on the infield that would class as his superior.

Washington Senators boss Clark Griffith acknowledged that Weaver "does bat .300, with his hands. But he bats a lot more than that with his brains.

He is my idea of a smart ball player; hustling, confident, in there all the time. He is a live-wire on the infield. I wish I had him on my ball club."[39]

In Lane's estimation, Weaver, "quite a remarkable fielder," was "quite an uncommon player." Indeed,

> Weaver is not a paper average payer. He is not a type of player to whose record paper averages do justice, any more than they do justice to the fiery impetuosity of Ty Cobb or the uncanny fielding wisdom of Tris Speaker. Weaver is a live wire, as Griffith says. He is quick as a cat, incessantly active, aggressive in his work, always hustling, always a thorn in the side of the opposing pitcher when at bat, always a hurdle in the path of the opposing batter when in the field. It is his active brain, his undaunted spirit, rather than his mere mechanical gifts that make Weaver a great player. Not that his mechanical gifts are not showy and flashy enough in themselves. But, showy as they are, they are thrown into the shade by that quick thinking and audacious mentality that make the star baseball player.[40]

* * *

In a stunning turn of events, the Cincinnati Reds captured the 1919 World Series, besting the favored Chicago White Sox in eight games. Most striking was the seeming ineptitude of key White Sox players, with Felsch batting .192, Risberg hitting .080, Gandil and Eddie Collins offering .233 and .226 marks respectively, and Leibold throwing up a .056 batting average. Cicotte dropped two games, one a blowout in the Series opener, while Williams lost three games, seemingly lacking control at opportune moments, which contributed to a 6.61 ERA. By contrast, Jackson batted .375, with 12 hits, six RBIs, and the lone home run either team belted. Weaver did almost as well at the plate, hitting .324 on 11 hits, including four doubles and a triple, but failed to drive in a single run. The White Sox pitching star was the unheralded Kerr, who won two games, one a three-hit shutout, the other a 10-inning affair. Chicago's fielding mastery was belied by a dozen errors, topped by Risberg's four, and costly positional miscues by the likes of Felsch and Jackson, who was not saddled with an official error. Weaver, on the other hand, played flawlessly in the field.

Chicago got blown out in games one, five, and eight, and batted a mere .224 against Reds' pitchers, who tossed a composite 1.63 ERA. Greasy Neale led Cincinnati with 10 hits and a .357 batting average, while Roush batted only .214 but scored six times and drove in seven of his teammates. The Reds' pitching staff was terrific, with Eller winning twice, and Ring, Ruether, and Sallee all contributing a victory apiece.

The Series began disastrously for the White Sox and scarcely improved thereafter. After Cicotte and Chicago were shellacked 9-1, *The New York Tribune* stated bluntly, "it is hard to imagine a great machine so hopelessly outclassed for even one game;" at the same time, Grantland Rice insisted that "the Sox have always been hard, game fighters, and they haven't quit." *The New York Times* reported that never in World Series history had a pennant winning squad "received such a disastrous drubbing in an opening game." The contest was so "one-sided," the *Times* declared, "that the heralded White Sox looked like bush leaguers." The overpowered Sox "were stunned and went down with no pretense of striking back." Troubled by the turn of events, Hugh Fullerton of *The Chicago Herald and Examiner* sat in the press box with Christy Mathewson and the two men marked plays that they viewed as questionable. The White Sox experienced another drubbing in game two; Lefty Williams, noted for his control, walked six, and despite giving only four hits, was defeated 4-2.[41]

Sportswriter Ring Lardner, as he passed through a train car carrying members of Comiskey's team, chortled,

> I'm forever blowing ball games,
> Pretty ball games in the air.
> I come from Chi
> I hardly try
> Just go to bat and fade and die;
> Fortune's coming my way,
> That's why I don't care.
> I'm forever blowing ball games,
> And the gamblers treat us fair.[42]

In the games ahead, a series of curious events continued to unfold, as indicated by contemporaneous news accounts. Game four ended in a 2-0 victory for the Reds, with both runs scoring thanks to two errors by Cicotte. Rice reported that except for that one inning, Cicotte "had the Reds badly baffled and bewildered." The final run scored on a double by Neale, over the head of left fielder Jackson. As the *Times* indicated,

> For some reason or other, Jackson, unnoticed, played in close back of shortstop when Neale, who is a heavy swatter, came to the bat. Neale's slant, which would ordinarily have been easy picking if Jackson had been playing back in his regular place, went over Joe's head and along he went through a lot of spiral evolutions to get the ball. It dropped to the turf just as he got his hands on it.

*The Sporting News* also indicated that if Jackson "been playing his normal position he would have been under the ball without trouble."[43]

Little helping matters, the *Tribune* suggested, was the fact that Cincinnati pitcher Jimmy Ring, in the eighth inning,

> struck out Joe Jackson and Hap Felsch with as much ease as if they had been a brace of bushers just up from the underbrush for a first whack at the real stuff.

When Ring hooked these two rare birds that close to the end of the trail, the big crowd emitted a hollow moan, indicating widespread woe. They knew then and there that the Red pitcher had their heroes in his clammy grip, with nothing whatsoever to be done about it except wait for the melancholy end.[44]

After Williams's control again deserted him in the sixth inning of game five — the *Tribune* said he "was wilder today than Tarzan of the Apes roaming the African jungle from limb to limb" — the White Sox confronted a 4-1 deficit. Buck Weaver was heard to say, "We are up against it, I admit. But the Reds have taken four games out of five. Why shouldn't we take four out of five? If we do as well in the balance of the series as they have done up to date we will win out yet." Christy Mathewson, who had earlier suggested that those who had bet on Chicago should "try to get out from under," sharply criticized the White Sox outfielders. Their performance, Mathewson wrote, "was a disappointment to me after hearing so much about their great work. The fielding of Felsch and Jackson was not up to the advertisement. Jackson allowed one to go over him without even seeming to get started after the ball until it was past him, and Felsch misjudged one hit by Roush that put an end to all doubt as the result ... after today, National Leaguers must reserve judgment as to their real ability." At the end of the eighth inning, *The Sporting News* noted, "Sox fans had quit — quit after their team had quit on them."[45]

Ironically, following game five, the National Commission indicated that the Series would prove "rich" for all players, with the winners slated to receive nearly $5,000 apiece and the losers over $3,200 each. These sums easily dwarfed the previous year's earnings and more than doubled some player salaries.[46]

After game five, J. G. Taylor Spink, editor of *The Sporting News*, spoke of how disappointing Chicago's performance had been. The White Sox, he wrote, had displayed a "failure ... to show a fighting spirit and a strength of attack that all their supporters had a right to look for." In fact, "that has been their lack," Spink insisted, "and that has brought them to the verge of defeat almost disgraceful."[47]

The October 9 issue of *The Sporting News* contained an editorial regarding developments on the field and the gambling that was flourishing in the stands. Gangs of what columnist Joe Vila called "hook-nosed gentry," the editorial noted, were present; such individuals were said to be in attendance "not as sportsmen but as a business." Talk abounded that "these well organized gentry" sought out any "inside stuff," to obtain an edge. Nevertheless, *The Sporting News* declared,

There is not a breath of suspicion attached to any player, nor a hint that any effort in any manner was made to influence a player's performance — not a chance for that — but there is repugnance among sportsmen that such organized methods of getting "dope" for gambling purposes should be practiced.

And more than that there is danger. There are not lengths to which the crop of lean-faced and long-nosed gamblers of these degenerate days will go. It is not a far step from getting a ball player off in a quiet corner and offering to make it worth his while to get information to getting another player off in a quiet corner and offering to make it worth his while to do something more serious.

The National Commission, the editorial continued, was responsible "to keep baseball clean for Americans — for that kind of Americans who don't organize betting syndicates and make a 'business' of anything there is a chance to filch a dollar out of, however, sacred it may be — to Americans."[48]

After taking games six and seven, the latter a 4-1 victory by Cicotte, Chicago was crushed 10-5 in the deciding contest, with Williams lasting only a third of an inning. In the October 16th issue of *The Sporting News*, Henry P. Edwards contended that the White Sox "beat themselves. Williams pitched bad baseball. Cicotte could brag of only one of his three sessions. Joe Jackson and Happy Felsch messed up more fly balls to their gardens in the eight games than they would do ordinarily in two entire seasons." By contrast, Edwards acknowledged, "We can give Dick Kerr, Ray Schalk, Eddie Collins and Buck Weaver nothing but praise for the manner in which they hustled and fought for victory, but only four men cannot win a World's Series when the entire opposition is hustling and trying the hardest to win." Grantland Rice saluted "the heavy hitting of Jackson, Weaver and Collins;" Buck, Rice contended, was "the main Sox Star, with Jackson leading in offensive playing."[49]

Edwards then discussed talk of unsavory dealings that was being bandied about. "Naturally, when so many players play so wretchedly there are bound to be ugly rumors placed in circulation, but such is the case after every big sporting event, and I feel sure that the American League officials will do their best to prove the falsity of the charges or, failing in that, to punish the guilty ones if, contrary to expectations, it is found that some of the players did not try sincerely to win for Chicago." Already, Charles Comiskey had offered $10,000 for evidence proving that some of his players had been on the take.[50]

In an editorial in that same issue, *The Sporting News* referred to "criticisms, alibis — and accusations" that had poured forth after the White Sox defeat. Referring to Cicotte and Williams, the paper insisted "none has the right to say he did not try, nor that any other Sox player did not try." The editors then denied that Williams should be coupled with Risberg as "Series goats."[51]

After the infamous set of contests with the Cincinnati Reds, in which the heavily favored White Sox failed to regain the world championship, dissension within team ranks continued to fester. Reports filtered out that Kid

Gleason and Ray Schalk had confronted various White Sox players, particularly Lefty Williams, because of their atrocious performances during the World Series. In the last few months of 1919, Comiskey continued to offer a $10,000 reward for evidence verifying that any of his players had thrown games.

Despite such concerns, which were shared by Comiskey and Kid Gleason, nobody associated with the Chicago management did something quite basic. Referring to White Sox secretary Harry Grabiner and Commy, among others, Bill Veeck later charged, "They never called in the players to warn them they were being watched nor did they direct the manager to warn them."[52]

\* \* \*

J. C. Kofoed, in the November issue of *Baseball Magazine*, pinpointed what he considered the reasons for the White Sox's shocking defeat in the 1919 World Series: "the Swede, whose lamentable weakness at bat, combined with Felsch's failure, Gandil's inability to hit in a pinch and the pitching crash of Cicotte and Williams." Indeed, "the demoralization of Happy Felsch was a terrible shock to Chicago." On the other hand, "at third base the Sox presented a candidate for the laurel crown," Kofoed noted. "'Buck' Weaver's fighting spirit, his exceptional playing of the bag and his punch at bat earned him a place in the Hall of Fame," although, like Schalk, Weaver failed to deliver the big blow when the White Sox were trailing. Other Chicago stars included Jackson, Kerr, and Schalk, Kofoed reported. Still, the journalist noted, Jackson's "hits were not particularly timely." In fact, "when safe blows were most vitally needed the Jackson-Felsch-Gandil combination was unable to connect." Furthermore, "Jackson pulled a bone" in throwing to home plate during the fourth game, a toss that Cicotte cut off. In Kofoed's estimation, the pitcher's "error was one of the hand; Jackson's one of the head."[53]

The following month's editorial in *Baseball Magazine* contested the notion, suggested by the likes of Hugh Fullerton, that the World Series might not have been played on the level. "If a man really knows so little about baseball that he believes the game is or can be fixed," the editorial charged, "he should keep his mouth shut when in the presence of intelligent people." Unfortunately, F. C. Lane declared, "this white souled reformer of crooked baseball is as blatant as he is ignorant." In fact, the initial three games were all decided by the failure of the losing team to produce timely hits. Lane asked, "Can any one imagine Joe Jackson or Eddie Collins or Roush or Groh failing to hit when a decisive game in the world's series is at stake?" The White Sox dropped game four because they couldn't hit Jimmy Ring and Cicotte committed a pair of untimely errors. "Either possibility is too absurb (sic)," Lane exclaimed, "to merit any consideration whatever." The next game also went to the Reds because Eller outpitched Williams. "Who fixed this game?," Lane asked. "Williams or the White Sox batters?" Game six went to the White

Sox, when Ruether, after being staked to an apparently insurmountable lead, "blew up." Again, Lane wondered, "Was Ruether fixed?" After Cicotte finally won one, the stage was set for the last game, which proved to be "a slugging match pure and simple." As three Chicago pitchers proved unable to hold back the Reds, Lane queried, "Were these ... Sox pitchers fixed? Fighting on their home grounds with the championship a possibility, were they likely to quit?"[54]

Only a pitcher, Lane contended, could throw a game. However, if he were throwing poorly, his manager would remove him. Thus, there would have to be "at least two pitchers in the plot." Lane argued that the catcher and infielders would hardly prove oblivious to such developments. Consequently, "the only way a game could be thrown with any degree of certainty," he insisted, "would be to have most of the players on a particular team involved as well as the manager." Even if "some enterprising genius could ever get a number of star players to throw a game" — which he considered "an unthinkable thing in itself" — Lane wondered "how long would that plot remain secret?"[55]

If discovered, the owner "would be ruined, the players would be blacklisted for all time." Lane reflected,

> And for what? How much could be won by throwing a game? A few thousand dollars? Would that pay the player for losing his means of livelihood for the balance of his career and being driven in disgrace from his chosen profession? Would it pay the owner for losing a half million dollar franchise and being branded as a crook? Even if players were dishonest, which they are not, they have sense enough not to run such risks, risks that are practically prohibitive. ... The possibility of fixing a baseball game is practically nil, for too many uncertain elements enter into the game and too many persons are involved in the plot.[56]

As talk of a White Sox fix unfolded, reports indicated that heavy betting had occurred throughout the Series, with the *Times* estimating that $2,000,000 was bet in New York City alone. A brief article in *The Sporting News* indicated how pervasive the problem was in another corner of organized baseball: the minor leagues. One veteran asserted, "I do know something has to be done about getting rid of the gamblers who infest minor league ball. The betting is something fierce. Down in our country oil men think nothing of betting $500 on a ball game." While declaring that the oil man was "generally regarded as a square sport," the veteran reflected "about the gambler who might take the oil man's bet and be too anxious to win it." Thus, he exclaimed, "Get the gambler out now. Get 'em out before something does happen."[57]

Hugh Fullerton of *The Chicago Herald and Examiner* remained determined to get into print his concerns about the World Series. His own paper feared libel charges, so Fullerton turned to *The New York Evening World*. There, on December 15, 1919, the first of a series of articles — which had been tempered — by Fullerton, explored the explosive issue of a possible World Series fix. Fullerton declared, "Baseball has reached a crisis. The major leagues, both owners and players, are on trial." Fullerton explained:

> In the last world's series, the charge was made that seven members of the White Sox entered into a conspiracy with certain gamblers to throw the series. Some of the men whose names are used are my friends and men I would trust anywhere, yet the story is told openly with so much circumstantial evidence and with so many names, places and dates that one is bewildered."

As for the accused ballplayers, Fullerton insisted, "If these men are guilty they should be expelled. If they are innocent they should be allowed to prove it and the persons who are responsible for the charges should be driven out of the sport forever."[58]

Investigations by Charles Comiskey and Kid Gleason, it was announced on December 16, had uncovered no evidence that White Sox players had laid down during the World Series. Nevertheless, news of a payoff by "a gambling syndicate" continued to circulate. On December 18, National Commission chairman Gary Herrmann declared that reports of Chicago players being bought off lacked foundation. Still, he indicated that moves would be undertaken to curb possible gambling abuses. "What gambling is done in baseball starts in ball parks," he stated. "There won't be any ball park gambling next season if I can stop it at the start."[59]

Starting that day and continuing for the next two weeks, the notion of a possible World Series scandal was again discussed, overshadowing ongoing power struggles involving major league moguls. The public was clamoring, Fullerton wrote in *The New York Evening World* on December 18, for "an entire cleaning up of baseball and a thorough investigation of the scandalous charges" that were circulating about the World Series. As for himself, Fullerton insisted, he was only demanding that the suspect players "be either convicted or acquitted." He certainly was engaged in no vendetta against longtime friend Charles Comiskey, who had suffered "a terrible blow" and appeared "badly broken in health and growing old."[60]

Two days later, Fullerton again declared that "a complete investigation" was necessary. The sportswriter had asked Judge Kenesaw Mountain Landis if he would assume "the responsibility of conducting an investigation if the powers of baseball are willing to submit the entire matter to him and assist him in bringing witnesses before him." He had no proof of wrongdoing on the part of any players, Fullerton admitted, but had heard gamblers indicate "that they had 'put over' the thing;" moreover, they had acquired financial backing due to the assumption "that they could control the players."[61]

By all accounts, Judge Landis stood ready to serve as an arbiter for the leaders of organized baseball. With baseball's honesty in question, the National Commission, W. J. Macbeth of *The New York Tribune* suggested, should explore accusations of a World Series fix. The National Commission, Macbeth noted, "is the supreme court of baseball, or is supposed to be." It possessed "unlimited funds" for office operations. "What better way could this money be employed," Macbeth asked, "than in clearing the great American game from suspicion?"[62]

As a veteran sportswriter, Macbeth found it difficult to fathom "that players would conspire to have games decided other than on their merits." To date, no direct evidence had been unveiled regarding crooked dealings by either of the participants in the just completed World Series. Nevertheless, he admitted, "there has been more than the usual amount of talk and gossip and rumor. The good name of the game has suffered as a consequence." While Charles Comiskey was supposedly investigating various charges, Macbeth called for the National Commission to take the lead. Indeed, he argued that organized baseball's governing body

> should not sit idly by and permit Comiskey to do the investigating. It owes it to the public and the great institution the triumvirate represents to help throw on the spotlight. No matter how ardent Mr. Comiskey might be in trying to hunt out artifice, it is easy to understand how the work would be hampered for him. The commission is in a much better position to turn loose gumshoe men.[63]

Furthermore, Macbeth contended, "the vast scandal emanating from the recent world's series may be only a tempest in a tea pot. But the very life of the game of baseball depends upon public faith in the innate honesty of the game." Gambling posed "the greatest menace to the health and welfare of organized baseball." The game's great popularity, Macbeth astutely noted, was the result of long and "conscientious endeavor" by both promoters and ballplayers, with the public apprised of "everything that had to do with the game's welfare." No player's integrity had been challenged for a quarter-of-a-century until Christy Mathewson recently had accused Hal Chase of "unsportsmanlike practice." Unfortunately, Macbeth declared, National League leaders "very unwisely" failed to inform the public of what had transpired. Thus, impressions of a "white-wash" emerged.[64]

Organized baseball, Macbeth warned, could only hold the public's confidence "by playing the political game openly and aboveboard." Now, "no greater opportunity to reassure the wavering faith of a credulous public presents itself than to have the National Commission clear for action against this latest scandal, the most serious ever charged against the honesty of professional players."[65]

Joe Vila referred to reports that a list of various individuals might unveil "collusion between professional gamblers and certain Chicago ball players."

Despite expressing skepticism, Vila admitted "baseball received such a staggering blow that the fans have a right to demand a public investigation of the so-called indictment." Vila then went on to say, "Personally I don't believe for a moment that anything was wrong in the World Series." However, because of all the scuttlebutt concerning a possible fix, he reasoned, a full airing of the accusations should be undertaken. If proven true, then "the magnates should resort at once to the blacklist." As for the Chicago players accused of wrongdoing, Vila suggested they sue for libel.[66]

White Sox catcher Ray Schalk, one Chicago area newspaper claimed, indicated that seven of his teammates would not return the following season. *The Sporting News* demanded that Schalk be less cryptic and more forthcoming. "Now what does Ray Schalk know," the paper asked, "that he should make the statement credited to him?"[67]

1919 came to end with Charles Comiskey renewing his offer of $10,000 for incriminating evidence damning his ballplayers. One rumor had Comiskey's players concocting a plan to throw games during the regular seasons. Another indicated that a pair of White Sox, as the World Series unfolded, had bet on the Reds.

CHAPTER EIGHT

# The National Commission and Baseball's Achilles' Heel

As the 1919 World Series had unfolded, controversies continued to swirl regarding the National Commission and Ban Johnson's role as a virtual baseball "dictator." A move remained in place to oust Chairman Gary Herrmann. *The Sporting News* reported on October 2 that the anti-Herrmann faction wanted to replace him with Big Bill Edwards, collector of the Port of New York, if Federal Judge Kenesaw Mountain Landis were unavailable. Saluting Herrmann's honesty and fairness, Joe Vila asked what would happen if Edwards or Landis were vilified for rulings involving baseball law. "It's a sure thing that Judge Landis will not take the big plunge," Vila wrote, while Edwards appeared unwilling unless "an iron-clad" ten-year contract, at a $25,000 annual salary, was offered. As matters turned out, American League president Johnson refused to support Edwards's candidacy.[1]

The ongoing breach between Ban Johnson and Yankee owners Jacob Ruppert and Til Huston — which involved litigation concerning the Carl Mays case — heightened in mid-fall. Johnson remained opposed to awarding New York its portion of World Series proceeds as the American League's third-place finisher, but the Board of Directors authorized payment of such funds. *The New York Times* felt compelled to deny that a third league, centered around the disenchanted Yankee, White Sox, and Red Sox franchises, was in the offing. The Federals' collapse, the *Times* noted, should dissuade intelligent business operatives from believing that another major league was viable. Once more, obtaining adequate facilities would be difficult, and not enough "high-class talent" existed to fill a third big league. A war would cost millions, although players would welcome the opportunity to garner "abnormal salaries."[2]

The November 13 issue of *The Sporting News* headlined, "Wanted, a Moses to Lead Them to Peace." Referring to the rift between Johnson and the American League powerhouses, Joe Vila dismissed talk of "the Pipe Dream League." Such a circuit, it had been suggested, could be comprised of the three clubs that wanted to oust Johnson, Jack Dunn's Baltimore franchise in the International League, and new teams shaped by Edsel Ford, Harry F. Sinclair, Price McKinney, and J. K. L. Ross, in Detroit, Pittsburgh, Cleveland, and Montreal, respectively. Vila, however, roundly denied such a possibility. Sinclair, after all, had already suffered through "another outlaw league," and was presently a co-owner of the St. Louis Browns; additionally, he was due nearly $100,000 as part of the settlement from the Federal League litigation. McKinney had earlier declined Johnson's offer to purchase the Indians "at any figure," as well as an opportunity to take over the New York Giants. Commander Ross and other wealthy Canadians had allowed Akron to obtain the Binghamton franchise in the International League for a mere $30,000. Edsel Ford might be interested but would probably encounter opposition from his father. Dunn, Vila indicated, "wouldn't go into an 'outlaw league' to save his life."[3]

"The war in the American League," Oscar C. Reichow contended, "grows in ferocity." Two of the leading antagonists, Ban Johnson and Charles Comiskey, had once been fast friends, but now the White Sox owner determined to oust his former compatriot. Comiskey indicated that he, Ruppert, and Frazee "intend to do everything possible to rid baseball of this impediment which we believe is now attached to it." Reichow termed the Johnson-Comiskey clash "child's play," which unfortunately, was transpiring "when baseball has a brighter future than ever before." The controversy, if it were prolonged, Reichbow believed, could wound organized baseball more grievously than the Federal League fight had, "because there is nothing that the fans loath more than internal scrapping."[4]

On December 10, at the Hotel Biltmore in New York City, the American League held "the most torrid session" in its history. "They rode over us with a steam roller," said Colonel Huston, "and we are gong to send the steam roller right back at them." At one point, Ruppert exclaimed, "You can't drive us out of baseball." The insurgents challenged the notion that Johnson was operating under a 20-year contract, signed in 1910, with a $30,000 annual salary. Unable to prevail, their lawyers served Johnson with papers, with the Yankees seeking damages regarding the Mays case and the expulsion of the American League president from office.[5]

The National League held its annual meeting the same day, with Gary Herrmann announcing that he would resign as National Commission chairman within 30 days. *The New York Times* indicated that while Herrmann's integrity had never been at issue, baseball magnates reasoned "that a neutral Chairman should rule baseball's highest court." Ban Johnson naturally opposed Herrmann's departure.[6]

In an editorial dated December 25, *The Sporting News* declared that baseball aficionados in Chicago, tired of the strife, welcomed a statement attributed to Judge Landis, which indicated he would take on the job himself. Purportedly, Landis would not decline "if properly approached and conditions were suitable." Such an appointment, the paper warned, would not rectify all of baseball's ills. Furthermore, discussion of a possible Landis chairmanship, *The Sporting News* cried, "is a good deal like asking somebody or other to become president of the League of Nations — or to accept the crown of Russia. There ain't no such animal, or if there is now there soon may not be." Such an analysis, the editorial continued, was not intended to reflect badly on Landis. "He'd be a fine man for the job, no doubt, but make the job first, then get the man. Unless the Judge understands this situation we'll say he hasn't been following baseball very closely of late, good fan though he may be."[7]

Al Spink of *The Chicago Evening Post* suggested that only Judge Landis's appointment as National Commission head could end the baseball war. As one baseball man informed Spink,

No one is favor of square dealing, honesty and decency should be opposed to the election of Judge Landis as chairman. No one who wants to see the affairs of the game placed on a fine, substantial basis, above and beyond the reach of men who have axes to grind or who are willing to sacrifice the good of the game for their own selfish ends, will oppose the election of Judge Landis as chairman of the commission.

Landis, if elected, would lift the game into its proper sphere, lift it out of the sea of discord into which it has fallen recently and place it where its progress would not be blocked as it has been by the bickerings and quarrels of the last two years. With Landis holding the reins, the politics of the game would be subordinated to the rear, and only the playing end would be considered. The game, as a result, would come out of the ditch in which it is now floundering and would prosper as it never has prospered before.[8]

In an editorial on January 8, *The Sporting News* reported that the selection of Landis to arbitrate the American League dispute had been considered. Supposedly, Landis, after examining all available evidence, was to decide if Ban Johnson should remain league president. If he determined that Johnson must resign, then the majority and minority factions were to cast aside their disagreements. If he called for Johnson to stay at his post, then the chances of a league schism would heighten. When Johnson urged that the Yankees owners be "retired," the efforts at compromise supposedly crumbled.[9]

Still, Henry P. Edwards of *The Cleveland Plain Dealer* indicated that National League owners, along with Charles Comiskey, Harry Frazee, and Jacob Ruppert, all strongly supported Landis. Edwards claimed,

> A man of Judge Landis' caliber is needed at the head of the commission. He has had a wonderful record on the bench and from the standpoint of integrity and ability is one of the biggest men in the United States. In addition, he is a great baseball fan and has been for the last thirty years. He had kept in touch with the national game and could step into the job without preparation.

*The Chicago Daily News'* Oscar Reichow, who like Edwards also regularly contributed to *The Sporting News*, indicated that Landis was willing to accept the position. That would be, Reichow argued, "for the good of the game." Frederick G. Lieb of *The Philadelphia Sun* and George Daley of *The New York World* seconded that notion.[10]

* * *

On January 8, Herrmann's resignation had been delivered, to become effective "at the earliest possible date" but, in any event, no later than a scheduled February 11 joint meeting of the American and National leagues. As Herrmann bluntly put it, "I have had enough of the annoyance of the present situation." Several names were broached as the possible replacement for the National Commission chairman, including Bill Edwards, John Farrell of the National Association, John Conway Toole, and Judge Landis. Ban Johnson was said to prefer the selection of Henry Killilea of Milwaukee. National League president John Heydler, reputed to have opposed Herrmann's retention, was quite pleased about the impending changes organized baseball would experience. The new chairman, Heydler believed, "must be a man powerful enough to reach out after any ball player, club owner or official of baseball who by his act or association or speech brings the national game into disrepute." Such an individual, he reasoned, must be able to keep baseball free from the kinds of scandals that had recently afflicted it.

> From now on the chairmanship of the Commission will be a real job, not a sinecure. I do not mean to cast any reflection on the diligence of Herrmann, as he has been a wonderful man for the game. I really regret to see him step out of the position, but times are changing in baseball and therefore changes are required in the governing body of the sport. The position is a tough one. The man who takes it will be required to stand for a lot of criticism, because he is going to get it, no matter what he does. That has always been the history of the job, but Herrmann weathered it nicely and, I believe, has always been fair.[11]

Heydler then posed the question of where "the right man" would be discovered:

> He ought to be unearther(sic) somewhere as this country is full of good baseball men. I have no idea who he might be. That will be up to the committee selected about a year ago to scour the country for men they thought qualified to be recommended to take the place. This committee has been at work. What progress has been made or what individual it has in mind I do not know, but I think that committee should be heard before a decision is made.
>
> We want the right man for that position. Things have happened in baseball recently that have to be stopped. The game has an exceptionally bright future before it and we cannot afford to permit the future to be wrecked. Gambling has done much to hurt the sport. But that will be stopped and we are going to extremes to stop it. Club owners, of course, will have to assist us, but if they do not we will have to take it upon our own shoulders to wipe it out of the ball parks. And that is a part of the responsibility that will befall the new chairman of the Commission.[12]

Who was such a man?, asked *The Sporting News*. To one columnist, "that man is none other than Judge Kenesaw Mountain Landis." The good judge was "all that President Heydler desires, and a little more. He is aggressive and loves the game of baseball as he does no other sport and, I believe, if persuaded to accept the position, would go a long way to devising some method to wipe out completely the gambling evil that threatens to ruin the game." Landis appeared to be favored by the committee selected to recommend a new National Commission chairman. "A better move for baseball," the sportswriter suggested, "could not happen." After all, "Landis is a man of national reputation, is known to be honest, fearless and one who deals with common sense." While some baseball folk would proclaim him "too radical," *The Sporting News* questioned such an evaluation, claiming that all who appeared before his court recognized that "they have to be fair and tell the truth." Yankee owners Ruppert and Huston expressed their support for Landis.[13]

So, once again, did Al Spink of *The Chicago Evening Post*. Spink quoted from one baseball man in Chicago who insisted that Landis's appointment

> will see major league baseball stock go up a kiting and, at least, double in value. Landis' election will give a great book to the sport and drive out politics, gambling and all other evils which are trying to creep in.
>
> But, greater than that. The presence of a man of the character of Judge Landis at the head of the game will give it a standing it has never approached before and place it in a position in the minds of all as the finest, healthiest and fairest outdoor sport in all the world.[14]

With the joint meeting of the majors slated for February 11 in Chicago, a plan was devised to place a player on the National Commission, along with the league presidents, a minor league representative, and a neutral chairman. A similar proposal, tendered by David Fultz of the Players Fraternity, had been ill-received by baseball owners; it was anticipated that the current suggestion would suffer the same fate.[15]

On the morning of February 11, it was announced that American League discord had ended. Ongoing litigation by New York against Ban Johnson was to cease. Carl Mays was reinstated as a member of the Yankees, who were named third-place finishers in the 1919 pennant chase, and hence, entitled to their proportional World Series receipts. An arbitration committee, effective for two years, was to be established. Yankee owner Ruppert continued to demand that Johnson's powers be curbed, with insurgents to receive their own representation on the National Commission.[16]

Other decisions affecting major league baseball were made at the joint meeting. Admission prices increased, with the old 25-cent bleacher seats discarded. Prices at the Polo Grounds likewise jumped, with only a few hundred 50-cent tickets to be available for each game, other bleacher seats set at 75 cents, and lower stand chairs costing $1, rather than 85 cents.[17]

The Joint Nominating Committee, made up of Ruppert, Detroit's Frank J. Navin, the Phillies' William F. Baker, and the Cubs' William Veeck, put forth five names as potential replacements for Commissioner Herrmann. They were Senator James A. Walker from Brooklyn, Bill Edwards, John Conway Toole, Harvey T. Woodruff, *The Chicago Tribune*'s sports editor, and Judge Landis. Herrmann offered Cap Anson as another possibility. However, on February 14, John Heydler indicated that Judge Landis had been eliminated as a possible replacement for Herrmann. Landis denied that he had been a candidate, asserting that no baseball official had spoken to him about the position.[18]

On February 25, talk now focused on Edwards and Woodruff, with Ban Johnson strongly preferring the latter. Heydler continued to insist that a new chairman had to be selected, for organized baseball, in his estimation, had experienced chaos ever since John K. Tener's departure from the National Commission in the midst of the Scott Perry controversy.[19]

W. A. Phelon of *Baseball Magazine* bemoaned Herrmann's passing, which he believed, left organized baseball bereft of "a capable chieftain." Herrmann had reportedly been informed that he could serve as "chairman for life at $20,000 per," provided he relinquished all control of the Cincinnati ball club; the 61 year-old owner of the current world champions was unlikely to agree to such terms. Judge Landis, Phelps indicated, "has the calibre and personality, but has stated that he would run the office with great dignity and would leave 'minor matters' to subordinates." Sportswriters John Foster and Irving Sanborn each possessed local support, while a series of attorneys — Toole, Henry Killilea, Walker — were being considered. Heydler was said to favor Bob Young, while Anson appeared willing to accept the post.[20]

* * *

The tumult surrounding the National Commission, both owners and sportswriters warned, prevented an examination of what they considered the game's most troublesome ailment: gambling. As 1920 began to unfold, so did additional rumors regarding the previous year's World Series. Hugh Fullerton, in his *Chicago Herald and Examiner* column, continued to question the integrity of the 1919 Series. In an editorial dated January 1, *The Sporting News* noted that one baseball owner, acknowledging the threat gambling operations posed, called for appealing "to the gamblers' patriotism and civic pride, on behalf of baseball as a national institution, that they keep their sinister touch off it." *The Sporting News* retorted, "A fat chance," and exclaimed that if no better solution could be concocted, "then the time has come to shut the gates of the parks." For "the professional gambler as we have known him considers nothing sacred if there is a chance for him to frame it."[21]

There existed only one means, the editorial argued, "to loosen the tightening fingers of the gamblers on baseball and that way is to smash that grip with a club." Baseball moguls afraid or unwilling to do so, *The Sporting News* offered, "have no place in baseball." As charges were flung, the paper declared, "the club owners have none but themselves to blame." Ban Johnson, in 1916, had urged that the problem be addressed but received no support.[22]

The editorial concluded:

> There may be nothing in the World Series' scandal — there has been no evidence, we think we can say, that is positive enough to convict any one of the crooked work on the playing field, but it's through no fault of the gamblers that there have not been games bought and sold. And does any one think gamblers would have grown bold enough to approach players if a club had been swung on them when they first saw the "possibilities" and got busy on the job when they learned indifference of magnates made the golden opportunity?[23]

Ray Schalk now denied that anything underhanded had occurred during the 1919 World Series. "I ... played to the best of my ability. I feel that every man on our club did the same, and there was not a single moment of all the games in which we all did not try." Schalk also refuted the notion that he had declared several White Sox would not be returning next season. As for Charles Comiskey, he was reported to be "tired of it all," having spent considerable sums of money investigating the supposed fix and uncovering nothing. Comiskey again expressed his readiness to hear information implicating any ballplayers, while affirming his determination "to keep the game clean and honest."[24]

"The first big task" of the new National Commission chairman, *The New York Times* reported on January 11, involved reducing gambling's impact on

Buck Weaver tossing ball, 1919. National Baseball Hall of Fame Library, Cooperstown, N.Y.

Buck Weaver in front of Chicago White Sox dugout, 1919. National Baseball Hall of Fame Library, Cooperstown, N.Y.

the game. Unsubstantiated but "insistent rumors" regarding the Cincinnati-Chicago World Series, the *Times* noted, led baseball officialdom to believe that "vigorous action" must be undertaken to placate fans. The present National Commission, headed by Gary Herrmann, the *Times* charged, "never took aggressive methods to curb the practice."[25]

In early March, *The Sporting News* editorialists chastised fellow newspapermen who were unhappy that they had not been fully apprised about the

Buck Weaver, 1919. National Baseball Hall of Fame Library, Cooperstown, N.Y.

dismissal of various players from organized baseball, an obvious reference to the likes of Hal Chase and Lee Magee. The public, so went the argument, had the right to know. *The Sporting News* was content with the National Commission's actions, and exhorted journalists to go after "the gamblers who are responsible for the fall from grace of certain ball players. ... Their names and their faces — who could not pick out those faces — are known everywhere followers of baseball congregate." Yes, crooked ballplayers should be targeted, *The Sporting News* agreed, "but don't forget to get the men with the faces who used the players as tools."[26]

Grantland Rice also argued for "the public's right to know immediately" who the accused players were, along with all the details surroundings the charges. "The semi-exposure" that unveiled no names, he contended, "did nothing to help clear up the shadow that has hovered over the game for several months." The inept handling of this case, Rice declared, demonstrated as never before "baseball's need of a strong entry at the head of the National Commission."[27]

That winter, the dark shadow of the ballplayer who long would have been selected as most likely to throw a game continued to shroud the national game. More purported machinations of Chase, reputed to have bet heavily on the 1919 World Series, began to be discussed. The Chicago Cubs gave outfielder Magee, an old crony of Chase's, his unconditional release. Angered, Magee hired an attorney and threatened on March 23 to reveal all he knew. "If I'm barred," Magee exclaimed, "I'll take quite a few noted people with me. I'll show up some people for tricks turned ever since 1908. And there will be merry music in the baseball world." *Baseball Magazine* insisted that Magee either "put up or shut up." On April 1, *The Sporting News* reported that Magee's attorney could "explode 'the biggest bomb in baseball history,' and take certain other players down with him in the ruins."[28]

On April 12, as the 1920 regular season approached, *The New York Tribune*'s W. O. McGeehan argued that its success rested "rested entirely with the players." Baseball had experienced some tough blows recently, including the Yankee-Ban Johnson war, "the scandal rumors" involving various White Sox players, and Magee's threat to unveil corruption. These developments, McGeehan reflected, "were not calculated to do the game any good." While the upcoming season promised to be baseball's "most wonderful" yet, both the players and owners needed to usher in various changes. The ballplayers, McGeehan insisted, possessed considerable responsibility for the game's well-being.

> It is up to the player now to see that his profession is kept above the breath of suspicion. Promoters have sounded the death knell of gambling. In every city will be pursued such a crusade against the vice as has been carried on for

several years past by the local clubs. The ball player can do much more than the vigilance of the owner by refusing to associate in any way with men of the gambling type.[29]

In the columnist's estimation, "the professional baseball player has been fast and loose with the welfare of his profession in recent years." Unfortunately, "too much of the mercenary has crept into the sport in the last ten years. Baseball has changed from a purely sporting promotion to a purely business proposition." While players were entitled to seek the highest salaries possible, the recent efforts of several players to repudiate their contracts could not be condoned.[30]

The owners too had to accept the need for major changes in the structure of the game. McGeehan wrote:

> To the magnates let us sound a warning. The fundamental principles of organized baseball are shaky. The complete reorganization of major and minor league baseball is inevitable if the game is to be saved. ...
>
> The attitude of contempt for majority opinion among the owners which certain of the mighty have maintained is deplorable indeed. It is a shame, approximating criminal neglect, that the office of chairman of the National Commission has been left vacant since early in February.[31]

# Chapter Nine

# The Sale of Babe

To its great advantage, major league baseball was about to experience a different kind of change in the game's very makeup. That transformation was spearheaded by a 25-year-old former stellar pitcher turned slugger whose star was soon to shine even brighter. On December 26, 1919, the Boston Red Sox and the New York Yankees finalized a deal that shaped those historic franchises for decades to come. Since its establishment as one of Ban Johnson's squads during the American League's inaugural season in 1901, Boston had compiled a record second to none. In various incarnations, Boston's Americans or Puritans or Red Sox had captured six pennants and five World Series; the New York Giants' John McGraw, in 1904, had refused to match his National League titlists with Boston's defending world champions. Boston's first championship teams featured third baseman Jimmy Collins, slugging outfielder Buck Freeman, and pitchers Cy Young and Bill Dinneen. The 1912 championship unit exhibited the superlative outfield play of Duffy Lewis, Tris Speaker, and Harry Hooper, and the strong right arm of Smokey Joe Wood, who threw 10 shutouts as he compiled a 34-5 record. Guided by manager Bill Carrigan, the 1915 and 1916 Red Sox teams relied on excellent pitching staffs, which included Ernie Shore, the white Rube Foster, Dutch Leonard, Carl Mays, and Babe Ruth. The war-riddled 1918 version of the Red Sox looked to the pitching of Mays, Ruth, and Sad Sam Jones, along with Babe's bat.

Begun as the Baltimore Orioles, one of the legendary teams of the late 19th Century, the New York Highlanders were established in 1903, because

American League president Ban Johnson wanted to compete with McGraw's enterprise. While the Orioles had been managed by McGraw, the Highlanders were led by Clark Griffith who nearly took them to the pennant in 1904. With right-hander Jack Chesbro winning a record 41 games, the Highlanders dropped a decisive contest to Boston, as their spitballing ace threw a wild pitch to allow the winning run in the ninth inning. In 1906, the Highlanders again came in second, falling three games behind Charles Comiskey's White Sox, despite 20-win seasons by Al Orth and Chesbro and a .323 average from their brilliant first baseman, Hal Chase. Another runner-up performance occurred in 1910, but New York finished a distant 14½ games behind the Athletics and were afflicted with dissension, purportedly piqued by Chase, who took over the managerial reigns late in the year. The next serious pennant run occurred in 1919, when the Miller Huggins-led Yankees came in 7 ½ back of Comiskey's White Sox. Aiding the Yankee drive were former Red Sox players Duffy Lewis, Ernie Shore, and Carl Mays, whose controversial demands had resulted in his departure from Boston.

* * *

Encountering severe financial difficulties, the bulk attributed to his New York theatrical productions, Boston owner Harry Frazee, in late 1919, decided to sell Babe Ruth to the Yankees. By late October, it had become apparent that "baseball's biggest attraction" would demand his salary be more than doubled. *The Sporting News* decried such a move: "Ruth, for reasons that seem good to himself, would make his contract a 'scrap of paper.'" But the paper also took Boston management to task, for having allowed Mays, who had been unhappy with his contract, to force a trade. Refusing to renegotiate with Ruth now, *The Sporting News* pointed out, would hardly be consistent with Boston's previous mode of operation.[1]

During the late fall, Ruth remained in the news, barnstorming in California where he received $500 per game. There was also discussion of a new league being established in New York that would pay him $20,000 a year. Most significant of all, James O'Leary suggested, was Ruth's examination of the Mays case. That would only lead Babe to believe "that a contract is not binding a baseball star when he chooses to disregard it and elects to shift to some other club." Ruth, like Mays, the sportswriter contended, might seek to join the Yankees. Thus, "we are reaping what was sown in the Mays case."[2]

On December 3, *The New York Times* declared that Ruth could soon enter the boxing ring. Over a 30 day span, former boxer Kid McCoy would help to train Ruth. If that report were favorable, a match would be sought by Al St. John with heavyweight champion Jack Dempsey. "I have always wanted to be a professional boxer," Ruth was quoted as asserting. "But I gave up any future I might have had in that game to play baseball." However, "if McCoy and St. John think I have any future, I am willing to do everything they ask."[3]

On December 25, the *Times* noted that Ruth had returned his contract to the Boston Red Sox, while demanding a $20,000 salary. Ruth also indicated that he would refuse to play for any other major league team. His business manager, John Igoe, now insisted that Ruth had no intention of entering the ring. Two days later, Ruth declared that he was "through with major league baseball," unless Boston management agreed to his salary demands. "I have several propositions on hand," Ruth pointed out, "any one of which would pay me more than $10,000 a year," his present salary. Denying he was planning to take up boxing, Babe did indicate that motion pictures might be in his future.[4]

In the meantime, Harry Frazee set up a meeting with manager Ed Barrow at the Hotel Knickerbocker in Manhattan. Frazee immediately told Barrow, "Simon, I'm going to sell Ruth to the Yankees;" the previous summer, Frazee had declined a $100,000 offer from Yankee owner Jacob Ruppert. Barrow replied, "I thought as much. I could feel it in my bones. But you ought to know that you're making a mistake." Frazee countered, "Maybe I am, but I can't help it. Lamin is after me to make good on my notes. Ruppert and Huston will give me $100,000 for Ruth and they've also agreed to loan me $350,000. I can't turn that down. But don't worry. I'll get you some ballplayers, too;" later, it was revealed that the Yankee owners took a $300,000 mortgage on the Boston franchise. Barrow responded directly, "Listen. Losing Ruth is bad enough, but don't make it tougher for me by making me show off a lot of ten-cent ballplayers that we got in exchange for him. There is nobody on that ball club that I want. This has to be a straight cash deal, and you'll have to announce it that way."[5]

On December 26, Harry Frazee and Jacob Ruppert crafted the most notorious contract in major league history, which resulted in "George H. Ruth" being traded to the New York Yankees. The amount of money involved far exceeded previous sales, including the Yankees' recent purchase of Carl Mays, the Indians' acquiring of Tris Speaker back in 1916 for some $55,000, Cleveland's earlier receipt of Joe Jackson, and Chicago's buying of Eddie Collins from the Athletics. Announcement of the latest Red Sox-Yankee deal was delayed for several days, allowing New York skipper Miller Huggins to talk with Ruth in California at the Griffith Parks golf course and get him to agree to terms. In an essay written on December 29 for *The Sporting News* entitled, "Ruth's Liking for Boston Is Pathetic," James O'Leary indicated that Frazee stood ready to trade or sell any Red Sox player besides Harry Hooper, including Ruth. An editorial in that publication suggested that the Yankees were ready to pay top dollar for the mighty hitter. Frazee reportedly was willing to ship out Ruth, because he had become "a drawback to the artistic success of the Red Sox team" and had alienated other players so that they were not giving their all.[6]

After Huggins prepared to sign Ruth to a $20,000 contract, the story broke on January 6 that the "baseball's super slugger" had been traded to the Yankees; this was, Ruth's new manager declared, "the biggest deal ever pulled off in baseball." Playing 77 games a season in the Polo Grounds with its inviting right field wall, the *Times* noted, could place Ruth's own home run record in jeopardy. Yankee president Ruppert declined to reveal the terms of the deal, declaring

> I am not at liberty to tell the prices we paid. I can say positively, however, that it is by far the biggest price ever paid for a ball player. Ruth was considered a champion of all champions, and, as such, deserving of an opportunity to shine before the sport lovers of the greatest metropolis of the world.
>
> It is not only our intention, but a strong life purpose, moreover, to give the loyal American League fans of greater New York an opportunity to root for our team in a world's series. We are going to give them a pennant winner, no matter what the cost. I think the addition of Ruth to our forces should (be) held greatly along those general lines. Yet the fans can rest assured we by no means intend to stop there. Eventually we are going to have the best team that has ever been seen anywhere.[7]

Babe Ruth in New York Yankee uniform, 1920. National Baseball Hall of Fame Library, Cooperstown, N.Y.

The addition of Ruth, *The New York Tribune* predicted, made the Yankees serious pennant contenders. Furthermore, he offered something that Yankee teams had long been lacking:

The Babe is one of the very most colorful players of the game's history. He is an unique character, always good for a quip or a laugh on his worst days, and for spread-lines every afternoon he happens to be himself. A big good-natured boy, with the strength of a Goliath and an idol everywhere the game is known, Ruth has still the biggest part of his career in prospect, provided he meets with no serious accident or illness.[8]

On January 7, Ruppert announced he had received a telegram from Huggins affirming that Ruth was looking forward to playing with the Yankees. Indeed, Ruth was already envisioning a full season at the Polo Grounds that would enable him "to set such a home run record in 1920 as has never before been dreamed of."[9]

In an editorial entitled "The High Cost of Home Runs," the *Times* warned that the transaction heightened "the concentration of baseball talent in the largest cities, which can afford to pay the highest prices for it." This was "a bad thing for the game," the *Times* conjectured, "and it is still worse to give a valuable player stranded with a weak club the idea that if he holds out for an imposing salary he can get somebody in New York or Chicago to buy his services."[10]

Abe Kemp, sports columnist for *The San Francisco Bulletin*, termed the transfer "of the mightiest slugger of them all ... the most stupendous deal that has ever been perpetrated in the history of the game." To fans in Boston, Kemp saw the move as "nothing short of a catastrophe." Moreover, "they will not forget, and already their howls of disgust and rage are being heard and bandied about." As for speculations that Frazee intended to leave baseball or refused to accept Ruth's demands, the sportswriter opted for the first possibility. Ruth, he claimed, "is worth every cent that he can get. He is the greatest drawing card in the game, and, irrespective of whatever amount is doled out to him on the 1st and 15th of each month, it comes back in the golden stream at the gate." The Yankee owners had made a wise investment, Kemp continued, but it was not good for the game. "It places the power in the hands of a few millionaires who can spend the money and not miss it, while it leaves the less fortunate magnates to scrape and dig as best they can, depending mostly upon a prayer to secure a first-class club."[11]

Attempting to justify the sale, Frazee contended that the Red Sox were quickly turning into "a one-man team." He charged,

> Ruth had become simply impossible and the Boston Club could no longer put up with his eccentricities. While Ruth, without question, is the greatest hitter that the game has ever seen, he is likewise one of the most selfish and inconsiderate men that ever wore a baseball uniform. Had he possessed the right disposition, had he been willing to take orders and work for the good of the club like the other men on the team, I would never have dared let him go. Twice during the past two seasons Babe has jumped the club and revolted. He refused to obey orders of the manager.

Ruth's antics, Frazee declared, had alienated his teammates. "Half the men on the team were not on speaking terms to the other half or to him because of his actions. He had the idea that the Red Sox could never play a game without him or at least win one, and he could do as saw fit." Only a monetary deal had been possible, Frazee insisted. Swapping players for Ruth would have wrecked the Yankee ball club. An attempted trade for the White Sox' Joe Jackson proved unrealizable, as did other attempts to obtain star ballplayers.[12]

Most Boston reporters and fans alike appeared deeply distressed by news of Ruth's departure from the Red Sox. One cartoon sketch was captioned "Think of the Baseballs Frazee Will Save." It highlighted the Boston owner with hatchet in hand — featuring a dollar sign — whacking away at a column propping up Fenway Park. That pillar contained Ruth's likeness and was emblazoned with the slugger's name. Other smaller pillars, already cut down, were named "Duffy Lewis" and "Mays." A sign indicated that Fenway was a "HOUSE FOR SALE," while there were additional for sale signs next to the Boston Public Library and the Commons. In the upper left-hand corner, a small figure was posing the question, "Anybody wanter buy a good-right eye?"[13]

An editorial in *The Boston Post* exclaimed,

> The sale of Babe Ruth to the New York Yankees will be a tremendous blow to the army of loyal fans who have stuck to the Red Sox through thick and thin, through good seasons and bad. Boston fans are bound to be disgruntled. A great star today is, generally speaking, above a mere purchasing price. The Red Sox roster today contains very few men whose services are sufficiently in demand to warrant other clubs giving up tried and true players in barter. What few players of this calibre are now numbered among the Red Sox must, it would surely seem, be retained if the club, now that Ruth is gone, is to keep from crowding the Athletics for eighth place in 1920. This is not the first time that Boston baseball has been shocked by the sale of a wonderful player — Cy Young and Tris Speaker went their ways, much to the disgust of the faithful, but the club did not suffer materially. But Ruth is different. He is of a class of ball players that flashes across the firmament once in a great while and who alone bring crowds to the park, whether the team is winning or losing.[14]

The *Boston Herald* was less judgmental in its evaluation of the deal.

> Stars generally are temperamental. This goes for baseball and the stage. They often have to be handled with kid gloves. Frazee has carefully considered the Ruth angle and believes he has done the proper thing. Boston fans undoubtedly will be up in arms but they should reserve judgment until they see how it works out.[15]

Boston Mayor Andrew J. Peters expressed his own displeasure regarding Frazee's decision to sell baseball's most exciting player.

The loss of Ruth is greatly to be regretted. He is a splendid ball player of natural ability and his timely and vigorous work at the bat will be sadly missed by the Boston fans. It is my hope that the money received for the sale of Ruth will be used in a manner that will have its result in Boston winning the championship. New York gains while Boston loses.[16]

Continuing his attempts to deflect criticism, Frazee indicated that Ruth had been seeking a trade to the Yankees for over a year. When Ruth was a holdout the previous spring, he had asked to be sold to New York. During a mid-season squabble with team management, Ruth again suggested that he be traded to Boston's American League rival.[17]

James O'Leary's column in *The Sporting News*, filed on January 12, offered that Frazee was compelled to deal Ruth once the slugger "regarded himself as bigger than the Boston Club, bigger than the game itself." He would have preferred players, not money, Frazee declared, but "Ruth could go only to one club." Only the Yankees could afford to pay what they had. As for the New Yorkers' decision, Frazee termed it "a big gamble," but one that would pay off if Ruth had a couple of great seasons with his new team. Promising that he would use the money from Ruppert to obtain other players, Frazee predicted the Red Sox would be "a stronger team next season" without Ruth.[18]

Stung by Frazee's comments, Ruth responded in kind, while indicating a readiness to play for the Yankees if only to show up the Boston owner:

Frazee is not good enough to own any ball club, especially one in Boston. On Babe Ruth Day Boston people packed the park. He reserved 15,000 seats and forced the ball players to pay for their wives. I paid for Mrs. Ruth. After the game I was called to his office, where he handed me a cigar and thanked me. That is a fair sample of his liberality. Because I demanded a big increase in salary, which I felt I was entitled to, he brands me as an ingrate and a troublemaker. The time of a ball player is short and he must get his money in (sic) few years or lose out. Any fair-minded fan knows that my efforts on the Boston club last season warranted a larger salary and I asked for it.

I have always hustled as hard as any man on the diamond. When not taking my turn in the box I played in the outfield, doing everything I could to make the club win. I don't like to play for Frazee. I like Boston and Boston fans. They have treated me splendidly and if it were not for Frazee I would be content to play with the Red Sox to the end of my baseball days. Frazee sold me because he was unwilling to meet my demands to alibi himself with the fans he is trying to throw the blame on me.[19]

The sale, *Baseball Magazine*'s W. A. Phelon noted, spotlighted both the Yankees and Ruth, while making "every holdout player on both circuits doubly determined to stick by his guns." The Yankees had long been "a poor second in popular affections" to the Giants. Their owners, Jacob Ruppert and

Til Huston, both "game sportsmen," were "eager to do anything, irrespective of expense, to make their luckless club a drawing card." Unless Ruth completely fizzled—and at the Polo Grounds, Phelon contended, "Babe should fairly rain home runs"—the transaction would more than pay for itself in extra admissions. But it would prove costly to all other ball clubs, who would have to deliver "a blamed sight more in money extorted by the hold-out birds."[20]

In the April 1920 issue of *Baseball Magazine*, leading baseball figures discussed the merits of the Ruth transaction. Not surprisingly, Colonel Ruppert saw it "as a ten-strike." Previously considering Ruth unattainable, Ruppert had discovered that Frazee was prepared "to do something drastic to his dissatisfied star." Consequently, Yankee management determined to obtain Ruth if Frazee were ready to move him, "no matter what colossal price might be set on the purchase." And "this price was a staggerer," an unprecedented sum for a baseball player, but appeared justified. Former National League president John Tener recalled Cap Anson, Ed Delahanty, and Nap Lajoie, but termed Ruth "the heaviest hitter I have ever known." While hearkening back to Sam Crawford, Detroit manager Hugh Jennings seconded that notion, stating that "Ruth is unquestionably the heaviest hitter I have ever seen. He drives the ball higher and makes it go further, in my opinion, than any other batter who ever lived." St. Louis Browns' skipper Jimmy Burke also declared that Ruth "drives it further than any man I ever saw." Moreover, Burke continued, Ruth was "the greatest hitter I have ever seen." Ed Barrow, Ruth's last manager with the Red Sox, stated that Ruth was "always dangerous but he is never better than with men on bases when the game is in the balance." Indeed, "Ruth rises to the occasion better in batting than almost any other player I have known."[21]

In a lengthy article, F. C. Lane sought to explain how Ruth became baseball's greatest slugger. Ruth's career, Lane declared, was "a veritable romance of the diamond." He then spun the Horatio Alger-like tale of Ruth's rise from poverty to become "universally recognized as the greatest player figure in the game." Not Frank Baker, but Babe Ruth, Lane wrote, deserved to be considered "the home-run emperor or czar or absolute monarch far above mere kingly rank." Indeed, "nothing in the whole history of baseball can compare with the amazing manner in which he shattered all existing home-run records last season."[22]

\* \* \*

Babe Ruth proved to be a perfect fit for America's greatest city. The April 1920 edition of *The New York Globe* discussed the city's hold on the rest of the nation; it might have been referring to the Babe:

New York is like Edgar Lee Masters' Spoon River. It is "Amerikee." Its tone is set by the people who come to it. Easy, vulgar, unproductive is here, therefore the vulgar come here; artistic fame is here, therefore the makers and lovers of beauty come here; excitement is here, therefore the people from the open country who think they have never seen enough or done enough come here.

New York sits upon the surplus wealth of America; it is Cinderella, the Fairy Godmother, the handsome Prince, and the wicked sisters all in one. It is the Isle of Circe and the land of heart's desire. Above all, it is the expression of the great suppressed wish of America. What millions on plain and mountain dream of doing, New York does. ...[23]

# CHAPTER TEN

# A Season of Courage: Rube Foster and a League of His Own

The new decade began far less auspiciously for African Americans in general. A report by the NAACP indicated that nine military veterans had been "lynched" over the course of the past year in the United States. Two had been burned, two suffered hangings, four were shot, and one was pummeled to death. A former soldier was killed because he failed to "turn out of the road soon enough for passing white men." Rumors existed of other, unsubstantiated lynchings in the American South. No prosecutions had been undertaken against any perpetrators.[1]

In 1919, an editorial in *The Chicago Defender* noted, "lynching mobs" had proved "more active and dastardly than in previous years," as Jim Crow measures pertaining to southern railroads remained in effect. "Race clashes" ensued in a number of northern communities, while "movements put on foot" to maintain residential segregation. African Americans were denied the right to vote and adequate educational facilities in various sectors of the land. "The white American" continued to believe, the *Defender* charged, that "our dark skins" afforded "him license to insult our women and browbeat our men."[2]

Through it all, Robert S. Abbott's publication exclaimed, "we have forged steadily ahead." As for the "new Negro," the *Defender* declared, we haven't such a critter, just the same old tinted individual roused into self-consciousness, awakened to his own possibilities, with stiffened backbone, with new ambitions, new desires, new hopes for the future. An individual that has proven that somewhere on this earth men and women are judged by their worth and not by their complexion. Our soldier boys found these places, it aroused them from their lethargy; and they returned home with a spirit so contagious the other ninety and nine got it. The yesterdays with us are passed; we are looking forward to the tomorrows.[3]

The editors of *The Chicago Whip*, a defiantly radical African American newspaper, also hearkened the arrival of the New Negro, while explaining how they identified with him. This required considerable courage, as harsh governmental raids were being undertaken against those condemned as "Reds" and anarchists:

The New Negro does not wish to overthrow the government by violence or force neither does he belong to any anarchistic order. The New Negro does wish the government to overthrow all agencies and forces that are depriving him of full American citizenship. We are dissatisfied with the treatment we are receiving. We want the existing order of social, economic and political affairs changed. The Negro wants to be treated as a man and consideration on the basis of merit and citizenship. The New Negro is disgusted with lynching and mob violence. He believes in defending his life and his home and all other sacred institutions. For this reason he is radical because the old regime is satisfied with "Uncle Tom" and "Aunt Liza" position (sic). We do not approve of direct action and sabotage. We do advocate intelligent collective bargaining and race solidarity.

The *Whip* sought for the African American to "have a man's chance." To that end, it urged, "Let radicalism arouse his slumbering soul."[4]

\* \* \*

Like the editors of *The Chicago Whip* and *The Chicago Defender*, Rube Foster clearly envisioned viable institutions that African Americans would own, control, and operate. Such self-empowerment, these men believed, would serve twin-fold purposes. It would give lie to long held theories regarding the supposed racial inferiority and necessary submissiveness of their racial kin. It would thereby set the stage for the day when segregation practices would be discarded altogether. Thus, Abbott's sportswriters, like Foster, long blackball's dominant figure, called for greater control of that game by African Americans.[5]

In early 1920, Foster was able to bring to fruition a dream he and other blackball visionaries had fastened onto: the formation of a Negro league. As the year opened, Foster was still urging other blackball moguls to recognize

Rube Foster, circa 1920. National Baseball Hall of Fame Library, Cooperstown, N.Y.

the need to follow organized baseball's lead. Their current practices, he warned on January 3, would ultimately reap no rewards. Raiding players from other teams was one of the most egregious examples. To Foster, "it has gotten so bad managers do not trust players, nor do the players trust the managers. It's folly for one to teach a player to jump and not pay the manager he leaves and expect that same player to be honest with him." By contrast, organized baseball retained the reserve clause that bound a ballplayer to a club until it released him. "Even the big leagues," Foster pointedly declared, "do not tamper with different clubs' players" but rather protected "each other's rights." Unfortunately, "our club owners," Foster wrote, "laugh at such protection and have year after year done just the opposite."[6]

Players had asked Foster if greater organization would curb their salaries. Responding, he noted that several individual major leaguers received more money than did "any three Colored clubs at the present time." If investments were shielded, Foster insisted, then more funds would be available for both ballparks and player development. Teams like the Indianapolis ABCs, Detroit Stars, Kansas City Monarchs, Royal Giants, and Cuban Stars had invested nothing "beyond their uniforms and advance money." Thus, they stood ready to damage other clubs, like Foster's team, with its considerable overhead.[7]

"We cannot get along without organization," Foster argued. "Neither will we have sufficient parks to play in to warrant paying greater salaries than we are at present unless we organize. There are thousands of dollars ready for such an organization. The money will naturally come from the whites." Cries would ring out, he predicted, "that it's a shame that all this money goes into the hands of the whites." However, Foster noted, "we will be the ones at fault. They can easily triple the present salaries and make money, as they will systematize it, build sufficient parks and give employment to many hundred Colored players."[8]

The current state of affairs, Foster prophesied, could not continue. Even present blackball standards would not be maintained for long, as park rentals had escalated and existing leases were only temporary. While "many Colored men with money have begged to get into the game," Foster recalled, "they want it patterned after the way leagues are conducted." As for himself, the blackball giant scowled,

> This will be the last time I will ever try and interest Colored club owners to get together on some working basis. I have so often been refused the necessary capital, not desiring to give to others the chance of monopolizing Colored baseball, but they are not going to continue to wait on me with their money. They can do so and leave me where I am. I have made the effort; it's now up to the ones that expect to permanently figure in baseball to get together.[9]

In his next editorial, Foster referred to his earlier call for two leagues, one in the east, the other out west, whose champions would meet for the world championship. Just such an approach, he bristled, "would have been the salvation of baseball." However, to date very little interest had been expressed in his plan. Members of the black community had supported blackball teams, Foster explained, "based solely on their loyalty to the Race." This could not continue indefinitely, for the people wanted greater professionalism, the kind that led graduates of the most distinguished universities to become baseball players. They made that choice "merely because it paid them better to do so." Black folk, Foster insisted, "can do the same thing, but only in patterning after the system of success" employed by organized baseball.[10]

He again referred to the disproportionate investments laid out by various blackball operators. Only the Lincoln Giants, St. Louis Giants, and Chicago American Giants, he underscored, possessed any tangible assets; those of his own ball club were greater than all the moneys expended on "the Colored parks combined." Foster closed with the following admission:

> I have fought against delivering Colored baseball into the control of whites, thinking that with a show of patronage from the fans we would get together. The get-together effort has been a failure. In justice to myself and the many players that will eventually benefit by ownership with system, money and parks, admitting that I cannot prevent it much longer, as in the past, I had better see that the snow does not stay in my yard after these many hard years of effort.[11]

On January 17, Foster reported recent efforts to meet with Nat C. Strong, a white booking agent and Eastern blackball's most powerful figure. Foster wanted to carve out an agreement to bring about improved working conditions, to hold salaries steady, and to allow teams to retain their present rosters. Strong purportedly responded that he wanted nothing to do with Foster's plan. The Chicago American Giants' boss quoted Strong as insisting "The men who are at present identified with the eastern clubs are an IMPOSSIBILITY ... (thus) there were several owners, managers and players they would never do business with again."[12]

The east-west divide, Foster explained, was "deeply rooted." Moreover, "there will be no peace until the men now connected give way to different owners." The crux of all difficulties was "the players (sic) question." Raids on other payrolls continued, although western teams did not tamper with each other's lineups. The sectional rift was so thorough that eastern and western teams refused to play one another, as did the top eastern squads. Speaking from painful experience, Foster related that if one took his team east and triumphed there, then owners in that region would strive to pirate away ballplayers, thereby engendering internal discord; thus, "you avoid going there."[13]

Had his proposal been accepted, Foster exclaimed, then "bitter feelings" could have been discarded and "a working agreement" devised "respecting each other's right." Also, all teams could have met, playing fields found, and a league constructed. Instead, "they refused such, desiring to fight each other. Now it's the survival of the fittest." Foster blurted out, "One would not think such IGNORANCE existed in the MODERN AGE." While ballplayers "had no respect for their word, contracts or moral obligations," Foster did not consider them "nearly as much to blame as the different owners of clubs."[14]

In an article in the February 1920 issue of *The Competitor*, C. I. Taylor, owner of the Indianapolis ABCs, also bemoaned the lack of organization afflicting blackball. Predicting that the upcoming season would "be the greatest in the history of the sport," Taylor declared his "faith in my people, and their ability to accomplish all things." Baseball, he continued, "is their national game because it is above all things an AMERICAN game. It abides deep in the sport loving natures of all Americans regardless of their creed or color." Thus, blackball's "chaotic condition" was all the more troubling. After all,

> We produce splendid players, men of brilliant talents, many of whom could play rings around the average ball players in the white leagues if they were given an opportunity. And we produce excellent teams, too, considering the very poor facilities we have in developing them as compared with the elaborate and carefully planned training camps that are maintained by the whites.[15]

However, the blackball version of the game grew "so slowly," Taylor reasoned, because of a "lack of organization! We have the goods, but we haven't got the organization to deliver them." For several years, Taylor, like Foster, had argued as much. Other refused to pay heed, dismissing Taylor as a "dreamer." His response was that "We will always be in the same boat unless we launch out into an organization." At last, it appeared that many heretofore reluctant sorts had also come to consider organization essential "if we are to make anything out of baseball for the black Americans." Taylor again urged Foster to take the lead in ushering in the greater organization blackball so desperately required.[16]

Led by Foster, midwestern blackball moguls finally agreed to meet in Kansas City, Missouri, in mid–February. Ira F. Lewis, writing in *The Competitor*, soon suggested that the attempt to bring about organized blackball "only needed Mr. Foster's aid to make the try a success." Lewis acknowledged that "to his undying credit let it be said that he has made the biggest sacrifice of anyone." After all, Foster's "position in the world of colored baseball was reasonably secure" throughout the Midwest. Possessing "an ideal park location" and "unlimited backing both in money and patronage," Foster could have long continued to operate in the same manner. However, Lewis noted, "he has seen the light,— the light of wisdom and the spirit of service to the public." Consequently, "from now on he will begin to be the really big man in baseball, he should be, by virtue of his knowledge of the game from both the playing and business ends."[17]

On February 7, the *Defender* indicated that the following figures would be present: Taylor, John Matthews of the Dayton Marcos, John Tenny Blunt of the Detroit Stars, J. L. Wilkinson of the Kansas City Monarchs, Charles Mills of the St. Louis Giants, Joe Green of the Chicago Giants, and, of course, Foster himself. Sportswriters who promised to attend included *The Indianapolis Ledger*'s Charles Marshall and A. D. Williams, *The Indianapolis Freeman*'s Dave Wyatt and Elwood C. Knox, and *The Chicago Defender*'s Cary B. Lewis.[18]

When the historic gathering took place at the Kansas City Y.M.C.A.'s Community Center at 18th and Vine, those individuals were joined by W. A. Kelly from Washington, D.C., and the St. Louis Giants' L. S. Cobb. Nominated by Blunt, Foster was elected temporary president at the first session on February 13, while Lewis was named secretary. The participants sought to devise the league Foster had long envisioned and looked to begin operations in 1921, which promised to be "the greatest" in baseball history. To the astonishment of those in attendance, Foster presented an incorporated charter for the National Negro Baseball League. The league, Foster unveiled, was already incorporated in Illinois, Michigan, Ohio, Pennsylvania, New York, and Maryland.[19]

Rube Foster and other blackball figures, circa 1920. National Baseball Hall of Fame Library, Cooperstown, N.Y.

During the two-day conference, journalists served as "arbitrators" for the blackball magnates. Unprecedented harmony and "good spirit," *The Chicago Defender* noted, reigned throughout the sessions. The newspapermen, chairman Foster declared, would resolve all disputes, choose player rosters, and draft league by-laws and a constitution. They were assisted by Elisha Scott, an attorney from Topeka, Kansas. Working throughout the night and into the early morning hours, the sportswriters and Scott established, in the words of the *Defender*, "the 'baseball bill of rights' to guide the destiny of the future league."[20]

At midday Friday, the constitution was ready to be examined by the blackball owners. They subsequently read and approved of the preamble, then scoured through the constitution, which, after considerable revision, was adopted. All managers were reported to have paid $500 entrance fees, tying them to the league, but later accounts suggested that Foster chipped in such an amount for any number of his colleagues. On the other hand, Foster also purportedly arranged for league equipment and balls to be purchased from him and was allowed to draw on deposit funds to cover necessary expenses.[21]

On February 21, the *Defender* indicated that "the Western Circuit, National Baseball League" would begin operations on April 1, 1921. The interval would allow ball clubs either to lease or purchase stadiums to host Negro National League contests. A number of road teams also reportedly agreed to participate and paid their entry fees. Even Foster's old antagonist, Nat C. Strong, delivered a letter indicating "that he was ready to do anything that would promote the best interests of baseball all over the country." After the Western Circuit established a foothold, Foster planned to call for league representatives to gather and include all large eastern cities.[22]

Player rosters were purportedly drawn to ensure some degree of balance, which required Foster to relinquish several of his American Giants. The Detroit Stars featured Pete Hill, Bruce Petway, Richard Whitworth, and Jimmy Lyons; the Kansas City Monarchs, John Donaldson, Joe Mendez, and Wilbur Rogan. The Chicago Giants included Walter Ball and John Beckwith, the St. Louis Giants got Tully McAdoo and Dan Kennard, while the Indianapolis ABCs received Oscar Charleston and William Dismukes. The American Giants remained strong, with Leroy Grant, David Malacher, and Cristobal Torrenti in their lineup.[23]

On March 6, the *Defender* discussed a meeting in Atlanta to create a new Southern league, inspired by "the National Western Baseball Circuit." Nashville, Birmingham, Knoxville, Chattanooga, Atlanta, Jacksonville, Montgomery, Pensacola, New Orleans, and Greenville, South Carolina — the home of Joe Jackson — were all represented. There was hope that Dave Wyatt, Cary B. Lewis, and Rube Foster would speak with the team owners, providing encouragement and inspiration for their endeavors. It was also anticipated that the Southern League would soon join Foster's organization.[24]

* * *

Two weeks later, the *Defender* predicted that 1920 "will be the greatest baseball season in the history of the American Giants." The roster included catchers Ray Brown and Tubby Dixon; infielders Grant, Bingo DeMoss, Bobby Williams, and Malarcher; outfielder Jude Gans, Torriente, Chaney White, and John Reese; and pitchers Tom Williams, Dave Brown, Tom Johnson, and String Bean Williams. Foster's club was said to be capable of defeating "any ball team in the country."[25]

All the while, Foster continued devising plans for the Negro National League, whose motto was "We are the ship. All else the sea." Organization, in his estimation, remained most vital of all, with unaffiliated teams to be treated as they were by the major and minor leagues. "Better baseball, better discipline and better standing" would supposedly result. The *Defender* particularly applauded Foster's decision to distribute stars around the league, thereby "equalizing the playing strengths" and ensuring increased attendance. Foster himself had shipped out Whitworth and Charleston, considered "the two greatest stars in the profession, both idolized by the fans and great drawing cards." Detroit magnate Blunt, to his credit, delivered Donaldson and Mendez, another pair of popular stars, to Kansas City, and received Lyons, in turn, from St. Louis owner Mills.[26]

Foster discussed what kind of team he was trying to put together in Chicago.

> We are making every effort to round out a winning combination for this fine baseball city, and I hope to be able to announce some names soon. The team we hope to put in the field this season will be one developed along safe and sane principles. I am not going to try any new-fangled system. Every man has his own ideas, and I have mine, but down at the bottom of it all the fans like the old base hit in the pinch, and the old fast one or curve that fools the batter with three on, two out, two strikes on the batter, and the hometown's favorite hurler in the box. New ideas may be pressed into service now and then, but the game is about the same as when I was in the limelight as a player.[27]

Following a visit by Foster to Detroit in late March, the *Defender* discussed the favorable impression he had made. Fans encountered "the congenial, business-like kind of a man who should be at the head of the new circuit." But he also left behind "an impression that baseball was something more than a mere recreation and pastime institution." Similarly, Foster conveyed to leading Detroit businessmen the value of their baseball franchise. Dave Wyatt saw the American Giants as determined "to play fast ball, keep things stirred up."[28]

On April 3, Wyatt analyzed the new league. Even two years earlier, he suggested, fans would have considered insane the possibility that stars like

Bill Francis, Whitworth, Hill, and Charleston could be transferred to other teams without heated protest from both owners and fans. Yet to ensure the Negro National League's success, Foster had recently handed over his leading pitcher and outfielder, along with one of his finest infielders, to rival squads. Wyatt sang the American Giants' owner's praises loudly:

> Foster has made more sacrifices for the good of the game than all the managers together, who at present constitute the personnel of owners and all those who may come. During the eleven or more years that he has headed a club the Chicago manager has been the chief benefactor to a few hundred players and promoters who have basked in the sunshine of baseball popularity at various times. He has been with player and owners alike, as well as the fans.[29]

Most recently, viewing organization of blackball as absolutely essential, he had made additional sacrifices. To that end, "Foster broke up one of the greatest playing machines of all time" so that blackball could be firmly established in Detroit.[30]

In Wyatt's estimation, "Foster has been the rock against which many a wave of adversity has been dashed to nothingness. He has weathered the storm of fierce criticism; he has sailed smoothly over the many obstacles that the combined power of his adversaries had placed in his path." As the 1920 season approached, Foster was "facing his greatest triumph, a realization of a life's dream." Still, "his hopes are not fully realized." Former antagonists were "gleefully parading under his baseball banner," but would the fans support this endeavor? Wyatt asked. Admission prices would surely be raised to cover increased salary, operating, travel, food, and hotel expenditures. For his part, Wyatt was certain that fans desired "good, fast, clean baseball," the kind that the Negro National League was certain to offer.[31]

* * *

While Foster and the other magnates of the Negro National League had called for beginning operations the following year, the new circuit's initial games were played in May 1920. On Sunday afternoon, May 2, the first contest was scheduled between C. I. Taylor's Indianapolis ABC's and Joe Green's Chicago Giants. Dave Wyatt reported that

> one of the largest and most enthused gathering (sic) of baseball devotees who ever assembled to do homage to the grand old national game witnessed the initial contests (sic) that ushered into being what is purported to be the most important and far-reaching step ever negotiated by the baseball promoters of our Race since the birth of the game more than forty years ago.

Veteran pitcher Walter Ball of the ABCs was bested by the youngster Ed "Huck" Rile, as the Giants prevailed 4-2. Indianapolis center fielder Oscar

Charleston, just transferred from the Chicago American Giants, was said to have "revealed streaks of his former greatness that made him the most feared man at the bat and on the base paths."[32]

On May 30, 228 delegates and members, representing almost 100 branches and nearly 30 states, gathered in Atlanta for the NAACP's 11th annual meeting. The Resolutions Committee urged that the entire American nation "consider the grievous injustices and discriminations heaped upon its colored citizens and ... hear their urgent demands." Black folk had to become politically involved, because of the realities confronting them: "lynching and mob violence, poor schools, 'Jim Crow' methods of travel, unequal justice in courts and in things economic, with disfranchisement in many states." The NAACP committee urged passage of federal legislation to attack the evil of lynching. It damned segregation ordinances as "illegal, unconstitutional and contrary to the spirit of true American democracy." It insisted on the upholding of the 13th, 14th, and 15th amendments to the United States Constitution. The committee called for equal spending on the education of black children — Jim Crow practices presently prevailed — and the providing of federal moneys for common school instruction.[33]

In the meantime, the American Giants steamrolled through the first part of the Negro National League's inaugural season, winning 18 of their first 20 games, building up a four game lead over the Detroit Stars. Indianapolis stood another two games back, while Kansas City, Dayton, and St. Louis had compiled losing records. The Cuban All-Stars had won only half of their first 18 contests, while the Chicago Giants, with their 1-8 record, were cellar dwellers.[34]

That month, *The Competitor* celebrated the "wonderful progress" of the Negro National League. Midwestern fans appeared willing to support the enterprise, as evidenced by attendance totals. Near the mid point of the league's first year of existence, the Chicago American Giants, guided "by that indomitable leader, Rube Foster," continued to lead the pack, with most other teams proving to be competitive, in their own fashion. The greatest impediment besetting the league, *The Competitor* charged, was "the unsportsmanlike, unbusinesslike and weak-kneed support" afforded it by African American newspapers in the region. At best, they were displaying "only half-hearted interest and support" in the new league. With two months of the season gone, no paper besides *The Chicago Whip* in league cities had published club standings or compiled batting and fielding averages. Indeed, little analysis had been drawn regarding league players or their performances.[35]

*The Competitor* faulted three sources for this state of affairs. Sportswriters had failed to keep track of statistics, in the manner of the major leagues. Newspapers appeared to expect special treatment from the league, not simply interviews and insider information. Various managers had possibly been remiss in providing accurate box scores. Regardless of who or what was to blame, *The Competitor* argued, "teamwork" was needed to help the new organization thrive.[36]

That summer, *The Chicago Whip* continued to propound the gospel of the New Negro, whom Rube Foster could be likened to. An editorial on July 10 cried out:

> The rumbling, roaring, rising, expanding voice of the American Negro is beginning to shake gently but perceptibly the foundations of the Southern Overlords, the Magistrates of the Lynch Law and the entire group of those afflicted with nightmares of perpetual White Supremacy. THE NEGRO IS BEGINNING TO THINK. THIS IS A REVOLUTIONARY EPOCH IN HIS AMERICAN EXISTENCE. He is beginning to analyze the race situation with keenness and far reaching insight.[37]

* * *

Near the close of August, the American Giants had carved out a comfortable lead in the Negro National League standings. Their 42-12 mark placed them 15 games ahead of the Detroit Stars, 17 in front of the Kansas City Monarchs, and 17½ ahead of the Indianapolis ABCs. Further back stood the St. Louis Giants, the Dayton Marcos, and the Chicago Giants.[38]

The Negro National League ended with no official standings released, but the Chicago American Giants — who had recently taken three of a five game set against the Stars and then trounced the ABCs 8-2 in the regular season finale — were proclaimed pennant winners. The American Giants were guided by southpaw Dave Brown's 10-2 record, third baseman Dave Malarcher, who batted .344, and centerfielder Cristobal Torriente, who led the league with a .411 mark. Tom Williams starred during league competition, compiling a 9-1 won-loss record, before splitting a pair of decisions in the post-season. The Detroit Stars had a number of the top players, including Jimmy Lyons, who stole more bases than anyone, 22, Edgar Wesley with his league-leading 11 home runs, and Bill Holland, the circuit's best pitcher, with a 17-2 won-loss record.[39]

The American Giants' first season in the Negro National League had proven quite successful, both artistically and commercially. Foster's team won every series from league members and also prevailed against Rogers Park of the City League, the Bacharach Giants, and the Knoxville Giants, reputedly the "colored champions of the South." Dave Wyatt asserted that the American Giants had "broken all records as a drawing card, having pulled the largest crowd ever at Kansas City, filled the Indianapolis park to capacity, jammed Navin Field ... and played to the largest week day crowd ever seen in the West at St. Louis." An estimated 200,000 spectators had show up at Schorling Park to watch their favorites perform.[40]

On Friday, December 3, the Negro National League bosses gathered at the Indianapolis Y.M.C.A. for their second annual meeting to discuss the inaugural season and plan for the future. In his opening address, chairman Rube Foster indicated that the year had been a good one, with over 616,000 fans attending league games and all clubs ending up in the red. The biggest news coming out of the conference involved the trade of Lyons, a .386 hitter, to the American Giants for outfielder Judy Gans and shortstop Young Riggins. The reserve clause, so controversial in the major leagues, was adopted by the magnates as part of a new league constitution. That clause, sportswriter Ira F. Lewis of *The Pittsburgh Courier* argued, was "in spirit the very heart of organized baseball." Players under contract who bolted from their old clubs would only have the option of quitting baseball altogether. League teams could refuse to take the field against any club not part of the National Association that violated this edict. The revised constitution, *The Chicago Defender* declared, would elevate blackball and draw thousands to league games who otherwise would never consider attending. Managers or owners were to be fined if ungentlemanly behavior, so damaging to the game, occurred.[41]

# CHAPTER ELEVEN

# A Season of Grace: Babe in Pinstripes

The first few months of 1920 alone would have enabled it to remain etched as a pivotal one in the national pastime's history. Just as the sport was experiencing a groundswell of popularity, organized baseball's governing body appeared increasingly dysfunctional. Holdouts and contractual disputes tore at the fabric of the National Commission and produced player movement of some note. The year opened with the announced sale of the game's greatest ballplayer to the New York Yankees, who would soon acquire the luster as the most storied major league franchise. Due to his own concerns about the cost of player raids and disorganization, Rube Foster, barely a month later, finally attained his heartfelt goal: the establishment of a Negro League spearheaded by African Americans.

During this same period, the notorious "freak deliveries," blamed by many for baseball's lack of scoring punch, threatened to become extinct, thereby setting the stage for an offensive explosion. In the June 1919 issue of *Baseball Magazine*, F. C. Lane argued for abolition of the spitball, which he termed "the villain of the diamond." It violated section four of rule 14, which declared that "in the event of a ball being intentionally discolored by rubbing it with the soil or otherwise, by any player — the umpire shall forthwith demand the return of that ball and impose a fine of $5 on the offending player." It was also, Lane contended, "unsanitary. ... In a game so healthy and wholesome and inspiring as baseball the spit ball is strangely out of place. Even its name is repulsive." Most significant, the spitball, he noted, "is dangerous;" it was extremely difficult to control, thereby endangering the batter's physical well-being. It was unnecessary too, with pitchers already possessing enough weapons at their disposal; the likes of Christy Mathewson, Walter Johnson, and Pete Alexander had never resorted to it. The spitball was damned by all fielders, who had to contend with its elusive quality. It had even haunted the finest spitball pitchers, including Jack Chesbro, whose wild pitch helped to doom his ball club at the height of a pennant race, and Ed Walsh, whose extensive labors wore down his seemingly tireless arm. Later that summer, former Cubs' owner Charles Webb Murphy called for the prohibition of all "freak deliveries." Murphy applauded the American Association's decision to ban all such "un-natural (sic)" pitches, which he deemed a victory for "lovers of clean baseball."[1]

Following the 1919 season, the push to ban "freaks" — "the spit, shine, talcum, emery, paraffine, licorice, resin and tobacco balls" — heightened in intensity. Ban Johnson, *The Sporting News*'s Joe Vila reported, was determined to get rid of those pitches. Like other critics, Vila contended that "doctoring the ball is cheap business. It has no place in America's greatest and cleanest pastime. It is trickery, not natural skill, and the sooner the rule makers stamp it out the better it will be for everybody excepting a few pitchers who will find themselves in tight fixes without the aid of such chicanery." Baseball moguls, the sportswriter declared, could "squelch these unsportsmanlike practices very easily if they will act without fear, favor or influence." Vila, along with other opponents of the freaks, suggested another benefit would flow from their abandonment: improved hitting. And "the baseball public," he insisted, "prefers heavy hitting to light stick work resulting from the extreme effectiveness of the pitchers, who have been permitted to augment natural ability with false skill."[2]

On February 9, 1920, the Joint Rules Committee — featuring Barney Dreyfuss, William Veeck, and chairman John Heydler — banned "freak deliveries," including the spitter; those violating the rule would be tossed from the game and issued a 10-game suspension. Seventeen current spitball pitchers, including Burleigh Grimes, were allowed to continue relying on the wet one. *The Sporting News* applauded the move, while contesting the notion that the new rules were unenforceable. *Baseball Magazine* was also pleased, declaring that the sport had "long been harassed by these weird inventions of the pitchers' ingenuity." The publication chortled that "more batting and fair-play for all" was now a preferred slogan. Devising its own, *Baseball Magazine* exclaimed, "'Down with the spitter and on with the base hit,' for a faster, livelier and more spectacular game."[3]

* * *

As the air was rife with discussion of the banned freaks and a supposedly livelier ball, 1920 witnessed the American League in particular offer more offense-laden baseball. Record team batting totals were shattered, with both the Indians and Browns bettering the .300 mark and the league, as a whole, hitting .284. American Leaguers belted a record 369 home runs, continuing the surge begun in 1919 when 240 four-baggers were hit in a shortened season, up from 96 in 1918, when admittedly even fewer games had been played. However, in 1917 — the last full American League season before the most recent one — only 133 home runs had been smacked.

Individual batting marks also jumped in 1920, with five players hitting over .370, topped by St. Louis' George Sisler with a .407 average and a record 257 hits. Cleveland's Tris Speaker, rebounding from an off-season in 1919 when he had hit only .296, batted .388, while Chicago's Joe Jackson posted a .382 total. Jackson's teammate Eddie Collins batted .372, just behind the newest Yankee, Babe Ruth. Nine players contributed over 100 RBIs, while an equal number scored over 100 runs. Five batters surpassed the 300 total base standard, as Sisler ended up at 399. Sisler's slugging average was an impressive .632, although that left him well behind the top slugger. Speaker's on base percentage was .483, again a distant second to the league leader.

While American League ERA totals continued their march upward begun the previous year, brilliant pitching performances were, nevertheless, produced. Indian right-hander Jim Bagby won 31 games, the Yankees' Carl Mays, 26, and Cleveland's Stan Coveleski, 24. Four White Sox starters — Red Faber, Lefty Williams, Eddie Cicotte, and Dickie Kerr — were 20 game winners. New York's Bob Shawkey garnered 20 victories and had the top ERA, 2.45.

The individual story of 1920, however, involved the record-shattering feats of Yankee outfielder Babe Ruth. His first year in a New York uniform was an epochal one, clearly among the greatest in major league history. In 142 games, which produced only 458 official at bats, Ruth rapped out 172 hits, including 36 doubles and 9 triples, on the way to the league's fourth best batting average, .376, and 388 total bases. Ruth scored 158 runs, drove in 137, walked 148 times, attained a .530 on base percentage — all new major league records — and even stole 14 bases. Most astonishing were his pure power numbers, as he compiled an unprecedented .847 slugging percentage and belted a hitherto unimaginable 54 home runs. Ruth's preeminence was such that Sisler, runner-up in the home run race, hit 35 fewer; Sisler's superlative slugging percentage was over 200 percentage points behind Ruth's; and even Ruth's bases on balls surpassed Speaker by more than 50.

* * *

**Babe Ruth in New York Yankee dugout, 1920. National Baseball Hall of Fame Library, Cooperstown, N.Y.**

During the pre-season, thanks largely to the purchase of Ruth, expectations ran high for Miller Huggins's New York Yankees. Huggins did have to contend with the retirement of third baseman Frank Baker, who was left to care for two small children following the death of his wife. The signing of Babe Ruth easily topped the news, with predictions that the Polo Grounds' right field wall would offer an inviting target for the game's premier slugger. The Yankee everyday lineup included first sacker Wally Pipp, a two-time American League home run titlist, second baseman Del Pratt, shortstop Roger Peckinpaugh, a .305 hitter in 1919, and outfielders Ping Bodie, Duffy Lewis, and Bob Meusel, a hard-hitting rookie from the west coast. The pitching staff revolved around submariner Carl Mays and Bob Shawkey, both already twice 20-game winners, along with 36 year-old Jack Quinn, who had once won 26 games for the Baltimore Feds, and first-year man Rip Collins.[4]

After acquiring Ruth — who had unsuccessfully battled with Harry Frazee for a share of the purchase price — from the Red Sox, Yankee owners Ruppert and Huston took out a $150,000 life insurance policy on their newest employee. New York had to overcome the beaning of Chick Fewster, a promising youngster who appeared ready to replace Baker at third base. Huggins now planned to play Meusel at the hot corner.[5]

Spring training proved difficult in other, unexpected ways for the New York Yankees, as Ruth, clearly pressing to prove his worth as the game's highest paid and most celebrated star, fell into a much publicized slump. Little helping matters, perhaps, was Ruth's determination to play center field, not only to aid the ball club but to prevent possible injuries from running into the nearby right field fence at the Polo Grounds. The experiment, *The New York Tribune*'s W. J. Macbeth suggested, appeared to be a marked success. This was hardly surprising to him, for Ruth seemed to be "nothing if not a big, grown up kid. Nobody in camp is working harder than he. He runs on every hit as if sprinting for a base knock in the real show and already runs them out well past second base." In the field, Ruth demonstrated "a judgment and speed" comparable to that of Sammy Vick, one of the fastest Yankees on the 1919 version of the team.[6]

On March 15, Joe Vila indicated that "the fans are beginning to expect too much from" the still struggling Ruth. Babe had to be prepared, Vila declared, for brickbats "from thousands of unreasonable bugs who will storm the Polo Grounds to see him perform. But if he crashes the apple like he did last year he'll own Broadway." Four days later, Ruth slammed a 477 foot homer off a Brown University pitcher in an exhibition contest; Ruth was reputedly the only player to have ever knocked one over the Yankee training lot fence.[7]

His new squad looked little better in dropping five straight games in late March to the Brooklyn Dodgers in Jacksonville, Florida. In the third contest, Ruth's frustration threatened to boil over, when, after striking out twice, he leaped over the left field fence to go after a fan in the bleachers who was calling him "a big cheese." After harsh words were exchanged, the 5'4" fan, pulling out a knife, exhorted Ruth to fight. Yankee pitcher Ernie Shore, a former Red Sox teammate of Babe's, got between the two men and convinced Ruth to head back to the field.[8]

Yankee co-owner T. L. Huston was displeased with Ruth's antics. "That kind of stuff will have to be stopped right away," he declared. "If criticism down here gets under Ruth's skin, what will he do in the big league parks? Star players always are subjected to a certain amount of abuse when they don't deliver every time up, and, if they are sensible, they realize that that is part of the game."[9]

*The New York Times*, on March 22, analyzed "the mote in Babe Ruth's eye." Ruth's performance at the plate in exhibition games had "been anything but impressive. Indeed, "it has been extremely disappointing." A simple case of "overeagerness" seemed to explain his dilemma, as he sought to own up to his slugger's reputation and to demonstrate that Yankee management had made a wise move in acquiring him. When Ruth stopped trying to belt the ball a mile, he "will begin popping the horsehide on the nose" once again.[10]

News accounts indicated that Frank Baker was experiencing a change of mind and intended to rejoin the Yankees for the 1920 season. *Baseball Magazine* viewed New York as a strong pennant contender, thanks to a beefed up pitching staff and powerful lineup. Huggins, the publication noted, might be able to rely on Ruth, Baker, Pipp, Lewis, Bodie, Peckinpaugh, Pratt, and Meusel. Together, they comprised "a murderous batting attack equalled (sic) by few clubs in recent years." Baker's reputed return, *The Sporting News* suggested, would enable New York to "terrorize American League pitchers." By the end of March, however, it was clear that Baker was not coming back. Naming Meusel his regular third baseman, manager Miller Huggins asserted that "the big fellow" could "hit a ball as hard and as far as Baker."[11]

March 25 proved to be a dark day for Yankee fans. The team suffered its fifth straight defeat at the hands of the Dodgers. Ping Bodie, refused permission to return to New York to attend to business affairs, angrily quit the team. During fielding practice, Wally Pipp was knocked out by a ball hurled down the first base line by catcher Muddy Ruel. In the first inning of the game, Chick Fewster was beaned by Jeff Pfeffer's speedy curveball. Ten minutes reportedly passed before Fewster was revived. Surgeons determined that Fewster, who was hemorrhaging, had suffered a fractured skull.[12]

On April 1, Babe Ruth finally belted his first home run as a Yankee against major league pitching. In the first inning of the seventh game of the New York-Brooklyn series, won by the Yankees 6-2, Ruth delivered a "gargantuan smash" that "fairly sang in the air as he leaned against it;" it sailed over the center-field wall, the first "out-of-the-grounds homer" ever hit at the Jacksonville lot. A week later, in Winston-Salem, North Carolina, Ruth knocked what should have been three home runs against Dodger hurlers. The first flew 75 yards past both fences of a half-mile race track, ending up nearly 600 feet from the plate, but was ruled a ground rule double. Another declared double went about as far as Ruth's center-field smash at Jacksonville. A final blow clearly was within fair territory but was judged beyond it by umpire Hank O'Day. On April 10, Yankee fans got their first look at Ruth in a New York uniform when the two teams continued their series at Ebbets Field. Ruth's appearance alone, The *Tribune* noted, would "give what was formerly a drab outfit considerable color."[13]

In a lengthy analysis, the *Tribune's* Ray McCarthy picked both the Yankees and Giants as likely pennant winners. Referring to baseball's unprecedented popularity, McCarthy predicted that the game's "greatest year" lay just ahead. 1920, he noted, would be the first since 1917 with a complete slate of games; it was also the first without "the additional burden of a war among the magnates." While acknowledging that "everybody is claiming the pennant for the Indians this year," McCarthy selected the Yankees with their "knock-out" pitching corps and everyday lineup further augmented by "the mighty Ruth." When Ruth began "his bludgeoning," McCarthy declared, "he may break up the league this year. Any one who thinks he won't hit has another think coming." Grantland Rice offered that "the flaming career of the spectacular Ruth will be followed by thousands who will never see him in action. But what he does or doesn't do will add a new interest to the various episodes of spring and summer."[14]

In the season opener at Shibe Park on April 14, Babe Ruth's New York Yankee days began inauspiciously, as reports incorrectly circulated that Frank Baker was about to rejoin the team. A headline in the *New York Times* rang out, "Babe Ruth's Muff Tosses Game Away." The wire service account from Philadelphia began,

> The petted Babe of the New York Yankees appeared today in the role of enfant terrible. When, with two of the Athletics retired in the final half of the eighth inning and the score a tie at one run each, Ruth gracefully stumbled backward and raised his capacious cupped hands heavenward for Joe Dugan's long fly, only to fluff the catch, 12,000 Philadelphians arose and volubly criticized New York's 'Who Will Win the Big League Pennants?,' methods of training children.

With a chill in the air, the sizable turnout was attributed to Ruth. But the star of the game was Athletics' pitcher Scott Perry, the subject of recent controversy involving the Boston Braves, Connie Mack, and the National Commission. Attention was riveted on Ruth, however, and both applause and cries rang out as he batted. Referring to the Yankee first baseman, who powdered a home run, fans exclaimed, "Pipp's crabbing your act, Babe," "He's stealing your stuff," "You haven't got a hit in your bag." Ruth did manage two singles in four at-bats, but was left stranded on each occasion.[15]

In the next game, the Yankees, behind 36-year-old right-hander Jack Quinn, beat the Athletics 4-1. Prior to the game, a group of Philadelphians presented Ruth with a parcel containing a small brown derby. Jeers immediately turned to cheers, when Ruth perched the hat on his head. Ruth's own performance was not up to par, as he whiffed three times at the plate, once with the bases loaded. *The Sporting News* noted that large crowds showed up to watch Ruth perform, but his "1920 debut was hardly an $137,000 affair." One unidentified veteran was heard to say, "Ruth is 'pressing the ball' too much. He may not get so many hits this year if he doesn't change his style."[16]

Miller Huggins took his "million dollar" ballclub to Boston, where the Yankees immediately dropped a doubleheader to the Red Sox in Ruth's first return to Fenway in an enemy uniform. In the opener, as Waite Hoyt blanked the Yankee on five hits, Ruth garnered a single and a double. The afternoon contest, won by Boston 8-3, saw Ruth bang out only a single in four at bats, with Carl Mays taking the loss. In the third game of the series, the Red Sox prevailed once more, 3-2, as Ruth failed to deliver and Herb Pennock held the Yankees to three hits.[17]

The Yankees continued to struggle early in the season, dropping four of their first six games, while the White Sox opened with four straight victories. With Ruth struggling, *The Sporting News* referred to his early performance as "something of a disappointment." New Yorkers, it indicated, were expecting home runs to abound in the right field stands. Thus, Joe Vila predicted, if Ruth "fails to win all the games single-handed there's going to be an outcry." Nevertheless, there were also sure to be thousands of diehard Yankee fans ready to accord Ruth "a glorious welcome." Furthermore, Vila wrote,

Ruth's presence at the Polo Grounds means intensified interest in the Yankees and the sport. If the King of Sluggers comes through he will be the pride of Broadway. If the Yankees are up there fighting with four western teams for the old banner there'll be a hot time in the big town.[18]

In its home opener on April 22, New York triumphed against the Athletics 8-6, with 25,000 in attendance. During batting practice, however, Ruth pulled a muscle and injured an already weakened left leg, as he sought to pound the ball over the fence. As the crowd screamed for him to belt one into the stands, Ruth "swung savagely" but missed, with "the force of his swing twisting him completely around." After discarding his bat, Ruth held his right side, moved behind the batting cage, and fell to one knee. As the *Tribune* noted, "Babe Ruth, the most expensive athlete in the national pastime, strained the broadest back in the business swinging at a wide one in practice." Determined not to disappoint the gathered throng, Ruth had a doctor, who indicated that he had strained ligaments near the short ribs, tape him up. As the game was about to begin, Ruth, who had difficulty walking, headed for center field. In the bottom of the first frame, a mighty roar went up as Ruth came to bat. The *New York Times* reported that "Manhattan has eagerly awaited the coming of this rare batting curio" since "the far-famed fence-buster" had been purchased by the Yankees. After striking out, Ruth "hobbled to the bench," and the team physician ordered him from the field.[19]

Two days later, it was announced that "the Goliath of Swat" would be sidelined for 10 days. Ruth had suffered a badly strained muscle, which W. O. McGeehan noted, was serious only to Yankee gate receipts. On a happier note, Ping Bodie abruptly returned to the Polo Grounds just as Miller Huggins softly asked, "Who will play center field?" Bodie replied, "I will," and a startled Huggins spotted Bodie in the room. A long talk ensued between the two men.[20]

To the astonishment of the rival Senators, Ruth came out of the dugout to pinch hit in the ninth inning of a close contest on April 26. "Supposed to be a pale and interesting invalid with his eleventh rib wrenched loose from its moorings," McGeehan exclaimed, Ruth "so startled the Senators that they tossed the game right back at the Yankees." Batting with Meusel and Bodie on base, Ruth crashed a ball to center, enabling the runners to advance. "The baleful presence of Babe Ruth also seemed to throw a scare into" Senators catcher Patsy Gharrity, who, in attempting to catch Ping off base, tossed the ball into center field, allowing Meusel to score. Pipp rapped a pitch at shortstop Jim O'Neill, who bobbled the ball, letting Ping cross the plate with the winning run. On April 29, Ruth got one hit in four times at bat against Walter Johnson, who beat the Yankees 2-1, striking out eight and scattering five hits.[21]

Notwithstanding Ruth's return to the lineup, the Yankees continued to struggle, posting a 4-7 record in their first eleven games, placing them ahead of only the 3-7 Athletics and the 0-11 Tigers. The surprising Red Sox led the league with a 10-2 mark, followed by the White Sox at 7-2, and the Indians, who were 8-3. In the middle of the pack were the 5-4 Browns and the 5-6 Senators. In the National League, the Reds had rebounded from their early rocky start to post an 8-3 record, a half-game better than the 8-4 Dodgers. While the Phillies, Pirates, Cardinals, and Braves were bunched around the .500 mark, the 4-8 Cubs and the 3-7 Giants were at the bottom of the standings.

On May Day, Babe Ruth belted his first home run as a Yankee — and the fiftieth of his career — in the midst of a 6-0 whitewashing of the Red Sox at the Polo Grounds. The *New York Times* celebrated Ruth's feat:

> Babe Ruth sneaked a bomb into the park without anybody knowing it and hid it in his bat. He exploded the weapon in the sixth, when he lambasted a home run high over the right field grand stand into Manhattan field. ... it was a sockdolager. The ball flitted out of sight between the third and fourth flagstaffs on the top of the stand.

In breaking the major league record the previous September, Ruth had hit the ball in the same spot. Joe Jackson was the only other player to accomplish that feat.[22]

The following day, Ruth's "daily home run," as *The New York Tribune* referred to it, lifted the Yankees to another victory over Boston. Said to "be one of the heftiest clouts driven even by the Babe himself," the hit soared as a line drive no more than 30 feet above ground to a spot between the right field wall and the bleachers. But absent a concrete impediment, it reputedly "would have crossed the Harlem River and proceeded to distant parts of the Bronx." Ruth's four-baggers, W. O. McGeehan exclaimed, "are not mere home runs with the crowd. Each home [run] seems to possess an individuality or eccentricity of its own. After the game the multitudes lingered in the lot to trace the path taken by the ball over the stadium or into the stands."[23]

On May 7, the Yankees' well-regarded business manager Harry L. Sparrow, who had helped finalize the deal that brought Ruth to New York, died from a heart ailment. Recommended by both his friend John McGraw and Charles Comiskey, Sparrow had been hired by Jacob Ruppert and T. L. Huston when they purchased the team in 1915. A then struggling franchise, the ball club had finished in the second division every year since 1911. Under Wild Bill Donovan, New York did somewhat better in 1915, finishing fifth, a distant 32½ games behind the pennant-winning Red Sox and their young southpaw pitcher Babe Ruth. The next season, the Yankees edged up to fourth place, a mere 11 games behind Boston. However, in 1917, they slid back to sixth, 28½ games in back of Comiskey's White Sox. Miller Huggins guided the Yankees to fourth place in 1918, 13½ from the league's top spot, occupied once again by the Red Sox. The past season had been the most promising, with New York taking the controversial third-place honors, 7½ games behind Chicago.[24]

In a three game set against the White Sox at the Polo Grounds, Ruth busted loose. In the opener, won by the Yankees 6-5, Ruth, McGeehan wrote, "ran amuck with a heavy piece of timber." He belted a triple and two homers, the last, off Dickie Kerr, flying into the upper right field seats. In the second contest, a 14-8 affair also taken by New York, Ruth "got his home run" — at Lefty Williams's expense — lofting it into the right field upper stands.[25]

Following the first two games, White Sox manager Kid Gleason predicted that Ruth, barring injury, would shatter his own home run record. "I have seen all the oldtime sluggers," offered Gleason, "but I can safely say — and I'll say it to any jury of judges who have followed the best — that Babe Ruth hits a ball harder than any man that ever played." Gleason continued to reflect, "Why his pop flies will carry most any major league right field fence or wall. On the Polo Grounds this year he'll make as many homers as he made all last year if he has the least bit of luck." Ruth appeared to have no flaws at the plate, Gleason suggested, as he could hit fastballs, curves, spitters, slow pitches, southpaws, and right-handers.[26]

* * *

On May 14, the Yankees seemingly suffered a major setback, one that was clearly the byproduct of Ruth's appearance in a New York uniform. The New York National Baseball Club, operators of the Giants, confirmed that the American League squad would not be allowed to play at the Polo Grounds after the current season ended. Rumors to that effect had floated for some time, but Giant president Charles A. Stoneham and McGraw made the definitive announcement. In response, Ruppert first asserted that the Giants were reneging on a promise that the Yankees could continue to rent the Polo Grounds for $65,000 a year; since 1912, the two teams had shared the ballpark. Then, he stated, "If the Giants do not want us any longer on the Polo Grounds there is no use trying to stay around where one is not wanted." Hardly surprised by the Giants' action, the Yankee owners had obtained options for a site to build a new ballpark by the start of the 1921 season. One was situated at Amsterdam Avenue and 137th Street, across from City College's Lewisohn Stadium, another at 11th Avenue and 57th Street, and two additional spots were supposedly located in Long Island City.[27]

Earlier, the Giants had been viewed as "a popular institution," but during the past several years, the Yankees' appeal had heightened in Manhattan. The addition of Ruth afforded the team baseball's greatest gate attraction. Clearly, the Giants' management was concerned about being displaced as the metropolitan area's most popular sports team. Rationalizing the refusal to continue the lease, Stoneham indicated that New York was a great city and, like Chicago, could easily accommodate two baseball stadiums.[28]

As if to underscore the Giants' concern about the Yankees' mushrooming popularity, a record crowd gathered at the Polo Grounds to watch the Indians, led by Ray Chapman's three hits and Jim Bagby's eight-hitter, blast the "Hugmen" 8-2. Carl Mays was bounced out of the game, after giving up five runs in the opening frame; the *Tribune* rang out, "$45,000 Pitcher Sent to Junk Heap in the first Inning." Ruth knocked a double off the right-field fence in three official at-bats, and came to the plate three times with no one aboard, which, as the *Times* indicated, was "something of a load off any pitcher's mind."[29]

But the biggest news involved the 38,000 fans who paid their way into the Polo Grounds, with another 15,000 or so denied entrance; the atmosphere was likened to "a real pre-world series." The timing was propitious for such a turnout, as the 11-12 Yankees, featuring "the game's greatest drawing card as a magnet" and having won four straight contests, were battling the Indians, atop the league with a 16-7 mark.[30]

Having belted five homers, Ruth was a full month ahead of his 1919 record-setting performance. An editorial in *The Sporting News* emphasized that Ruth "has found himself" and was smacking home runs longer and more frequently than before. Referring to the gracious way Ruth responded to the brown derby incident at the beginning of the season, the editorial praised the slugger:

> The Babe is young and still has far to go, but he is learning wisdom, and under handicaps, as a popular hero must be handicapped. He has had bad advice in some matters, "friends" will continue to advise him badly, but each day their counsel will have less influence on him. The Babe is developing and along the lines that are destined to make him the popular hero he should be.
> We have faith in the future of Ruth, not only as a home run hitter, but as a man of parts, for he has been put to the test and has endured it.[31]

With pressure brought to bear by National Commission members Ban Johnson and Gary Herrmann, an agreement was reached on May 21 to allow the Yankees to play at the Polo Grounds in 1921. Ironically enough, given his recent squabbles with Yankee management, Johnson undoubtedly performed the largest role in convincing Stoneham and McGraw to allow the American League squad to return for another season. It remained clear, however, that the Yankees were still going to construct their own park.[32]

Warding off a knee ailment and a bout of croup, Ruth, that "pale and interesting invalid," on May 23, cracked "his longest home run to date," a towering shot that cleared the right field seats by some 40 feet. Ruth, *The New York Times* exclaimed, had "returned to violent health." This was the fourth occasion in which he had driven a ball out of the Polo Grounds, each further than the one belted by Joe Jackson. A number of long-time spectators at the park insisted that Ruth's latest was "the most vehement smash ever made in a league park," and clearly the "hardest ever hit" at the Polo Grounds. "Bedlam in its wildest hours" reportedly "had nothing on that crowd which had seen a ball hit as only Ruth can hit it." Ruth's first six homers of the season had all been hit at the Polo Grounds, flown over the right field fence, and soared past the lower stands.[33]

An estimated 18,000 spectators witnessed Ruth's wallop, the same number that saw him drive a ball into the upper stand at the Polo Grounds three days later. Ruth, W. O. McGeehan declared, could knock homers into that spot and not simply fire them out of the ballpark. There, the sportswriter chortled, the expenses that Yankee management had "to make for implements used in the national pastime" could be minimized.[34]

The following day, Ruth produced a pair of homers against Boston, propelling New York to a 6-1 victory. Treated to a "royal procession" by the 12,000 fans in attendance at Fenway, "the battering Babe" delivered "wallops that will go down in the baseball history of the Republic," the *Times* insisted. In the process, Ruth tied yet another home run record, as he hit four in the last three games, equaling the mark set by Ned Williamson in 1884. In addition, Ruth "made one of the most brilliant catches ever seen at Fenway Park," racing in front of center fielder Ping Bodie to knock down a vicious liner with his left hand, and then snaring the ball with his bare hand before it fell safely to the ground. The next day saw "the menace of the mastodonic mauler" receive two walks, along with a single, which helped the Yankees prevail by a 4-3 count.[35]

On May 31, both the *Times* and the *Tribune* waxed eloquent about baseball's brightest star. Referring to Ruth's recent slugging barrage, the *Times* predicted that he was likely to "go far beyond the mark which a year ago was regarded as the last word in home run hitting." His 11 homers in May established yet another home run record, surpassing the nine he had crushed the previous July. Should Ruth better his own single season homer total, the *Times* offered, crediting the Polo Grounds' right field wall with that accomplishment would hardly be fair. Most of Ruth's homers to date would have soared out of the park in any major league stadium. Terming Ruth "the greatest attraction in the history of the game," the *Times* declared that "the most valuable ball player the sport has yet produced" made the Yankees a bona fide pennant contender.[36]

The *Tribune's* W. O. McGeehan wrote:

Baseball no longer is the chief attraction at the ball parks. Babe Ruth is. Paraphrasing the late lamented Mr. Shakespeare, Babe Ruth doth bestride the narrow baseball diamonds like a colossus. Undoubtedly, he is the hardest hitter of all time. Even the veterans admit that, the veterans who would never before admit the superiority of the Cobbs, the Speakers and the other more or less modern baseball players in their own particular branches of the intricate national pastime.[37]

McGeehan then referred to a discussion by three of the celebrated Orioles of the late 19th Century. Wilbert Robinson, now managing the Brooklyn Dodgers, insisted that Ruth "could hit a ball twice as hard as any of the old-timers. Delehanty [sic]? Pooh, don't make me laugh! Two of his best wouldn't equal one of Ruth's long hits." Joe Kelly, a Yankee scout readily agreed. "Ain't it the truth? At last the old-timers have to admit that one of the kids has the best of the old fellows beaten." Willie Keeler, a great hitter in his day, chimed in, "The hardest hitter the world has ever seen, and he ought to last, too, for some years to come."[38]

Recalling a comparison drawn between Cobb and Ruth to the latter's detriment, McGeehan considered that "extremely unfair." For his part, he considered Ruth to possess "quite as much baseball intelligence" as the Tiger star.

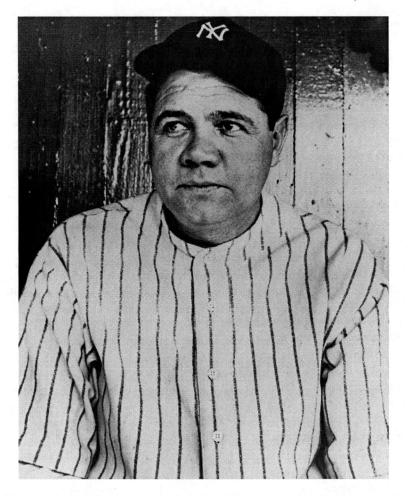

**Babe Ruth, 1920. National Baseball Hall of Fame Library, Cooperstown, N.Y.**

Furthermore, he saw the Yankee slugger as a "far more value" member of his team, which "Ruth is willing to play for and with." While Cobb cavalierly avoided spring training, Ruth "reports cheerfully ... and works just as enthusiastically as the youngest recruit who is trying to earn for himself even a place on the bench."[39]

Wrapping up his analysis, McGeehan declared,

Ruth has considerable force of character. He suddenly became a national idol. Yet it has not spoiled him so far, and I do not think that it will. He does not pose and he does not play to the galleries. Of course, he must glory in his achievement, this boy who was reared in poverty and suddenly shunted into more limelight than has come to many a general, statesman or movie star, but he takes it all gracefully and with a native intelligence that shows character. And force of character is the essential to success, even in professional sports. You will realize this if you will look over the list of the real successes in professional baseball. This Colossus of Baseball is standing on a crude pedestal, but it seems to me a very firm one.[40]

That same day, the Yankees took a pair from the Senators 7-6 and 10-7, running their winning streak to eight. Ruth went hitless in the opener, but made a spectacular, over-the-shoulder catch near the right center field fence, thereby robbing Joe Judge of a seemingly surefire triple. In the second contest, Ruth got his only hit of the day, "plastering the ball against the frieze over the upper right field stands." He produced against Walter Johnson, who had gone the entire 1919 season without relinquishing a homer. Ruth delivered just as fans were crying, "Ruth ain't had a home run all day."[41]

With Bob Shawkey suspended due to an altercation with an umpire, Ruth volunteered to pitch in the Washington series. Batting cleanup, he contributed a single and a double, while lasting four innings, during which time he walked two, gave up three hits, and allowed two runs. As the Yankees pounded the Washington pitchers for 17 hits and 14 runs, Ruth received the victory in his lone pitching performance of the season.[42]

In another doubleheader against the Senators on June 2, Ruth spanked three more home runs, giving him 15 for the year, putting him 12 homers and nearly two-and-a-half months ahead of the previous season's pace; indeed, in 1919, he had failed to reach that total until mid–August. In the first game, won by the Yankees 10-1 to stretch their winning streak to 10, "the unmatchable" Ruth belted two, to the delight of 28,000 patrons at the Polo Grounds. The *Times* referred to "the swaggering swat king" in the following fashion:

A modern Goliath of the bludgeon is Ruth. He is hitting them harder and sending them further every day. He has become a national curiosity, and the sight-seeing pilgrims who only flock into Manhattan are as anxious to rest eyes upon him, as they are to peek at the Woolworth building or the bungalows of the impressive rich on fifth Avenue.[43]

Propelled by Ruth, the New York Yankees, over a seven game span, batted .362, producing 92 hits — 39 were extra bases, including 13 home runs — and 62 runs; more than 108,000 fans had turned out to watch the slugfest. Bob Meusel hit .500, with a double, four triples, and two homers; Roger Peckinpaugh batted .484, topped off by seven doubles, one triple, and a home run; and Duffy Lewis chalked up a .393 mark, with three doubles and a homer. Ruth added a .357 average with three doubles and four home runs; he had now raised his season average to .328. Discussion of a livelier ball abounded, with many pointing to an improved grade of wool and horsehide. Others argued that the ban on freak pitches was having an impact. When asked about "the epidemic of long pastes," American League president Ban Johnson indicated that the baseballs being used during the 1920 season contained "a better quality of horsehide ... we are using Australian wool yarn, plucked from the back of the Australian kangaroo, and everybody knows how far the kangaroo can travel."[44]

In Philadelphia, Thomas Shibe, whose firm, A. J. Reach Co., manufactured all major league baseballs, insisted that the home run surge was not due to any change in the ball's composition. "The baseball used this year," he declared, "is the same as used last year and several seasons before that. The specifications this year called for the same yarn, the same cork centre, the same size and weight of rubber and the same horsehide. It has not been changed one iota and no effort has been made to turn out a livelier ball." Rather, the abolition of the freaks had made the difference. "With all freak deliveries dead and the spitter almost dead, the batsmen are able to hit the ball more solidly."[45]

After besting the Athletics, 12-6, before a crowd of 30,000 at the Polo Grounds, the Yankees slipped into first place, a half game ahead of the Indians. At this early point in the season, Grantland Rice was predicting that Ruth would hit forty homers. On June 13 in Cleveland before 28,000 spectators, "the superslugger" produced his 17th of the season, as the Yankees moved back within a half game of the league-leading Indians; the spectators reportedly "went into spasms of delight over the mammoth slam." The *Times* indicated that "the contagion of Babe Ruth's remarkable popularity spread like wildfire" before the largest crowd ever to congregate in League Park. The 14-0 debacle, in which Shawkey blanked the Indians, proved costly as Duffy Lewis pulled a ligament in his knee, removing him from action for about three weeks. "The ever willing infant," as the *Tribune* referred to Ruth, replaced Lewis in left field. In that game and in the next day's affair against the Indians, Ruth received intentional passes, despite a new rule that attempted to disallow them. Stan Coveleski shut down Murderers' Row, 7-1, putting the Yankees another game behind the Indians.[46]

Sizable crowds and Ruthian heroics again were present as the Yankees traveled to Comiskey Park for a crucial series with the White Sox. New York took the opener, 7-4, as Bob Shawkey outpitched Red Faber and Ruth smacked his 18th. In the next game, the Yankees again prevailed, 7-2, with Carl Mays scattering seven hits while Lefty Williams was rocked for Ruth's 19th home run. That three run shot, W. O. McGeehan reported, was belted "into the teeth of a howling gale from the stockyards" into public playgrounds outside the stadium. "The irresistible Babe," the *Times* indicated, raged like "a young hurricane" to produce the most mammoth clout ever witnessed at

Charles Comiskey's home park. Yankee co-owner T. L. Huston was said to carry "a 'ruthometer,' a machine for the registering of home runs." Purportedly, after Ruth's latest smash, Huston was heard to say, "There isn't any way of keeping count on them. No telling when he will smash them out. It is no season for mathematics."[47]

The third game was also won by the Yankees, as Shawkey outdueled Dickie Kerr, 3-2. Ruth managed only a single in three official at bats and, in the ninth, received a walk, to the dismay of the gathered throng. Patrons supposedly yelled, "Let him hit it" and "began to walk over to the box office to demand their money back." The series finale went to the White Sox, 6-5, as 25,000 fans watched Ruth lapse into semi-consciousness in the second inning after both Buck Weaver's errant toss during a double play attempt and his fist landed on Ruth's head. Dazed, Ruth soon had to leave the game.[48]

\* \* \*

The luminous quality of Ruth's 1920 batting performance was increasingly obvious. Grantland Rice referred to him as "the super-star in an age of stars." In an editorial filed on June 20, W. O. McGeehan declared that "trooping around with the Yankees clinches the conviction that Babe Ruth is a bigger show this year than baseball itself." Sixteen road games had resulted in a turnout of over 200,000, far surpassing what New York had previously drawn in its away games. The revived interest in baseball was a factor, but Ruth, McGeehan wrote, "is to a great extent responsible for the big crowds."[49]

In an interview with Ruth conducted around the same time, *Baseball Magazine*'s F. C. Lane explored the game's greatest phenom. The story began during batting practice at the Polo Grounds with Yankee pitcher Ernie Shore exclaiming, "It's the Babe again! He's poled another one into the bleachers. They'll need to put more timbers under this stand to hold up the crowd that will be out to see him Sunday." Lane contended, "No other diamond hero, past or present, ever swayed the crowd as does this once homeless inmate of a poor boys' industrial school in Baltimore." Whether Ruth caught or muffed a fly ball, Carl Mays suggested, the fans would yell "just as loud." Lane agreed, arguing that "Babe has reached that curious height of fame where the manner in which he parts his hair or ties his shoe-laces have [sic] become matters of public moment." At mid-game, Ruth doubled and Shore noted, "He might just as well have struck out. The crowd doesn't pay to see two-baggers from him. The crowd is just as thirsty for home runs as he is and he eats and sleeps and dreams home runs." After Ruth struck out leading off the eighth, one third of the gathered throng headed for the exits. "Can you imagine that?" asked Mays. "One man out in the eighth and they are through for the day. They know Babe will not come up again and they have seen what they paid to see. When Babe is through, they are through." No literary accolades, Lane offered, demonstrated so eloquently "the tribute to Ruth."[50]

In Lane's estimation, no baseball star had ever shown more brilliantly:

> Big, burly, battering Babe Ruth has overthrown all rivals, overturned all precedents and now monopolizes the game as no other player, past or present, has ever done. Take the giddy speed of George Sisler, the canny craft of Eddie Collins; more, take the peerless player of all time, the Georgia Wizard, Ty Cobb, himself; stand them together in a group on one side and on the other place the rugged, lonely figure of Babe Ruth, and see which group calls forth the lustier yells. As a betting proposition lay your money on Babe Ruth. It may be a triumph of brawn over brain. It may suggest the dominance of mere brute strength over intelligence. It may show a preference for the cave man over the finished artist. It may be what you will. But rest assured it's a fact. Babe Ruth is the uncrowned king of the diamond, the master figure of the baseball season, the big noise in the biggest game on earth.[51]

To Lane, Ruth was like a mountain peak, as he "towers at present above the baseball horizon." His powers, "his amazing talents," appeared limitless:

> He has played the role of giant who, striding brusquely into the well-ordered arena of established custom, has gone about overturning moss-covered precedent, and shattering records. Babe is particularly good at shattering records. His favorite stunt is to break a record so old that it has grown mouldy and crumbly, setting up a brand new one of his own creation in its place and then, in a fit of dissatisfied petulance, thrusting that new-made record roughly one side to make room for a still fresher creation.[52]

Ruth's 1920 accomplishments had proven even more remarkable than those of the previous season. Indeed, they appeared, Lane wrote, "wholly unparalleled almost super-human." His former boss, Jack Dunn, termed Ruth "the greatest natural ball player that ever lived. He's not only a batter that simply can't be equalled (sic), he's a remarkable fielder as well." Tiger manager Hugh Jennings declared that "Ruth is a curious example of one of the best pitchers in the league who is so good in other respects that you can't afford to let him pitch." Ed Barrow, who had managed Ruth in Boston, stated, "I have always thought that Babe had the makings of a remarkable first baseman, if he ever had a chance to show it." Yankee skipper Miller Huggins posed the question, "How shall I describe Babe Ruth's batting? Take all the adjectives there are in the language which could be used to describe a slugger, plaster than all on and then wish there were a few more for good measure. You can't describe him, you can't compare him with anybody else. He's Babe Ruth."[53]

Ruth attempted to explain his own batting prowess. "The stronger a man is and the heavier he is," he indicated, "the harder he can lean on a baseball, and height is something." He acknowledged that he employed probably the heaviest bat in the game, 52 ounces. "My theory is that the bigger the bat the faster they travel, not the bat, I mean, but the ball." Furthermore, "the harder you grip the bat the faster the ball will travel. When I am out after a homer, I try to make mush of this solid ash handle." Proper footwork and eye coordination were also important.[54]

* * *

"The mighty Babe," *Baseball Magazine* declared, was "the huge noise of 1920." He was "the biggest drawing card baseball has known in many seasons, and all through the matchless, magnetic power of the Home Run Drive!" On June 25, 20,000 fans watched as "Mr. George Herman Ruth, home run king and slugger extraordinary," drove "two prodigious circuit clouts" into the cheap seats. *The New York Times* referred to one smash off Boston southpaw Herb Pennock as "the longest and highest ride that a ball has ever had within the Polo Grounds inclosure." Ruth's four-baggers accounted for all the Yankee runs in a 6-3 loss to the Red Sox, putting his season total at 22. New York skipper Miller Huggins and his minions, sportswriter R. J. Kelly suggested, would "probably have to call out the state militia to handle the crowd" likely to jam into the park to watch the Yankees in their upcoming games.[55]

Three days later, W. O. McGeehan predicted that the 1920 Yankees would undoubtedly shatter all attendance records. Attendance was up throughout the majors, but baseball magnates were not wholly pleased by this state of affairs. For as the next season approached, there would likely be many contracts refused by ballplayers seeking big salary increases. McGeehan believed that both players and management made telling points regarding contractual matters. Yankee owners Ruppert and Huston, for instance, had invested heavily in their team when its "following was about the size of a skeleton platoon." They gambled when they purchased Babe Ruth, and paid him a record sum, although there was no guarantee that he could duplicate his 1919 feats. They expended considerable resources in fighting to retain Carl Mays. Having "played the game in a big way ... now they are beginning to see some profits in sight."[56]

But a ballplayer for his part recognized the brevity of a major league career and was "entitled to get what he can get when the getting is good. A played out baseball player is about as dead as a played out mine. The hero of a decade ago has his memories, of course, but he can't eat them." Not surprisingly then, "the tug-of-war will be on," McGeehan noted, "when the springtime comes again, gentle Annie, and let's hope that they don't break the rope."[57]

The same soaring attendance figures foretelling such labor unrest, *The Sporting News* indicated, aptly demonstrated that spectators much preferred free-swinging games to low-scoring contests. Was there any question, the paper asked, about what type of ball had engendered such excitement? "Have the fans shown any signs of deserting Ruth or Sisler or Hornsby as heroes, and flocking to the worship of the pitchers who have put over such rarities as shutout games?" *The Sporting News* bellowed, "On with the hits, and let the fans be merry."[58]

On July 7, with the Yankees primed for a lengthy home stand, Ruth escaped injury when his new automobile crashed as he ran it off the road after leaving Washington for Philadelphia. Two days later, Ruth, notwithstanding a sprained wrist, produced his 25th homer of the season, as New York defeated Detroit 9-3. Prior to the game, the Knights of Columbus awarded fellow member Ruth a diamond-studded watch fob. Teammate Ping Bode joked, "If any one handed me a cluster of sparklers like that, it would be my luck to have them turn out to be ice. The best I get for hitting home runs is a box of socks." To date, Ruth had hit 13 homers against right-handers, 12 off south-paws.[59]

The Yankees had now played half their scheduled games, with Ruth on a pace to hit 50 home runs. They stood at 50-27, a half game behind the Indians, whose 49-25 mark topped the league. The defending American League champion White Sox were in third with a 45-29 record, four full games in back of Cleveland.

Ruth smacked his 27th homer on July 11 and received three walks, leading the Yankees to a 6-5 victory over Detroit. A large crowd watched as the "king of all home run hitters and greatest walker since the palmy days of Dan O'Leary and Edward Payson Weston, starred in both specialties." In the first inning, Ruth walked on four pitches from Howard Ehmke, drawing the wrath of the "disgusted fans." After Ruth homered in the third, he was again walked on four pitches in the fifth inning, as "another howl of derision swept from the stands to the pitching mound." After the same result occurred in the seventh, Ehmke was razzed even more loudly. As the *Times* put it, "Every last mortal in that gathering of 35,000 wanted to see Babe hit, and the idea of one man blocking the will of the populace was more than the crowd could bear. Ehmke reached a new mark in extracting jeers, hoots and hisses from a Polo Grounds crowd."[60]

Appropriately enough, Ruth's record-tying 29th homer on July 15 enabled the Yankees to defeat the St. Louis Browns 13-10 in the 11th inning of a slugfest. Fans poured out of the stands to greet him. "The epoch-making clout" landed some three feet from beneath the top of the grand stand roof and no more than six feet from the end of the stand. It was the first hit allowed under a new league rule that afforded the batter a homer even if a runner ahead of him scored the winning run. Ruth's pace remained far ahead of 1919, when he had hit but 11 at the same stage of the season.[61]

"Amid a deafening din such as only 28,000 delirious fans can make," Ruth shattered the 30 home run mark on July 19 in the opener of a double-header against the White Sox. Ruth appeared just as pleased as the crowd, the *Times* reported:

> While the fans howled in glee, tossed hats around the stand in reckless aban-don and made the big stand a mass of waving arms, Ruth completed his jour-ney to the plate and then beamed back with a smile that spurred the crowd on to a great exertion, if that were possible. Doffing his cap, the conventional response which usually stills a cheering crowd of fans, had no effect here. Sev-eral times on his way to the bench Ruth bowed his acknowledgments, but the din continued after he disappeared in the dugout. His march to left field at the close of the inning was the signal for another outburst, and, the applause was renewed when he came in after the White Sox had been retired in the fourth inning.

In the ninth inning, Ruth delivered off Dickie Kerr once again, but the White Sox prevailed 8-5, after losing the first game 8-2 to Bob Shawkey. The four day affair with the White Sox ended on July 20, as a record 128,000 specta-tors witnessed the two teams split the series.[62]

With their third straight victory over the Indians, triggered by Ruth's 33rd homer, the Yankees, on July 23, briefly took over the top spot in the league standings. Cleveland rebounded in the series finale, as "an army of base-ball fans, numbering more than 50,000" sought admission into the Polo Grounds. With some 15,000 turned away, 37,000 watched as the Indians, allowing only single-run homers by Meusel and Ruth, won 4-2.[63]

In the Yankees's 100th game of the season, Ruth added his 36th home run, as New York pounded the Browns at Sportsman's Park 19-3. Heading the Yankee 21 hit parade was Ruth's "titanic larup over the right-field bleach-ers." The *Times* reported that "the slam was the biggest ever seen in this neck of the woods." The following day, Browns hitters returned the favor, push-ing around Yankee pitchers in a 13-8 shellacking that saw Ruth hit his 37th.[64]

On August 1, a record 40,000 showed up at Comiskey Park to watch Ed Cicotte and the White Sox defeat the Yankees 3-0. The August 2 edition of *The New York Times* indicated that the New York Yankees were now the "great-est drawing card in baseball history." Attendance marks had been broken in five American League cities and nearly equaled in another. In each case, the visiting team was Miller Huggins's squad, featuring Carl Mays, Bob Shawkey, Bob Meusel, and, of course, Babe Ruth.[65]

A crowd of 25,000 saw Ruth belt his 38th homer of the season on August 2, as the Yankees routed Lefty Williams. While Jack Quinn tossed a shutout,

Ruth was again the fan favorite, with the bleacher crowd according him a rousing reception. His home run ball, moreover, was tossed back to him; he returned the favor by throwing a new ball into the stands.[66]

On August 6, Ruth surpassed the heretofore unimaginable 40 homer run barrier in an 11-7 victory over the Tigers. As 10,000 fans at Navin field "howled with glee," a pair of "man-sized home runs" were delivered by the "human howitzer."[67]

* * *

Ten days later, in the midst of a contest between the Yankees and Indians, Cleveland shortstop Ray Chapman was killed by a pitch that crushed in part of his skull, the errant throw tossed by Carl Mays, known for his underhand delivery and nasty disposition. Many experts reasoned that the blow would prove crippling for the Indians.[68]

The pennant race, which saw Cleveland, Chicago, and New York bunched tightly together at the top of the standings, remained one of the tightest in American League history. Not surprisingly, Speaker, who had been batting near .400 all season, experienced depression but continued to spearhead the Indian squad. The White Sox benefited from excellent pitching by Cicotte, Williams, Faber, and Kerr, and the powerful sticks of Jackson, Collins, and Weaver. The Yankees, led by Ruth's phenomenal slugging, relied on quality pitching from Shawkey, Quinn, and Mays, whose mound work appeared unaffected by the tragedy.

*Baseball Magazine* increasingly featured Ruth in a series of essays and editorials. Shortly after the Chapman beaning, the publication celebrated the Yankee star:

> The Busting Babe has become a baseball idol such as the game's whole history cannot show. He's the Whole Works, the Main Squeeze, and the Big Attraction. In other words, it has been settled, for all time to come, that the American public is nuttier over The Home Run than the Clever Fielding or the Hitless Pitching. Viva el Home Run, and two times viva el Babe Ruth, exponent of the Home Run, and overshadowing run!

The New York Yankees, it was said, could only be referred to as "Babe Ruth and Company" during the summer of 1920. Yet even without Ruth, *Baseball Magazine* asserted, the Yankees would have been recognized "as notable sluggers."[69]

In an interview that appeared in *Baseball Magazine*, White Sox catcher Ray Schalk indicated "that there isn't any way to fool Babe Ruth. ... If he has a batting weakness, I don't know what it is. And further, I will go on record with the statement that there is absolutely no rule or set of rules which can

**Babe Ruth with Red Grange, circa 1920. National Baseball Hall of Fame Library, Cooperstown, N.Y.**

be laid down as a guide for pitching to Babe Ruth." Indeed, in Schalk's estimation, Ruth was "the most terrific slugger who ever lived." Schalk found it difficult to conceive that any other hitter could accomplish the feats that Ruth had. Furthermore, "the only man who can break Babe Ruth's records," he decreed, "is Babe Ruth himself."[70]

*The New York Times*, as it had throughout the 1920 American League race, continued to extol Ruth's batting feats. The report of an August 19th contest with the Indians that produced yet another Ruthian clout began in the following manner:

> His Royal Nibs, Babe Ruth, the Bazoo of Bang, edified a crowd of 18,000 spectators at the Polo Grounds yesterday with his forty-third home run of the season. It was a splendiferous spank and came in the fourth inning off Ray Caldwell. The ball disappeared over the roof of the right field stand and landed somewhere in Manhattan field. ...
>
> It is some time since Babe promulgated one of his excursion wallops on the home terrace and the overjoyed crowd sent forth great volumes of vocal approval. Hats went up in the air, cheers echoed over Harlem and there was a riot of noise which lasted several minutes.
>
> So great was the excitement following the home run that it killed Theodore Sturm of Bellrose, L.I. who was sitting in the box back of third base. He succumbed to heart disease.[71]

Troubled by an infected right wrist that put him out of action in late August, Ruth had added only one more homer before belting a pair against the Red Sox on September 4. "The mighty Behemoth of Bangs" had now hit more home runs than any other player in a season of organized ball. In 1895, Perry Werden had stroked 45 homers for the Western League's Minneapolis franchise. After his slow start, Ruth had pounded the ball so consistently that his batting average also stood at .378, tied with Joe Jackson for the third best mark in the league, behind only George Sisler and Tris Speaker.[72]

The Indians, White Sox, and Yankees remained bunched at the top of the American League standings as September unfolded. To Cleveland catcher Chet Thomas, New York appeared "like the figure of a big, bulky batter thundering out home run drives every day or so to the end of the chapter." Already possessing "enough great clubbers to cause any team trouble in Peckinpaugh, Pipp, Bob Meusel, Ping Bodie and the rest," the Yankees, Thomas suggested, "added to this a whole carload of dynamite when they signed Babe Ruth." Before the season began, he predicted, to the amusement of various friends, that Ruth would smack 40 homers. Thomas admitted,

> I am not so certain now that Babe is human. ... For Babe can hit anything, even though he isn't expecting it. I have seen him shift his swing when he thought a fast ball was coming and drive a curve out of the lot. He hits a ball so hard that it does things which no other batter can make it do. Line drives from his bat over the infielders heads will frequently take a quick drop to the ground and carom off at all kinds of freak angles. If he hits the ball on the ground, it seldom bounds true, because he puts such a tremendous amount of English on it with that big war club of his and the infielder who tries to stop

it is taking all kinds of chances with broken fingers and broken shins. The outfielders have to play so far back that a single from Babe is good for a double any day, but what are those outfielders to do? If they play in he will knock the ball so far over their heads that he will get to third or perhaps go all the way around on the hit. He is a problem which nobody can solve.[73]

Thomas then noted that he had argued with other players about Ruth:

I said Ruth was the greatest batter in the game. No one could take exception to that. I further said that he was the greatest batter who ever lived. There was no dissenting voice. But then I got a little ambitious and claimed that no batter in the future would ever be able to equal him. There some of the boys took me up and said I was biting off more than I could chew. That may be so. I am not a prophet. ... But I wish someone would describe to me just the kind of batter along in 1940 or maybe 1999, who will take Babe Ruth's record away from him. If he ever happens he will be some freak. It would take a man 7 feet tall, weighing 300 pounds and able to lift a piano with either hand to drive a baseball any further than Babe Ruth can drive it.[74]

* * *

To the Yankees' chagrin, outfielder Ping Bodie's season ended on September 8, thanks to an ankle injury suffered in an exhibition contest. Bodie was batting .295, with 26 doubles and 12 triples having helped to produce 79 RBIs. New York suffered another setback the following day, losing a 10-4 bout against the Indians, despite Ruth's 47th homer of the year.[75]

That same day, in the midst of breaking news about purported gambling escapades involving major league baseball, another story had Ruth and three teammates seriously injured in either an automobile or train wreck. Gamblers, it was reported, had put out such news to increase betting odds in a game pitting the Yankees against the Indians.[76]

That crucial series began with New York perched just below Cleveland and Chicago in the American League standings. The Indians won the opener 10-4, with Ruth getting his 47th homer; the Yankees rebounded to take the next game, 6-1, as he hammered his 48th, a two-run shot, in the first inning. He crushed his 49th in a 4-2 victory over the Tigers on September 13.[77]

Three consecutive defeats to the White Sox that soon followed all but doomed the Yankees' pennant hopes. The last game, a 15-9 slugfest, saw 43,000 spectators moan — notwithstanding Chicago's quest for another league title — as Ruth received a base on balls and managed only a single in four official at-bats. Ruth had enabled the Yankees to remain competitive, Joe Vila underscored, thanks to "his wonderful batting and influence." Ruth had also "proved to be the biggest paying investment in the history of baseball and he deserves all the popularity that he now enjoys." Thanks to him, the Yankees had reaped greater financial riches during the 1920 season "than any other major league club since baseball was born."[78]

W. O. McGeehan, writing in *The New York Tribune* on September 20, reported that Ruth was displaying his finest qualities "not as the home run hitter and the great ball player, but as a man." On a recent western road trip, Ruth had taken along Brother Matthias and the boys' band from St. Mary's Industrial School in Baltimore to raise building funds for the institution, which had recently experienced a devastating fire. While the band held concerts, Ruth served as a drawing card. In the midst of a boat ride from Cleveland to Detroit, Ruth had affirmed, "I want to say that this is a great school. It did a lot for me when I was just as little as the littlest chap in that band. Brother Mathias taught me how to play baseball and everything else that I know. I am never going to forget what they did for me and I am never going to forget my school." To McGeehan, "this was Babe Ruth at his best and his biggest, and as he spoke with that simple earnestness and utter self-consciousness he did not seem unlike the sainted rail-splitter himself."[79]

In the first game of a doubleheader at the Polo Grounds against the Senators on September 24, Babe connected in the opener, cracking the 50 home run mark; he then added another home run in the second contest, which helped New York win 2-1, to salvage a split. The *Times* reported the historic event:

> A crowd of 25,000 fans blazed into hysteria when the Mauling Monarch passed the fiftieth mark and gave the slugger a whoop and a hurrah he will never forget. The crowd was in full cry as Ruth cantered over the plate, smiling a smile as broad as his massive shoulders and raising his cap to the populace. It was one of those events in sport which will furnish chatter for years to come.
>
> Baseball has never before developed a figure of such tremendously picturesque proportions as this home-run king of the Yankees. With no weapon but a primitive club, he has manipulated it in a manner which would make the famed clubbers of the Stone Age look like experts in battledore and shuttlecock. Ruth has hit almost as many home runs as Heinz has pickles. In fact he is a greater pickler than the world has ever before known.[80]

As the pennant chase's final days unfolded, the Yankees remained stuck in the same position they had occupied for some time, just short of both the Indians and White Sox. As stories of a World Series scandal broke, Ruth hit another pair of homers to lead New York over Philadelphia, 3-0. On September 29, the Yankees' season wound to a close, as New York took two from Connie Mack's ball club, with Ruth hitting number 54 in the opener.[81]

The Yankees ended up with a franchise best mark of 95-59, which left them a game behind White Sox and three back of the Indians. Collectively, the Yankees batted .280, had a league-best .426 slugging percentage, and belted a league record 115 home runs, far surpassing the Browns' total of 50 round-trippers. The Phillies led the National League with 64 homers, topped by Cy Williams's 15, which afforded him individual honors. New York second baseman Del Pratt batted .314 and drove in 97 runs. Third baseman-outfielder Bob Meusel hit .328, with 83 RBIs in an abbreviated campaign. First baseman Wally Pipp and shortstop Roger Peckinpaugh each scored over 100 runs. Yankee pitchers excelled too, leading the league with a 3.31 mark. The controversial Carl Mays won 26 games and had a .703 winning percentage, both second best in the American League, and tossed six shutouts, more than any other pitcher. Bob Shawkey went 20-13, was third in strikeouts with 126, and had the league's lowest ERA, 2.45. Jack Quinn added a 18-10 record, while Rip Collins was 14-8.

But the individual star of the 1920 season was unquestionably Babe Ruth. W. A. Phelon, writing in *Baseball Magazine*, referred to Ruth as "the Goliath, the Sampson, the Superman of the season. He gave the final proof that the American public worships The Solid Bliff. Even as the fans adore a knockout fighter, so they adore the man who can crash the home run drives. And Babe certainly crashed 'em."[82]

W. J. Macbeth of *The New York Tribune* deemed Ruth "the most spectacular player of all time." He then declared, "Never before in the history of baseball and seldom in any other sport has arisen such a colossus of wonderment and veneration as the big fence." By contrast, John B. Foster, the editor of *Spalding's Official Base Ball Guide*, spoke of Ruth's influence on the game:

> It was the most marked demonstration of personal achievement arousing popular enthusiasm since the days when Mathewson was riding on the crest of the wave of public fervor, and it was far more forceful in effect than the triumph of Mathewson, because an heroic batter, by the very nature of his skill, calls for the greatest acclaim. The time was ripe for him to come. The war was over. Base Ball was good but not better than good. It rolled in a rut and Ruth lifted it out of the rut.

Through it all, Irving B. Sanborn noted, Ruth "remained the same likeable, boyish athlete he was, and by that very fact made himself hosts of new friends and admirers."[83]

# Chapter Twelve

# A Season of Fortitude: Tris's and Robbie's Men of Summer

The 1920 major league season, both glorious and troubled, did not conclude with a league or World Series title for Babe Ruth or Buck Weaver; however, before it ended, Rube Foster had captured the championship for the Negro National League's inaugural campaign. While Wilbert Robinson's Brooklyn Dodgers grabbed the National League pennant, the American League was won by Tris Speaker's Cleveland Indians, who went on to take the World Series in the seventh game of a best-of-nine format. Breaking the Boston-Philadelphia-Chicago stranglehold on the American League pennant, Cleveland had overcome a bundle of not inconsiderable impediments. These included Ruth's record-shattering performance and the New York Yankees' resurgence; an exceptional, but divided and soiled ball club in the form of Charles Comiskey's Chicago White Sox; and the death of one of the league's brightest and best-loved stars at the hand of a player who was perhaps the least-liked in the majors. Then, seemingly short-handed, the Indians, with their great star and manager warding off severe depression, bested the Dodgers, who featured a top-flight pitching staff and had won their second title for Robinson in five years.

In the tightest three-team race since the 1908 season, the Indians, with a 98-56 record, lived up to their pre-season favorites' role to capture the 1920 American League crown. In the process, they edged out the strife-torn White

Sox by two games and the Ruth-led Yankees by three. The Indians were spearheaded both off and on the field by center fielder Speaker, who batted above the .400 mark for much of the season, before cresting at .388, finishing as runner-up in the league batting race to George Sisler. The league leader in doubles with 50, Speaker also was second to Ruth in runs scored with 137 and on base percentage, .483, fourth in total bases, 310, and slugging average, .562, and fifth in hits, 214. Among his 69 extra base hits were 11 triples and eight homers, which helped to produce 107 runs batted in. Also surpassing the 100 RBI total were third baseman Larry Gardner and outfielder Elmer Smith. Cleveland compiled a team batting average of .303, with Gardner, Smith, outfielder Charlie Jamieson, catcher Steve O'Neill, and the late Ray Chapman also bettering the .300 mark. Amazingly enough, the Indians failed to take the team batting title, losing that honor to the fourth-place St. Louis Browns, who batted .309, thanks largely to Sisler's batting feats. Cleveland's 35 homers were well back of New York's 115 and behind Chicago's 37.

Indian pitchers were also league runner-ups in earned run average, posting a 3.41 record, behind the Yankees' 3.31 mark but ahead of the White Sox's 3.59 total. Cleveland's and the American League pitcher-of-the-year was righthander Jim Bagby, who won 31 games, had a league best .721 won-loss percentage, 48 games pitched, 30 complete games, and 339⅔ innings thrown. Nearly as good was righthander Stan Coveleski, whose 24 wins were just edged out by the Yankees' Carl Mays for the runner-up spot, and who led the league in strikeouts, 133, opponents' batting average, .243, and fewest hits per game, 8.11. The third Indian 20 game winner was yet another right-hander, Ray Caldwell, who tossed 20 complete games, and produced a .667 winning percentage. The lone productive southpaw on the Cleveland pitching staff was Duster Mails, a late call-up from the minors, who went 7-0 with a 1.85 ERA in nine appearances.

The National League race was tight for much of the season, before the Dodgers, with their 93-61 record, pulled away from the Giants and Reds, who finished seven and 10½ games back, respectively. By all accounts, the senior circuit's baseballs were not quite as lively as the American League's although its batting marks were also edging upward. The sixth-place Cardinals had the league's top team batting average, .289, led by Rogers Hornsby's .370, but the Dodgers' .277 tied them for second best with the Reds. The long-ball remained the exception in the National League, with the Dodgers producing only 28 home runs, topped by outfielder Zach Wheat's nine, the league's sixth highest total. Wheat led Brooklyn in batting with a .328 average, fourth in the National League. Outfielder Hy Myers hit .304 and led the team with 36 doubles, 22 triples, and 80 runs batted in. The only other Dodger regular batting over .300 was first baseman Ed Konetchy.

Along with Robinson's stewardship, pitching was Brooklyn's strength, as attested by a league-best 2.62 ERA. The 26-year-old spitballing right-hander

Burleigh Grimes was the staff ace, posting a 23-11 mark, with the league's best won-loss percentage, .676, in addition to a 2.22 ERA, 303⅔ innings pitched, 25 complete games, 131 strikeouts, and five shutouts. Other contributors included 16 game winner Jeff Pfeffer and Leon Cadore with his 15 victories, plus Al Mamaux and southpaws Sherry Smith and Rube Marquard, who all won in double figures. Smith's 1.85 ERA was better even than league leader's Pete Alexander, but he lacked the requisite number of innings to qualify for the title.

The 1920 World Series, won by the Indians in seven games, proved to be exciting, nevertheless. It featured three victories by Cleveland pitcher Coveleski, the first home run in World Series competition by a hurler, Bagby, the initial grand-slam, hit by the Indians' Elmer Smith, 15⅔ consecutive scoreless innings thrown by Mails, and the only unassisted triple play in post-season competition, turned by Cleveland second baseman Bill Wambsganss.

* * *

Following the close of the 1919 season, the Cleveland Indians eagerly awaited the next year. Since the addition of Tris Speaker to the ball club in 1916, Cleveland had moved out of the league's cellar to become a contender over the course of the past three years. Speaker's brilliant initial campaign with the Indians, in which his league best .386 batting average finally broke Ty Cobb's near decade-long stranglehold on the American League crown, had only lifted Cleveland to sixth place. Yet the Indians' 77-77 record was 19 games better than the previous year's mark and placed Cleveland but 14 games behind the pennant-winning Red Sox. In 1917, Speaker's .352 average, coupled with Bagby's 23 wins, propelled the Indians into third place, with an 88-66 record. The following season, Cleveland, led by Speaker and Coveleskie, who produced 22 wins, finished in second place, only 2½ games in back of the White Sox. Then in 1919, the Indians had ended up in second place, 3½ games behind the American League champion White Sox. After Speaker had replaced Lee Fohl as manager, the Indians, winning at a .650 clip, compiled a 39-21 record. Not surprisingly, particularly given Chicago's disastrous performance in the World Series, expectations ran high for Cleveland as 1920 arrived. Even New York's acquisition of Babe Ruth failed to dampen the Indians' high hopes.[1]

The Indians appeared remarkably well-balanced, with a strong everyday lineup, good reserves, and a fine pitching staff. First baseman-outfielder Joe Harris refused to come to terms with Indian management, but Doc Johnston was coming off a season when he batted .305. Second baseman Bill Wambsganss added speed on the base paths and a solid .278 average. Third sacker Larry Gardner, another .300 hitter, had led the Indians in runs batted in with 79. Shortstop Ray Chapman, along with Speaker the heart of the team, had batted .300 with ten triples. Elmer Smith had hit .278, while Speaker, in a down year for him, batted .296, with 38 doubles, 12 triples, and 83 runs scored. Charlie Jamieson appeared ready to replace the fading Jack Graney in the outfielder, while catcher Steve O'Neill, one of the game's finest, had hit .289, with 35 doubles. Former Red Sox pitching great and now outfielder Smokey Joe Wood was expected to be the key reserve, along with a soon-to-be benched Graney.

Indian pitchers, as a group, looked equal to most any staff in the league. Coveleski, a back-to-back 20-game winner, remained the ace, while Bagby had won 17 games during the past two years, following a 23 game season in 1917. Guy Morton and 20-year-old George Uhle each had won 10 games in 1919, while Elmer Myers and Ray Caldwell were expected to contribute as well.

One obvious advantage Cleveland had over ballclubs, and particularly Chicago, was the absence of team disharmony. By all accounts, owner Jim Dunn had cultivated a good relationship with his players. Consequently, there was little discussion of holdouts within the Indian camp — Harris was the major exception — in contrast to both participants in the last World Series and most other major league squads. Referring to the Yankees, Speaker was heard to exclaim, "We'll be fighting them every inch of the way for that old flag. If I get a good lefthander we'll breeze home."[2]

In late March, Speaker expressed some concerns about being the top-heavy favorite. While convinced that his squad was the American League's finest, Speaker attempted to quash the notion that the Indians couldn't lose. Yankee outfielder Duffy Lewis, sidelined because of blood poisoning, visited the Indians' camp and informed Tris, "Mighty fine looking ball club you have, Spoke." The Indian manager responded, "There you go. Trying to make it tough for me by saying we ought to win the pennant, I suppose." Lewis retorted, "Well, the team that beats you out will win it." Tris even felt compelled to rein in Indian owner Dunn who was gushing about his team's chances. "There's another one of them, helping put the handicap on us," Speaker indicated, before taking Dunn aside to talk with him.[3]

* * *

Prior to the start of the 1920 season, most prognosticators saw the Brooklyn Dodgers as a fourth or fifth place team only. Wilbert Robinson's team had surprised the experts before, taking the 1916 season, led by the big bats of first baseman Jake Daubert and outfielder Zach Wheat and right-handed Jeff Pfeffer, a 25 game winner with a 1.91 ERA. After dropping the World Series in five games to the Boston Red Sox, the Dodgers had plummeted into seventh place in 1917. The following year, Brooklyn again finished in the second division, despite the fine pitching performance of Burleigh Grimes, who produced a 19-9 record with a 2.13 earned run average. Once again, Daubert and Wheat had bettered the .300 mark, with Wheat, who hit .335, winning the league batting title. That fifth place finish was repeated in 1919, placing the Dodgers a full 27 games behind the Cincinnati Reds, despite a .263 team batting average, tied for second best in the league. Like Speaker, Wheat slid below the .300 level, hitting .297, with 11 triples. Outfielder Hy Myers led the team in batting with a .307 mark and was tops in the league with 14 triples and 73 runs batted in. New first baseman Ed Konetchy hit .298; second baseman Jimmy Johnston, .281; shortstop Ivy Olson, .278, with a league best 590 at bats and 164 hits; and outfielder Tommy Griffith, .281. Third base and catching had proven to be trouble spots, but Robinson was about to reshape his squad, relying on reserve infielder Pete Kilduff and catcher Otto Miller.

Jeff Pfeffer, returned from military service, regained his spot as Brooklyn's top pitcher, devising a 17-13 record with a 2.66 ERA. Leon Cadore was 14-12, with an even better 2.37 earned run average. Burleigh Grimes, experiencing arm troubles, had slumped to 10-11, while Al Mamaux was 10-12 with a 2.67 ERA. Other significant contributions had been made by southpaws Clarence Mitchell and Sherry Smith, as the Dodger pitchers produced a team 2.73 ERA, one of the top marks in the National League. Lefty Rube Marquard had missed most of the season with a broken leg.

Unlike the Indians but similar to the White Sox and Reds, Brooklyn experienced some labor disputes. Cincinnati, in 1919, had a $93,000 player payroll, but $165,000 was being demanded heading into the new season, with batting champ Edd Roush a prominent holdout. Zack Wheat and Hy Myers, Brooklyn's heaviest hitters, both threatened to remain on their farms where they anticipated large profits. Tommy Griffith also indicated that his business operations were succeeding too nicely for him to return to baseball. By early March, with Wheat, Myers, and Griffith now in camp, the Dodgers' two-time 20-game winner Pfeffer still had failed to come to terms. There was talk of an impending trade with the Cardinals, with Pfeffer to be swapped for left-hander Ferdie Schupp and an outfielder. The other major topic involved Robinson's decision to try out Jimmy Johnston at third base.[4]

Similar to the Indians, the Dodgers or Superbas as they were often called had a generally happy pre-season, including a successful series against the Yankees. As Opening Day approached, *The New York Tribune* analyzed Brooklyn's chances. In Grantland Rice's words,

> Brooklyn had a weird combination for a second division club. She had a club that tied the champion Reds in team batting with a fine pitching staff, a mixture that ordinarily is always good for 1, 2, 3, even with other pronounced weaknesses.

Infield loopholes permitted many a game to drift through, but this season finds Robby with a better looking club in every way—a stronger outfield, a more settled infield and enough good pitchers to carry two ball clubs through this year.

Thus, Rice presciently suggested that "Brooklyn has a great chance this season if she will only take it, if her entries are willing to hustle and make a fight of it." He could not foresee how "a hard hitting club with a fine pitching staff" would fall back into second division.[5]

Robinson, Ray McCarthy noted, was "relying on his pitching staff to bring him another pennant this year." The Dodger manager pointed to his pitchers' impressive showing in an extended pre-season series with the Yankees, while declaring that they would become even more potent down the road. Robinson was counting on Mamaux, Cadore, Grimes, Pfeffer, and Smith to win at least 15 games apiece.[6]

* * *

Both the Indians and Dodgers got off to quick starts on April 14, Cleveland blanking St. Louis 5-0 and Brooklyn squashing Philadelphia 9-2; no home runs were hit in either contest. Stan Coveleski struck out seven and gave up only five hits to the Browns, shutting down the heart of the lineup in a game that lasted 1 hour and 35 minutes. George Sisler and Baby Doll Jacobson both went hitless in four at-bats and Jack Tobin and Ken Williams each produced solitary hits in a like number of plate appearances. For the Indians, Ray Chapman, Elmer Smith, Doc Johnston, Steve O'Neill, and Coveleskie all knocked out a pair of hits.[7]

In a contest that lasted seven minutes longer than the Cleveland-St. Louis affair, Leon Cadore scattered eight hits while beating the Phillies. The Dodgers, *The New York Times* reported, "displayed the same vim that had marked their preliminary campaign." Brooklyn battered around Philadelphia Eppa Rixey, led by Ivy Olson, Zach Wheat, and Ed Konetchy, who got two hits apiece, and Hy Myers, who belted a triple and scored three runs.[8]

After the first 2½ weeks of the season, Cleveland had amassed a 9-3 record, which placed it just behind Chicago and surprising Boston in the American League standings. Over in the National League, Brooklyn stood at 8-4, one game behind front-running Cincinnati. The Dodgers' last bout had ended in a stalemate that was called for darkness. The most remarkable features of the 1-1 game were its length and the role played by starting pitchers Cadore of Brooklyn and Joe Oeschger of Boston; the two had just waged an 11 inning duel, won by Cadore a week and a half earlier. The latest contest lasted a record 26 innings, all of which were hurled by Cadore and Oeschger. After the Dodgers scored to open the fifth inning, the Braves knotted the score in the bottom of the sixth. From that point forth, goose-eggs went up on the scoreboard. Brooklyn managed just nine hits, Boston 15.[9]

While Tris Speaker's 1919 performance on the playing field had been disappointing — it was the first time in a full season that he had failed to crack the .300 mark — his current play was sensational. Grantland Rice, in his column for *The New York Tribune*, called attention to that fact on May 6. Since becoming a regular for the Red Sox in 1909, Speaker had become, Rice contended, "the greatest outfielding star in baseball, ranked by many as the greatest outfielder, from a defensive viewpoint, that ever played the game." Tris possessed an uncanny ability not only to go after the ball but to position himself. A brilliant hitter as well, Speaker in 1916, his first year with the Indians, had interrupted Ty Cobb's batting championship run. At present, he was performing a new role, as player-manager of the Cleveland Indians. While a decade earlier, Frank Chance, Fred Clarke, and others had held such twin roles, Tris was now "the last field manager left." The Phillies' Gavvy Cravath was also a player-manager, but at 39 had relegated himself to a subordinate role on the bench. As Rice put it, "Speaker alone is leading his team, and out there absorbing base hits and delivering winning blows at one and the same time."[10]

Speaker, Rice indicated, seemed certain to succeed as the Indians' field boss. After he took control of the squad the previous year, it had performed superbly. Early into his first full year as Cleveland's manager, Rice declared, "Speaker has had his machine working smoothly. He has had his men hustling in an age where hard work seems to have gone out of fashion and any extra effort is held to be old-fashioned and not worth while." Thus,

> The delegate from Cleveland, Ohio, and Hubbard City, Tex., is proving himself to be a manager of rare merit.
>
> The recipe is simple — to know baseball and to know how to lead men. Speaker is well fixed both ways. He had keen intelligence, a lot of magnetism, and he has studied his profession as closely as the oldtimers did when baseball was at least 50 per cent sport.
>
> And unless he has some bad luck he will more than likely give Cleveland the first pennant she has ever known and thereby take his place in Ohio history with an Irishman named Pat Moran.[11]

At the season's one month mark, Cleveland was leading the American League with a 16-6 record, which placed it 1½ games ahead of still surprising Boston, and four up on Chicago. Over in the National League, the Reds were on top with a 15-9 record, 1½ games in front of the Braves, and two ahead of the Pirates and Dodgers, who had amassed 11-9 totals.

Even the weather, which caused postponements, seemed to be working in Cleveland's favor. Rainouts enabled Speaker to turn to his two big arms,

Coveleski and Bagby, and their victory totals continuing piling up. Still, during the early season, the Indians appeared to rely on heavy hitting. In a nine game stretch between May 29 and June 4, Cleveland pummeled opposing pitchers for 66 runs and 110 base hits; their opponents did almost as well, collecting 52 scores and 108 hits. Even Coveleski appeared to falter and, other than Bagby, the Indian pitchers had fared poorly.[12]

Prior to the games on Sunday, June 6, Cleveland maintained a now half game lead over the Yankees. The Indians were stationed at 27-15, the Yankees at 27-16. Boston had begun to fall off the pace, but still held the third position at 22-17. The White Sox were only in fourth place, with their 23-19 record placing them four full games back of the Indians. With their 24-15 mark, the Dodgers had rushed to the top of the National League standings, mere percentage points ahead of the 25-16 Reds. Lusty batting averages were being recorded by hitters in both leagues, with Speaker's .380 leading the American and Rogers Hornsby's .392 the best in the National. Indian first baseman Johnston was hitting .374, putting him third behind Chicago's Joe Jackson. Shortstop Ray Chapman was batting .323. Zach Wheat, at .309, was the only Dodger hitter over the .300 plateau. Bagby possessed a 9-1 record, tying him for the league lead in victories with the White Sox's Lefty Williams.[13]

At the season's midpoint, both the Indians and Dodgers maintained first place in tight pennant races. Cleveland's 51-26 record placed it a half-game ahead of New York, while the White Sox were four back. Brooklyn had a 44-32 record, which put it a game on top of the Reds. Phelon viewed Cleveland as "playing steady, relentless ball," topped by Speaker's "terrific batting." The Indians, Phelon argued, required "one new pitcher, if a real winner," to "cinch the flag." However, lacking such a hurler, "Cleveland, though still a logical winner," he warned, "will have a rough road to tread." It was precisely "great pitching," Phelon declared, that had "brought Brooklyn to the front and may keep Robbie's people there." He asked, "What other club in either league can show such a front of pitchers? Men who were way off-grade last season, or were stiffened by war-drill, have come back better than ever; injured men have recovered; there isn't a bad pitcher in the flock, and Robbie has seven of them going at a winning clip!" Helping too was "the rejuvenation of the ancient Konetchy," the Dodger first baseman who had "been massacring the ball, pounding with direful vigor, and when the hits counted."[14]

In Speaker's estimation, the White Sox remained the team to beat. A still confident Speaker told *The Sporting News*,

> The Indians are the best club in the league, and I can't see how the White Sox or the Yanks will beat them out of the pennant. You'll notice I mention Chicago first and New York second. Well, that's just the way I have doped them all along. I figured if the Sox had the harmony they would be harder to beat than the Yanks.

If we come home within two games of the lead after this Eastern trip we'll make them both go some to beat us. I don't want to claim any pennants in July, and I don't want anyone to think I am over-confident, but I honestly believe we will be out in front by seven or eight games on the first of September. Then — well, they will have their work cut out for them to catch us.[15]

As for Speaker, who had recently established a new major league record with 11 consecutive hits, he continued to set the pace for the front-running Indians. By the end of July, Speaker had taken over the top spot in the American League batting race, with a blistering .413 average. Bunched together, but some 20 points behind, were Babe Ruth, George Sisler, and Joe Jackson. The pennant chases remained tight too, with the Indians two games ahead of the Yankees and 4½ up on the White Sox; the Dodgers stood 3½ in front of the Reds.[16]

More and more, Cleveland's pitching began to improve, with Ray Caldwell and Guy Morton beginning to follow the example set by Bagby and Coveleski. The Indians continued their heavy hitting and seemed to possess a fine blend of experience and youth. Wilbur Wood indicated as much when, on July 19, he referred to the 29 year-old Ray Chapman. The Indian shortstop, Wood noted, "is playing better ball than at any time in his career and it will be a long while before any rookie has a chance at his job."[17]

* * *

The 1920 major league season was unalterably marred due to the fatal blow suffered by Chapman in a rainy afternoon game at the Polo Grounds on August 16. Chapman froze as a pitch from submariner Carl Mays raced at his head, resulting in a severe fracture and cranial bleeding. A midnight operation at a local hospital failed to save the young star, whose loss threatened to paralyze his Indian teammates and, particularly, his good friend Tris Speaker.[18]

Three years earlier, *The Sporting News* had contained an editorial that referred to Mays as one "whose chief point of effectiveness in the past was alleged to be deliberate intention to 'dust them off.'" Ty Cobb had accused Mays of throwing at his head, while during spring training in 1917, Boston manager Jack Barry reportedly had to order the star pitcher not to keep firing "close to the heads" of Dodger batters; eventually, Barry opted not to send Mays again against Brooklyn during the series. Then, early that season, the Boston pitcher beaned the Athletics' outfielder Buck Thrasher. Mays "nearly killed Thrasher," the paper charged, "by driving a ball into his cranium and the 'accident' came at such a time when the Mackmen were in a batting rally, that it looked very suspicious." *The Sporting News* had proclaimed that Mays "is as deadly in his aim as ever." The editorial urged an examination of charges that Boston hurlers were deliberate beanballers: "There is no place in baseball for a pitcher who would deliberately take chances on killing or injuring an opposing player just to secure the slight advantage of making him plate shy."[19]

Following Chapman's death, an early move to bar Mays from organized baseball soon fizzled out. Speaker lent no support to such an effort, declaring, "I consider it an accident, pure and simple. Any attempt to create animosity or bitterness out of this would be unfair to the game of baseball; also it would be unfair to the memory of the dead boy, my friend, who was a square player, a square man and a true sportsman." Sportswriter Joe Vila, an eye witness, denied that Mays had tossed a bean ball.[20]

Mays, who was denounced for having delivered "the pitch that killed," expressed his own sentiments:

> If I were not absolutely sure in my own heart that it was an accident pure and simple I do not think that I could stand it. I always have had a horror of hitting a player ever since the accident to Chick Fewster. I liked him very much. When he was hurt by a pitched ball it affected me so that I was afraid to pitch close to a batter. This fear affected my work.
>
> In the early part of the season I could not do my best. I kept them on the outside because whenever I felt that the ball was going close to a batter's head I saw a picture of poor Fewster lying beside the plate. I had to fight that down. I had to play the game.
>
> Poor Chapman was one of the hardest batters I know of to pitch to. He had a peculiar crouch. He bent low and his head was close to where a curve might break. Babe Ruth's batting position is a little like this.
>
> I have often dreaded pitching to Ray Chapman for that reason. As I remember it, the ball that I pitched was a straight one on the inside. While I was holding the ball I felt a roughened place on it. This may have turned it into a "sailer," though it was not my intention to pitch it. ...
>
> After Chapman was taken off the field word was sent back to me that he was all right and for me not to worry, as I continued with the game. John Henry, the Washington catcher, who went out to the clubhouse to see him, told me that Chapman was all right and that he said for nobody to worry about him.
>
> As to my pitching in the future I do not think that this thing will unnerve me. My conscience is absolutely clear. If it was not I could not think of ever going near a baseball park again. It was an accident for which I am absolutely blameless.[21]

As *The New York Times* indicated, reports mistakenly indicated that Mays had blamed home plate umpire Thomas Connolly for not removing the deadly ball, which contained a rough spot causing it to move erratically. Connolly's colleagues William Evans and William Dinneen blasted the Yankee hurler:

> No pitcher in the American League resorted to trickery more than Carl Mays in attempting to get a break on it which would make it more difficult to hit.

Until the new pitching rules came into force which put a severe penalty on a pitcher roughening the ball, Mays constantly used to drag the ball across the pitching rubber in order to roughen the surface. Hundreds of balls were thrown out every year because of this act.

Additionally, team owners had recently complained to American League president Ban Johnson that too many balls were being discarded. Responding, Johnson ordered umpires to keep balls in play as long as possible, provided they were not dangerous.[22]

Johnson little helped matters in the Mays-Chapman affair, when he stated,

> I could not conscientiously attempt to make any trouble for Mr. Mays. But it is my honest opinion that Mr. Mays never will pitch again. From what I have learned he is greatly affected and may never be capable temperamentally of pitching again. Then I also know the feeling against him to be so bitter among the members of the other teams that it would be inadvisable for him to attempt to pitch again this year, at any rate.[23]

*New York Tribune* columnist W. O. McGeehan noted that a few folk in organized baseball were determined "to be cruelly unfair" to Mays, "whose tragic ill fortune" had resulted in Ray Chapman's death. McGeehan bluntly stated, "To intimate in any way that this was not an accident is cowardly and unsportsmanlike." League president Ban Johnson, McGeehan insisted, must ensure that Mays "gets a square deal for the sake of the game." *The Sporting News* denied that anyone was accusing Mays of directly intending to harm any batter, but pointed to his frequent brushes with hitters. "There are few who do not feel that Mays took the chance and made the batter take the chance," the paper asserted, "and there are many who wag the head and say such a thing as has happened was bound to happen some day." By late August, talk of a boycott against Mays had fizzled out.[24]

In the meantime, concerns that the Indians would fall out of the pennant race proved wrongheaded. The loss of Chapman was indeed considerable. At the time of the fatal blow, he was batting .303, with 27 doubles, eight triples, 97 runs scored, and 49 driven in. *The New York Tribune* believed that Chapman's absence would cripple the Indians, for he was, in the words of the paper, "one of the steadiest players on the team." The *Tribune* referred to him as "an infallible infielder and a reliable hitter, the strongest in their infield," and far more skilled than any possible replacement on the Cleveland bench.[25]

The fatality was the first ever suffered by the major leagues. Ironically, Chapman was, as the *Tribune* noted, "one of the best-liked players in professional baseball," while Mays was one of the least favored. Chapman, who had recently married and planned to enter his father-in-law's business, had only reluctantly agreed during the off-season to play one more year. The mass turnout by Indian personnel and community folk at Chapman's funeral at St. John's Roman Catholic Cathedral in Cleveland demonstrated the grief they suffered and the load his team had to bear heading into the final weeks of the 1920 season.[26]

On the morning of August 20, thousands attended the service, presided over by the Reverend William A. Sculler, the diocese chaplain. Pallbearers included Chapman's closest friends on the Indians, Tris Speaker, Steve O'Neill, and Joe Wood, along with former Cleveland player Tom Raftery. During his sermon, Dr. Sculler declared,

> Chapman played the game of life as he played the game of his profession, cleanly and honestly. He was our friend as a ball player and as a man. Sterling athlete that he was, he never knew defeat. Courageous and with an indomitable spirit, he played his part in life honorably and he was a shining type of typical American youth and a great example for others. Clean, wholesome, gentle and true, he was the idol of this city as a ballplayer, but above all was his gentleness and kindness as a man.[27]

*  *  *

The pennant races continued, with Ray Chapman's team remaining deeply enmeshed in a three-team fight in the American League, while the Dodgers continued to battle with the Reds and the onrushing Giants in the National. W. A. Phelon, discussing Cleveland's situation, indicated that "a deplorable accident" felling its "great shortstop, Ray Chapman," might "seriously impair its chances. … Chapman was the life of the Cleveland infield, a great batsman. There is nobody ready to replace him, and this misfortune must have almost broken Speaker's heart." Bagby and Coveleski appeared "badly overworked," but the team's hitting, especially Speaker's, "was enough to save game after game and keep the club going furiously."[28]

Over in the National League, the Reds were beginning to falter, as their pitching was hardly up to the 1919 standard. The Giants, under John McGraw, were surging, with improved pitching and the fine performance of Frankie Frisch, their "brilliant young infielder." Brooklyn's pitching, its mainstay throughout much of the season, was also weakening, at times appearing to be "composed of Burleigh Grimes and a prayer."[29]

With less than a month to go in the regular season, the Indians and Dodgers had regained the leads in their respective leagues. The Indians, as of September 10, were a mere three percentage points ahead of the White Sox and eight better than the Yankees. The Dodgers were only one percentage point in front of the Reds, while the Giants were continuing to move up fast. Soon, Brooklyn pulled away from the pack, while Cleveland, Chicago, and New York continued to jockey for position. Three straight defeats to the

White Sox at Comiskey Park a week later appeared to doom the Yankees, who slipped into third place, albeit just in back of both Cleveland and Chicago. The Reds continued their slide, enabling the Giants to move into second place behind the Dodgers in the National League.

Yet even as the pennant races, particularly in the American League, remained riveting, the unveiling of purported gambling scandals began to overshadow events on the playing fields. Still, on September 27, *The New York Times* reported that "Brooklyn's baseball dementia" surpassed inflationary pressures as the Robins and Rube Marquard beat the Giants 4-2 in the final game of an important series. Thousands were denied admission, as some 25,000 filled the Polo Grounds. After the game, hundreds of Brooklyn fans waited around to greet their conquering heroes.[30]

*The New York Tribune*'s W. O. McGeehan roundly applauded the Brooklyn manager for his team's success:

> Wilbert Robinson, with no particular baseball team, is sitting very comfortably on top of his league. This is not the first time that our Uncle Wilbur had made the experts look silly with no particular baseball team. The secret of it seems to be that Robinson is a natural leader of men, one of those men who has the big human understanding that permits him to take the "cast-offs" and restore their faith in themselves.

McGeehan then noted that the Brooklyn squad was indeed "an aggregation of 'cast-offs.'" That was true even of his pitchers, who afforded him the best shot at winning the World Series. It was Robinson, McGeehan insisted, who "made them, as the old song has it, what they are to-day, and he is satisfied." On paper, his infield was "terrible," but it had held together during pivotal series.[31]

The columnist then reasoned that Brooklyn had a good shot at winning the World Series. Pitching counted in such contests, and Robinson, McGeehan contended, "has about as formidable a pitching staff as there ever has been in any league." He then declared, "It would be a fine thing if this grand old man of the game could crown his long association with the game with a world's championship. For in baseball there has been no squarer and fairer player and manager than this same Uncle Wilbert Robinson, of Flatbush and Baltimore."[32]

As the Dodgers headed toward a title, two unlikely figures — both late-season call-ups — kept the Indians in the American League pennant race. The Cleveland debuts of both Walter "Duster" Mails and Joe Sewell had proven inauspicious, but eventually the pair provided Tris Speaker with the left-handed pitching and shortstop play his team had been lacking. In his first outing, Mails was blasted by Washington. In his initial fielding opportunity in the major leagues, Sewell threw errantly and had trouble handling balls cleanly. In his second time on the mound, Mails shut down the Browns 7-2 and then beat the Athletics 5-2. While Sewell continued to have troubles in the field, he rapped out 10 hits in his first 24 at-bats for a .417 mark.[33]

In nine appearances, eight as a starter, Mails went 7-0, with six complete games and a pair of shutouts. While Harry Lunte had been unable to fill the breach left by Ray Chapman's passing, Sewell, just called up from the minors, batted .329 in 70 official plate appearances; his defense, however, continued to be erratic at best. Still, even at this early point in his career, Sewell displayed a trait he would be recognized for: an ability to stave off strikeouts; only four times had pitchers been able to fan him.[34]

Brooklyn, closing with 23 wins in its last 29 games and a 93-61 record, finished seven games ahead of New York and 10½ better than Cincinnati. The American League race remained tighter and was not decided until the season's final week. Then, on September 28, with Cleveland and Chicago still vying for first place, Charles Comiskey announced that seven of his players, accused of engaging in a fix to throw the 1919 World Series, were suspended for the season's duration. Comiskey declined offers by New York's Jacob Ruppert and Boston's Harry Frazee to borrow players to play out the schedule. The front-running Indians went on to take the American League title, ending up with a 98-56 total, two games better than the White Sox and three up on the Yankees. But as preparations began for the Cleveland-Brooklyn showdown, the scandal involving the 1919 World Series remained very much in the forefront of the news.

# CHAPTER THIRTEEN

# A Season of Infamy: Gambling and the Chicago White Sox

In 1920, Rube Foster, Babe Ruth, and the New York Yankees, far more than the pennant-winning Indians and Dodgers, reshaped baseball in their own fashion. During that same year, the team that had previously been the fans' favorite wrestled with the demons of advancing age, rule changes, internal strife, and the cancer that had long imperiled the national pastime. Nevertheless, until the very end of the 1920 regular season, Charles Comiskey's Chicago White Sox remained highly popular and in the running for another American League title. Still, it was increasingly clear that the White Sox, like John McGraw's New York Giants, had been somewhat eclipsed by the road show and Polo Grounds feats of the Ruth-led Yankees. Also, sportswriters, for the first time, seemed somewhat less inclined to wax poetic about the Old Roman as hints of a 1919 World Series fix continued to be bandied about.

On the surface, the 1920 version of the White Sox appeared to be thriving nicely, at least until the season's ill-fated final week. On its way to a 96-58 mark, Chicago featured a pitching staff with four 20-game winners: Eddie Cicotte, Lefty Williams, Dickie Kerr, and Red Faber, who had rebounded from arm ailments. Faber was fourth in the league with 23 wins and strikeouts, 108, and second in both innings pitched, 319, and complete games, 28. Kerr was third in winning percentage, .700, Williams was second in strikeouts with 128, and Cicotte had the fourth best win-loss mark, .677. White

Sox batters compiled a lofty .294 average, headed by Joe Jackson, who adapted readily to the livelier ball by hitting .382, producing a slugging percentage of .589, and knocking 42 doubles, all third best in the league, driving in 121 runs and shaping a .444 on-base percentage, the fourth best marks, leading the league in triples with 20, scoring 105 runs, and even rapping a dozen homers, a career best. Eddie Collins hit .372 and had a .438 on-base percentage, fifth best in the American League, was runner-up to Sisler with 224 hits, and scored 117 runs, fourth highest in the league. Happy Felsch batted .338, with 115 RBIs, while Buck Weaver hit .331, produced 208 hits, 34 doubles, and 8 triples, scored 102 runs, drove in 74, and stole 19 bases. First baseman Shano Collins, who had replaced Chick Gandil, batted .303 with 10 triples, the same number as Swede Risberg; Eddie Collins, Felsch, and Jackson also ended up in double figures for three-baggers.

Yet even in the midst of such pitching and batting prowess, which kept Chicago in a riveting pennant race alongside Cleveland and New York, rumors floated about games the White Sox played loosely, as well as regarding the just completed World Series. Indeed, no team was more apt to be the subject of such talk than the Comiskey-driven Sox, notwithstanding the paeans that had been crafted by sportswriters about "the Old Roman." Salary disputes had been contentiously drawn out for the past three years, in particular. Holdouts were not uncommon, featuring the likes of Joe Jackson, Happy Felsch, and, most frequently, Buck Weaver. Team dissension and divisions were clearly present, with Jackson, Felsch, Risberg, Gandil, Cicotte, and Williams arrayed against another faction headed by Eddie Collins, whose salary, at various points, more than doubled that of other star Chicago players. Weaver at times appeared to be the odd man out; at other points, he seemed to be close to the first group.

\* \* \*

Expectations ran high for the Chicago White Sox from the day Eddie Collins was purchased from Connie Mack's Philadelphia Athletics on December 8, 1914, until the 1920 season wound to a close. The 1915 White Sox were led by Collins, who batted .332, first baseman Jack Fournier, who hit .322, the second and third best marks in the league behind Ty Cobb, and 24 game winners Jim Scott and Red Faber. Chicago finished with a 93-61 record, 9½ games back of Boston. The next year, the White Sox were again runner-ups to the Red Sox, and were once more guided by Collins, who hit .308, Felsch with a .300 average, and Joe Jackson, traded from the Indians the previous August, who batted .341. Chicago's top pitcher was Cicotte, whose .682 win-loss percentage led the league, while his 1.78 ERA was just behind Babe Ruth's. The 1917 White Sox swept to the American League pennant and then beat McGraw's Giants in the World Series, leading many observers to believe that a dynasty was in the offing. The team appeared strong all around, featuring an infield of Gandil, Collins, Risberg, and Weaver, and an outfield of Felsch, Jackson, and Nemo Leibold, plus catcher Schalk, the game's finest. A first-rate pitching staff was headed by starters Cicotte and Faber, Lefty Williams, and Reb Russell, and reliever Dave Danforth. The draft and the decision by several White Sox to enter the shipping yards or industrial plants to avoid military service crippled the 1918 squad, which finished sixth, a distant 17 games behind the Red Sox. The end of the war virtually allowed for the 1917 team to be reconstructed, with the same everyday lineup in place. The top Chicago pitchers, and two of the league's finest, were Cicotte and Williams, while Faber hobbled through the season, a failing only somewhat offset by Dickie Kerr's impressive rookie season. While some sportswriters forecast a weaker performance by the White Sox in 1920, the Chicago ballplayers appeared able at times, in the manner of the previous year, to play wondrously when they wanted to.

That was, however, precisely the dilemma that Comiskey, manager Kid Gleason, and players like Collins and Schalk had to contend with. As the end of the 1920 campaign approached, these White Sox stalwarts believed that certain of their compatriots had not given their all at various points during the previous regular season, the World Series, and the current year. Ire over contractual negotiations, general disgruntlement regarding Comiskey's stewardship, and an affinity for gamblers had dangerously melded together, thus ensuring the ruin of what once had promised to become a sports dynasty.

Charges of corruption had afflicted organized baseball since it first emerged after the close of the Civil War. An 1865 contest between the New York Mutuals and Brooklyn Eckfords was marred by the determination of three Mutual players to throw the game. But with a dearth of quality ballplayers, the two teams allowed the fixers to play again and downplayed the incident. The great Cincinnati Red Stockings of 1869-70 suffered one tie in the midst of a long winning streak, but that stalemate occurred because of a reputed $60,000 that had been bet by gamblers, including the Troy Haymakers' owner John Morrisey. Fearing a loss, Morrisey ordered his players off the field in the 6th inning of a stalemated game. Gambling remained popular at baseball parks, as represented by betting pools through which both owners and players backed their opponents.

The charter of the National League, formed in 1876, mandated that gambling be prohibited. Yet founder William Hulbert "ran with a fast crowd. He piled up some gambling debts." The Haymakers now were said to be fully in the control of gamblers. Charges that a contest between the Philadelphia Athletics and New York Mutuals had been fixed led to calls for their ouster from the league. Then in 1877, Hulbert kicked four members of the Louisville Colonels, including star pitcher Jim Devlin, out of the league for throwing games. Five years later, Dick Higham was expelled for crooked umpiring. Charges were leveled in 1891 that the New York Giants had allowed the Boston Red Stockings to win a number of contests to prevent the Chicago White Stockings and their first baseman-manager Cap Anson from taking the pennant. Two years later, Baltimore players were said to have offered a $500 bribe to Pittsburgh pitcher Red Ehret to drop an important game; Oriole captain Wilbert Robinson acknowledged that $100 had been paid to Ehret, but to win the contest.

Gambling flourished at ballparks and among players, who continued to bet on their own teams, in the early years of the 20th Century. The number of fixed games mounted, Bill James has contended, in the 1916-18 period. Salaries in major league ball had recently increased thanks to competition from the Federal League. That league's demise, coupled with an economic downturn, left some players in more precarious economic situations. With horse race tracks closed because of American involvement in World War I, gamblers turned more readily to the baseball diamond. They hobnobbed easily with such players as Hal Chase, Lee Magee, and Carl Mays. Chase, in particular, acquired a reputation as one whose honesty could readily be called into question. Starting in 1909, accusations began to be made that Prince Hal, a seemingly peerless first baseman and gifted batsman, bet heavily on games, sometimes against his own ballclub. In 1913, New York Yankee skipper Frank Chance informed sportswriter Heywood Broun that Chase was tossing games; Broun wrote up the story and Chase was traded to Charles Comiskey's White Sox.

Eventually, America's greatest sports scandal would revolve around Comiskey's Chicago franchise. In the midst of the 1917 pennant chase, most of the White Sox players had contributed $45 apiece to a fund that was doled out to members of the Detroit Tigers for having defeated the Boston Red Sox in a crucial series. While Eddie Collins and Ray Schalk joined in, an injured Buck Weaver refused to do so. The practice of rewarding other teams for besting one's closest competitors was hardly novel. At the tail-end of the 1919 season, after the White Sox had clinched the title, they supposedly reciprocated by dropping a pair of games to the Tigers who were vying with the Yankees for third place. Joe Jackson, Happy Felsch, and Chick Gandil all supposedly played out of position to enable the Tigers to prevail.[1]

By the advent of the 1919 World Series, the White Sox players were an increasingly unhappy lot. They had been infuriated by Comiskey's "reward" of a stale case of champagne after winning the 1917 pennant. Many were angered even more by Commy's miserly approach in determining salaries. Yes, Eddie Collins had his $15,000 salary. But Ray Schalk received less than half that, a bit over $7,000 as part of a three-year, $21,250 package. The great Joe Jackson and top-notch third baseman Buck Weaver were each getting only $6,000 a year. That was still $1,000 more than pitching ace Eddie Cicotte and $2,000 better than first baseman Chick Gandil. Happy Felsch, a terrific center fielder, was paid a mere $3,750 a year, while the White Sox's leading southpaw pitcher, Lefty Williams, got only $3,000. Shortstop Swede Risberg's contract called for a $2,500 annual payment, less even than reserve infielder Fred McMullin, who was paid $2,750.[2]

Furthermore, there were the charges and invectives Comiskey had hurled the way of some for avoiding military service during the 19-month period of the United States' involvement in World War I. Comiskey compounded that situation by continuing to badmouth certain players for a while even following the Armistice.

\* \* \*

The editors of *Baseball Magazine*, while acknowledging the danger posed by gambling, were greatly offended by talk of a World Series frame-up by Hugh Fullerton, *The Chicago Herald and Examiner* sportswriter. In a lengthy editorial, F.C. Lane took Fullerton to task. Baseball had been on trial, Lane acknowledged, during the past season. It had more than met the test, he argued, attaining unprecedented popularity. Lane saw the upcoming season, which promised to be the majors' first full one since 1917, as certain to continue baseball's greater prosperity.[3]

Gambling, Lane continued, was "a prevalent evil in all sports. In some it is the paramount issue." Horse racing, he contended, was "a magnificent sport" that required "the betting glamour." Wrestling was tainted by continuous rumors of fixed bouts. Boxing had also been scarred, with the results of certain heavyweight championship fights called into question. Baseball, by contrast, was "the cleanest of all professional sports, the freest from deserved criticism, the most above suspicion." Inevitably then, Lane wrote, muckrakers turned to that sport.[4]

Recently, "a giddy screed," Lane charged, had been issued "from the facile pen of Hugh Fullerton." Lane was troubled by the possibility of Fullerton serving as a baseball arbiter, for as he saw matters, "we know of no one less competent by clear reasoning and fairness of vision to pass judgment on so broad a question." As for driving anyone out of the game, Lane called for that fate to befall Fullerton. Lane wondered why Fullerton gave so much credence to the words of gamblers, with whom the sportswriter had supposedly "been consorting rather freely."[5]

Considering Fullerton's charges to be unbelievable, Lane asserted that baseball "is on trial" and had been urged to conduct "a sweeping investigation." But what, he asked, "is the end of all this?" Did baseball have to carry out an investigation on each occasion that a gambler criticized players or when Fullerton called for that to occur? If so, he warned, "baseball had better set

Buck Weaver batting, 1920. National Baseball Hall of Fame Library, Cooperstown, N.Y.

aside a commission to sit in perpetuity on the claims of gamblers and Mr. Fullerton. They will be kept busy three hundred and sixty-five days a year and on leap years three hundred and sixty-six."[6]

Referring to Fullerton as "a visionary and erratic writer," Lane condemned "the contemptible way in which he deserted the sport which has given him a living for many years, in the dark days during the war. The slanderous libels with which he reviled the game, the owners, and the players on that occasion will long be remembered by thousands of persons who read them with supreme disgust."[7]

Concluding his diatribe, Lane made telling observations of his own:

> There may be a few players in baseball crooked enough to throw a game, if they could and dared. There will always be a few crooks in every sport. The inherent difficulty of throwing a game, however, is so great ... that it makes the risk practically negligible. Mr. Fullerton knows this as well as any one and for that reason his wholesale vicious charges are all the more inexcusable.[8]

In its very first issue of 1920, *The Sporting News* contained a feature editorial warning that the "cancer" of gambling had to be dealt with. The paper's editorialists declared forthrightly, "There is only one way to loosen the tightening fingers of the gamblers on baseball and that way is to smash that grip with a club." Furthermore,

> We want to say right here that the situation has pretty near reached the point where the club must be swung and will be swung with strong hands if those hands can be set free from would-be manaclers. The ugly stories in connection with the recent World's Series are only a chapter in this history that will be written of the efforts of the gamblers to get hold of baseball. Alleged dealings between players and gamblers were hinted weeks before the World's Series was played, and the White Sox players weren't the ones mentioned then, by name or by insinuation.[9]

The editorial continued:

> There may be nothing in the World's Series scandal — there has been no evidence, we think we can say, that is positive enough to convict any one of crooked work on the playing field, but it's through no fault of the gamblers that there have not been games bought and sold. And does any one think gamblers would have grown bold enough to approach players if a club had been swung on them when they first saw the 'possibilities' and got busy on the job when they learned indifference of magnates made the golden opportunity?[10]

A week later, *The Sporting News* presented a front-page article discussing Ray Schalk's denial that he had predicted several teammates would not be returning to the White Sox. "I played in that World's Series and played to the best of my ability," related Schalk. "I feel that every man on our club did the same, and there was not a single moment of all the games in which we all did not try." *The Sporting News* suggested that "if there had been anything wrong going on, it is a certainty he would have detected it, as he is too smart a catcher to let any crookedness escape him." In the same vein, the report noted that "Eddie Collins, also one of the brightest and cleverest players in the American League, was on a line with the plate and could easily see if anything out of the ordinary was taking place."[11]

* * *

Prior to the start of the 1920 season, the Chicago White Sox had to contend with more than rumors of a World Series fix. Once again, a series of holdouts, involving first baseman Chick Gandil, third sacker Weaver, and shortstop Risberg, among others, threatened the team's very makeup. "Salary disputes," like gambling, *Baseball Magazine* acknowledged, were "a perpetual plague in baseball. The first player who ever drew his semi-monthly envelope, accepted it in the firm belief he was underpaid." However, "this complaint, which has long been chronic, is now developing acute symptoms. The world-wide labor unrest which has cursed every industry from Russia to Australia has found, in professional baseball, a fertile field for its misspent energy."[12]

The previous year, *Baseball Magazine* noted, players willingly cooperated with owners, even though wages were reduced. However, having witnessed "colossal crowds and wild tales of the owner's profits," the players now demanded salary increases. They recognized that playing careers were short, injuries could befall them at any point, and others, who performed less capably, had more generous contracts. But the team owner, much reviled by players and the public alike, the publication declared, was "probably the most misunderstood individual in baseball." In fact, "most of the owners are public-spirited citizens who have risked large fortunes in an uncertain business." If players were apprised of all business matters, such as the need to offset financially troubled years with more successful ones, *Baseball Magazine* suggested, then considerable animosity could vanish.[13]

Gandil, just coming off one of his finest campaigns, with a .290 mark, now walked away from the White Sox. Gandil, sportswriter Oscar C. Reichow reported from Pasadena, supposedly considered himself ill-treated by Charles Comiskey. In early March, Gandil visited the Cubs' training camp in Pasadena, California, and announced his retirement. Unhappy with the contract that had been tendered him, Gandil was opting to stay on the West coast with his family. His wife was not enamored with the East and had evidently convinced Chick to remain in the West where his financial opportunities were greater.

Gandil indicated that he had been tendered an offer to manage a club in Idaho for more money than Comiskey would pay him.[14]

In the middle of the month, the White Sox began spring training in earnest, with Gandil, Buck Weaver, and Swede Risberg considered holdouts. Comiskey had recently traveled out to California where all three were staying. Reserve infielder Fred McMullin was also in California, but it was presumed that he would be in camp shortly. Pitching ace Eddie Cicotte had agreed to join the team train, just before it was departing from Chicago.[15]

Comiskey, while supposedly conducting the investigation regarding the 1919 World Series, attempted to placate his discontented players. Joe Jackson received a three-year, $24,000 package. Cicotte's salary was doubled, to $10,000, as was Lefty Williams's, to $6,000. Happy Felsch was now to be paid $7,000. Risberg got $3,250, McMullin, $3,600. A year earlier, the now unhappy Weaver had signed a three-year contract, set at $7,250; more remarkable still, on Harry Grabiner's salary list for 1920 a notation indicated, "10 Days' clause out."[16]

Three days after training camp began, Weaver showed up, but soon departed for Chicago to talk with Comiskey. While Buck demanded a salary increase or a trade to the Yankees, White Sox team secretary Harry Grabiner indicated that Weaver, like the team, was expected to honor a contract. "Weaver himself asked for a long term contract last spring, and he got just what he wanted. If we had a bad season financially he would not expect us to ask him to take a cut in salary. We are willing to do our part, and he must do his if he wishes to play ball." Backing up Grabiner's stance, Comiskey declared,

> Weaver signed a three year contract at his own demand and without my consent last spring, and he will live up to it or stay out of organized baseball for the rest of his life.
>   He told me last spring all about his opportunities to make up in Wisconsin, where he went during the war, and I advised him to stay there if he thought it was best for him. While I was out of town he came back and signed for three years with Kid Gleason and Harry Grabiner. If I had been there he would have had only a one year contract. Now he will have to live up to the terms he dictated if he wants to play in organized baseball.[17]

Referring to Weaver's contractual dispute, *The Chicago Whip* spoke of him almost reverently:

> Buck Weaver, the best third Baseman in Base Ball the Best Dispositioned Ball Player, a man who builds rather than tears down, a man who helps put the Winning Germ in Gutless men, has quit the White Sox. A Ball Player whose value is more to Comiskey, than a deck of Eddie Collins a player who never

caused dissension for any owner, a better hitter in all just as finished a player, and who has made Eddie Collins look better than he really is. His refusal to help the Wonderful Eddie Collins to draw his big juicy salary is but natural. Unless Buck comes to terms it is good bye "pennant Hopes." ... He has the Ball Club with him to a man, so the battle is on. Comiskey can do more with him in a minute than anyone else can in a month. It is a great guy Comiskey has not in Camp.[18]

On March 27, Reichow, still stationed in California, discussed Weaver's latest demands. "We read out here," Reichow wrote, "with much disgust of Buck Weaver's desertion of Kid Gleason's clan, and his trip to Chicago to demand a new contract from President Comiskey, despite the fact that his contract has two years more to run." To Reichow, Weaver's move seemed to parallel his friend Babe Ruth's, who had apparently advised the White Sox third baseman when the two palled around together during the off-season. Reichow warned, "If Weaver gets away with it the club owners might as well abolish contracts entirely, because innumerable similar cases are almost bound to follow." The sportswriter recalled how Comiskey had dealt with Hal Chase in a similar situation several years earlier and wondered if the White Sox owner "still has the courage to demand that a player live up to his word."[19]

The previous spring, Reichow reminded his readers, Weaver had "bellowed about not getting enough money." Threatening to depart the major leagues, Weaver held out until Comiskey came through with a three-year contract. At the time, Weaver was placated and, Reichow noted, he "played wonderful ball for the Sox." Now unhappy once again, Weaver wanted his contract torn up and a more generous one crafted in its place. "I always knew Buck as a square man," Reichow declared, "but when he chooses to throw honor to the winds I fear he will find the road rough and rugged."[20]

By April 1, Weaver was back at the White Sox camp in Waco, Texas. All his teammates, except for Gandil, had also returned to the fold, and *The Sporting News* predicted another big year for Comiskey's crew. Oscar Reichow foresaw a three team race, with the White Sox, Indians, and Yankees battling for the pennant. With the return of Red Faber to form, Gleason promised to have "a wonderful hurling staff," led by "that great veteran, Eddie Cicotte," that could keep the White Sox competitive.[21]

Grantland Rice viewed both Chicago teams as lacking requisite balance. Each, he declared, boasted "at least four stars of outstanding note — four of the greatest in baseball." While the Cubs had Pete Alexander, Jim Vaughn, catcher Bill Killefer, and shortstop Charlie Hollocher, the White Sox featured Cicotte, Schalk, Collins, and Weaver, "with Joe Jackson in the offing." Rice believed that the White Sox had "an exceptional amount of battery strength," when Cicotte, Williams, or Kerr was throwing to Schalk; he failed to count on Faber to bounce back from his injury-plagued 1919 season. The White

Sox infield included "Collins and Weaver, two luminaries," while first and third base stood as potential trouble spots.[22]

Rice's colleague Ray McCarthy was less hopeful about the White Sox's chances. The World Series setback and "ugly rumors" of a fix, McCarthy contended, had not well served Chicago's American League representative. W. A. Phelon evidently agreed, predicting there was "a big chance that the White Sox will come far short of their 1919 playing standard."[23]

* * *

No matter, Chicago began the season with a rush, sweeping its first six contests and going 8-2 to hold first place in the American League. Lefty Williams held the Tigers to four hits in an 11-2 rout in the opener, while Cicotte tossed a 4-0 shutout in the second game. Despite the ban on the shine ball, Cicotte remained, *The Sporting News* asserted, "one of the smartest pitchers in baseball." Chicago hardly appeared to be the "wrecked" squad some had predicted during the off-season.[24]

Yet even as the White Sox got off to a fast start, they remained a deeply troubled lot. As Eliot Asinof has so eloquently pointed out, symptoms of loose play cropped up as early as the seventh game of the season. With a 6-0 record, Chicago was favored over Cleveland as a new series began. Suddenly, however, betting odds shifted in the Indians' favor. The game initially went well for the White Sox, with Red Faber holding a 2-1 lead into the eighth inning. Then, on a relay from outfielder Joe Jackson, Swede Risberg threw the ball wildly, preventing either Buck Weaver or Ray Schalk from snaring it. The runner scored and Cleveland eventually triumphed in the ninth.[25]

At various points during the season, similar scenarios unfolded. Hardly surprising then, talk of a World Series scandal refused to abate entirely. On May 6, *The Sporting News* produced a front-page article with the headline ringing, "Why Do Honest Ball Players Stand for Crooks in Ranks?" Oscar Reichow considered it "unfathomable," in the wake of allegations about the World Series, "why the ball players in the major leagues have not taken some action toward keeping the Great American Game free from crookedness." Not only baseball moguls, but the players — if they were only courageous enough — Reichow asserted, should strive "to rid the sport of the men who have no scruples about throwing honesty to the winds. This type of player, we all know, ought to be tarred and feathered and run out of the country." He coldly asked, "Why shouldn't the players take it upon themselves to eliminate the crooks?" Baseball, Reichow continued, was "their bread and butter," affording them a wealth of commercial opportunities. Furthermore, "baseball gives players a national reputation," which also compelled them to oust their crooked counterparts.[26]

The following week's issue of *The Sporting News* contained another lead article calling for a "crusade against gamblers." Municipal detectives, National League president John Heydler reported, were being turned to. Led by owner Barney Dreyfuss, Pittsburgh had virtually rid itself of the problem, doling out several thousand dollars in fines. Dreyfuss, it was said, "likes to see the ponies run, but baseball is a sport and virtue with him. He knows that piker gamblers and betting can do the game almost irreparable harm." Horace Stoneham had closed the doors of the Polo Grounds to "known gamblers." The Cubs' Bill Veeck and White Sox boss Charles Comiskey appeared unwilling to tolerate gamblers. As a result, Reichow declared, "there is less betting on ball games in Chicago than any other city in either major league circuit," as had been the case for several years.[27]

In that same edition, Joe Vila discussed the fate of Heinie Zimmerman. A one-time triple crown winner, three-time RBI champ, and lifetime .295 hitter, Zimmerman had been out of the majors since John McGraw dumped him and Hal Chase late the previous season. While Zimmerman would fill a pressing need of the Giants, Vila indicated, McGraw, who dearly loved to win, refused to take the third baseman back. Vila applauded McGraw and the Giant owners "for their determination to rid their club of disloyal players."[28]

* * *

By mid-May, the White Sox remained in a battle with the Red Sox for second place behind the Indians. The starting pitching was quite strong, with Williams said to be "pitching the best ball of his career" and Faber continuing his "corking comeback." The hitting was potent indeed, with Jackson, Felsch, and Weaver all "knocking the stitches out of the ball." Weaver was shuttling between shortstop and third base, due to an injury to Risberg. Kid Gleason refuted notions that Cleveland had a better club this time around or that his club was a troubled one:

> They counted us out for two reasons: one, that dissensions would break us up, the other that we had no pitching staff left. It so happens that there isn't any dissension around. And it happens also that we are getting better pitching this season than we got a year ago. And with Schalk, Collins, Weaver, Joe Jackson and Felsch, among others, still around, I can see no reason to take a running jump into the lake yet. Besides, we'd like another shot at the Reds.[29]

In his column on May 16, Grantland Rice discussed one of his favorite ballplayers, the Chicago third baseman:

> If we had to cast a vote for the Hustlin' Kid in the Ancient Order of Sons of Swat it would likely go to Buck Weaver, of the White Sox.

Weaver is and has been to the White Sox what Johnny Evers was to the old Cubs, an everlasting inspiration in the way of pep.

He is not only a great ball player but a great fighter, one who seems to give 103 per cent of everything he has to each contest.

Whether it's an ordinary scrap or a world series the general idea is about the same to Buck — give 'em all you got.[30]

Four days later, *The Sporting News* featured a front page photograph of a smiling Weaver and a caption entitled, "WORTH MOST ANY PRICE." The paper declared that

Weaver is having a wonderful year with the Chicago White Sox and his good work and fine spirit deserve more than passing notice. ... He started out in his old brilliant style at third, then shifted to short when Risberg was hurt, where he has been even more a star, if possible. Not only is his fielding spectacular, but he is hitting at a tremendous clip, giving Joe Jackson a run for the honor of being the leading swatsmith on Kid Gleason's fast-going bunch of "wrecks."... He made as good at one position as he had at the other and at either position many rate him the premier in his league.[31]

\* \* \*

Following a meeting in Chicago, Johnson, Stoneham, McGraw, and Cincinnati Reds' president Gary Herrmann announced on May 21 that detective agencies would be employed to curb baseball betting. Three days later, as part of a concerted drive against gamblers, four arrests were made at the Polo Grounds and 47 at Cubs Park. On May 27, five more gamblers were removed from the Giants' ballpark. The next day, another half-dozen were arrested at the Polo Grounds.[32]

After a jury in Lee Magee's suit against the Chicago Cubs found for the defendants on June 9, a *Baseball Magazine* editorial chortled,

The bubble of player dishonesty has been exploded. It was a beautiful bubble while it lasted, painted with all the tints of malice and slander which the malignant ingenuity of Hugh Fullerton and his tribe of muckrakers could devise. It sought to involve the entire baseball structure in a wholesale denunciation of dishonesty. It assailed the integrity of the World's Series itself.

However, now "that vicious campaign" had apparently "simmered down to the Magee case." *Baseball Magazine* exclaimed, "If you seek a striking example of anti-climax here it is." And Magee, who had threatened to "name names," had failed to do precisely that.[33]

To F. C. Lane, "the player, as a class, has been vindicated just as everyone knew he would be. The player is essentially honest and in the few cases where he is not it has never been possible for him to do much damage to any save himself." Magee had not injured the game, Lane declared, in contrast to "sensational writers like Hugh Fullerton — men for whose actions there was not the slightest excuse."[34]

* * *

After their early torrid start, the Chicago White Sox had struggled — perhaps due in part at least to occasionally indifferent play — notwithstanding powerful hitting by Joe Jackson, Eddie Collins, Happy Felsch, and Buck Weaver. With over a third of the 1920 season completed, Chicago's record stood at only 29-25, which placed it just above Boston in the American League standings. Leading the race with a 36-17 mark were the Indians, 7½ games ahead of the White Sox; the Yankees were in second place, thanks to their 37-20 record, which left them two games behind.

Within two weeks, however, the White Sox had won 10 of 12 to close within five games of Cleveland, which still led the Yankees by 1½ games. *The Sporting News* indicated that, once again, the White Sox were talking about a pennant drive. Everywhere, it seemed, Chicago, due to its sluggish performance and perhaps because of continuing questions about the 1919 World Series, was being written off. While first base was proving to be a sore spot, White Sox hitters, especially Eddie Collins, Jackson, Felsch, and Weaver, were "clubbing the ball vigorously enough to keep any team close to first place." Furthermore, Oscar Reichow noted, "not only are Gleason's athletes doing damaging work with the hickory but they have not lost any of their pep that characterizes their playing on the field. They are a fighting tribe because Gleason insists on it." Provided the pitching held up, the White Sox would remain a factor in the pennant race. And to date, Cicotte, Williams, and Kerr had indeed been pitching well.[35]

As of early July, the White Sox were stationed in third place, which appeared not to faze Kid Gleason. Oscar Reichow deemed this a better team than the 1919 version because of the deeper pitching, thanks to Red Faber's "wonderful" mound work. The White Sox also seemed determined to battle to their last out, as attested by ninth inning homers by Eddie Collins and Joe Jackson that won separate ballgames.[36]

Yet Chicago continued to struggle. Throughout the season, Eliot Asinof charges, various White Sox players threw games, purportedly fearing what gamblers might do if they refused to. *The Chicago Tribune's* Jim Cruisenberry recognized that the White Sox appeared even more split into cliques than the previous year. Near the end of July, Cruisenberry and Ring Lardner were lounging in a Manhattan hotel room, as the Yankee-White Sox game had been rained out. They received a phone call from Kid Gleason, inviting them to Dinty Moore's, a haven for sports fans in New York City. "I'm at the bar with Abe Attell," Gleason declared. "He's talking, and I want you to hear it. I won't let on that I know you." After they arrived, Gleason asked Attell, "So it was Arnold Rothstein who put up the dough for the fix?" The former boxing champion replied, "That was it, all right. You know, Kid, I hated to do that to you, but I thought I was going to make a bundle, and I needed it." But with the threat of libel suits, Gleason's story was not aired, to his dismay.[37]

On August 2, Chicago completed its 100th game of the season, a 7-0 pasting before 25,000 fans at Comiskey Park at the hands of the Yankees, who featured a home run by Babe Ruth. Still stationed in third place, the White Sox had compiled a 61-39 record, which placed them 3½ games behind the Indians, who, in turn, were one game up on the Yankees. By now, Shano Collins was filling in nicely for the departed Chick Gandil at first base, while Nemo Liebold was no longer platooned in right field. The pitching was first-rate, the team healthy, and, as W. A. Phelon noted, "the old spirit" apparently "restored." The White Sox were performing at a better clip than the 1917 squad and almost as proficiently as last year's team. Thus, Phelon exclaimed, "Hard to stop 'em when they are that way."[38]

The August 12 issue of *The Sporting News* included an editorial discussing Hal Chase's latest machinations. Chase had become a one-third owner of the San Jose team in the independent Mission League, with other investors insisting that "he was repentant." Moreover, the paper claimed, "it would be unfair to punish him for sins committed outside of California." Once again, however, Chase, the former "Prince Hal," was being accused of seeking to fix games.[39]

At this point of the season, the White Sox slipped past the Yankees into second place, a mere game behind the Indians. The fatal blow suffered by Cleveland shortstop Ray Chapman threatened to doom Tris Speaker's squad and enable Chicago to grab another title. The White Sox players, Oscar Reichow reported, "were wrought up over" Chapman's death. Deeply saddened, some initially demanded that Yankee pitcher Carl Mays be banned from baseball. After cooling off, they realized that such a call amounted to accusing Mays of intentionally injuring Chapman. The loss of their stellar shortstop, Reichow claimed, "seriously cripples the Indians' chances of taking the pennant." By contrast, the White Sox now appeared to be on a roll. Yet Chicago never pulled away in the race, due to the fact, Eliot Asinof suggests, that certain members of the team continued throwing games, thus enabling Cleveland to remain close.[40]

In his column on August 25, Grantland Rice particularly praised Buck Weaver yet again. The Chicago third baseman, Rice declared, was "replete with nervous energy — full of steel springs. But he is a great fighter and a great ball player." Rice then observed, "A ball club that carries Weaver, Collins and Schalk has a lot of nervous or nerve-driving power to carry it along."[41]

On August 30, Chicago and Boston began a three game series at Fenway, with the White Sox a half-game in front of the Indians. Lefty Williams dropped the opener, 4-0, while Eddie Cicotte lost a 1-0 lead in the third inning on an error by Joe Jackson and then the game in the seventh when the pitcher fell apart, enabling Boston to prevail 7-3. Jim O'Leary, a sportswriter for *The Boston Globe*, exclaimed to a friend, "Why, they're playing just like they did in the World Series!" Schalk, as the home-plate umpire noted, vented his anger at Cicotte. Dropping the third game, the White Sox dropped behind Cleveland in the standings.[42]

Back in Chicago, Eddie Collins told a seemingly resigned Comiskey that the Boston series had been fixed. Later, Collins remembered the following scenario:

> It was in Boston the incident happened that cost us the 1920 pennant. Some gamblers got panicky that we'd win again and they must have gone to the players they had under thumb and ordered the rest of the games thrown. We were leading by three games with seven to go. We knew something was wrong but we couldn't put the finger on it. The feeling between the players was very bad. Dickie Kerr was pitching for us and doing well. A Boston player hit a ball that fell between Jackson and Felsch. We thought it should have been caught. The next batter bunted and Kerr made a perfect thrown to Weaver for a force-out. The ball pops out of Weaver's glove. When the inning was over Kerr scaled his glove across the diamond.
>
> He looks at Weaver and Risberg who are standing together and says, "If you'd told me you wanted to lose this game, I could have done it a lot easier." There is almost a riot on the bench. Kid Gleason breaks up two fights. That was the end. We lose three or four more games the same way.[43]

Collins's recollections were recorded nearly 30 years later and contained some obvious factual errors, including those involving the league standings as the season neared a close. His are virtually the only impressions that Buck Weaver ever did anything on the playing field but play as hard as he was capable of. Indeed, shortly after the Boston series, Grantland Rice determined to settle the question of the game's top third baseman. The Giants' Frankie Frisch appeared to be the player of the future, while Heinie Groh remained a fine hitter and fielder. At present, Weaver was out-hitting both by at least 40 points. To Rice, Buck was "also one of the game's hardest hustlers and best fielders." Thus, "to name any other third baseman above the Sox star is an act that could hardly be justified by the dope."[44]

* * *

A recent article in *The Sporting News*, which discussed a Coast League bribery scandal, blamed the ballplayers for failing to tackle the gambling problem. Stationed in San Francisco, Seal Rock declared, "The astonishing thing is that so many ball players, innocent themselves of wrong things, knew that others were guilty, that bribes were being offered, and kept the matter from the club magnates and the league head." They evidently had feared that the innocent would be caught up in a dragnet alongside the guilty, thereby dooming baseball. Rock wrote, "They know differently now. Baseball is bigger than the crooks and gamblers and it will survive when some of the misguided players who forgot all sense of decency and honesty are in the ash heap."[45]

On September 4 a story broke that eventually resulted in a reexamination of charges involving the 1919 World Series. William Veeck, president of the Chicago Cubs, began to explore accusations that members of his team had recently thrown a game to the Phillies; as a consequence, professional gamblers had reportedly "cleaned up." Promising to explore the matter fully, Veeck stated, "My impression has been that there was less gambling this year than ever before. I thought that might be attributed to the fact that we went after some fellows pretty hard last year." Veeck, of course, was referring to Hal Chase and Lee Magee. The Chicago-Philadelphia contest in question was won by the Phillies 3-0, despite manager Fred Mitchell's decision to replace pitcher Claude Hendrix with his ace Pete Alexander. Veeck and Mitchell opted for that course after being warned that Hendrix, pitcher Paul Carter, and infielder Buck Herzog were in on a fix. As matters turned out, Hendrix, previously a fine pitcher with the Pirates, the Chicago Whales in the Federal League — where he won 29 games one season — and the Cubs, would not pitch in the majors after the 1920 season; Carter and Herzog similarly would not return to the big leagues. On September 5, an announcement was made that the Chicago chapter of the Baseball Writers' Association would examine whether the Chicago-Philadelphia game had been fixed.[46]

The following day, W. O. McGeehan, *The New York Tribune* columnist, analyzed the issue of baseball and gambling. He wrote, "Baseball is the only professional sport that has stood the test of a half century. It is more popular to-day than at any time in its history. It is popular because the public has faith in the honesty of the game. If it had not been kept absolutely pure baseball would have gone done in a crash long ago." Many magnates and a few stars like Ruth and Cobb were reaping great financial rewards from the game's success. Lesser players were also making more money than they would likely attain off the playing field. McGeehan reasoned, "One would think, then, that the baseball players would strive to keep the game as sweet and pure as it always has been." However,

> there is an undercurrent of gossip going the rounds that is none too reassuring for the future of the game. The scandal associated with the last world's series between the Reds and the White Sox developed nothing tangible, and so the public forgot. A few of the National League players against whom the finger of suspicion was pointed were quietly dropped last spring.

Now, new charges had arisen concerning a possible fix. The 1920 season, McGeehan remembered, had been favored by the kinds of three-team pennant races that had been absent from the game since 1908. "It is to be hoped," McGeehan concluded, "the pennants are decided strictly on merit. The game can tolerate no monkey business."[47]

Analysts applauded Veeck for seeking to determine the veracity of the accusations; by inference, at a bare minimum, they seemed to be criticizing Charles Comiskey and other baseball insiders for having failed to pursue the 1919 World Series story more diligently. On September 7, a grand jury in Chicago was instructed by Judge Charles A. McDonald to investigate the charges. McDonald, whose name had been tossed about as a possible baseball commissioner, told the grand jurors that baseball pools constituted a "pernicious influence" and "should be wiped out and the promoters thereof should be indicted and prosecuted." McDonald discussed why the issue of gambling had to be grappled with:

> Baseball is our national sport. Its purpose is to furnish wholesome recreation and entertainment to the public. It has become a part of the every day life of every lover of clean sports in the country.
>   This popular interest in the game is due primarily to the fact that heretofore organized baseball has always been conducted in such a manner as to inspire the confidence of the public in the honesty and integrity of the respective players and those interested in promoting the game.[48]

As the American League race remained tight, Elbert Sanders in *The Sporting News* contended that "a fight is just what the White Sox like." Moreover, Sanders predicted, "that fighting spirit will show best in a hard race." While Eddie Collins was on roll, "Jackson, Weaver and Felsch" needed to "perk up and get into the stride" they had experienced earlier. If they did so, Sanders declared, "there is nothing that will stop the Sox from clinching the championship this month."[49]

On September 12, Oscar Reichow reported that Kid Gleason was attempting to tackle the problem of his team's inconsistent play. Gleason's star pitcher, Eddie Cicotte, had lost a pair of games Reichow agreed "that should have been won;" believing Cicotte was out of shape, the White Sox manager ordered him to show up at Comiskey Park each morning for practice. "This is something unusual for a veteran like Cicotte," Reichow declared, but demonstrated Gleason's determination to goad his team. The batting of Joe Jackson, Eddie Collins, Buck Weaver, and Shano Collins remained potent, but the pitching had not been steady, as of late.[50]

Two days later, Grantland Rice announced his all-star team for 1920. Included on his roster were catcher Ray Schalk, second baseman Eddie Collins, and third baseman Buck Weaver. As for Weaver, who was clearly outhitting Heinie Groh, Rice declared, "the game has no harder worker." Even though Joe Jackson was hitting over .380, Rice refused to place him on his squad. Outfielder Ross Youngs, the sportswriter declared, was "a much better defensive player than Jackson, and there is a good bit of logic in the claim that he is a better all around man," an intriguing statement.[51]

After a three game sweep of the Yankees, who had temporarily moved into first place, the White Sox appeared to have righted themselves. Cicotte, *The Sporting News* noted, was engaged in "a comeback," while both Dickie Kerr and Red Faber pitched terrifically. All the while, however, storm clouds continued to gather over Charles Comiskey's ball club.[52]

In Judge McDonald's courtroom, the investigation of possible fixes involving baseball games proceeded apace. Impressed, Reichow, who had earlier favored Kenesaw Mountain Landis, now supported McDonald's selection as National Commission chairman. After all, Reichow noted, "McDonald is a Chicago man. This is his home, and this is where the National Commission belongs for more reasons than one. It is the greatest baseball city in the country."[53]

That very city continued to host the grand jury investigation of alleged gambling incidents involving baseball. The scope widened on September 19 to include the 1919 World Series. That evening, subpoenas were issued requiring the following to appear before the grand jury: American League president Ban Johnson, National League president John A. Heydler, White Sox skipper Kid Gleason, Chicago White Sox president Charles A. Comiskey, Chicago Cubs president William L. Veeck, a series of Chicago area sportswriters, and New York Giant pitcher Rube Benton. It was also indicated that additional players would likely be summoned, as well as some figures who had recently left the majors: Hal Chase, Lee Magee, and Heinie Zimmerman.[54]

Ban Johnson indicated that his league would seek congressional legislation criminalizing betting on baseball contest. The hope was that pools would thereby be eliminated. Only in such a manner, Johnson asserted, could the game be free of gambling. "The Federal government should intervene itself in this matter," he said. "The public believes in the integrity of baseball and it should be protected by Federal laws."[55]

CHAPTER FOURTEEN

# The Scandal Unveiled and One Innocent Amid the Black Sox

As the 1920 season wound to a close, organized baseball's Achilles' heel, its longtime, dark, dirty secret, threatened to overshadow the sensational yet tragic year that the majors had experienced. With a livelier baseball, batting averages and ERAs had both increased markedly, particularly in the American League. There, Babe Ruth's home run binge was the biggest individual story, but the batting feats of George Sisler, Tris Speaker, Joe Jackson, and Eddie Collins could hardly be ignored. Rogers Hornsby had become the National League's best and heaviest hitter, although he was a year removed from the period when his diamond feats became more remarkable still. Even in the midst of the batting splurge, notable pitching accomplishments were being attained, with Jim Bagby winning 31 games, Carl Mays 26, Stan Coveleski 24, and a quartet of White Sox becoming 20-game winners. In chalking up 27 victories, Pete Alexander won pitching's triple crown in the National League, while Wilbur Cooper captured 24 games and Burleigh Grimes, 23.

The pennant races in both leagues proved stirring throughout most of the season, with the Dodgers eventually coming out on top in the National League, beating out the Giants and the defending champion Reds. In the

American League, the contest went down to the wire, with the Indians nipping both the White Sox and the Yankees, the closest three team race since 1908.

Yet even before Cleveland and Brooklyn had clinched the pennants, the excitement regarding the impending World Series was at least somewhat tempered, because of revelations coming out of Chicago. Under Cook County Judge Charles A. McDonald's direction, a grand jury investigation of an alleged attempt to fix a single contest between the Cubs and Phillies soon broadened to include a series of other events, most notably the 1919 World Series.

Even while those games had been played, there had been discussion and rumors that something amiss was taking place. Gambling activity proved heavy and the odds rapidly shifted to Cincinnati. The contests themselves, for some at least, appeared curious, to say the least, with the heavy-hitting and slick-fielding White Sox inexplicably bumbling altogether, while their two best pitchers got whipped in five of six affairs; four of those, moreover, were blowouts. Fine fielders like shortstop Swede Risberg, Joe Jackson, and Happy Felsch performed, in several incidents, no better than did bush leaguers. Time after time, clutch hitters like Chick Gandil and Felsch failed to deliver. Most surprising of all, 1919's best pitcher, Eddie Cicotte, got blown out in game one and then literally threw away the fourth contest, while Lefty Williams, usually sure of control, was wild and hittable enough to drop three straight outings.

Rumors floated that the White Sox were battling against one another more fiercely than their opponents on the baseball diamond. Stories began to crop up that gamblers on the east coast or in the midwest had paid several Chicago players — including some of the game's finest — to throw the World Series. Charles Comiskey offered to pay, first $20,000, then half that amount, to anyone uncovering information that any of his ballplayers had deliberately failed to give their all.

During the off-season, as had been the case a year earlier, signs were clearly present that Comiskey's ball club was deeply troubled. First baseman Chick Gandil refused to play for Comiskey any longer, remaining on the west coast with his family. Infielders Swede Risberg, Fred McMullin, and Buck Weaver threatened to hold out as spring training approached. Weaver's demand for a new contract was the most serious, yet he eventually came into camp. Once the season started, the White Sox played brilliantly at times, but there were instances when the performance of certain ballplayers proved questionable to various observers. Still, Chicago battled with both the Indians and Yankees for league honors until the greatest scandal in American sports history began to unravel.

\* \* \*

"The last world's series between the Chicago White Sox and the Cincinnati Reds was not on the square," Assistant State's Attorney Hartley Replogle charged on September 22. "From five to seven players on the White Sox are involved." Initiating an investigation into alleged baseball gambling, the Cook County grand jury questioned American League president Ban Johnson, Chicago Cubs president William Veeck, and Chicago White Sox president Charles A. Comiskey; other scheduled witnesses included National League president John Heydler and New York Giants pitcher Rube Benton. Subpoenas had also been issued for the Giants' manager John McGraw, White Sox catcher Ray Schalk, Barry McCormick, who had umpired the August 31 contest between the Cubs and Phillies, and former journalist William Birch. Repolgle anticipated calling Giants president Charles Stoneman and newspaperman Joe Vila. While the questioning had occurred behind closed doors, Johnson acknowledged testifying as to his belief that various games had been thrown during 1919. That had led, Johnson indicated, to the ouster of certain ballplayers from the major leagues. By one account, Comiskey informed the grand jury that he had withheld World Series checks from various players while an investigation was being undertaken. He also spoke of his $10,000 offer to anyone who uncovered evidence of wrongdoing by White Sox players.[1]

During his testimony the following day, Benton stated that Hal Chase had made some $40,000 through "wise bets" on the 1919 World Series. Prior to testifying before the grand jury, Benton indicated that Chase and Buck Herzog had promised him "easy money" to toss a game against the Chicago Cubs. After talking to the grand jury, Benton repeated his earlier accusations, while now adding that Heinie Zimmerman had termed him "a poor fish" with "four hundred bucks ... waiting" if he threw the contest. Herzog reportedly strongly denied the charge.[2]

Also, on September 23, Ban Johnson informed reporters, "I heard several weeks ago a vague statement that the White Sox would not dare win the pennant this season. That statement was repeated several times, and within the last few weeks it has been hinted, more or less openly, that the Sox would not dare win because the gambling syndicate would tell what it knew of certain players in the Cincinnati-Sox world's championship games in 1919."[3]

A New York Times editorial on September 24 indicated that major league baseball "has been almost wholly free from serious charges of corruption" during the past four decades. The game had thrived as Americans were certain "of the purity of the national sport." Thanks largely to that confidence, baseball had become "a great and profitable industry." Now, however, the Times declared, "the sure-thing gamblers have tampered with the game." Should the prosecution demonstrate the authenticity of charges made about the 1919 World Series, the editorial maintained, then "it is the worst thing that has ever happened to professional baseball." If proven to be true, the Times declared, "the guilty men will undoubtedly be blacklisted." For "it is a matter of self-preservation as well as of honor and of pride in the national game to stamp out every vestige of crookedness."[4]

That same day, grand jury foreman H. H. Brigham told reporters that information had been presented indicating who had fixed the 1919 World Series. Acting at the behest of a gambling ring, that individual had purportedly tendered an offer to White Sox players to throw games. The testimony to date had led the grand jury to subpoena Arnold Rothstein, a major New York "sportsman" who was the controlling owner of the Havre de Grace racetrack, former major league pitcher William Burns, and ex-featherweight boxing champion Abe Attell. Brigham had earlier asserted that "crook work" had indeed impacted baseball.[5]

Away from the Chicago courthouse, Charles Comiskey blasted Ban Johnson for providing little help to investigate the charges directed at some of his ballplayers. Comiskey indicated that he had heard, following the 9-1 blowout in the first game of the 1919 World Series, certain White Sox were in on a fix. He immediately ordered Kid Gleason "to safeguard the series as much as possible." On the morning of game two, Comiskey informed National League president Heydler of the rumors. He also instructed Gleason "to take out any ball player who did not appear to be doing his best." After the Series, Comiskey undertook his own investigation into the possibility of a fixed World Series. Now, he promised to provide "every assistance" to the Cook County Criminal Court "to turn up any evidence of crookedness that exists affecting the honesty or integrity of the great American pastime — baseball." Comiskey then declared, "I'll go further, if any of my players are not honest I'll fire them, no matter who they are and if I can't get honest players to fill their places I'll close the gates of the park that I spent a lifetime to build, and in which, in the declining years of my life, I take the greatest measure of pride and pleasure."[6]

Rube Benton also claimed that a $100,000 pool had been delivered by a Pittsburgh gambling syndicate to various White Sox players to "lay down" so that a Reds' victory would be assured. This information, Benton indicated, was obtained during a visit to his home by "a betting commissioner" from Cincinnati. Benton then stated,

> We discussed various players on the team. Buck Weaver's name was not mentioned, nor were the names of Jackson, Eddie Collins, John Collins or Ray Schalk. Five players were mentioned by Hahn in the course of the conversation. Four are: Eddie Cicotte ... Claude Williams ... Chick Gandil ... and Hap Felsch. ... I do not recall the name of the fifth man.[7]

*The New York Tribune* and *The New York Times* now printed the names of the players whose 1919 World Series checks had been held up by White Sox management. They were Cicotte, Williams, Felsch, Weaver, Swede Risberg, Jackson, Gandil, and Fred McMullin.[8]

On September 25, former Cubs owner Charles Weeghman claimed that professional gamblers began plotting, in August 1919, to frame that year's World Series. Weeghman related how he had encountered Chicago gambler Mont Tennes at the Saratoga racetrack. Tennes informed him "that a well-known New York gambler had told him that seven White Sox players had been 'fixed' to throw the series." When asked if he had relayed the information to league president Heydler, Weeghman admitted, "I think I did tell him, although I do not know how soon, because I was at Saratoga and having a pretty good time. It might have slipped my mind because I thought so much of baseball that it seemed impossible to me that any player or set of players could be bribed to throw a series."[9]

Indicating that his grand jury testimony would be illuminating, Ray Schalk declared, "It is up to the baseball players themselves to protect the sport. If they are going to drag me into this I am going before the grand jury and tell all I know. I will mention the names of men on my own team."[10]

On September 26, National League president John Heydler acknowledged that Charles Comiskey and White Sox manager Kid Gleason had been convinced, following the first contest of the 1919 World Series, that the games were "fixed." When he informed Ban Johnson about the Chicago management's suspicions, the American League boss expressed little enthusiasm for undertaking an investigation. Heydler also revealed that Rube Benton had indicated former major league pitcher Jean Dubuc was apprised by William Burns about a World Series fix. Heydler further noted that Lee Magee had confessed to both him and Cubs owner William Veeck that he had been involved with Hal Chase in an attempt to throw a game. By contrast, Heydler was unwilling to verify if Heinie Zimmerman had similarly been involved in such an effort.[11]

As Heydler viewed matters, the New York Giants had been more vigilant than any other ball club in attacking the gambling problem. "McGraw deliberately wrecked his pennant chances," Heydler declared, "by getting rid of Chase and Zimmerman because of their alleged gambling and game-throwing." It was Chase, not Buck Herzog, whom Benton had pointed to, Heydler recalled, when they discussed efforts to fix a game between the Cubs and Giants. Benton, the starting pitcher in that contest, had been ordered by McGraw "to either win or buy a ticket home."[12]

The New York Tribune also reported that White Sox infielders McMullin and Weaver had denied participating in schemes to drop World Series games. Leaks from the grand jury, however, indicated that McMullin had served as the "go-between" for gamblers and his teammates. After Chicago whipped Detroit 8-1, behind Eddie Cicotte's seven-hitter, a reporter attempted to talk with Weaver about the scandal. In Eight Men Out, Eliot Asinof indicated that Weaver denied any wrongdoing, declaring, "Look I didn't get no money. Not from nobody!"[13]

In his brilliant examination of the 1919 World Series, Asinof claimed that Weaver refused to go along with the fix. This was something that Chick Gandil and the other conspirators were clearly aware of. Weaver's love of the game was seemingly too great, too pure even, to allow him to do anything but play his hardest:

> Each year, he's played his heart out. Every game was THE game. Every swing was real. The old, worn piece of dirty leather on his left hand was a tool of his greatness, and he slapped it, fondled it, oiled it with genuine concern. Relentlessly he would concentrate on every pitch. Life was this momentary thing, over and over again. He would set himself loose, yet alert, sharp as a tack. Nothing else mattered but the round white ball and that split second when it moved at him, sometimes with the speed of a bullet. He loved it. He loved the quickness of his body, his instinct to lean one way or the other in anticipation of a hit at him.[14]

News reports indicated that Ban Johnson had just returned from New York City, where he had met with gambling kingpin Arnold Rothstein, the purported mastermind behind the World Series fix. After speaking with Rothstein, Johnson indicated, "I felt convinced he wasn't in any plot to fix the world series. He did admit that he heard of the fixing." Nevertheless, Rothstein supposedly bet on the White Sox to take the first game, before switching to the Reds for game two. Rothstein denied having "won an enormous sum on the series," but was aware that Abe Attell was involved in efforts to carrying out a fix.[15]

Johnson's own role in the now unfolding investigation, Charles Comiskey suggested, was hardly above reproach.

> I will say this. There's one man working on this investigation and I did think he was sincere in it for a time, but I believe now he's using it for his own personal gain. It was a terrible thing to see a story printed of crookedness on the White Sox recently, just before they went into a tough series against New York; but it was still worse to follow with a statement of blackmail of my players by gamblers just before they went into the series against Cleveland, a club in which this man is interested.
> I refer to Ban Johnson, the President of our league.[16]

Elbert Sanders, writing in *The Sporting News*, defended Johnson for having long toiled "diligently" on the gambling issue. "Far seeing as he is," Sanders declared, "he had been after his magnates for several years, issuing warning upon warning against the growing evil of betting on ball games." Unfortunately, however, "the smug magnates saw no great danger in the betting that was becoming more of a nuisance, even if not apparently a danger, all the time." By contrast, Sanders blasted Comiskey, with the kind of criticism the Chicago owner previously had been immune to:

Charles A. Comiskey makes a rather sorry figure trying to lay the blame for his White Sox not being cleaned out last fall on the shoulders of Ban Johnson — for certainly it was Commy's first duty, and everybody can imagine what a howl would have gone up from Commy's associates had Johnson ordered dismissal of a single White Sox last fall, at a time when he was grappling with Comiskey in the Mays case war.

Still, Sanders acknowledged that even his harshest foes would neither accuse Comiskey of accepting overt dishonesty on the part of team members nor claim that he would hesitate, because of financial considerations, to usher them from the game.[17]

Also, in *The Sporting News*, James C. Isaminger blamed organized baseball for having downplayed the Hal Chase affair. It was the responsibility of the owners, Isaminger asserted, to ensure that the game remained clean. Furthermore, "the public is in no humor for baseball politics at this stage."[18]

In his column for *The New York Tribune*, W. O. McGeehan, on September 27, wrote that "so far nothing tangible, nothing coherent, has come out of the grand jury investigation into the charges of crookedness in the last world's series." To date, McGeehan claimed, "baseball is the one clean professional sport." While nothing to the contrary had now been proven, he argued, "the baseball fans want to know the whole truth. If the whole truth does not come out of this investigation then the game will suffer. If there is any evidence that players have been tampered with and that games have been thrown those players must be expelled from organized baseball. The game must be cleaned up."[19]

Crooked ballplayers, *The New York Times* agreed, would have to "be expelled from the game for all time." The present investigation into alleged fixes involving baseball, the *Times* argued, would benefit the sport. While a temporary blow would thereby be received, "baseball itself is too big an institution to be permanently crippled by the actions of a few players who betray their trust for the sake of money." The vast bulk of ballplayers were honest, the *Times* continued, and "the game can well spare the crooks, regardless of their ability on the diamond."[20]

Professional gamblers, the *Times* indicated, had long sought to carve out a niche in baseball, but generally to little avail. During the past two years, "some crooked ballplayers" had set the stage for "the sure thing gentry" who were seeking "big cleanups." After the present inquiry was concluded, the *Times* hoped that crooked and honest players could be separated. "A sport that has honesty of endeavor as its crowning virtue has been contaminated by crooks," the *Times* acknowledged, "but in the main it will be found to have been as honest as the American public has always regarded it."[21]

In Philadelphia, on September 28, more revelations were forthcoming about the World Series fix. He and former big leaguer Bill Burns, ex-boxer

Billy Maharg admitted, had helped to trigger the conspiracy that purportedly led eight Chicago White Sox to throw the 1919 World Series. Maharg revealed that the first, second, and eighth games of the Chicago-Cincinnati affair had been thrown. White Sox pitching ace Ed Cicotte had tendered the offer to toss the World Series to the two men in a New York hotel room. The players were promised $100,000 but only received a tenth of that amount. Former boxing champ Abe Attell amassed a considerable fortune for himself and a group of New York gamblers but reneged on his promises to the players. Attell cleaned up, in large part because he devised a fake telegram that supposedly verified Arnold Rothstein's bankrolling of the scheme. Maharg and Burns, expecting a fix in the third contest, bet heavily, with disastrous results.[22]

When informed about Maharg's accusations, Charles Comiskey sent a wire asking the former pugilist to testify before the Cook County Grand Jury. Promising to pay Maharg $10,000 if his charges panned out, Comiskey also again declared, "Furthermore, I'll see that every player implicated is fired from organized baseball forever."[23]

Responding to Comiskey's charges that he was seeking to benefit from the scandal, Ban Johnson stated,

> This is not a time for quibbling and side issues. The integrity of professional baseball is on trial before a Grand Jury of Cook County and we are content to abide by its investigation and decision. It is the only sane and thorough method of unraveling a mass of appalling charges.
>
> If the allegations are true, then the guilty must be brought to the bar of justice. There was a time the authorities of the game could have controlled the gambling situation, when it was in the spawning period. Today it has grown to such proportions that the hand of a stronger and sterner power has been invoked.

Johnson then expressed his astonishment that newspapers would give any credence "to the vaporings of a man whose vindictiveness toward the President of the American League has been so long and thoroughly known."[24]

The American League pennant race, on the morning of September 28, remained one of the tightest on record. The Indians stood at 94-54, while the White Sox were at 95-56, a half game and six percentage points back. The Yankees, with their 93-59 record, were three behind and close to being eliminated mathematically. If Chicago won the title, Comiskey indicated, all members of his ball club, including those suspected of engaging in the World Series fix, would play against the National League champion Dodgers. All, he declared, were entitled to the presumption of innocence until their guilt was verified.[25]

Comiskey's pennant hopes were dashed that very day when the Cook County grand jury indicted seven present White Sox and one former team member for conspiring with gamblers to throw the 1919 World Series. *The New York Tribune* noted that among those charged were "stars of the first magnitude and some of them for years have been idols of the fans." Those charged included Eddie Cicotte, Lefty Williams, Joe Jackson, Happy Felsch, Buck Weaver, Chick Gandil, Swede Risberg, and Fred McMullin. With but three games remaining on Chicago's schedule, all those indicted, other than light-hitting reserve infielder McMullin and the retired Gandil, were having big seasons as the White Sox vied for their third pennant in four years. Both Williams and Cicotte were 20-game winners. Jackson was batting .382, third best in the league, with a career high 12 homers and 121 RBIs. Weaver was having his best year, hitting .331, with 34 doubles, 208 hits, 102 runs scored, and 74 RBIs. Felsch too was experiencing his finest season, with career peaks of 14 homers, 115 RBIs, and a .338 batting average. Risberg, despite missing several games due to injury, was hitting .266, with 10 triples and 65 RBIs.

The story now broke that both Cicotte and Jackson had confessed to having received $10,000 and $5,000 respectively to help fix the 1919 World Series. Cicotte was said to have broken down before the grand jury, "My God I think of my children. I never did anything I regretted so much in my life. I would give anything in the world if I could undo my acts in the last world's series. I've played a crooked game and I have lost, and I am here to tell the whole truth. I've lived a thousand years in the last year." In the opening game, Cicotte indicated, "I wasn't putting a thing on the ball." Then, in game four, the pitcher acknowledged, he deliberately committed two errors to cost Chicago another contest. Cicotte blamed Risberg, Gandil, and McMullin for pressuring him for a full week prior to the start of the World Series. Needing to pay off a $4,000 mortgage on a farm, Cicotte agreed to the fix. He met with the other indicted White Sox shortly before his first outing, when it was agreed to throw the games. As for himself, Cicotte cried out, "I had sold out 'Commy.' I had sold out the other boys, sold them for $10,000 to pay off a mortgage on a farm, and for the wife and kids." Cicotte admitted, "I've lost everything — job, reputation and friends. My friends all bet on the Sox. I knew it, but I couldn't tell them that the Sox would lose. I had to double-cross them. I'm through with baseball. I'm going to lose myself and start life over again."[26]

He had been promised $20,000, Jackson related, but received only $5,000 from Lefty Williams. He and his fellow conspirators, Jackson revealed, attempted unsuccessfully to throw game three, but Dickie Kerr's three-hit shutout precluded that possibility. That resulted in gamblers double-crossing the players "for 'double-crossing' them." Almost pathetically, Jackson declared, "They've hung it on me. They ruined me when I went to the ship-yards. But I don't care what happens now. I guess I'm through with baseball. I wasn't wise enough, like Chick, to beat them to it. But some of them will sweat before the game is over." As for himself, he planned, Jackson reported, to remain near his "protectors until this blows over. Swede is a hard guy."[27]

On leaving the courtroom, Jackson purportedly encountered a group of kids who plaintively asked, "It isn't true, is it, Joe?" By one account, their fallen hero responded, "Yes, boys, I'm afraid it is." Silently, the youngsters moved aside, letting Jackson pass.[28]

Facing the possibility of five-year prison sentences and fines as high as $10,000 apiece, the indicted players were now suspended from the Chicago White Sox. Acting at Comiskey's behest, attorney Alfred S. Austrian mailed the following letter to the eight ballplayers:

> You and each of you are hereby notified of your indefinite suspension as a member of the Chicago American League baseball club.
>
> Your suspension is brought about by information which has just come to me directly involving you and each of you in the baseball scandal (now being investigated by the present grand jury of Cook County) resulting from the world series of 1919.
>
> If you are innocent of any wrongdoing you and each of you will be reinstated; if you are guilty you will be retired from organized baseball for the rest of your lives, if I can accomplish it.
>
> Until there is a finality to this investigation it is due to the public that I take this action, even though it costs Chicago the pennant.

Comiskey, in the words of *The New York Times*, thus proceeded in "wrecking the team he had given years to build up and almost certainly forfeiting his chances to beat out Cleveland for the American League pennant."[29]

Yankee owners Jacob Ruppert and T. L. Huston wired a telegram to Comiskey, delivering the following offer:

> Your action in suspending players under suspicion, although it wrecks your entire organization and perhaps your cherished lifework, not only challenges our admiration but excites our sympathy and demands our practical assistance. You are making a terrible sacrifice to preserve the integrity of the game. So grave and unforeseen an emergency requires unusual remedies.
>
> Therefore, in order that you may play out your schedule and, if necessary the world's series, our entire club is placed at your disposal. We are confident that Cleveland sportsmanship will not permit you to lose by default and will welcome the arrangement. We are equally certain that any technicality in carrying it out can be readily overcome by action of the part of the National Commission.[30]

After being apprised of both his indictment and subsequent suspension, Buck Weaver denied any involvement in the campaign to fix the 1919 World Series or receipt of ill-won funds. "I batted .333 (actually .324) and made only four (actually 0) errors out of thirty chances (actually 27) in the world series," asserted Weaver, whom the *Tribune* referred to as "one of baseball's leading third basemen." "That should be a good enough alibi."[31]

That evening, Comiskey made another statement to the Associated Press:

> The consideration which the grand jury gave to this case should be greatly appreciated by the general public. The Hon. Charles A. McDonald, Chief Justice, and the foreman of the grand jury, Harry Brigham, and his associates who so diligently strove to save and make America's great game the clean sport which it is are to be commended in no uncertain terms by all sports followers, in spite of what happened to-day. And, thank God, it did happen! Forty-four years of baseball endeavor have convinced me more than ever that it is a wonderful game and a game worth keeping clean.
>
> I would rather close my ball park than send nine men on the field with one of them holding a dishonest thought toward clean baseball — the game which John McGraw and I went around the world to show to the people on the other side.
>
> We are far from through yet. We have the nucleus of another championship team with the remainder of the old world's championship team.[32]

Also, that evening, White Sox players not involved in the fix held a celebration dinner, with Eddie Collins, Eddie Murphy, Amos Strunk, Nemo Leibold, and Shano Collins present. "We've known something was wrong for a long time, but we felt we had to keep silent because we were fighting for the pennant." Although unable to be on hand, Red Faber and Ray Schalk telephoned in support of the "clearing of the atmosphere." Chicago manager Kid Gleason asserted, "We're going to win the pennant and then the world's series, in spite of this." Happy "that it's all cleared up," Gleason declared, "The men on my team now are real men and real ball players."[33]

On September 29, reports from the Cook County Grand Jury continued to make for front-page headlines. Two gamblers were indicted: Boston's Joseph "Sport" Sullivan — the same figure whom pitcher Carl Mays had once been associated with — and an individual only referred to as "Brown." The more riveting news involved the confession of Lefty Williams, who indicated that he had received $10,000 after the fourth game of the series. He then delivered half that amount to Jackson. Denying that an actual meeting of the indicted ballplayers had taken place prior to the start of the World Series, Williams declared that the various players "just dropped in one a time" to Chick Gandil's room. Among those present, in addition to Williams himself, were Eddie Cicotte, Gandil, Happy Felsch, and Buck Weaver. When queried as to how much Weaver had been paid, Williams replied, "I could not say." Williams was then asked, "Did he tell you how much he got?" Williams responded, "He never did." Williams also named Sullivan and Brown as involved in the fix; they were reported to be associated with a New York gambling ring and to be confederates of Abe Attell, the so-called "chief of fixers."[34]

Happy Felsch also presented his own confession, although not in the grand jury setting. "Well, the beans are all spilled, and I think I am through with baseball. I got my $5,000, and I supposed the others got theirs, too," declared Felsch.

> I don't know what I'm going to do now. I have been a baseball player during the best years of my life, and I never got into any other kind of business. I'm going to hell, I guess. I intend to hang around Chicago a while until I see how this thing is going to go. Then maybe I'll go back to Milwaukee.
>
> I wish that I hadn't gone into it. I guess we all do. We have more than earned the few dollars they gave us for turning crooked.[35]

Then, Felsch attempted to refute the notion of any unsavory play by the White Sox during the current season. "The talk that we 'threw' games this year is bunk. We knew we were suspected and we tried to be square. But a guy can't be crooked part of the time and square the rest of the time. We knew that sooner or later somebody was going to turn up the whole deal."[36]

Declaring that he had not wanted to participate initially, Felsch stated, "I had always received square treatment from 'Commy' and it didn't look quite right to throw him down." After agreeing to the fix, Felsch was handed $5,000 in a dirty envelope from Williams, as he had informed Judge McDonald. "He said he didn't care what I got," Felsch related, "that if I got what I ought to get for crabbing the game of the kids I wouldn't be telling him my story."[37]

Grand jury foreman Harry Brigham delivered his own early assessment of the World Series fix. The players were "apparently only tools of a gambling ring," which had made inroads throughout professional baseball. Brigham declared,

> It is plainly evident that some of those boys yielded to the influence of those whose names doubtless will appear in the list of defendants later on. I sympathize with some of them. They were foolish, unsophisticated country boys who yielded to the temptations placed in their path by professional gamblers.
>
> I hope the cleansing process of this investigation will extend to all the sore spots in the sporting world.[38]

Comiskey now estimated his monetary loss, considering the value of the seven players who had been on the White Sox' 1920 roster, at $230,000. Jackson, Weaver, and Felsch, in his estimation, were all worth $50,000, while Cicotte and Williams had a market value of $25,000 apiece. Risberg's valuation was set at $20,000, McMullin's was half that amount.[39]

The Chicago owner admitted, "It's been tough, but I feel better this morning. I am glad the worst is over. The boys who are left are clean; they have never sold a ball game and they never will." Kid Gleason asserted that his team was still in the pennant race and would do everything it could to win, despite the loss of so many key players. Among the remnants of his once powerful ball club were some who charged that certain of their teammates had been seeking to prevent Chicago from repeating in the American League.[40]

No one cared what happened, Ed R. Hughes of *The San Francisco Chronicle* indicated, to the indicted ballplayers. "They are dead so far as baseball is concerned." However, "everyone who loves his country should care a great deal whether or not baseball itself is to survive. Baseball means something to this country, and the game itself is bigger than the crooks who have tried to ruin it." Hughes also focused on the dilemma that Buck Weaver had faced the previous fall:

> Honest ball players have held off in the past, deeming it dishonorable to "snitch" on a fellow player, but with the life of the game itself in the balance the time has come for the honest players to flock together and kick into deserved oblivion the crooks that are befouling the sport which has been well named the "national game" of the United States.[41]

St. Louis Browns owner Phil Ball had a solution for the players who had engaged in the World Series fix. "There is no room in baseball for crooked players," he declared. "Throw them out and keep them out."[42]

That solution alone would hardly satisfy *The Los Angeles Times'* editorial staff. To save the "American institution" of baseball, the *Times* argued on September 30, required "fumigation" of gamblers. However, "outraged justice will not be appeased," the paper contended, "until those crooks are doing forced labor in a penal institution. They must be made to know that one does not debauch an American ideal, either of government or sport, with impunity." The *Times* suggested that "the weight of public contempt" had already "crushed" the ballplayers who had been in on the fix. Broke, they would leave prison in the same fashion, "slinking in the shadows." In the *Times'* estimation, "they are as dead to the life they once knew as though in their graves; for it was their own future that they gambled away when they played the game slackly because they were paid for it."[43]

In his column on September 30, Grantland Rice discussed the dilemmas major league baseball was confronting.

> Baseball, as the national game of 110,000,000 people, faces a serious struggle to get back into the open again.
> If the game were not so firmly intrenched (sic) in the souls of the multitude and if it were not generally understood that a vast majority of players were honest, the struggle to get back would be even more serious than it is — if not altogether hopeless.

But, even as it is, there are thousands upon thousands of loyal fans who have been badly stunned.

For years they have thundered not only their belief in baseball's complete honesty — but they have shown how it was impossible to throw a game. Not physically impossible — but too uncertain a proposition for gamblers to take up.

But a professional gambler can wreck any sport in the world — even baseball.[44]

Rice then contended that "an aggressive, active National Commission" could have prevented any new scandals from arising. Unfortunately, however, major league baseball lacked a chairman and the moguls made little effort to rectify the situation. "So they attempted to cover up the fire. Or rather they attempted to put out the fire by covering it up." Now fully in place, the scandal, Rice predicted, "is going to do a lot of damage before the finish." To date, it had caused many to distrust the game. The scandal's total obliteration required the fullest investigation possible, topped off by "prison sentences for every ballplayer and every gambler involved." This was necessary, Rice believed, because

those mixed up in this crookedness are worse than thieves and burglars. They are the ultimate scum of the universe, and even the spotted civilization of the present time has no place for them outside of a penitentiary.

The only complaint in this case would come from the thieves and murderers, who might have a just kick in being forced to associate with the crooked gamblers and the crooked ballplayers convicted of the dirtiest crime in sport.[45]

After completing a four game series sweep against the Browns, the Indians now held a 1½ game lead over the White Sox. The Yankees had finished at 95-59 and thus were eliminated, for Cleveland had already compiled 96 victories.

On September 30, Judge Charles A. McDonald, Chief Justice of the Cook County Criminal Court, vowed to continue the inquiry into baseball gambling. He made that assertion following State's Attorney Maclay Hoyne's observation that valid indictments would be difficult to draw up against the players. Charles Comiskey's business operations, McDonald charged, had been injured with his attorney now placing the loss at $500,000, the majority attributed to the White Sox' drawing power.[46]

Assistant State's Attorney Hartley Replogle issued his own statement:

We have now discovered that baseball games have been bought and sold, by unscrupulous gamblers and baseball players. There must be no repetition of this scandal. Congress should pass an act making it a felony for any one to offer a bribe or a gratuity to any baseball player playing interstate baseball to play our national game other than on its merits, also making it a felony for any such player to accept such a bribe or gratuity. Let Congress act.[47]

Two incidents related to the ongoing investigation demonstrated its considerable impact. In Chicago, Buck Herzog, on leaving Joliet Park after the completion of an exhibition contest, was stabbed three times by an irate fan who went after him, hollering, "Here are some of those crooked Chicago ball players!" In Boston, newsboys blasted the indicted White Sox for having cast a "murderous blow at the kids' game." By contrast, these members of the Roosevelt Newsboys' Club praised Ray Schalk and Dickie Kerr "for their manly stand against the Benedict Arnolds of baseball."[48]

After taking State's Attorney Hoyne to task, *The New York Times* discussed how significant the revelations of baseball corruption were:

JACKSON and FELSCH and CICOTTE and WEAVER and the rest of them were heroes to the boys of America. They belonged to the goodly fellowship that includes pirates and Indian fighters, super-detectives and, more recently, aces of the air service. To hear that they sold a world's series is as bad news to the boys of America as if one of our modern historians should discover that DANIEL BOONE had been bought by the Indians to lose his fights in Kentucky, or that PAUL JONES had thrown the Serapis-Bonborgme Richard battle for British gold.

On city corner lots, in small towns and country villages, on diamonds improvised by farm lads in the stubblefield, millions of boys have spent the energy of their growing years in the wild hope that some day they, too, might take their places in the fellowship of the big-league elect. Most of them eventually outgrew the ambition, but it did them no harm. And now they find that some of their heroes were only crooks, and contemptible, whimpering crooks at that. They did it for their wives and children or to lift a mortgage from the old farm. They had scruples about going in, and their guilty knowledge was an awful load on the conscience, but they all kept quiet till they had been found out; then they did what they could to get off easily by betraying each other.

Perhaps the law has no punishment for them. Leave it to a vote of the fans, and they would be punished.[49]

Talking to reporters, Buck Weaver insisted,

I've been wrongfully accused and I intend to fight. I shall be in major-league baseball next year, if not with the White Sox, then with some other team. They have nothing on me. I'm going to hire the best lawyer in Chicago to defend me, and I'm going to be cleared.

Look, I know you have to put in local color in an interview. But print what I say, and don't say I'm prematurely aged over this thing. Don't say my shoulders are drooping, my head hanging, and my back humped. I'm no condemned criminal and I don't like being pictured as one![50]

When informed that Weaver and Chick Gandil were among the suspect players, minor league catcher Joe Jenkins, a reserve catcher on both Chicago's 1917 world championship and 1919 pennant winning squads, was taken aback:

> I was certainly surprised to read where 'Buck' Weaver and 'Chick' Gandil were brought into the mess. There was always a suspicion about some of the other men named, but those two were not thought of. Weaver hit well and played a great game at third base, while Gandil hit in most of the runs for us and one could not tell by his playing there was anything wrong.[51]

\* \* \*

On October 1, State's Attorney Hoyne exclaimed, "I have evidence that 1920 games were 'fixed' and I have information that the forthcoming world's series was to be 'fixed.'" Having succeeded so well the previous fall, gamblers intended once again, Hoyne warned, "to pollute the national sport." Fearing that very possibility, *The New York Times* called for making the bribing of players in organized baseball a capital offense, as it strikes "at the very heart of this nation." The following day, the Cook County grand jurors now comprised a special jury empowered to investigate more fully the baseball scandal.[52]

That same day, Kings County District Attorney Harry E. Lewis indicated that his investigation had failed to unveil "a single suspicion" of an effort to fix the 1920 World Series among the Brooklyn Dodgers. Instead, Lewis noted, "I think it would be very dangerous for any gambler to approach any one of them with a dishonest suggestion."[53]

As for those who "sold out" the game, Yankee owner Jacob Ruppert, like Charles Comiskey, insisted that "they are forever out of organized baseball. They will never have a chance to return. They won't be able to hold up their heads again." Baseball, he declared, "must be kept clean."[54]

On October 4, the day before the World Series opened, White Sox reserves Byrd Lynn and Harvey McClellan charged that some of the indicted ballplayers threw games during the 1920 regular season. Chicago lost the pennant, they claimed, because

> certain players ... didn't want us to win. We soon noticed how carefully they studied the score board — more than even the average player does in a pennant race and that they always made errors which lost us the game when Cleveland and New York were losing. If Cleveland won — we won. If Cleveland lost — we lost. The idea was to keep up the betting odds, but not to let us win the pennant.[55]

In an interview with *The Sporting News*, one player reported,

When we started on our last trip East we have every reason to believe we were on our way to win a pennant. Then Cicotte and Williams seemed to go bad without reason; Jackson, Felsch and Risberg began dumping the ball to the infield every time we have a chance to score runs. Some of us always had believed we were sold out in the World's Series. When the players showed they meant to beat us out of getting in on this one we decided to act. Cicotte was told he would have to win a certain game or he would be mobbed on the field by the honest players on the team — he won it.[56]

Another account also had White Sox players complaining about the antics of various teammates during the 1920 season. "We would have won the pennant in a walk," they reported, "if those fellows had played fair." Cicotte was warned that he had better win one particular game, and as the story went, the pitcher had a choice to make. He could choose "between double-crossing his gambler partners and taking a licking from his team mates." Consequently, "he decided, naturally, to double cross."[57]

Also, on October 4, Chicago owner Charles Comiskey announced that he was delivering a $1,500 bonus to ten ballplayers who had not been involved in the 1919 World Series fix. In a note to the players, Comiskey declared,

As one of the honest players of the White Sox team of 1919 I feel that you are deprived of the winner's share of the world's series receipts through no fault of yours. I do not intend that you, as an honest ball player, should be penalized for your honesty or by reason of the dishonesty of others, and therefore take pleasure in handing you $1,500, being the difference between the winner's and the loser's share. I wish you all the luck possible and hope that the future will bring nothing but happiness to you and yours.

In response, the players — who included Ray Schalk, Red Faber, Dickie Kerr, and Eddie Collins — indicated that they wanted "the world to know the generosity of our employer."[58]

In his column for *The New York Tribune*, W. O. McGeehan contended that "the entire nation is shocked" by the grand jury revelations. While American big business operations and political machinations were often viewed as suspect, "it was a tradition that the American national game was absolutely straight." But now it was clear that crookedness existed "and on a big scale, in professional baseball." This was all the more troubling, McGeehan suggested, because

the game has been so much of a part of the national life that the whole country is concerned. They will demand an accounting of their stewardship from the magnates to whom the national game has been intrusted (sic). For the national game is not entirely the property of the owners of baseball clubs and of baseball parks. Aside from the schools, the games of a nation play the most important part in the development of its people. Corruption in a nation's sports is of almost as great concern as corruption is its educational system.[59]

\* \* \*

On October 7, *The Sporting News* discussed National League president John A. Heydler's declaration that White Sox officials knew of the fix shortly after the 1919 World Series. An editorial mistakenly asked why Charles Comiskey was kept in the dark about "all this terrible thing — for there is no one who would say had he known he would not have been quick and determined in his action?" After all, *The Sporting News* incorrectly reasoned, the Old Roman, notwithstanding his faults, "with his pride, and the glory he took in his baseball career, and that of his White Sox, would not have allowed a crooked ball player to wear his colors, nor would he have counted the cost — had he known of that player's crookedness."[60]

That same issue contained an article comparing the present scandal with the one that had beset the National League during its infancy over forty years earlier. Paul W. Eaton singled out Chicago's third baseman for particular consideration:

> Take the case of Buck Weaver, an easy going, happy-go-lucky chap, without enough business instinct to take care of his own money. He seems to have hesitated considerably before he was coaxed to go in, if it should be proved that he did go in at all.

Also expressing a certain sympathy for Eddie Cicotte, Eaton hoped that the courts would recognize that varying degrees of guilt should be assigned to the players. Nevertheless, he then wrote, "But this is a case where organized baseball cannot show leniency even to those it might like to extend to it. It is compelled, in self defense, and for self preservation, to expel them from the game for life. To condone any such offense would quickly kill the game."[61]

The following week, *The Sporting News* presented a lengthy article entitled, "Chicago Fans Grieve Most for Weaver and Still Hope for Him." News of Weaver's purported involvement in the scandal had most affected those who followed the White Sox:

> Weaver was an idol on the South side, not because of his personality, but because of the aggressiveness with which he played. Few more aggressive ball players ever have been in the American League. It was though he could not loaf in a ball game if he tried, because he loved to win too much. He always tried, was ever ready to take advantage of an opponent's mistake and enthused beyond compare when it fell to his lot to drive home a run or win a ball game. It was this unlimited interest, this determination and this dexterity that caused the followers of the White Sox team to place such implicit faith in his honesty.

When rumors emerged about which players might have been involved in a fix, "Weaver's name was one that was never mentioned."[62]

While Weaver insisted he was innocent, Oscar C. Reichow continued, Chicago fans argued that "he made the mistake of his life" in not informing Comiskey after the first contest in Cincinnati had been thrown. Reichow contended, "He should have protected the fair name of the national game and at the same time kept the finger of suspicion from pointing strongly at him. I addition, he could have saved his reputation, moral character and decency of the players who are now out of baseball for all time."[63]

Weaver's protestations of innocence soon compelled W. A. Phelon of *Baseball Magazine* to reexamine painstakingly the 1919 World Series records. Having done so, Phelon reported,

> I'll say close analysis fails to show a darned thing on Weaver. The confessions so far made have him pinned pretty tight — but the scores don't show it. If he played crooked, he must have done it in a strangely clever, hidden, most insidious way. Can it be possible that Weaver, intending to play crooked ball, mechanically played blamed good ball in spite of himself?

As Phelon indicated, Weaver fielded flawlessly, got 11 hits, including four doubles and a triple, and was robbed of four other extra-base hits and another single by great Reds' fielding.[64]

On October 27, White Sox secretary Harry Grabiner made an entry into his diary regarding a conversation between Weaver and Rosenbaum. Weaver acknowledged having attended a meeting in which talk unfolded about throwing the 1919 World Series. Offered $5,000, Weaver was said to have taken the "matter under consideration but refused to be a party to same." Chick Gandil told Weaver that the fix was on "regardless of his connection," but "he refused to be a party to same." At the same time, Weaver refused to inform on his friends and teammates. He also indicated that Fred McMullin had "approached him during 1920 season to throw a game for 500 which he refused."[65]

On October 30, *Collyer's Eye* offered a front page story in which Eddie Collins charged that certain of his teammates had thrown games during both the 1919 World Series and the past season. Collins claimed that he was aware of such schemes during Chicago's first at-bats in the initial frame of game one against Cincinnati. After Nemo Leibold singled, Collins, in attempting to bunt his teammate along, forced him at second. Weaver was up next and delivered the hit-and-run signal. When Collins took off, Weaver failed to take a swipe at the plate. After being tagged out, Collins "accused Weaver of not even attempting to hit the ball." In addition, Collins claimed, "Weaver and Cicotte 'threw' many games during 1920." The Boston series was the most egregious of all to Collins, who called it "the rawest thing I ever saw." He then exclaimed, "If the gamblers didn't have Weaver and Cicotte in their pocket then I don't know a thing about baseball."[66]

# CHAPTER FIFTEEN

# Savior of the Game: Baseball's Great Dictator

The unraveling of the 1919 World Series scandal caused both sports-writers and baseball insiders to demand a revision of the seemingly impotent National Commission. Many blamed its weaknesses for having spawned the culture of cover-ups, evasions, and dissembling that had enabled crooked ballplayers and gamblers to fix games. Now, it was increasingly clear that America's greatest sporting event, the World Series, was hardly immune to such developments. Fearing for not only the well being but the very viabil-ity of organized baseball, baseball men and reporters insisted that the game's governing body be transformed. Caught up in the circle of events was the ongoing power struggle pitting American League president Ban Johnson — long viewed as baseball's czar — and a group of loyal supporters against his implacable foes. For a brief spell in the fall of 1920, there was talk of reconfiguring the American and National leagues, of even replacing them with one twelve-team unit.

The result of these enterprises was the appointment of Judge Kenesaw Mountain Landis as commissioner of major league baseball. The powers granted to Landis would be considerable, yet it was quickly evident that he was determined to widen their scope still further. Fearing the kind of public backlash that had resulted in Landis's selection in the first place, owners generally caved in, enabling the commissioner to be viewed as the dictator of

Judge Kenesaw Mountain Landis, 1920. National Baseball Hall of Fame Library, Cooperstown, N.Y.

baseball. They did so as well because Landis proved to be a master at working the public relations angle, presenting himself as the repository of the time-honored values associated with the national game. Landis thus acquired a power base of his own, yet he was astute enough to recognize that it rested ultimately on the good will of the moguls themselves. Thus, the seemingly stolid standards he demanded of players did not always have to be attained by the men who paid their salaries and reaped whatever profits baseball amassed during a troubled, but generally golden period. Those standards, as matters bore out, were not always locked into place, even pertaining to ballplayers. Landis wielded the clubs of temporary suspensions, fines, and banishments, and he did so in the same arbitrary, at times, seemingly irrational manner, he had employed in his federal courtroom. All the while, print journalists continued to sing his praises as the man who saved major league baseball and restored the faith of the American people in the grand old game. Moreover, that game, throughout his tenure, remained determinedly segregated, with Landis demanding that Jim Crow barriers be held aloft.

* * *

Militantly intolerant and certain of his own moral rectitude, Kenesaw Mountain Landis undoubtedly watched with delight as 1919 gave way to the new decade. The raids then unfolding against radicals of various stripes must have pleased him greatly. After all, Landis had recently exploded on being informed that Victor Berger had won a special election to regain the congressional seat denied him by the House of Representatives. Landis had exclaimed, "It was my great disappointment to give Berger only 20 years in Leavenworth. I believe the law should have enabled me to have had him lined up against a wall and shot."[1]

On January 1, 1920, State's Attorney Maclay Hoyne orchestrated a series of such raids throughout Chicago in a purported effort "to wipe out Bolshevism and anarchy in this community." Chicago, *The New York Times* asserted, had long been viewed as "the centre (sic) of the nation's radical activities." Beginning in the afternoon and extending deep into the night, some 300 raids were undertaken. This occurred, Hoyne indicated, without the support of the Wilson administration. He charged, in fact, that "the Reds" had received advance notice of the impending assaults from someone associated with the Justice Department. Among those arrested were prominent figures in the Communist Labor Party and the I.W.W. Those individuals and the 200 or so other individuals who had been taken in custody, Hoyne insisted, were part of "a gigantic conspiracy ... to overthrow the United States Government." Furthermore, "the headquarters of many of the Red organizations in this conspiracy are located in Chicago." The conspirators sought, Hoyne claimed, "to establish ... a Soviet form of Government."[2]

The following day, 25 agents from the federal Bureau of Investigation, along with 50 Chicago policemen, conducted additional raids that resulted in 100 arrests. The agents were ordered to disregard the previous day's raids orchestrated by State's Attorney Hoyne and to visit every site on a government list of "alien agitators."[3]

Similar raids were carried out in scores of municipalities throughout the nation. The *Times* estimated on January 3 that nearly 2,600 arrests had been made, 700 in New York City alone. Aliens, it was anticipated, would be treated in the fashion of Emma Goldman and Alexander Berkman who, along with 200 other deported radicals, were presently aboard the so-called "Soviet Ark" on their way to Russia. U.S. citizens who were being rounded up were expected to face trials for anarchy under criminal syndicalism statutes or conspiracy charges.[4]

In response to the ferocity of the raids, a backlash soon ensued. On January 20, 1920, a coalition of liberals and radicals, headed by the Boston Brahmin Roger Nash Baldwin, founded the American Civil Liberties Union. The ACLU's Statement of Purpose proclaimed "that all thought on matters of public concern should be freely expressed, without interference. Orderly social progress is promoted by unrestricted freedom of opinion." To support First Amendment rights, the ACLU dedicated itself to "an aggressive policy of insistence." In May, Assistant Secretary of Labor Louis F. Post explained why he refused to allow the deportation of several hundred aliens ensnared in the dragnet. In June, Federal Judge George W. Anderson bitterly condemned the Justice Department's "lawlessness. ... A mob is a mob, whether made up of government officials acting under instructions from the Department of Justice, or of criminals, loafers, and the vicious classes."

\* \* \*

While the red scare petered out, albeit not completely, another federal judge, one who had staunchly supported the activities associated with it, was increasingly in the public spotlight. As the hysteria regarding a purported radical conspiracy to overthrow the U.S. government waned, another, very different kind of crusade was about to begin. That involved an effort to clean up the national game, associated by its champions and acolytes with America's very well-being. Editorialists and baseball officials alike considered that essential, in the wake of charges of corrupt dealings that were furiously unfolding as the summer, and consequently, the major league season of 1920 neared an end.

On September 30, National League president John A. Heydler called for the formation of a new governing body for major league baseball; the committee was to feature three members, as proposed by A. D. Lasker, a major stockholder in the Chicago Cubs. "The disclosures at Chicago," he declared, "show the futility of an organization like the National Commission ruling an activity of such country-wide interest as baseball." Heydler then referred to the fact the former National Commission chair Gary Herrmann had been president of the Cincinnati Reds, when that team met the Chicago White Sox during the now infamous 1919 World Series; Herrmann reasoned that the Reds' success on the diamond could be attributed to superior play alone. Of equal significance, American League boss Ban Johnson was engaged in a long-running feud with White Sox owner Charles Comiskey. All of this led Heydler to proclaim that

> baseball must be controlled by a body that is not hampered by bias. The controlling organization must be one with powers to enforce rigid discipline and compel every one (sic) connected with the sport — league Presidents, club Presidents, managers and players alike — to carry out the orders on every matter in which the good of the sport is concerned. It must be a body that can say to a league President, 'Do this,' with the knowledge that he must obey."[5]

On October 1, the management of the New York Giants, Pittsburgh Pirates, and both Chicago teams urged the creation of a tribunal, comprised of baseball outsiders, to rule the game. This was necessary, John McGraw, Barney Dreyfuss, William Veeck, and Charles Comiskey contended, so that baseball could "continue to exist as our national game." Owners and players alike had to recognize, they argued, "that the game itself belongs to the American people." Among the names bandied about as possible board members included California Senator Hiram Johnson, General John J. Pershing, General Leonard Wood, former Secretary of the Treasury William McAdoo, Chief Justice and former president William Howard Taft, and Judge Kenesaw Mountain Landis.[6]

Both Grantland Rice and W. O. McGeehan of *The New York Tribune* also demanded that organized baseball undergo dramatic transformations. Rice insisted that "a national tribunal with a national figure as chairman, must be arranged at once if baseball is to be saved." The National Commission, McGeehan declared, should be discarded. As evidenced by the present scandal, he insisted, that body remained "enmeshed in its own petty politics, and they are none too savory." Driven by financial considerations, he contended, "it lacked the slightest human understanding or sense of sportsmanship." The magnates had determined that new leadership was required, McGeehan continued, which obviously did not bode well for American League chieftain Ban Johnson. A new governing body was required, composed of individuals "everyone will trust," the journalist proclaimed, "to supervise all baseball and to settle all baseball problems." Pointedly, McGeehan indicated that the magnates had promised to establish "a new national body;" this "is a promise that they will be made to keep, for the American public," he warned, "will accept no half-way reforms and no compromises with old powers of baseball, blind to the needs of the game."[7]

As the 1919 World Series fix continued to be unveiled, *Baseball Magazine* revisited its earlier condemnations of those, particularly Hugh Fullerton, who had charged ballplayers with throwing games. On October 4,

Fullerton demanded "an apology and a refraction." Refusing to respond to Fullerton, F. C. Lane declared that his publication claimed the right "to defend the game from muckraking attacks." Lane repeated his charge that Fullerton's "attack was vicious, premature, unfounded," based on "gamblers' rumors and bar-room conversation." In this instance, "Mr. Fullerton merely made a wild, hazardous guess and for once in his life he guessed right."[8]

*   *   *

For a brief spell, news of the White Sox scandal appeared to slacken somewhat as the 1920 World Series unfolded. The Series opened in Brooklyn on October 5, with Stanley Coveleskie holding the Dodgers to five hits to trump Rube Marquard in a 3-1 ballgame. Brooklyn bounced back in game two, as Burleigh Grimes shut out the Indians to earn a 3-0 victory over 31-game winner Jim Bagby. The Dodgers took the Series lead with a 2-1 win in the next game, also played in Brooklyn, as left-hander Sherry Smith held the Indians to three hits. Ray Caldwell started for Cleveland, but was replaced in the first by Duster Mails, who threw 6⅔ scoreless innings. The Indians knotted the Series with a 5-1 win at League Park, behind Coveleski's five-hitter; Leon Cadore was knocked out of the box early in the game. Bagby avenged himself against Grimes in game five, as the Indians won easily 8-1. The last two games were shutouts: Cleveland triumphed 1-0, as Mails's three-hitter bested Smith, and Coveleskie won yet again, beating Grimes 3-0.

Brooklyn's Zach Wheat batted .333 and Ivy Olson hit .320, but the Dodgers collectively managed only a .205 mark against Indian pitching. Cleveland was led by the .333 marks posted by Charlie Jamieson and Steve O'Neill, while Tris Speaker, Elmer Smith, Joe Evans, and George Burns all hit at least .300. Indian pitching was superb, topped by Coveleski's three wins and Mails's 15⅔ consecutive scoreless innings hurled. Most attributed Cleveland's World Series success to Speaker, who managed a series' high six runs scored while operating from his center field post and the dugout. *Baseball Magazine* would later proclaim Speaker "the star of the 1920 baseball season." In addition to the Indians' mound work, the 1920 World Series is best remembered for the unprecedented unassisted triple play turned by Cleveland second baseman Bill Wambsganss and Smith's grand slam homer, the first in the history of the fall classic.[9]

Yet even in the midst of the World Series, rumblings of discontent with organized baseball's leadership continued to be heard. Representatives from the Boston Red Sox and both New York City and Chicago teams met in Chicago on October 5 to explore the possibility of reorganizing professional baseball. In a meeting two days later in New York City, National League club presidents and John A. Hedyler appeared to favor the so-called Lasker Plan to have a neutral group of three individuals supplant the National

Commission as baseball's high court. Concerns about the gambling revelations had led to a determination that the game be cleaned up. One mogul explained, "The game of baseball is too great an institution to permit it to be placed in jeopardy by a few who can be tempted with bribes. We are determined to clean house."[10]

On October 11, W. O. McGeehan again called for the abolition of the National Commission. However, he noted that "the old guard" appeared determined to oppose any changes in the structure of organized baseball. Its members seemed to believe that the revelations coming out of the Chicago grand jury would soon be forgotten and impressive attendance figures maintained. McGeehan reminded his readers that National Commission had been so ensnared "in its own petty politics that it did nothing while the game was being debauched." Players who had thrown games were whitewashed, as the "magnates took the word of Hal Chase against that of Christy Mathewson." At present, McGeehan charged, the National Commission was "a thing without a head, a discredited and impotent relic of a ruling body in baseball."[11]

Change was absolutely essential, McGeehan indicated:

> The fans will accept none of the protestations of the old line magnates. They know that the vaporings that came from the old National Commission mean nothing at all. It took the National Commission one year to learn that a world's series had been made the field for gamblers' manipulation. It took them over two years to learn that certain players had been selling baseball games day by day for whatever was offered.

Cuttingly, McGeehan concluded, "The so-called practical baseball men have all but killed the game. It needs new blood and ideals to bring back the lost faith of the fans."[12]

Ban Johnson remained bitterly opposed to the possibility of restructuring the National Commission, which he had long dominated. While Johnson argued against the holding of a joint meeting of American and National league representatives, John A. Heydler responded, "Our people will be there. They are firm in the belief that public sentiment will brook no delay where such vital matters as the good repute of the national game, the protection of all honest players and the protection of immense property rights are concerned."[13]

Meeting in Chicago on October 18, a full complement of National League delegates, along with representatives from the Chicago White Sox, New York Yankees, and Boston Red Sox, called for the abolition of the National Commission. They urged the total reorganization of baseball and the selection of a three-person tribunal lacking financial interests in the game. Most significant, National League president Heydler declared,

We want a man as chairman who will rule with an iron hand. I'll be glad to take orders if I am told something is wrong at a certain place and instructed to clean it up.

Baseball has lacked a hand of that type for years. It needs it now worse than ever. Therefore, it is our object to appoint a big man to lead the new commission.

Referring to the events in the Cook County grand jury room, Heydler insisted, "We must have a commission with a chairman at the head invested with the power to clean house of the men with dishonest tendencies. The men indicted but not found guilty on trial do not belong in baseball."[14]

By the following day, Heydler and the supporters of the Lasker Plan were talking about forming a new, 12-team league. Denying any hostility toward Johnson and his supporters, the so-called "Loyal Five," Yankee co-owner Ruppert subsequently stated, "We are but anxious to have the welfare of the game placed in the hands of men who, as national figures, will guarantee to the country at large the honesty and integrity of a sport whose fair name had been so sullied by a few dishonest players."[15]

In a scathing essay in *The Sporting News*, Joe Vila, who had testified in Chicago, dismissed the Lasker Plan as a foolish undertaking that would only underscore the fact baseball moguls could not care for their own enterprise. The national pastime's honesty, he charged, could be preserved only by the players who had to expose and refuse bribes. Vila went still further, however, blasting club owners:

Magnates who have openly winked at public betting in their ball parks, who have tampered with players belonging to rivals, who have encouraged contract jumping and who have tried to cover up crookedness at the expense of the gullible public have no place in organized baseball. Yet club owners suspected of committing these crimes against baseball are howling loud for "reforms" and are playing dirty politics to get even with the upright individuals who have tried for years to suppress existing evils.

Vila then singled out Charles Comiskey and William Veeck, both sponsors of the Lasker Plan, for insisting that they were unaware of "the shady ball players" who were throwing games. Furthermore, Comiskey had failed to suspend suspect players until they were indicted by a Cook County grand jury.[16]

Baseball fans, W. O. McGeehan continued to argue, expected major changes in organized baseball. A "baseball war," he warned, would further damage the game. McGeehan then charged, "Even 'Babe' Ruth cannot revive the interest that died such violent death when it was shown that a world's series had been hawked and sold by gamblers, and that the National Commission was so tangled in its own politics that it could not save the game."[17]

On October 22, General James W. Wadsworth, father of the United States Senator by the same name, offered his services on a new baseball commission. "I am too fond of baseball," the general declared, "believing in it, not only from a clean sport point of view, but also as a great help to the physical development of young America, to see it go down in the estimation of the public."[18]

News accounts indicated that Federal Judge Kenesaw Mountain Landis had been offered the chairmanship of the National Baseball Commission, with a $25,000 annual salary. While denying that Landis had been tendered such an offer, Alfred Austrian — the attorney for the Chicago White Sox — acknowledged, "Judge Landis has been mentioned frequently as an ideal man for the place."[19]

That same day, additional indictments were issued by the Illinois grand jury against Abe Attell, William Burns, and Hal Chase. Four days later, Arnold Rothstein and St. Louis Browns' second baseman Joe Gedeon testified, but no indictments were forthcoming against either individual. Ban Johnson proclaimed Gedeon, who evidently knew of the fix, "entirely innocent," while Alfred Austrian declared that "Rothstein, in his testimony today, has proved himself guiltless."[20]

Frank G. Menke, in *The Sporting News'* October 28 edition, continued the paper's defense of Ban Johnson and its questioning of Comiskey's motivations, something that would have been unthinkable just a short time before. A year ago, both *Collyer's Eye* and sportswriter Hugh Fullerton, Menke pointed out, had charged that the 1919 World Series was fixed. The publication named the very players recently indicted by the Cook County grand jury. Comiskey, notwithstanding his own suspicions, had proceeded to defend his players, while offering a $10,000 reward for evidence authenticating their guilt. Menke now asked, "What are we to think of Comiskey?" For, if he genuinely believed that his players had thrown the Series, "why didn't he act then?" Furthermore, "why did he permit men to remain in the line-up through 1920 whom he suspected — and who were charged with baseball crookedness by various writers?" Menke then posed a particularly damning question, "Doesn't it seem that if somebody is to be condemned that Comiskey, lovable and wonderful a man though he may be personally, is that man?" Comiskey, notwithstanding his concerns, had relied on the suspect ballplayers during yet another pennant chase during the 1920 season, which garnered $500,000 in profits for his ball club.[21]

On November 4, *The Sporting News* contained a biting analysis of the man it had once portrayed as the most beloved in baseball. The most striking of the grand jury revelations, the paper declared, was

> that one of the magnate idols — Charles A. Comiskey — is not the noble figure that he was supposed to be. ... Comiskey, who was given information of the

rottenness within his ball club, suppressed it, because the players involved had "cost him a lot of money." He protected his investment at the expense of the public, to the shame of baseball, and to his own final confusion and confounding — all the dust he could stir up by posing with his associates as a "reformer" has been blown aside and the scene is laid before the world.

What remained was "a wreck of the 'Old Roman' baseball once knew and admired."[22]

Comiskey felt compelled to respond to such charges, triggered by accusations from H. C. Redmond that a year ago, he had apprised the White Sox owner of the fix and the players involved. Redmond's tale, Comiskey indicated, was so "vague and uncertain" as to be worthless. His own investigation into the 1919 World Series — costing around $10,000 — continued, lasting until the past May. After his attorney, Alfred S. Austrian, secured the confessions of the accused ballplayers, Comiskey suspended them. He undertook this action although it might have cost him a pennant and resulted in several hundred thousand dollars in property damage. Comiskey asserted, "I took my loss without pang or a bit of sadness, other than that occasioned by ascertaining the fact that those in whom I had put full faith and trust had violated the confidence I had reposed in them."[23]

The next day, Buck Weaver and Fred McMullin appeared at the office of the State's Attorney in Chicago, where they posted $10,000 bonds in response to the indictments charging them with conspiring to fix the 1919 World Series. "The charges against us are a fabrication, and we can prove it," Weaver informed newspapermen. "We ask the baseball public to withhold judgment."[24]

The special grand jury investigating baseball issued its final report on the morning of November 7. Although it had uncovered evidence "that some games were thrown by players," the grand jury found "the practice was not general and the leaders in organized baseball may be relied upon to keep the game above suspicion." The grand jury urged passage of federal legislation "making the offering or accepting of a bribe a criminal offense." It then declared,

> The young player from the minor league or from amateur baseball who enters the major leagues should realize that he occupies a position of trust, and has entered upon an honorable career, and he must therefore conduct himself in a manner that will make his occupation one of integrity and high standing. If the game is conducted on a basis that inspires public confidence, young men and boys will be encouraged to play the game more and more, thereby developing in the youth of the country sound bodies and sound minds and, what is more, sound morals and better citizens.
>
> The jury is impressed with the fact that baseball is an index to our national genius and character. The American principle of merit and fair play must prevail, and it is all-important that the game be clean, from the most humble

player to the highest dignitary. Baseball enthusiasm and its hold upon the public interest must ultimately stand or fall upon this count.

Baseball is more than a national game; it is an American institution, having its place prominently and significantly in the life of the people. In the deplorable absence of military training in this country, baseball and other games having "team play" spirit offer the American youth an agency for development that would be entirely lacking were it relegated to the position to which horse racing and boxing have fallen. The national game promotes respect for proper authority, self-confidence, fairmindedness (sic), quick judgment and self-control.[25]

At a meeting on the evening of November 8 attended by supporters of the Lasker Plan, Judge Kenesaw Mountain Landis became the unanimous choice to serve as chairman of professional baseball's new Board of Control. Landis's term of office was to run seven years, with a $50,000 annual salary compensation. Plans were also discussed to devise a 12-team league, following the admission of the first club of the "Loyal Five" to break away from Ban Johnson.[26]

The American League president responded by threatening to place new ball clubs in Chicago, Boston, and New York, to replace the White Sox, Red Sox, and Yankees, respectively. "We are prepared to give them all of the battle they want," asserted Johnson. "War, in my judgment, is the best cleanser. I am for it, as I believe it will clean up baseball like it cleans up everything else. What the game really needs is to be cleansed of some of its undesirable club owners, who have been a detriment because they openly allowed gambling in their baseball parks." Referring to the "Loyal Five" as "the only decent element in the major leagues," Johnson insisted that "they have fought with me to stamp out the gambling evil. I got no assistance whatever from the others." Johnson then sought to garner support from the minor leagues, whose owners had long sought representation on the National Commission.[27]

Ballplayers, Abe Kemp of *The San Francisco Bulletin* suggested, "would relish a baseball war." Salaries would jump dramatically, as open bidding ensued. However, the baseball war, by November 10, threatened to subside. The 16 major league moguls agreed to meet in Chicago and seek to resolve points of contention. Both league presidents, along with attorneys, stenographers, and others who had attended recent meetings, would be excluded. In *The New York Tribune* on November 13, W. J. Macbeth reported that the conference was taking place that day. As Macbeth saw matters, Ban Johnson and the "Loyal Five" were surrendering fully to the other baseball moguls, having failed to convince the minor leagues to back their side. All parties appeared to have agreed on the selection of Judge Landis as head of a baseball board of control.[28]

* * *

"Peace was restored in organized baseball today," raved leading newspapers across the country, as Judge Landis accepted the offer to lead the board controlling baseball. Landis, it was agreed, would remain on the federal judiciary, where he received a $7,500 salary. He was to be afforded "one-man control" of organized baseball, serving on the board of control by himself. His annual salary as baseball's "supreme arbiter" was set at $42,500, plus a $10,000 allowance, for a seven-year term. *The New York Times* referred to Landis — whom it called "the eminent jurist" — "as arbitrator, a one-man court of last resort" and baseball's "dictator."[29]

Following their conference, several owners had headed for Judge Landis's courtroom where he gaveled them to be quiet and made them wait until a bribery case was disposed of. On meeting with them in chambers, Landis initially turned down the offer, declaring that he "loved his position as judge" too dearly to depart from the bench. Eventually, Landis succumbed, providing that he could hold both positions simultaneously, with the baseball salary reduced by the amount his federal judgeship afforded him. At that point, Landis happily accepted their offer, declaring, "I'm ready to go to work at once. All you have to do is name the time and establish me in office." Later, he walked with Washington owner Clark Griffith, an old friend, and stated,

> Grif, I'm going to tell you just why I took this job. See those kids down there on the street? See that airplane propeller on the wall? Well, that explains my acceptance.
>
> You see, that propeller was on the plane in which my son, Major Reed Landis, flew while overseas. Reed and I went to one of the world's series games at Brooklyn. Outside the gate were a bunch of little kids playing around. Reed turned to me and said: "Dad, wouldn't it be a shame to have the game of these little kids broken? Wouldn't it be awful to take baseball away from them?" Well, while you gentlemen were talking to me, I looked up at this propeller and thought of Reed. Then I thought of his remark in Brooklyn. Grif, we've got to keep baseball on a high standard for the sake of the youngsters — that's why I took the job, because I want to help.

It was precisely for that reason, a *St. Louis Globe-Democrat* editorial contended, that Landis could best serve his country as baseball czar: "It may truthfully be said that baseball has a stronger influence upon the sport standards, and therefore the personal integrity standards, of America than any other sport."[30]

In his official acceptance, Landis spoke in the following manner:

> I have accepted the chairmanship of baseball on the invitation of the sixteen major league clubs. At their request and in accordance with my earnest wishes

I am to remain on the bench and continue my work here. The opportunities for real service are limitless. It is a matter to which I have been devoted for nearly forty years. On the question of policy, all I have to say is this. The only thing in anybody's mind now is to make and keep baseball what the millions of fans throughout the United States want it to be.

Thus, as *The New York Times* saw it, Landis was accepting the undertaking "as a public trust."[31]

As the *New York Tribune* reported, Yankee co-owner T. L. Huston called Landis "the one man able to act as sole arbiter" of baseball disputes. A series of problems afflicted baseball, said Huston, none more serious than gambling. "This evil," he declared, "must be crushed and crushed instantly." As for those ballplayers who consorted with gamblers, Huston declared "there can be but one fate — expulsion from the ransk (sic); 'blacklist,' if you will. The game must be divorced from everything that smacks of the gambling evil." The *Tribune* insisted, "a policy of 'thumbs down' will be pursued in regard to those players of the White Sox or other clubs that have been implicated in the gambling expose. These men are to barred forever from the profession." Similarly, "the magnates themselves will have to keep as pure and undefiled as the players."[32]

Glowing editorial tributes poured forth for organized baseball's new boss, with the *New York Times* declaring that "the crooked players and battling club owner will have no place in the game in the future. The sport at last is in the hands of the public, as personified by Judge Landis, and he knows enough of its recent past to make certain that there will be no recurrence in the future." However, the *Times* also called for Landis to resign his federal judgeship before taking on his new job. Landis expressed no concerns about handling both positions simultaneously, for he could attend to baseball matters on the weekend or take a train into Manhattan within 20 hours.[33]

Traveling to Cincinnati on November 20, Landis conducted his first official business as baseball czar, speaking with former National Commission chairman Herrmann about transferring records to the new headquarters in Chicago. Landis was heard to say, "We have got to have a higher standard of integrity and honesty in baseball than in any other walk of life — and we are going to have it. We are determined to heal the wounds suffered by the great national game and maintain the sport in the place it deserves in the heart of America."[34]

On November 22, W. O. McGeehan applauded Landis's appointment. The *New York Tribune* columnist suggested that the selection of Landis already "seems to have cleared the atmosphere considerably." Public confidence in baseball, badly tattered by the grand jury revelations in Chicago, appeared to be rebounding. Yet a pressing need existed, Oscar C. Reichow insisted in *The Sporting News*, for Landis to pursue the gambling issue, which had been placed

**Judge Kenesaw Mountain Landis with granddaughter, 1920. Chicago Historical Society (DN 071727).**

on the backburner for some time now. Reichow expected the Achilles' heel of baseball to be dealt with differently under Landis's supervision. Baseball moguls, Reichow insisted, "cannot go too far in giving the judge the powers to act where the integrity of the sport is at stake. They ought to go the limit in letting him handle any situation that may arise that reflects on the honesty of the sport."[35]

Following a walking conversation with Landis, Dean Snyder declared that the judge was viewed as "the Moses of baseball" because "the whole American public has faith" in him. Snyder quoted Landis as stating, "I can't think of anything more tragic than the crippling of baseball, can you?"[36]

F. C. Lane and *Baseball Magazine* also expressed enthusiastic support for Landis. Lane wrote, "It is a sublime tribute to the ability and integrity of Judge Landis, that, wholly inexperienced and untried as he is in his new position, such absolute power has nevertheless been bestowed upon him. No greater compliment could possibly be paid him."[37]

While in New York City to watch the Army-Navy gridiron contest, Landis affirmed on November 28 that "the keynote of the entire newly outlined plan is to rid our great national game of the sinister and oppressive burden of gambling." Baseball had to be freed of the professional gamblers, Landis reasoned, but even "friendly betting" was potentially troublesome.[38]

The next day, Reichow stated that Landis "will be death on ball players who even harbor a thought of throwing a ball game to make a bit of 'easy money.'" To Reichow, the stakes were high: baseball's very integrity. Undoubtedly recognizing this, the moguls chose Landis, considering him "the one man who is capable of handling the gambling situation from A to Z."[39]

In a similar fashion, Joe Vila contended that Landis and the club owners could demonstrate their commitment to reform "by driving all of the rascals out of the game." But it was "up to the players themselves," Vila suggested, "to purge baseball of dishonesty." He referred to Buck Weaver, who had recently declared in an interview, "I'll never be called a squealer." Weaver

**Judge Kenesaw Mountain Landis, 1920. National Baseball Hall of Fame Library, Cooperstown, N.Y.**

claimed that "he took no bribe money and played honestly." Nevertheless, Vila charged, "he cannot deny that he knew what was going on."[40]

To Landis, Harry F. Pierce of *The St. Louis Star* suggested, professional gambling was the biggest issue the national pastime had to contend with. "If more stringent laws are needed to prevent gambling in baseball, they can be had through either state or federal statutes," Landis suggested. "I don't believe there would be any difficulty in having such legislation introduced in Washington, for decent people are too fond of the game to pass up an opportunity to do what they can for the game." Landis also argued that "every appearance of evil" had to be blotted out; thus, betting between friends that occurred in the stands during ballgames should be stopped. "To eliminate this sort of thing, and I think it is highly important that it be eliminated, I have great faith in the loyalty of the fan for one thing and such other influences as can be devised."[41]

On December 12, a tentative new agreement was devised by major league tycoons, who named Landis the "First High Commissioner" of baseball and instructed him to administer the revised baseball laws. Much was expected of Landis, W. O. McGeehan reported. "He has built up for himself a reputation for fairness and farsightedness." The *Tribune* indicated that the powers afforded baseball's new boss — he drafted them — were sweeping indeed.

These included the right to investigate at the behest of others or on his own volition "an act, transaction or practice charged, alleged or suspected to be detrimental to the best interests of the national game of baseball." The club owners would have to sustain the powers granted the commissioner, Vila suggested, or demonstrate that "his selection as their Moses was merely a sort of camouflage to hush up their scandal." American League president Ban Johnson had indicated his approval.[42]

* * *

The naming of Kenesaw Mountain Landis as commissioner of major league baseball pleased those who thought that he could help clean up the national pastime. They were particularly concerned about both baseball's now tarnished image and whether the sport could thrive in the manner that had appeared all but certain when the guns of war were silenced back in November 1918. Potentially serious problems, however, loomed ahead, as evidenced by newspaper accounts printed during 1920's final days. Landis's appointment and the dissipating of the Lasker Plan hardly brought peace inside the American League. The "disloyal three"— the Yankees, Red Sox, and White Sox — continued to heap abuse on president Ban Johnson, demanding his ouster, or at a minimum, a drastic reduction of his powers. Johnson responded with attacks of his own, particularly those directed at his old friend and now inveterate foe, the suddenly vulnerable Charles Comiskey. The *Tribune's* W. O. McGeehan charged that Johnson's "mud-throwing" directed at Commy was "remarkably mean and cowardly;" he also indicated that Comiskey's reputation was "too well established" for him to suffer as a consequence.[43]

The contentious nature of player salaries continued to shadow organized baseball. At the end of November, news accounts indicated that the Players' Fraternity was being revived. Support for unionism was strong, one star was said to have indicated, in both major and minor league ranks. A new Fraternity was to be run by the players themselves, with top-line stars leading the charge. W. J. Macbeth, writing in the *Tribune*, termed "a union scale of wages in baseball" impractical. As he put it, "There is only 'Babe' Ruth. There is but one Ty Cobb. There is only one Speaker, one Sisler or one Alexander." Nevertheless, Macbeth foresaw trouble ahead as few players had signed their contracts for the upcoming season. [44]

At the same time, the lawsuit by the former owners of the Baltimore Federal League team continued to work its way through the courts. In early December, organized baseball won a reversal in the District Court of Appeals in Washington, D.C., of a lower court ruling that granted treble damages to the plaintiffs following an $80,000 jury verdict. Two and a half weeks later, however, it was announced that the Baltimore stockholders planned to appeal the District Court's determination. Thus, concerns remained that organized baseball might yet be proclaimed a "trust." Still, Paul W. Eaton, writing in *Baseball Magazine*, shared the delight of many of his colleagues that the District Court had ruled organized baseball was not involved in interstate commerce.[45]

In an editorial dated December 16, *The Sporting News* refused to join in the celebration about the appellate court decision. The newspaper particularly focused on the reserve clause that seemingly bound a player to a team in perpetuity; furthermore, it warned that no court would uphold that union. Judge Landis had so reasoned, *The Sporting News* suggested, when he deliberately refused to issue a ruling in the Federal League suit.[46]

The full ramifications of the 1919 World Series scandal still had to be grappled with as demands for the indicted players' banishment coincided with their own efforts to remain in the game they loved but had recently disgraced so horribly. No one would fight harder to do so than Buck Weaver, who, the *Tribune* noted on Christmas Day, 1920, "points to his record in the big series in question." Weaver, W. J. Macbeth admitted, "certainly played the most sensational ball of any party concerned and with apparent will that fooled every spectator if, indeed, he were dishonest." His play had induced critics to proclaim him the finest third baseman in baseball.[47]

In devising *Baseball Magazine*'s "All America Baseball Club of 1920," F. C. Lane placed Babe Ruth, Tris Speaker, and Edd Roush in the outfield, while indicating that two other ballplayers might have been considered for the honor: Joe Jackson and Happy Felsch. However, "the records of these two men ... ," Lane indicated, "is forever blotted out in the infamy they have brought upon themselves." While Lane selected Heinie Groh at the hot corner, he admitted that another choice also might have been made.

At third base there *was* a player who was one of the greatest stars who ever filled that position. We say there *was* such a player. What his future status may be we do not know, but he is at present involved in one of the deepest disgraces that have ever blotted the record of the National Game. Until he can clear his name of that blot, we believe that all right-thinking fans will agree with us that George Weaver can have no proper place on an All Star team.[48]

## CHAPTER SIXTEEN

# *The Season After*

1920 had proven to be a remarkable one in baseball annals. It opened with the sale of the game's greatest star, Babe Ruth, to the New York Yankees. Within a month, Rube Foster, along with erstwhile friends and antagonists, founded the Negro National League. During pre-season, rules changes continued to take hold, including the banning of most trick pitches, although certain pitchers who relied on the spitter were grandfathered in. Another change that would affect the game, most notably the American League version during the impending season, involved a somewhat livelier ball that helped to augment both run production and earned run averages. While blackball appeared more organized than ever during this period, the National Commission, lacking a commissioner and, increasingly, the support of any number of baseball men, foundered mightily. As it did, rumors abounded that a fix had occurred during the 1919 World Series, but organized baseball seemed incapable of responding to the quandary.

The 1920 regular season proceeded apace, with the American League experiencing a spirited three-team race, involving Cleveland, Chicago, and New York, while the National witnessed Brooklyn and Cincinnati vie for the top spot, with the Giants becoming a contender in September. By that point, a series of historic events had occurred: the longest game in major league history, Walter Johnson's first and only no-hitter, the lone fatality in a big league contest, superlative pitching by the Indians' Jim Bagby and the Cubs' Pete Alexander, and unprecedented batting feats by teams and players alike, topped off by Ruth's unparalleled performance at the Polo Grounds and around the American circuit.

With barely a month before the season's finale, less happy news began to break about gambling, thrown ballgames, and even a tossed World Series. A Cook County grand jury began to hear tales of how the 1919 World Series games between the Chicago White Sox and Cincinnati Reds had been fixed. Some of baseball's greatest stars, including Chicago right-hander Eddie Cicotte, southpaw Lefty Williams, left fielder Joe Jackson, center fielder Happy Felsch, and third baseman Buck Weaver, were subsequently indicted for having conspired to drop the World Series to the Reds. Reports from Chicago overshadowed the conclusion of the pennant races, won by Cleveland and Brooklyn, and the subsequent meeting of Tris Speaker and Wilbert Robinson's squads. In the meantime, demands for the fixers' permanent expulsion from the game abounded, as did charges that the National Commission had foundered altogether. Fearing a public backlash, moguls selected an old friend, Federal Judge Kenesaw Mountain Landis of Chicago, to become Commissioner of organized baseball. Broad, sweeping powers were afforded Landis, with the expectation that the longstanding gambling bugaboo would at last be dealt with.

\* \* \*

As the new year began, the fallout from the now infamous Chicago-Cincinnati World Series hardly slackened. On January 12, 1921, representatives from the American and National leagues accepted a new national agreement that named Judge Landis commissioner and granted him expansive powers. Before signing the document, Landis insisted on the rewriting of permissive contractual language that allowed the commissioner, following the investigation of any matter considered injurious to baseball, to "recommend such action as he deemed advisable." Landis declared,

> You have told the world that my powers are to be supreme. To give me the power merely to 'recommend' takes all power out of my hands. I will retire from the room, gentlemen, and you can discuss this matter. But I want you to know that either I must have power to take such action as I wish or else you had better seek a new Commissioner. I wouldn't take this job for all the gold in the world unless I knew my hands were to be free.

The word "take" was soon substituted for "recommend." Landis now possessed, *The Sporting News* reported, "the power of baseball life or death over any person, high or low connected with the game."[1]

On January 30, Landis spoke at the First Presbyterian Church in Evanston, Illinois. "Now that I am in baseball, just watch the game I play. If I catch any crook in baseball, the rest of his life is going to be a pretty hot one. I'll go to any means and to anything possible to see that he gets a real penalty for his offense."[2]

Two weeks later, Landis, in the midst of the general celebration about his appointment, suffered something of a setback. Representative Benjamin Welty of Ohio moved to impeach him for neglecting his duties as a federal judge in taking on the responsibilities of baseball commissioner. Strikingly, Welty included a provision condemning Landis "for injuring the national sport of baseball" by helping to cultivate the impression "that gambling and other illegal acts in baseball will not be punished in the open forum as other cases." In the Senate, N. B. Dial of South Carolina urged passage of legislation preventing Landis and other federal judges from obtaining outside salaries. Dial also blasted Landis's decision to release a bank clerk who had embezzled from his employer, supposedly because of his meager salary.[3]

Soon, Harvey Brougham, in an article in *Overland Monthly*, painted a blistering tale of "America's erratic judge." To some, Brougham, Landis was "the embodiment of the Good Samaritan." But to others, "he is a poseur, more interested in advertising his unique personality than making himself a credit to his high office" as a federal judge. Brougham concluded that Landis was "constitutionally unsuited for position. He lacks some of the qualities essential in a calm judge, with sound judgment and a minimum of prejudice. He is more of a politician than a lawyer." Criticism of Landis had mounted, Brougham noted, since he failed to resign his judgeship following his appointment as baseball commissioner. As a consequence, "the Judge is in danger of being regarded henceforth as a popular idol with feet of clay."[4]

Notwithstanding Brougham's charges, Landis clearly felt compelled to pursue any number of leads involving reputed gambling incidents. In a meeting at the Auditorium Hotel in Chicago on February 19, Landis interviewed Chicago second baseman Eddie Collins regarding rumors that the White Sox, in the midst of the 1917 pennant race, had paid Tiger players for defeating the Red Sox. The collection, Collins recalled, had occurred after Chicago clinched the title. Six days later, Detroit pitcher Hooks Dauss acknowledged that a pot had been paid to certain Tiger players, but only for winning contests against Boston. Former Tiger pitcher Bill James spoke with Landis the following day and seconded Dauss's recollections.[5]

In the meantime, the eight indicted White Sox players — Buck Weaver had unsuccessfully sought to have his case severed from the others — were placed by Commissioner Landis on an ineligible list. To be removed from the list would require the showing of "a clean slate" regardless of how matters were resolved in court. Landis appeared to have acted in this manner due to a delay in the trial of the Chicago ballplayers. The postponement of the trial led Charles Comiskey on March 13 to proclaim,

> Those players are on my ineligible list. It was not necessary for Judge Landis to put them on his, but I am glad he did, as it justified my position. There is

absolutely no chance for any of them to play on my team again unless they can clear themselves to my satisfaction of the charges made against them by three of their teammates.

Three days later, Comiskey severed his formal ties with the accused players, by giving them their unconditional release.[6]

Unable to obtain a delay, the prosecution, on March 17, opted to terminate the cases against the eight Chicago players. Within a day, however, a second investigation was initiated involving the 1919 World Series. Then, on March 26, 144 indictments against 18 individuals were handed out. In addition to the ballplayers, Sport Sullivan, Abe Attell, Bill Burns, and Hal Chase were indicted.[7]

On April 7, Landis placed New York Giant outfielder Benny Kauff, once known as "the Ty Cobb of the Federal League," on the ineligible to perform list. Kauff had been charged with the theft and possession of an automobile. Indictment did "not imply guilt," Landis acknowledged, but it did suggest, in his eyes, that "there is probable cause to believe the accused guilty."[8]

The following day, one news report indicated that three of the indicted White Sox — Joe Jackson, Swede Risberg, and Claude Williams — were forming their own team. Happy Felsch and Fred McMullin also planned to join the squad. Investment broker George M. Miller, who was financing the enterprise, was seeking to line up opponents from independent ball. By now, editorialists and columnists were referring to the accused players as "the Black Sox." When Jackson, Williams, Felsch, and Buck Weaver subsequently played against a semi-pro team, *The Sporting News* headlined the event, attended by some 3,000 spectators, "Just like Nuts Go to See a Murderer."[9]

\* \* \*

As the 1921 regular season approached, the New York Yankees and their greatest star were very much in the news. They had been so, in fact, throughout the off-season, even during the dark days when the 1919 World Series fix was being uncovered. In late October, two major announcements were made by Yankee co-owner Jacob Ruppert. Miller Huggins, the so-called "Midget Manager," signed to lead the Yankees for another year, while Ed Barrow, who had guided the Boston Red Sox for the past three seasons, was named New York's business manager. In mid–December, the Yankees and Red Sox pulled off yet another trade. Second baseman Del Pratt, a .314 batter, light-hitting catcher Muddy Ruel, reserve outfielder Sammy Vick, and pitcher Herbert Thormahlen went to Boston, while New York received catcher Wally Schang, a .300 hitter the past two seasons, infielder Mike McNally, and pitchers Waite Hoyt and Harry Harper. The 21-year-old Hoyt was coming off a 6-6 campaign but possessed tremendous potential. Indeed, Huggins saw the young right-hander as the key to the entire deal.[10]

Yankee owners Ruppert and T. l. Huston announced on February 7 that a new $2,000,000 stadium, seating 75,000, would be constructed in the Bronx. The site was a ten-acre plot of land, centered around Amsterdam Avenue and 163th Street, where a Jewish orphan asylum was presently situated. Purchased from the William Waldorf Astor estate, the grounds were situated across the Harlem River from the Polo Grounds. A week later, Colonel Rupert was informed that the Yankees' lease on the Giants' ballpark would be extended through the end of 1922. Joe Vila now reported that Yankee management, to ensure easy access through the "I" subway, would locate the triple-deck stadium on East 161st Street, a bare 200 yards from the Harlem River.[11]

F. C. Lane now posed the question, "Can Babe Ruth Repeat? Will the redoubtable hero of the big war club who drove out a thunderous salvo of fifty-four home runs in 1920 be able to equal or excel that performance in 1921?" Answering his own query, Lane indicated that "What Babe Ruth may do only Babe Ruth can determine. For he alone among players past or present scorns all bounds and limits and fairly revels in performing feats that for any other player would be sheer impossibility." The previous spring, in a conversation with Ivan Olson, the Brooklyn shortstop told Lane, "This man Ruth is all they claim for him. In fact I believe he will do greater things than he had done so far. I wouldn't know where to set a limit on his powers." Lane saw matters somewhat differently:

> Babe broke the home run record, yes; but he did more, much more. He pulverized that record. He ground it to impalpable powder and scattered it to the four winds. He annihilated that record. He exceeding (sic) the former high mark by so prodigious a margin that the record, though only a year old and one of his own making, sinks into ridiculous obscurity. Yes, Babe annihilated the old record. And in its place he hung a new record; a record so lofty, so seemingly beyond the reach of human endeavor that we are led to wonder if even he can ever equal that mark again!

Still, Lane reasoned that if Ruth remained healthy he could "considerably exceed" his 1920 performance. In the process, he would not compete against other ballplayers, but rather "will race against time. He will race against Ruth, the Ruth of 1921 against the Ruth of 1920."[12]

Given the furor regarding the gambling scandals, Ruth's performance on the playing field and the public's perception of both him and the game appeared essential to baseball's well-being. Lane seemed to recognize as much, declaring that "Babe Ruth and Baseball are partners once more at the same old stand." Baseball as an institution, Lane wrote, was "an unwieldy impersonal sort of thing." By contrast, "Babe to the public eye is the visible personification of baseball." Lane continued, "Never before has a player possessed quite the force of personality, quite the seemingly limitless capacity to do wonderful and unheard of things which Babe shows to so amazing a degree." Happily, "Babe Ruth stands forth in the limelight as the great prototype of the game whose records he has enriched by some of its proudest trophies. Babe and Baseball are quite properly linked. For in the public interest Babe and Baseball are one."[13]

A record opening day crowd turned out at the Polo Grounds on April 18 to watch the Yankees crush the Athletics 11-1, behind Carl Mays's three hitter and Ruth's five hits, which included two doubles. While the crowd was disappointed that Ruth had failed to hit one out of the ballpark, he produced five homers within the next two weeks, and, as Robert W. Creamer has noted, hit no fewer than 10 a month for the rest of the season. In contrast to his slow start in 1920, Ruth batted .400 early in the campaign.[14]

Even more strikingly than in 1920, Ruth's batting feats, as *Baseball Magazine* indicated, appeared to have set off a "home-run epidemic." The publication noted that "the lively ball has become an obsession in the game." The National League baseballs appeared more juiced up than during the previous year and home run totals in both circuits escalated sharply. In 1920, National Leaguers belted 261 round-trippers, while their American League counterparts smacked 369. In 1921, those totals would jump to 460 and 477, respectively. Individual marks, however, did not increase so dramatically as the top sluggers in the National League, New York's George Kelly and St. Louis' Rogers Hornsby, were the only batters who produced as many as 20 homers. Over in the American league, the Browns' Ken Williams, the Yankees' Bob Meusel, the Athletics' Tilly Walker, along with Ruth, hit that many.[15]

\* \* \*

In the meantime, a report filed in Chicago on June 27 again suggested Buck Weaver's determination to separate himself from his co-defendants. During the reconvened trial, Weaver, like Chick Gandil, was said to have sat apart from his former teammates. Moreover, "Weaver passed the others as he came in, but did not speak to them. He is said not to be on speaking terms with the other players, due to his refusal to play independent ball here with them. Weaver was surrounded by friends who joked with him, but the other players refused to talk."[16]

*The New York Times* noted, on June 30, that Jackson, Felsch, Risberg, Williams, and Gandil were playing independent ball on the weekends to "overflow crowds." Indicating that they had signed one-year contracts, Jackson claimed, "We are making more money than we did with the White Sox, and I, for one, am well satisfied." While Jackson and Williams were running a poolroom, Buck Weaver was co-owner of a drug store. "Buck, however, wants to play in organized baseball again and is confident that eventually he will be reinstated," the *Times* reported. "He is not playing independent baseball with the others, saying his drug store takes up all of his time." Eddie

Babe Ruth batting, 1920. National Baseball Hall of Fame Library, Cooperstown, N.Y.

Babe Ruth going up to bat, 1920. National Baseball Hall of Fame Library, Cooperstown, N.Y.

Cicotte owned a farm near Detroit and was reportedly "interested in a garage." Defense attorney Ben Short downplayed notions that the players were being richly compensated, indicating that they were receiving between $2,700 and $2,900.[17]

On July 10, Detroit owner Frank Navin reminded American League president Ban Johnson, who was tracking down stories of the 1917 pot paid by the White Sox to the Tigers, that moguls had engaged in similar practices. "As you know," Navin wrote, "it was a common practice in those days for club owners, especially Mr. Lannon (sic) of Boston, to frequently wire ahead to different clubs and promise the pitchers from one to five hundred dollars to defeat our club when we were in the race. You will remember that you objected very much to this action at the time."[18]

In early July, the impaneling of potential jurors in the Black Sox case began. The case against Fred McMullin had been dropped because of insufficient evidence against him. Refusing to sit alongside the other defendants, Weaver made no effort to acknowledge them. Then, on July 11, White Sox manager Kid Gleason entered the courtroom, along with Eddie Collins, Dickie Kerr, Red Faber, Ray Schalk, Roy Wilkinson, and Harvey McClellan, all of whom had been called as defense witnesses. Swede Risberg burst out with, "Hello, Kid, how's the boy?" Gleason responded, "Pretty good, Swede — how's yourself?," and the two shook hands. Then, Gleason exclaimed, "And there's old Buck Weaver! Stacking up pretty good, Buck?" Weaver replied, "Sure," and then Faber and Kerr proceeded to tickle their old teammate. Expressing displeasure at having witnessed the friendly exchanges in the courtroom, Thomas Rice caustically wrote, "Birds of a feather flock together."[19]

On July 27, Judge Friend indicated that he would award a new trial to Buck Weaver, Happy Felsch, and St. Louis businessman Carl Zork if guilty judgments were handed down against them. As Friend noted, "There has been so little evidence presented against these men that I doubt if I would allow a verdict of guilty to stand if it were brought in." Still, "as some evidence has been brought against them, I will not dismiss them unless the State is willing to nolle prosse."[20]

Despite being handicapped by the mysterious loss of evidence, including the confessions of three ballplayers, the prosecution remained determined to pursue the case. Speaking for the prosecution, Edward Prindeville stated,

> Baseball is about the only sport we have left that is not censored. If the game is to be conducted in the same manner as the 1919 world's series was conducted, you will find it will soon be restricted as was horse racing and prize fighting: either that or legislated out of business.
>
> Gambling is the root of the whole trouble. Unless the gamblers can bet on the games there would be no object for them to buy the players, heart and soul.

Unless the gamblers can make money by betting on fixed games, there is no market for dishonest ball players to sell their honor.

Prindeville then asked for five-year prison sentences, coupled with $2,000 fines, to be levied against the defendants.[21]

Six of the defendants were reported to be planning to barnstorm major league cities. If acquitted, they intended to seek use of Comiskey Park for their opening contest. Buck Weaver was said to be "the only defendant who does not intend to join. He expects to apply for reinstatement in the American League."[22]

In his column for *The New York Tribune* on August 1, W. J. Macbeth asserted that Weaver, although "implicated in the world's series scandal of 1919, has been whitewashed in the eyes of the law." Macbeth predicted that the Black Sox might well "escape the fingers of the law." Moreover, the sportswriter charged, "these shameless men, who already have been condemned forever in public opinion have the nerve to ask that major baseball parks be thrown open to them for exhibition purposes." Nevertheless, Macbeth warned, "the Black Sox will soon fight out the weight of public opinion. They will require no major league field. They will never attract a corporal's guard of fair-minded sportsmen." Macbeth then concluded with the following observation: "Presuming all are acquitted it will give Judge K. M. Landis an opportunity to prove himself the savior of baseball. I am sure the Commissioner will never tolerate the presence of any one against whom suspicion pointed so strongly appearing in organized baseball."[23]

On August 2, in the trial involving conspiracy to defraud the public through the fixing of the 1919 World Series, the seven remaining former White Sox, along with two others, were found not guilty. Requiring but one ballot, the jury made its determination following fewer than three hours of deliberation. Cheers filled the courtroom along with cries of "Hooray for the clean Sox!" An obviously pleased Judge Hugo M. Friend thanked the jury for its decision, deeming it a fair one. Several of the players immediately raced over to shake hands with the jurors. Even the bailiffs joined in the celebration as hats and papers were flung about. Buck Weaver and Swede Risberg, *The New York Times* reported, appeared the most animated, "grabbing each other by the arms and shouting." Weaver declared, "I knew I'd be cleared, and I'm glad the public stood by me until the trial was over." Defense counsel Harry Berger called the verdict "a complete vindication of the most mistreated ball players in history."[24]

The very next day, Commissioner Landis, American League president Ban Johnson, and White Sox owner Charles Comiskey all issued statements that, in spite of the verdict, the ballplayers would not be readmitted to organized baseball. Landis proclaimed,

Regardless of the verdict of juries, no player that throws a ball game; no player that undertakes or promises to throw a ball game; no player that sits in a conference with a bunch of crooked players and gamblers where the ways and means of throwing games are planned and discussed and does not promptly tell his club about it, will ever play professional baseball.

Of course, I don't know that any of these men will apply for reinstatement, but if they do, the above are at least a few of the rules that will be enforced. Just keep in mind that, regardless of the verdict of juries, baseball is entirely competent to protect itself against crooks, both inside and outside the game.

Yankee owners Jacob Ruppert and T. L. Huston applauded this statement, indicating that it "has our unqualified support. These ball players must be barred from the national game at all hazards. Their own confessions make them impossible."[25]

President Johnson declared:

The trial of the indicted players and gamblers which closed yesterday uncovered the greatest crime it was possible to commit in baseball. The fact the men were freed by a Cook County jury does not alter the conditions one iota or minimize the magnitude of such offenses.

The energetic prosecution of the State clearly indicates that crimes of this character will not be permitted to go unchallenged.[26]

Chicago White Sox players on trial with their attorneys, 1921. Chicago Historical Society (ICHi-28764), photograph by *Chicago Daily News* (SDN-62959).

Comiskey added this note: "Cicotte confessed to me that he had been 'crooked' and implicated seven other players. Until they all are able to explain this to my satisfaction none of them will play with the Sox." His manager, Kid Gleason, was heard to say that if the players reentered organized baseball, "then I am through with the game." Comiskey also declared that he was ready to respond to any demands made by the ousted players.[27]

Buck Weaver, attorney Michael J. Ahern asserted, had a legitimate contractual claim. His other attorney, Thomas Nash, stated that he would "put Weaver back in organized baseball." One report noted that Weaver, who continued to hold a half-interest in a South Side drug store in Chicago, hoped to play ball with the Cleveland Indians or New York Giants. Subsequently, Weaver sued the White Sox for $20,000 in back pay.[28]

A *New York Times* editorial expressed satisfaction with the turn of events. The jury determination made sense, the *Times* suggested, as little evidence existed against some of the players and even the confessions of others did not prejudice the jurors against them. However, virtually everyone would also be pleased, the paper suggested, by Commissioner Landis's fiat. The old National Commission would likely have "exhausted its energies in twiddling its thumbs" and then deciding it could not overturn the jury verdict. "But the new high Commissioner is not much troubled by that respect for quibbles and technicalities which is the Western idea of justice. He goes straight to the essential rights and wrongs in the good old Oriental manner — the manner of Haroun-Al-Raschid."[29]

Charles A. McDonald, chief justice of the Cook County criminal court who had initially presided over the Black Sox case, also expressed a certain satisfaction with the apparent results. Although somewhat disappointed that the jury had decided in the manner it had, he believed that the prosecution and investigation "put the fear of God and the law in the hearts of the crooked gamblers and shady players and has purged baseball for a generation to come." He was also delighted that baseball leaders "have decided for all time to keep shady players from the game. I am sure the young men and boys of the country will welcome the purging and will again have confidence in the great American sport."[30]

Landis's decision to banish the Black Sox for life from organized baseball has always been viewed as one of his most courageous decisions by those who celebrate his stewardship of the national game. Yet given the demands made by sportswriters and baseball moguls alike, Landis could hardly have acted otherwise. Later, critics would contend that Joe Jackson, whose statistical numbers topped all others during the 1919 World Series, had not been treated equitably. At the time, however, greater concerns were expressed about Buck Weaver, who was viewed as a ballplayer's ballplayer and who was considered to have played as hard as ever during the ill-fated Series. Like

Landis, many contended that Weaver knew of the plot to throw championship games to the Reds. Unlike baseball's new commissioner, not all seemed to believe that Weaver's playing career consequently should be ended.

* * *

More happily, the remainder of the 1921 major league season revolved around the man, who, in the words of F. C. Lane, "inaugurated the era of the Homer and, more than any other one person, revolutionized baseball." As the Black Sox scandal appeared to have been resolved, Babe Ruth maintained a record pace of belting round-trippers. All the while, as Lane recorded, Ruth had turned into "a national idol," perhaps at the very time when baseball most needed one:

> Babe cannot move along a New York street without being almost instantly recognized by someone. Immediately the news spreads with lightning swiftness and a crowd collects. Babe's daily progress might literally be described as a battle with crowds of admirers. People who wouldn't know the name of their own congressman, if it was mentioned, know all about Babe Ruth and press forward for a nearer glimpse. Audacious souls who would meet a millionaire in his private office without hesitation, try to summon up courage to shake him by the hand. Newsboys stare at him speechless, with open mouths. Taxicab drivers make way for him. The whole world has gone suddenly daffy about Babe Ruth.[31]

Shattering baseball standards, Ruth had "taught everybody else," Lane noted, "something of the possibilities of home-run hitting." Yet he remained "so far superior to any of his followers that there is no comparison." Ruth had accomplished such feats despite the manner in which pitchers responded to him: "Never give him anything that he wants. Place the ball where he least likes to have it. Make things as hard as possible for him. If nothing else, can be done, deliberately pass him. Give him no chance to hit. And as for the outfielders, lay back against the fences."[32]

On September 15, Ruth broke his own major league home run record, by belting his 55th in the opening game of a doubleheader against the St. Louis Browns. He hit his 59th in the season finale, helping the Yankees to beat the Red Sox 7-6, which enabled New York to win its first American League pennant. The Yankees ended up at 98-55, 4½ games ahead of the defending World Series champion Indians. Charles Comiskey's White Sox, with a 62-92 record, finished in seventh place, 36½ games in back of New York. In the National League, John McGraw's New York Giants compiled a 94-59 record, placing them four games ahead of the Pirates and seven up on the Cardinals.[33]

Ruth's 1921 batting marks were, overall, even more remarkable than during the previous season. Along with the new home run record, he scored 177 runs, drove in 171, and produced 457 total bases, also all new major league standards. In addition, Ruth received 144 walks, had an on-base percentage of .512, and a slugging percentage of .846, which were second only to the records he had established the previous year. In batting .378, third in the league behind Detroit's Harry Heilmann and Ty Cobb, Ruth garnered 204 hits, 16 triples — only two less than the league leaders — and 44 doubles, placing him second to Tris Speaker's 52. Many baseball historians consider Ruth's 1921 season the greatest in major league history.

Although the Yankees took a 3-2 lead in the best of nine game series from the Giants, Ruth's badly infected arm precluded him from appearing in the last three contests, except for one unsuccessful at-bat as a pinch-hitter, all won by McGraw's team. In the games that he played, Ruth knocked out five hits in 16 at bats for a .313 mark, scored three runs, and drove in four, while crushing his first home run in World Series competition.

The post-season proved to be less auspicious as the two men clashed who now were viewed as organized baseball's greatest figures. Some indeed referred to them as the saviors who helped the national pastime overcome the Black Sox scandal, one through his seemingly iron will and the other thanks to his magical bat. Judge Kenesaw Mountain Landis and Babe Ruth battled over the right of a ballplayer from a pennant-winning squad to barnstorm in the off-season. Also involved was the commissioner's continued determination to display, as he had through his banishment of the Black Sox, that he had established the boundaries for organized baseball. Those boundaries, Landis intended to demonstrate, applied even to the sport's most popular and greatest star. Significant too, only Babe Ruth now contended with Commissioner Landis for the title of baseball's most important figure.

Shortly after the end of the championship affair, Babe Ruth, along with Yankee teammates Bob Meusel and pitcher Bill Piercy, began a barnstorming expedition in defiance of a rule, carved out in 1911, preventing players from World Series teams from doing so. A headline in *The San Francisco Bulletin* rang out, "Ruth Defies K. M. Landis ... Trouble Is Now Brewing." On being informed of Ruth's action, Landis thundered,

> Baseball law must be enforced. Ruth on the face of the evidence, violated provisions of the baseball law that I had no hand in making. I inherited the rules of the game when I became head of baseball, and I am going to see that the rules are enforced.
>
> I want to give this message to law-abiding baseball players and to the public: Baseball law will be enforced.[34]

As a series of exhibition contests were cancelled, Ruth announced, nevertheless, that he would play in a game in Elmira, New York. "I still think I am in the right and Judge Landis is wrong," declared Ruth. "I see no reason why this rule should be invoked against us when Sisler of St. Louis and others who shared in the world's series money are playing exhibition games unmolested by Judge Landis. I see no reason not to play." Ruth went on to claim that the mandate was "unfair, unjust and un-American."[35]

Even Ruth's enormous popularity failed to safeguard him from the editorial attacks now visited on him. *The San Francisco Bulletin* claimed that Ruth had wrongly defied the commissioner. It also reported that the Yankees were already seeking an outfield replacement, perhaps the White Sox' Harry Hooper. "If the axe falls, and the Babe gets his," the *Bulletin* predicted, "baseball writers and the fans will be back of Landis almost to a man. The attitude here is that the whole affair need never have come to a head if Ruth hadn't acted like a great big kid and gone off to play toy baseball in a great huff, just to show Landis he wasn't afraid to."[36]

*Baseball Magazine*, which had just recently exalted Ruth as the greatest phenomenon ever to grace the diamond, now condemned him roundly. "It is too bad that Babe should have pulled up stakes and endangered his reputation with the show," declared F. C. Lane, "thus making himself a menace." Ruth's actions, Lane charged, "cannot be disregarded any more than an elephant which has broken loose and gone rambling aimlessly over the

Babe Ruth, Bob Meusel, and Judge Landis, 1922. National Baseball Hall of Fame Library, Cooperstown, N.Y.

countryside, is a menace that can be disregarded." Judge Landis recognized, Lane continued, "the welfare of organized baseball demands discipline." The editorial concluded with the following observation:

> Judge Landis was chosen to govern baseball with a strong hand. That was for the security of discipline. But, in a larger sense, if we understand the situation, he was chosen to preside over the general welfare of baseball to the end that the game might proper and to the end that it might best serve the needs of the community as the true National game.[37]

With pressure mounting and turnout slackening, Ruth's tour ground to a halt. Ralph S. Davis, writing in *The Sporting News*, insisted that the slugger "be severely disciplined," while demeaning Ruth in the manner that a number of writers were giving vent to. Davis also seemed to suggest that punishment of Ruth would serve as a warning to players, who appeared increasingly restive in the wake of a number of rulings by the commissioner, including one placing Bennie Kauff on the permanently ineligible list. Perhaps sensing that restiveness, Yankee magnates Jacob Ruppert and T. L. Huston indicated their support for Landis in meting out punishment to their star player. Putting Ruth in his place, Frank G. Menke indicated, might be welcomed.[38]

On December 5, the edict came down from the commissioner's office, resulting in Ruth, Meusel, and Piercy being forced to hand over their World Series shares. More important, the three ballplayers were suspended until May 20 of the 1922 season. In delivering his decision, Landis not only referred to baseball law but to the key question: "Which is the bigger, baseball or any individual in baseball?" The next day, perhaps as part of a deal crafted with Yankee management, Landis announced that Ruth was nevertheless eligible to play in New York's exhibition contests.[39]

* * *

Never entirely ignored by major leaguers, much to the chagrin of the new commissioner, were the practitioners of blackball. A host of exhibition games continued to pit players from organized baseball against stars who, because of color barriers, were precluded from competing against them in an official capacity. No one had fought harder to send black ballplayers against their better know white counterparts than Rube Foster, now heading into his second season of the president of the Negro National League. Ira F. Lewis, writing in *The Competitor*, sang his praises:

> Rube Foster ... is slowly but effectually working towards an ideal. Mr. Foster has seen through the periscope of his uncanny vision and foresight the possibilities of colored baseball, as a business venture which almost staggers the

imagination of the man who looks upon the sport as a plaything.

The Windy City leader is working towards the establishment of a real major league with franchises in the principal cities of the East and Middle West; or, two leagues, comprised of cities of the East in one and cities of the West in the other. Smaller cities to be formed into minor circuits. Under this plan could be worked out the general scheme of organizing practically the entire country and especially the South, into a general plan of ORGANIZED COLORED BASEBALL.[40]

The June 1921 issue of *Baseball Magazine* included a rare look at the segregation barriers that prevented blacks from competing in

Judge Kenesaw Mountain Landis tossing out ball at 1922 World Series, 1922. National Baseball Hall of Fame Library, Cooperstown, N.Y.

the major or minor leagues. The publication applauded efforts by Andy Lawson, the leading sponsor of the Continental League, to allow blacks into his organization. F. C. Lane recognized Lawson's "evidently sincere attempt to give the colored ball player a chance." Lane continued:

> The brand of Cain rests heavily on the Negro in this country. Through no fault of his own, life for him is beset with heavy handicaps. In this land of vaunted freedom he finds only the shadow of the substance. Equal opportunity for all, the slogan of the loud-mouthed campaign orator has only a far away and empty ring in his ears.
> At every turn, in every industry, the Negro is at a disadvantage. And nowhere is that disadvantage more cruelly oppressive than in professional sport.[41]

To the delight of Rube Foster, who remained committed to battering down those racial barriers and stereotypes, 1921 proved to be one in which many blackball stars were competing in his brand of organized baseball. Also satisfying was the continued dominance of Foster's own Chicago American Giants, who, on the strength of a 41-21 record and .661 winning percentage, swept to their second straight championship, beating out the Kansas City Monarchs, whose lengthier 50-31 schedule translated into a .617 won-loss percentage. The third-place St. Louis Giants took top individual honors, as Charles Blackwell batted .448, Oscar Charleston hit 15 homers, and right-handed pitcher Bill Drake produced a 20-10 record. The American Giants were led by center fielder Cristobal Torriente, who hit .338, and leftie Dave Brown, who notched an 11-3 won-loss record.

Significantly, the Negro National League continued to provide a model of organizational stability for blackball participants. *The Chicago Defender*, on November 26, termed the league "a wonderful success," athletically speaking. Commercially, it had not succeeded as mightily during its second campaign, because of poor weather conditions and depressed economic circumstances. Consequently, gate receipts were down approximately 25 percent. Only Chicago thrived at both the box office and cash register.[42]

In a series of four articles, which appeared in December issues of the *Defender*, Foster discussed what the league required to thrive. Organized blackball, he noted, demanded a "business system in the handling of the affairs" of the various clubs. It also needed managers with "brains, patience, endurance and an open mind to deal with all the players on a ... club squarely." Although he had handled temperamental stars, none, Foster insisted, had proven difficult to manage. In fact, he said, "I have not had one to disobey any instruction given him." Indeed, "to be frank and honest, all of my players play baseball as if they had no mind of their own or did not know what to do." Relying on extensive training, he had schooled them in the Foster system. Gaining the players' confidence, he never belittled them. He also got to know them personally, visiting their homes, learning about their temperaments and habits, and discovering what they found most appealing. His method had proven successful, Foster suggested, for "I know of no man who has the respect that will surpass the respect I receive from the ball players."[43]

Yet Foster worried that the players were "doing much to ruin the profession they have chosen as a livelihood; their conduct is far beneath their profession; they have not even the confidence of their conscience." Thus, they broke contracts, jumped from one ball club to the next, and seemingly held up their teams for ransom. "Our players," Foster claimed, "are harder to handle than the white players. It seems characteristic of our race to act according to the size of the attendance: the larger the attendance the worse our actions. We don't feel that we have had a good afternoon until we show off to the multitude how bad we can be."[44]

# CHAPTER SEVENTEEN

# *Legacies*

In 1920, those involved with professional baseball had to contend with the unholy trinity of American mythology, class, and race. So recently removed from a major war, Americans seemingly looked to baseball as a repository of time-honored values and virtues. On the diamond, so went the argument, wholesome competitiveness could reign freely. Heroic figures and teams, moreover, were expected to uphold organized baseball's finest traditions, not only throughout the regular season but during America's greatest sporting event, the World Series. As that year's slate of games was played, larger-than-life figures sprang forth, in keeping with the history of a sport that had placed Cap Anson, the old Baltimore Orioles, Christy Mathewson, Connie Mack, Cy Young, and Walter Johnson, among others, in a rhetorical Hall of Fame. Tris Speaker, Jim Bagby, Pete Alexander, and, above all else, Babe Ruth, had seasons for the ages, while old-line stars like Walter Johnson and Ty Cobb temporarily lost a bit of their luster. With the fatal beaning of their fine shortstop Ray Chapman, the Cleveland Indians were considered heroic in their own fashion, but were never viewed as one of the great baseball teams, as Charles Comiskey's White Sox so recently had been.

That squad, of course, had been riddled with dissension because of anger over Comiskey's pay scale, the favoritism displayed the likes of Eddie Collins, and the owner's treatment of ballplayers who had declined to enter America's armed forces during World War I. That upset had translated into a willingness to throw the World Series, a decision made by some of baseball's biggest stars, including Eddie Cicotte, Lefty Williams, Happy Felsch, and Joe Jackson. The discontent over salaries and organized baseball's infamous reserve clause continued to result in contract squabbles and talk of players' involvement with gamblers. Others were increasingly displeased about the inequitable distribution of resources that enabled the New York and Chicago teams to stockpile talent.

While discussion of a Hall of Fame during that era never involved Rube Foster, blackball, to its everlasting credit, was never marred with the brush of crooked dealings. The national game, so popular and troubled as 1920 rolled around, remained for "whites only," at least in its official capacity. Both the major and minor leagues kept out some of the greatest players, managers, and administrators, including someone like Foster who had been blackball's top pitcher and was still its leading field boss. Black ballplayers were barred, although the lucrative nature of barnstorming led to a series of games involving major leaguers and their ebony-skinned foes. At the same time, black moguls frequently rented big league ballparks, which also placed money into the coffers of those involved with organized baseball. Concerned that profits were escaping the black community and hoping to demonstrate the absurdity of Jim Crow practices, Foster, in 1920, finally established the Negro National League. All the while, he retained hope that someday the color barriers in organized baseball would be lifted.

Myth-making, class considerations, and racial realities thus remained intertwined in a manner that clearly affected baseball and paralleled their presence in American life. Myths enabled Americans to place baseball giants on a kind of pedestal, while engaging in hero-worship. Nevertheless, the crosses of gambling, class, and race had to be borne in a sport that was viewed as an essential part of the American experience.

As the triad of mythology, class, and race continued to swirl about the national pastime, 1920 proved to be a formative moment. That year forever changed the careers and lives of four of the most important figures ever to grace baseball diamonds: Buck Weaver, Kenesaw Mountain Landis, Babe Ruth, and Rube Foster. These gentlemen helped to sustain the myths, while some at least ultimately challenged class and racial barriers; however, not all benefited from their individual efforts. Ruth became baseball's highest-paid star, his salary not surpassed in real dollars until the advent of free agency. Player discontent over salaries, coupled with the gambling culture that permeated the major and minor leagues, led to Weaver's expulsion. Foster, due to racial barriers, was never even allowed entrée into organized baseball. Landis, for his part, acted to sustain those very barriers, while helping to mythologize the game, particularly at the professional level.

The revelations of the 1919 World Series fix resulted in Weaver's suspension from the Chicago White Sox, which, by the summer of 1921, proved to be permanent from organized baseball altogether. Thus, one of the greatest third basemen ever to play the game, and a man who had just come into his prime, would never again compete at his sport's highest level. For the next three and a half decades, he struggled mightily to regain his good name, but remained instead on baseball's permanently ineligible list.

Federal Judge Kenesaw Mountain Landis, who placed him on that list, notwithstanding a jury determination that Weaver had not conspired to throw the 1919 World Series, rode growing concerns about the game's very well-being to its highest post. As baseball's long-time commissioner, Landis ruled the sport, at various points, as if it were his personal fiefdom. In the process, as he attempted to address the blight of gambling, Landis helped to restore public confidence in organized baseball. Nevertheless, his rule proved to be arbitrary, capricious, and, at times, injudicious. It was also characterized by Landis's determination to maintain silence about baseball's other great shame: the color barrier that prevented some legendary ballplayers, managers, and magnates from competing against their white brethren in the major or minor leagues.

Landis's seemingly righteous control of the game, which received such favorable press, extended even to its single greatest star and the most spectacular performer in all of American sports history. Determined to barnstorm after the 1921 World Series, Babe Ruth clashed with the pugnacious little judge, and soon paid the price. Landis suspended the spectacular home run king, perhaps costing him yet another run at a long ball record. Yet Ruth rebounded in 1923 to have one of his finest seasons and remained baseball's most luminous light for the next decade. Certain standards, both single-season and career, that Ruth established, would later be broken; others, remain unreachable as a new century unfolds.

The records of another key baseball man are scattered, at best, having occurred outside organized baseball's realm. Rube Foster, like Ruth, was at one time a superlative pitcher and a fair hitter too. Foster, while still pitching at a high level, became blackball's greatest manager, creating his own legendary Chicago American Giants. Similar to Landis, Foster became head of a professional organization, the Negro National League. Foster not only served as league president but largely shaped and molded it during its first years of existence. As a consequence, he helped to keep black ballplayers in the public limelight, albeit in the shadows of the organized baseball that Landis presided over, Ruth dominated, and Weaver was cast out of.

Repeatedly, Buck Weaver sought reinstatement into organized baseball from a series of commissioners, starting with Landis. Those requests were invariably turned down, as Weaver continued to be stigmatized by his association with the Black Sox because of "guilty knowledge." After meeting with Weaver in December 1921, Landis issued a press release snidely declaring,

"Birds of a feather flock together. Men associating with gamblers and crooks could expect no leniency." Weaver's own personal sense of honor, curiously, had doomed him. As he explained on January 13, 1922, "The only doubt in my mind was whether I should keep quiet about or tell Mr. Comiskey. I was not certain just what men, if any, had accepted propositions, whether they accepted. I couldn't bring myself to tell on them, even had I known for certain. I decided to keep quiet and play my best." For the powers that be in organized baseball, some of whose own hands were stained by the tar of "guilty knowledge," that was hardly enough. On December 11 of that year, Weaver was barred forever from organized baseball.[1]

Landis responded in different manners to Weaver's petitions, sometime ignoring them and on other occasions firing back notes rejecting out of hand the pleas for reinstatement. As word of other possible scandals, which involved Weaver's teammates but also Tris Speaker and Ty Cobb, threatened to unravel five years later, Buck again asked Landis to reconsider his stand. The commissioner replied that time, "I regret that it was not possible for me to arrive at any other conclusion than that set forth in the decision of Dec. 11, 1922, that your own admissions and actions in the circumstances forbid your reinstatement." Once more, Landis damned Weaver for failing to come forward: "You knew your club officials were seeking to ascertain the facts, but you kept still." Following Landis's death in 1944, Weaver made additional requests to the commissioner's office to be removed from the permanently ineligible list. His last attempt to do so occurred in a letter dated January 29, 1953, but was summarily turned down.[2]

On January 31, 1956, Weaver suffered a fatal heart attack. Former teammates Ray Schalk and Red Faber each referred to him as "the greatest third baseman I ever saw." Schalk recalled, "That incident caused Weaver the tortures of hell." Faber remembered Buck as "a wonderful competitor, a fellow who played baseball because he loved it." Weaver's former manager Pants Rowland called Weaver "the greatest third baseman of all time." Not denying that Weaver's refusal to talk merited some punishment, Rowland also remembered, "Squealing in those days was considered almost a crime in itself. And Buck ... simply didn't know how to cope with such a situation or the slick operators." Furthermore, "Weaver was the only one who stepped right up and protested his innocence."[3]

Agreeing with such assessments, Ty Cobb exclaimed,

> I can't speak for the others who were involved, but they'll never get me to believe that Buck Weaver was guilty of anything. Buck just wasn't the type to be in on a crooked deal like that and certainly there wasn't anything wrong with the way he played in the 1919 Series. If you'll just look up the records you'll find that he was one of the Series' biggest stars.
>
> To my way of thinking, those figures speak for themselves. I just can't imagine any one who was trying to throw a game playing the kind of baseball Weaver did against Cincinnati.

> Besides, I know Weaver as a man of excellent character. It wasn't in him to cheat and even if he had tried to kick one away it certainly would have showed up. By that I mean he was such a flawless player that a false move by him would have been recognized at once.

After proclaiming him "the greatest third baseman I ever saw," Cobb declared, "It was a shame that he had all that trouble. Weaver had at least another five or six great years ahead of him and had his career not been ruined by that scandal he would have ranked right along with Honus Wagner as one of the greatest infielders of all time." Then, Cobb concluded, "It was a real tough break. And, like I said, I'll never believe Weaver had it coming to him."[4]

Following Weaver's death, a series of sportswriters likewise proclaimed both his legendary ball-playing and his general innocence, notwithstanding "guilty knowledge" of the World Series fix. Terming him "the greatest third baseman I have seen," Sec Taylor insisted that he "had no part in the attempt to throw the Series." Weaver refused to play the part, Taylor wrote, of "stool pigeon." Hugh Brown, in *The Philadelphia Evening Bulletin*, indicated that Weaver's "stylish antics at third base were copied by all small-fry dreaming of a big league career as an infielder." For many an impoverished lad, Brown recalled, "Weaver was THEIR idol, not Eddie Cicotte or Joe Jackson." Campaigns have been undertaken, including one orchestrated by Hall of Famer Ted Williams, to clear Joe Jackson's name, but little has been done regarding Buck Weaver.[5]

Kenesaw Mountain Landis appeared wholly self-assured of his own righteousness, whether that involved damning socialists, Wobblies, or those he saw as crooked ballplayers including Buck Weaver. Landis resorted to blacklisting to rid the National Game of unsavory play, yet he did so in the same erratic way that he presided over his courtroom. Thus, the eight "Black Sox" were permanently barred from organized baseball, but, curiously enough, not the infamous Hal Chase, who undoubtedly would have had more to say about underhanded play on the diamond than virtually anyone. On the other hand, Chase's one-time confederate, Lee Magee, was banned. So were various baseball men, who were accused of fixes, bribes, negotiating with an "outlaw" squad, or even participating, as Benjamin Kauff supposedly had, in an auto theft ring. Ironically enough, Dickie Kerr, one of the "Clean Sox" stars of the 1919 World Series, was temporarily suspended for having played against some of the Black Sox, while engaging in a contract dispute with Charles Comiskey. Yet Rube Benton, who was kicked out of the National League for possessing knowledge about the 1919 World Series fix and failing to report a bribe involving Chase, was reinstated by Landis. Giants owner Charles A. Stoneham, who was involved in highly questionable "bucket shop" brokerage houses and was a gambling associate of Arnold Rothstein, was left untouched by the commissioner; Landis failed to act even following Stoneham's indictment for perjury and a series of other embarrassing revelations. Such incidents led *The Sporting News'* Frank G. Mince to ask in late 1923, "Has Landis Spoiled Chance to Be of Service to Game?" And in 1927, when reports of both the payoff to Tiger players by the 1917 White Sox and a purported betting incident involving Cobb, Speaker, Smokey Joe Wood, and Dutch Leonard surfaced, Landis effectively carved out a statute of limitations regarding such incidents. In 1943, the commissioner did bar Philadelphia Philly owner Bill Cox, who was accused of placing bets on his own ball club, from organized baseball.[6]

As for Landis, he remained a controversial figure in his own right and was forced to resign from the federal bench in 1922. His stewardship of organized baseball was mixed at best, occurring during a period of tremendous popularity, economic depression, and a world war. To his credit, Landis helped to restore baseball's good name; still, even that feat was tarnished by his reluctance or outright hostility to opening up the gates of the major and minor leaguers to black ballplayers. Indeed, Landis strove mightily to prevent exhibition contests matching up his players and those who played the blackball version, perhaps fearing that whatever success the dark-skinned athletes would attain might lead to heightened calls for their admission into organized baseball. Landis presented himself as the new baseball czar, freed various players from being relegated to the minors almost indefinitely, but was forced to give way as Branch Rickey began devising an intricate farm system to groom ballplayers for his St. Louis Cardinals. Landis happily watched as the antitrust suit against organized baseball, which had earlier visited his courtroom, was tossed aside in a curious decision issued by the United States Supreme Court, presided over by the same William Howard Taft who was once considered for the post of baseball dictator. Judge Landis was still ruling over the game when President Franklin Delano Roosevelt declared that it should continue, even in the midst of world-wide conflagration. Landis's death on November 25, 1944 enabled baseball magnates to take back control of the game. Leading to the appointment of Happy Chandler as his successor, it also set the stage for the shattering of Jim Crow strictures in organized baseball.[7]

Throughout a good part of Landis's tenure, the game thrived mightily, thanks in no small measure to Babe Ruth's sheer brilliance. Following his epic 1920 and 1921 campaigns that led many sportswriters to proclaim him the greatest player in the game's history, Ruth appeared all-too mortal during his 1922 season, shortened because of the suspension levied by Commissioner Landis. Playing in only 110 games, Ruth lost his home run title, hitting only 35, drove in but 99 runs, batted only .315 in the regular season, and then flopped miserably against the Giants in the World Series. He rebounded in 1923, with what some then considered his finest season. Babe opened the year by hitting the first homer at the new Yankee Stadium — called "The House

That Ruth Built." He went on to attain his highest batting mark ever, .393, regained the home run crown with 41 belts, and garnered a record 170 walks. Babe also led the Yankees to their first World Series title, as he smashed three homers and batted .368 against John McGraw's Giants. The Yankees came up two games short to the Washington Senators in 1924, but Ruth won his only batting title with a .378 mark and led the league with 46 homers. The following year was his most difficult one yet, as an out-of-shape Ruth was afflicted with physical ailments, played but 98 games, hit only 25 homers, drove in a scant 66 runs, and batted a mere .290, while New York plunged to a seventh-place finish. The Yankees rebounded with another pennant in 1926, as Babe led the way by notching a league best 47 homers and a .372 batting average. 1927 witnessed Ruth crash the 60 home run barrier, as his 110 win Yankees rolled to a pennant and swept the Pirates in the World Series. The Cardinals were the hapless victims the next year, as Ruth produced 54 homers and a .323 batting average in the regular campaign. The following three years saw the Yankees finish as a distant runner-up, in third place, and again in second, but Ruth remained at the top of his game, smacking league-leading totals of 46, 49, and 46 homers, respectively, with batting averages of .345, .359, and .373. Starting in 1930, his $80,000 salary surpassed the amount paid the President of the United States. New York was back on top in 1932, Ruth's last great year, when he hit 41 homers — albeit a distant second to the Athletics' Jimmy Foxx — batted .341, and belted a home run in the World Series that might or might not have been a called shot. Ruth's pair of homers in the four game sweep of the Cubs were the last of 15 he produced in World Series competition. The next two years were less happy ones for both the Yankees, as they finished runner-up each time, seven back of the pennant winners, and Ruth, whose home run totals dropped to 34 and 22 and his batting averages to .301 and .288. Unable to receive the appointment as New York manager he so desperately desired, Ruth finished his career back in Boston, playing the first few weeks of the 1935 season for the moribund Braves, where he hit the last six of 714 career total homers. His other lifetime numbers included a .342 batting average, 2,873 hits, 2,174 runs scored, 2,213 runs batted in, 2,056 walks, a .690 slugging percentage, and an on-base percentage of .474, all truly Ruthian numbers.[8]

Official records, by contrast, are sporadic at best for blackball's greatest pitcher of the early 20th Century, its top manager and its most creative administrator, Rube Foster. Still, from 1920-1922, the first three years of the Negro National League, Foster's Chicago American Giants swept to the pennant. Their third title was the result of a 36-23 record, which bested the twin 46-33 marks of the Indianapolis ABCs and the Kansas City Monarchs. Blackball historian Norman "Tweed" Webb declared that Foster's American Giants, from 1910-22, comprised "the greatest black team I ever saw." In 1923, the aging American Giants finished at 41-29, only good enough for runner-up honors, alongside the Detroit Stars, and behind the Kansas City Monarchs. The following season, Foster's team, thanks to a 49-24 mark, again came in second, in back of the Monarchs. During the 1925 split-season, the American Giants finished with a cumulative record of 54-40, placing them in fourth place.

While the Negro National League that he, more than any other individual, had birthed, nurtured, and sustained, appeared to be succeeding, Foster's vision remained larger. He continued to hope for an end to the Jim Crow barriers that prevented blacks from entering organized baseball. At times, Foster appeared to move incrementally in an effort to challenge the segregative realities that kept stars like Oscar Charleston, John Henry Lloyd, and Martin Dihigo from competing on a regular basis with the top white ballplayers. After Judge Landis became baseball commissioner, Foster visited him, hoping to obtain permission to use major league stadiums. On meeting the head of the Negro National League, Landis exclaimed, "Why, I know you: You're Rube Foster." The request was denied. On another occasion, Foster again went to see Landis, after the commissioner halted a series of games between the Chicago American Giants and an all-star squad led by Detroit outfielder Harry Heilmann. "The very idea, Judge, that you can cancel this game," Foster complained. "This is a chance that we have every year to play against your fellows, make a little extra money. Why do you do this?" Landis reportedly replied, "Mr. Foster, when you beat our teams it gives us a black eye."[9]

By the mid-twenties, Foster was obviously more frustrated than ever by the failure to contest Jim Crow baseball. He supposedly sought out the assistance of old friends, New York Giants' manager John McGraw and American League president Ban Johnson, in an effort to contest the segregation that afflicted the national pastime. By one account, Foster hoped that Johnson would let American League teams battle against the Chicago American Giants when they had no games scheduled but were awaiting encounters with the White Sox. Another story had Foster planning to put a white ballplayer on his team. In the meantime, as his American Giants struggled in the first half of the 1926 season, the over-taxed powerful league boss was crippled with mental illness. With a 57-21 record, the Chicago American Giants, now guided by Dave Malarcher, again came in second behind the Monarchs, taking them into the black World Series.[10]

Thus, Foster never steered his own team into the black World Series, another dream of his for so many years. The first such games were played in 1924, as the Monarchs bested the Eastern Colored League champion Hilldale Daisies. The same two teams met the next season, with Hilldale prevailing. Foster's American Giants finally reached the black World Series in 1926, but Dave Malarcher had taken control of the team, and guided it to a victory over the Bacharach Giants, as he did again in 1927. The league broke down by the end of the decade, a condition heightened by both Foster's absence and the advent of the Great Depression. The fate of his league was undoubtedly not revealed to Foster who had been confined to the state mental ward in Kankakee, Illinois, where he died on December 9, 1930. The Negro National League went out of business in 1932, but was reborn a year later.

His friend and colleague Dave Malarcher discussed Foster's impact on the national game.

> Foster had had an opportunity to leave Negro baseball and go into white semi-pro baseball because he was the leading drawing card outside of the major leagues back in those days when he was pitching. But Rube told me he refused to go because he knew that all we had to do was to keep it up to a high standard, and the time would come when the white leagues would have to admit us. The thing for us to do, he said, was to keep on developing, so that when that time did come, we would be able to measure up.

Sportswriter Ric Roberts of *The Pittsburgh Courier* similarly considered Foster's most significant contribution to the national game "the organization, the perpetuation of black baseball."[11]

*  *  *

In 1936, the year following his retirement from major league baseball, Babe Ruth was selected as one of five charter members of the Baseball Hall of Fame. Some 226 members of the Baseball Writers' Association of America voted for the inaugural class that also included Ty Cobb, Honus Wagner, Christy Mathewson, and Walter Johnson. Amazingly enough, Cobb was left off five ballots, while Ruth and Wagner were absent from 11, Mathewson from 10 more. Johnson got 189 votes, but Nap Lajoie, Tris Speaker, Cy Young, Rogers Hornsby, and Mickey Cochrane, who rounded out the top ten in the initial balloting, came up short. Joe Jackson got a mere 2 votes, but Hal Chase received 11 and did even better the following year. Lajoie, Speaker, and Young all made it in 1937, as did Ban Johnson, who was selected by the Centennial Committee, but Pete Alexander, Eddie Collins, and George Sisler, were among those who failed to do so. In 1938, Alexander was the only player selected, as Ray Chapman received the lone vote he ever garnered, while the following year, Collins, Sisler, and Willie Keeler made it. Hornsby had to wait until 1942 to become that year's lone inductee. Landis was elected to the Hall in 1944, a month following his death. Carl Mays, notwithstanding five 20-game seasons and a lifetime 208-126 record, received his only half-dozen votes 14 years later.

Hall of Fame members have also been chosen by special committees, including the Centennial Commission (1937-1938), the Old Timers'

Committee (1939-1949), the Veterans Committee (1953-present), and the Negro Leagues Committee (1971-1977). In 1937, the Centennial Committee selected American League founder Ban Johnson. The Old Timers' Committee elected Charles Comiskey in 1939, while Judge Landis was voted in five years later. The Veterans Committee, in 1977, slated Chapman's replacement, Joe Sewell, for induction, and in 1981, finally welcomed Andrew "Rube" Foster into the Hall of Fame. To date, some eight decades after his stellar playing career ground to a halt, George "Buck" Weaver, arguably the lone innocent among the Black Sox, has yet to receive a single vote for induction into the Hall of Fame.

# *Notes*

## 1. *America's Greatest Game*

1. John Thorn, "Our Game," in *Total Baseball: The Official Encyclopedia of Major League Baseball*, Sixth Edition, ed. by John Thorn et al. (New York: Total Sports, 1999), pp. 4–5; "Our Reason for Being," *Baseball Magazine* 2 (February 1909): no page number.

2. George Landor Perin, "Why Our Parson Likes Baseball," *Baseball Magazine* 2 (February 1909): 62–63; Christy Mathewson, "Baseball in Its Worthier Aspect," *Baseball Magazine* 2 (March 1909): 19, 21.

3. Walter Camp, "The American National Game," *The Century Magazine* 79 (April 1910): 936–48.

4. W. A. Phelon, "The Baseball Melting Pot," *Baseball Magazine* 5 (October 1910): 32–37.

5. David L. Belding, "The Athletics in Cuba," *Baseball Magazine* 6 (May 1911): 69–70; A. D. Roberds, "Baseball in Cuba," *Baseball Magazine* 5 (April 1911): 6–12.

6. Roberds, "Baseball in Cuba," pp. 6, 11–12.

7. Phelon, "Baseball Among the Magnates," *Baseball Magazine* 8 (February 1912) pp. 4–5.

8. Phelon, "Baseball in Cuba," *Baseball Magazine* 9 (May 1912): 33–36.

9. F. C. Lane, "Gridiron v. Diamond," *Baseball Magazine* 8 (December 1911): 21–25.

10. I. B. Sanborn, "Is Baseball on the Square?," *Baseball Magazine* 8 (January 1912): 61–62; Phelon, "Baseball among the Magnates," 4–5.

11. "Editorials," *Baseball Magazine* 9 (August 1912): 11.

12. Ibid., pp. 11–12.

13. Lane, "Baseball's Greatest Danger," *Baseball Magazine* 9 (September 1912): 45–53.

14. Ibid., pp. 46, 48–50.

15. Ibid., pp. 50–53.

16. "Is Professional Baseball Wholesome?," *The Outlook* 102 (October 1912): 329–30; H. Addington Bruce, "Baseball and the National Life," *The Outlook* 104 (May 17, 1913): 104–07.

17. Simeon Strunsky, "The Game," *The Atlantic Monthly* 114 (August 1914): 248–51.

18. "World Series Reform," *Sporting Life*, December 5, 1914, p. 10.

19. "Base Ball Pools," *Sporting Life*, June 5, 1915, p. 14.

20. "Editorials," *Baseball Magazine* 9 (June 1912): n.p.

21. "Personal Glimpses," *The Literary Digest* 45 (December 7, 1912): 190–92.

22. "Editorials," *Baseball Magazine* 10 (December 1912): 11–13.

23. "Fraternity Receives Recognition," *The Sporting News*, January 15, 1914, p. 4.

24. Lane, "Is There Room for a Third Big League?," *Baseball Magazine* 13 (June 1914): 43–52.

25. Ibid., p. 52; Sanborn, "Chase Could Not Wait His Ten Days," *The Sporting News*, June 25, 1914, p. 1.

## 2. The People's Judge

1. John T. McCutcheon, "Kenesaw Mountain Landis, Judge," *Appleton's Magazine* 9 (October 1907): 418–27.

2. Ibid., pp. 423, 427.

3. Jerome Holtzman, *The Commissioners: Baseball's Midlife Crisis* (New York: Total Sports, 1998), pp. 19–20.

4. Ed Fitzgerald, "Judge Landis: The Man Who Saved Baseball," *Sport* 8 (June 1950): 52–53.

5. "Organized Ball Forced into A United States Court," *Sporting Life* (January 16, 1915, 2; Vila, "Feds Pull Greatest Bone in All Their Erratic Career," *The Sporting News*, January 14, 1915, p. 1; "Our Own Part in It," *The Sporting News*, January 14, 1915, p. 4; "Base Ball Writers O.B.," *The Sporting News*, January 14, 1915, p. 3; "The Greatest Danger of All," *Sporting Life*, January 23, 1915, p. 12.

6. "Trust Case in Judge's Hands," *Sporting Life*, January 30, 1915, 1–3.

7. "Judge Kenesaw M. Landis," *The Sporting News*, January 28, 1915, p. 2.

8. "Fed Suit Dwindles to a Plea 'To Make 'Em Leave Us Alone,'" *The Sporting News*, January 28, 1915, p. 5.

9. "Press Box Pickups at Landis Park," *The Sporting News*, January 28, 1915, p. 5.

10. David Pietrusza, *Judge and Jury: The Life and Times of Judge Kenesaw Mountain Landis* (South Bend, Indiana: Diamond Communications, Inc., 1998), p. 157; J. G. Taylor Spink, *Judge Landis and 25 Years of Baseball* (St. Louis, Missouri: The Sporting News Publishing Company, 1974), p. 41.

11. Lane, "The Famous Federal Suit," *Baseball Magazine* 14 (March 1915): 65.

12. "Editorials," *Baseball Magazine* 15 (September 1915): 17–18.

13. "Peace Reigns in Game and Organized Ball Is Supreme," *The Sporting News*, December 30, 1915, p. 3; "Provisions of the Peace Pact," *The Sporting News*, December 30, 1915,

p. 3; "Baseball Law Again Reigns," *The Sporting News*, December 30, 1915, p. 4; Pietrusza, *Judge and Jury*, p. 157.

14. Robbins, "Outlaw Anti-Trust Suit Is Dismissed by Judge Landis," *The Sporting News*, February 10, 1916, p. 1.

15. I. E. Sanborn, "Judge Landis Dismisses," *Sporting Life*, February 12, 1916, p. 5; "Judge Landis' Hint," *Sporting Life*, February 29, 1916, p. 2; "The Tribute from Landis," *The Sporting News*, February 17, 1916, p. 4.

16. "The Trouble Baltimore Breeds," *The Sporting News*, January 13, 1916, p. 4; "The Gentle Holding Game," *The Sporting News*, February 3, 1916, p. 4; "A Sympathy Strike in Baseball," *The Sporting News*, December 7, 1916, p. 4; Robert F. Burk, *Never Just a Game: Players, Owners, and American Baseball to 1920* (Chapel Hill: The University of North Carolina Press, 1994), p. 214; "Requests of the Fraternity," *Sporting Life*, January 20, 1917, p. 2.

17. "Editorial Comment," *Baseball Magazine* 18 (March 1917): 101–102.

18. Vila, "Vila Back to Pay Respects to Fultz," *The Sporting News*, January 18, 1917, p. 1.

19. "Fultz Is Ready to Call Off His Strike," *The Sporting News*, February 8, 1917, p. 1; "Players' Fraternity News," *Sporting Life*, February 24, 1917, p. 7; "All Players Released from Pledge," *Sporting Life*, p. 7; Harold Seymour, *Baseball: The Golden Age* (New York: Oxford University Press, 1989), p. 242; "Organized Ball in Full Power Again," *Sporting Life*, February 24, 1917, p. 2; "The Fraternity's Future," *The Sporting News*, January 25, 1917, p. 1.

20. "The Excuse for the Hold-Out," *Sporting Life*, March 17, 1917, p. 2.

21. "Editorial Comment," *Baseball Magazine* 18 (April 1917): 167; Lane, "The Players' Strike," *Baseball Magazine* 18 (April 1917): 173–78.

22. "The End of the Baltimore Federal League Club's Suit," *Sporting Life*, June 23, 1917, p. 4.

23. "Editorial Comment," *Baseball Magazine* 18 (April 1917): 168.

24. "Honorable Kenesaw Mountain Landis," Kenesaw Mountain Landis Scrapbook, Chicago Historical Society; "'Copperheads' Flayed by Federal Judge Landis in Stirring Speech," June 2, 1917, Landis Scrapbook.

25. Pietrusza, *Judge and Jury*, pp. 112–13.

26. "1,100 Hear Forceful Talk by Judge

Landis," November 1917, Landis Scrapbook; "Landis Smites Profiteers in Patriotic Talk," *The Chicago Daily Tribune*, December 5, 1917, Landis Scrapbook.

27. Seymour, *Baseball: The Golden Age*, pp. 369–370; Pietrusza, *Judge and Jury*, pp. 119–35.

28. Ron Fimrite, "His Own Biggest Fan: Baseball's First Commissioner; Kenesaw Mountain Landis Was Part Hero, All Ego," *Sports Illustrated* 79 (July 19, 1993): p. 76; "'Damn the Hyphen,'" *The Chicago Tribune*, August 5, 1918, Landis Scrapbook.

29. "Too Optimistic by Far," *Sporting Life*, April 1, 1916, p. 2; "Call Off the Base Ball Strike," *Sporting Life*, February 10, 1917, p. 2.

30. "Military Training at Camps No Joke," *Sporting Life*, March 17, 1917, p. 2; "Probable Bad Effect on War on All Sports but Base Ball," *Sporting Life*, April 7, 1917, p. 2; "How Will the War Affect Base Ball This Season?," *Sporting Life*, April 21, 1917, p. 2.

31. Robbins, "Military Idea Game's Saviour (sic) since Declaration of War," *The Sporting News*, April 12, 1917, p. 1.

32. "Editorial Comment," *Baseball Magazine* 19 (May 1917): 227.

33. "A Plea for Sport during the War," *Sporting Life*, June 30, 1917, p. 4; "Editorial Comment," *The Baseball Monthly* 19 (June 1917): 294; August Hermann, "Base Ball Is a War Game," *Sporting Life*, July 14, 1917, p. 4.

34. William A. Sunday, "A Defense of the Grand Old Game," *Baseball Magazine* 19 (July 1917): 364.

35. Robbins, "War Really Aid to Baseball Interest," *The Sporting News*, August 23, 1917, p. 1; Robbins, "Commy Wants Military Day an Annual Feature in American," *The Sporting News*, August 30, 1917, p. 1.

36. Robbins, "Commy Stands Pat for Rights of Fans to Their Baseball," *The Sporting News*, December 13, 1917, p. 1; Robbins, "Nation's Fighting Men Have Message for Baseball Fans," *The Sporting News*, December 27, 1917, p. 1.

# 3. The Old Roman's Club

1. Lane, "Who Will Win the World's Championship?," *Baseball Magazine* 20 (November 1917): 136–39, 178–80.

2. "Baseball Men Think Comiskey Will Roll President Johnson," *St. Louis Republic*, October 28, 1907, Charles Comiskey Papers, National Baseball Hall of Fame Library.

3. "Comiskey Feted," *The Sporting News*, December 1, 1906; George C. Rice, "The Old Roman," *Baseball Magazine* 1 (June 1908): 47–49; Frank B. Hutchinson Jr., "Charles Albert Comiskey — The Man," *Baseball Magazine* 2 (April 1909): 52–54.

4. Hutchinson, "Charles Albert Comiskey," pp. 53–54.

5. Hugh S. Fullerton, "Comiskey," *Baseball Magazine* 5 (August 1910): 1–6.

6. "The Hall of Fame for the Immortals of Baseball," *Baseball Magazine* 6 (May 11): 85–86.

7. William A. Phelon, "The Great American Magnate," *Baseball Magazine* 10 (January 1913): 17, 23.

8. "The Tour of the World," *Sporting Life*, March 14, 1914, p. 4.

9. "White Sox and Giants," *The Indianapolis Freeman*, March 14, 1914, p. 7; Hugh C. Weir, "The Real Comiskey," *Baseball Magazine* 12 (February 1914): 21–23.

10. Ibid., p. 25; "Charley Comiskey Best Liked Magnate in Game," *New York Evening Journal*, February 26, 1914, Comiskey File.

11. William A. Phelon, "The Federal League and Other Problems," *Baseball Magazine* 13 (September 1914): 33.

12. William G. Weart, "Loss of Collins Wakes up Laggard Quaker City Fans," *The Sporting News*, December 17, 1914, p. 1; "American League to Fore with Two Big News Stories," *The Sporting News*, December 17, 1914, p. 3; Robbins, "Chicago Can Dream of Anything Now," *The Sporting News*, August 26, 1915, p. 1; "The Famous Joe Jackson Deal," *Baseball Magazine* 16 (March 1916): 30–32; Damon Runyon, "The World of Baseball: Charles Comiskey Not a Piker," *Sporting Life*, August 21, 1915, p. 3; "You Can't Buy Pennant Winner," *The Indianapolis Freeman*, October 9, 1915, p. 7.

13. "There Is but One Joe Jackson," *The Sporting News*, July 6, 1916, p. 4.

14. John J. Ward, "The American League's Premier Catcher," *Baseball Magazine* 18 (November 16, 1916): 33; "When the 'Browns' Were World's Champions," *Baseball Magazine* 18 (February 1917): 37; Robbins, "Hopes Never Were so High for a Pennant for White Sox," *The Sporting News*, March 8, 1917, p. 1; Robbins, "Military Idea Game's Saviour," p. 1; J. C. Kofoed, "What's the Matter with Base Ball?," *Sporting Life*, June 16, 1917, p. 3.

15. Robbins, "Rowland's Thanks for Winning Eight Straight — Fired Again," *The Sporting News*, May 24, 1917, p. 1.

16. "Now Comes Real Grief for Commy," *The Sporting News*, September 27, 1917, p. 1; "Editorial Comment," *Baseball Magazine* 20 (December 1917): 194; William Evans, "Charles Comiskey, the Prince of Magnates," *Baseball Magazine* 20 (December 1917): 209–11, 241–43.

17. Irving M. Stein, *The Ginger Kid: The Buck Weaver Story* (Dubuque, Iowa: The Elysian Fields Press, 1992), p. 96; George Weaver salary sheet, Buck Weaver Player File, National Baseball Hall of Fame Library.

18. Robbins, "Now It Is Chicago's Turn to Talk of Its Own World's Series," *The Sporting News*, May 6, 1915, p. 1; Robbins, "Mental Suggestion All the Thing Now," *The Sporting News*, May 20, 1915, p. 1; "Edwards Thinks Well of White Sox," *The Sporting News*, May 20, 1915, p. 2.

19. Robbins, "Third Base Causes Rowland No Worry," *The Sporting News*, March 23, 1916, p. 1.

20. Ibid.

21. Robbins, "White Sox Safe in Windy City Favor," *The Sporting News*, April 6, 1916, p. 1; Robbins, "Rowland Now Facing Real Acid Test with Chicago White Sox," *The Sporting News*, May 25, 1916, p. 1; Robbins, "Cheery Note from White Sox Booster," *The Sporting News*, June 8, 1916, p. 1; Robbins, "Robbins Defends White Sox for Not Making Walkaway," *The Sporting News*, September 7, 1916, p. 1; Robbins, "Robbins Inclined to Do a Bit of Hedging," *The Sporting News*, October 5, 1916, p. 1.

22. Robbins, "White Sox A Team Opposed to Strike," *The Sporting News*, January 18, 1917, p. 1; Robbins, "Uncle Sam's Nephews Won't Give up Baseball for War," *The Sporting News*, February 8, 1917, p. 1; Robbins, "Ban and Commy Not Worried over War," *The Sporting News*, February 15, 1917, p. 1.

23. Robbins, "First Cry of Quit Is Sent from Chicago," *The Sporting News*, August 16, 1917, p. 1; Whitman, "Hub Banks on That Long Stay at Home," *The Sporting News*, August 30, 1917, p. 1.

24. John J. Ward, "Who's Who on the Diamond: Thumbnail Sketches of Well Known Players," *Baseball Magazine* 19 (September 1917): 502–03; "Comments from the Winning Players," *Baseball Magazine* 21 (December 1918): 22.

25. Ward, "Who's Who on the Diamond," p. 503.

26. Lane, "Who Will Win the World Championship?," pp. 136–38; Vila, "All Talk in Gotham of World's Series," *The Sporting News*, September 13, 1917, p. 1.

27. "Buck Weaver as told to Hal Totten," in My Greatest Day in Baseball: *Forty-Seven Dramatic Stories by Forty-Seven Stars*, ed. John P. Carmichael (New York: A. S. Barnes & Company, 1945), pp. 42–43.

28. Ibid., pp. 43–45.

29. Ibid., pp. 45–47; William G. Weart, "Unfair Tactics Stir White Sox to Life," *The Sporting News*, October 18, 1917, p. 1.

30. Lane, "The All-American Baseball Team," *Baseball Magazine* 21 (December 1918): 219.

31. Robbins, "Nothing but Draft for Commy to Fear," *The Sporting News*, November 22, 1917, p. 1; "Buck Weaver as Told to Hal Totten," pp. 44–45; "Comiskey Richest Baseball Man Who Got Start Wearing Spikes," n.d., Comiskey File; "Current Sporting Gossip," n.d., Comiskey File; Donald Gropman, *Say It Ain't So, Joe! The True Story of Shoeless Joe Jackson* (New York: Citadel Press, 1995), pp. 153–154.

32. "Looking over Past Year in Baseball," *The Sporting News*, January 3, 1918, p. 2; George S. Robbins, "Commy a Booster for Plan to Pension Players in Service," *The Sporting News*, February 7, 1918, p. 1; W. A. Phelon, "In the Swirl of the Baseball Tide," *Baseball Magazine* 20 (January 1918): 274; Lane, "Baseball's Bit in the World War," *Baseball Magazine* 20 (March 1918): 390–91.

33. "Editorial Comment," *Baseball Magazine* 20 (April 1918): 263–64; George S. Robbins, "Crowder Order Not a Hit with Anybody," *The Sporting News*, May 30, 1918, p. 1.

34. Phelon, "The Passing Month," *Baseball Magazine* 20 (March 1918): 413; Phelon, "Who Will Win the Pennants?," *Baseball Magazine* 21 (May 1918): 135; "Retreats to a Ship Yard," *The Sporting News*, May 16, 1918, p. 1; Phelon, "Major League Baseball in the Balance," *Baseball Magazine* 21 (September 1918): 403.

35. George S. Robbins, "Desertions Rouse Old Roman's Anger," *The Sporting News*, June 20, 1918, p. 1.

36. Ibid., pp. 404–05; "The Month in War," *Baseball Magazine* 21 (August 1918): 355; Peter T. Dalleo and J. Vincent Watchorn III,

"Slugger or Slacker?: Shoeless Joe Jackson and Baseball in Wilmington, 1918," *Delaware History* 26 (Fall 1994): 95–123; Francis C. Richter, "Review of the 1918 Season," *The Reach Official American League Guide for 1919*, ed. Francis C. Richter (Philadelphia: A. J. Reach Company, 1919), p. 12.

37. Phelon, "Final Echoes of the 1918 Season," *Baseball Magazine* 22 (November 1918): 31.

38. Stein, *The Ginger Kid*, p. 113.

# 4. The Biggest Man in Baseball

1. "Editorial Comment," *Baseball Magazine* 21 ( July 18, 1918): 269.

2. Harry R. Stringer, "Baseball for Our Soldiers and Sailors," *Baseball Magazine* 21 ( June 1918): 217–18.

3. George S. Robbins, "Baker Rule a Blow to Nation's Morale," *The Sporting News*, July 25, 1918, p. 1.

4. Lane, "A Rising Menace to the National Game," *Baseball Magazine* 21 (August 1918): 345–47, 372; Lane, "Baseball's Future," *Baseball Magazine* 21 (September 1918): 407.

5. George S. Robbins, "Robbins Offers Plan to Make Professional Game Essential," *The Sporting News*, October 3, 1918, p. 1; Paul W. Eaton, "Washington Wants Baseball to Go On," *The Sporting News*, October 10, 1918, p. 1; George S. Robbins, "Fling the Ball Park Gates Open Next Year, Says Commy," *The Sporting News*, October 24, 1918, p. 1.

6. Lane, "The Future Prospects of Major League Baseball," *Baseball Magazine* 22 (November 1918): 19–20; "Editorial Comment," *Baseball Magazine* 22 (December 1918): 74.

7. Charles W. Murphy, "Baseball a War Time Necessity," *Baseball Magazine* 22 (December 1918): 87; Frederick E. Parmly, "Baseball Will Win the War," *Baseball Magazine* 22 (December 1918): 106, 108.

8. Frederick G. Lieb, "Harold Chase," *Baseball Magazine* 5 (September 1910): 51–53; "The All America Base Ball Team," *Baseball Magazine* 6 (December 1910): n.p.; "Who's Who on the Diamond," *Baseball Magazine* 6 ( January 1911): 67; "All-America Baseball Nine," *Baseball Magazine* 8 (December 1911): 13.

9. "Pulling for Chase to Clear Himself," *The Sporting News*, August 22, 1918, p. 2; "Charges against Chase Cap Climax in Season of Shocks," *The Sporting News*, August 22, 1918, p. 2; Phelon, "Closing Events of 1918 Baseball Season," *Baseball Magazine* 21 (October 1918): 483; Francis C. Richter, "Review of the 1918 Season," p. 13.

10. Francis C. Richter, "Review of the 1918 Season," pp. 8–10.

11. "Hard to Dope out in International," *The Sporting News*, April 23, 1914, p. 5; "No Tears Shed as Dunn's Team Goes," *The Sporting News*, July 16, 1914, p. 3; "Lannins' Grays Lead," *The Sporting News*, August 27, 1914, p. 1.

12. Kal Wagenheim, *Babe Ruth: His Life and Legend* (New York: Henry Holt and Company, 1992): p. 26; "Lannins' Grays Lead," p. 1.

13. A. H. C. Mitchell, "Causes of Red Sox Success," *Sporting Life*, October 9, 1915, p. 6; Francis Eaton, "No Limit for Lannin in Making Red Sox a Winner," *The Sporting News*, July 23, 1914, p. 1.

14. Babe Ruth contract, January 6, 1916, Babe Ruth File 19, Sporting News Archives, St. Louis, Missouri; Cover of *Sporting Life*, March 4, 1916, p. 1; John J. Ward, "The Coming Southpaw," *Baseball Magazine* 17 ( July 1916): 43–46; Lane, "The Foremost Pitching Staff of the American League," *Baseball Magazine* 17 (September 1916): 77; "This Pair Being Put to Severe Test," *The Sporting News*, September 21, 1916, p. 3.

15. Lane, "Is Batting Doomed?," *Baseball Magazine* 17 (August 1917): 68–73.

16. Lane, "The All-America Baseball Club," *Baseball Magazine* 17 (December 1916): 48–52; Sanborn, "All-Star Baseball Team," *The Sporting News*, November 9, 1916, p. 7; "Grantland Rice's All-Star Team," *The Sporting News*, November 23, 1916, p. 7; Edwards, "An All-American Star Team," *The Sporting News*, November 30, 1916, p. 6.

17. Whitman, "Ruth Counted Big Ace for Jack Barry," *The Sporting News*, May 10, 1917, p. 1; Whitman, "Let Those Who Doubted Barry as a Leader Look at Record," *The Sporting News*, May 17, 1917, p. 1.

18. "Babe Ruth is one of the greatest pitchers" box, *Baseball Magazine* 20 (February 1918): 336.

19. Ernest J. Lanigan, "Casual Comment," *The Sporting News*, January 3, 1918, p. 6.

20. "No Rule Changes and Fans Must Wait for More Batting," *The Sporting News*, March 7, 1918, p. 5.

21. Burt Whitman, "Barrow Wins His Cross as Real Major League Leader," *The Sporting News*, May 23, 1918, p. 1; "Must Be So, since Babe Says It," *The Sporting News*, August 8, 1918, p. 5; Phelon, "In the Swirl of the Baseball Tide," *Baseball Magazine* 21 (October 1918): 340.

22. Lane, "The Season's Sensation," *Baseball Magazine* 21 (October 1918): 471; Whitman, "Barrow Had Feared Pitching Collapse," *Sporting Life*, May 16, 1918, p. 1.

23. Ibid; Edward G. Barrow, "When a Pennant Is Almost Won," *Baseball Magazine* 21 (October 1918): 461; Edward G. Barrow, *My Fifty Years in Baseball* (New York: Coward-McCann, Inc., 1951), 89–95; Lee Allen and Tom Meany, *Kings of the Diamond: The Immortals in Baseball's Hall of Fame* (New York: G. P. Putnam's Sons, 1965), p. 202.

24. "It's Something New that Ruth Introduces," *The Sporting News*, September 19, 1918, p. 6.

25. "George S. Robbins, "Chicago to Show Boston Fine Points in World's Series," *The Sporting News*, August 29, 1918, p. 1; Phelon, "Who Will Win the World's Championship," *Baseball Magazine* 21 (October 1918): 466–69, 499–500.

26. Lane, "The Cubs against the Field," *Baseball Magazine* 21 (October 1918): 455; "Ruth Wins Hair-Line Verdict in a Battle with Vaughn," *The Sporting News*, September 12, 1918, p. 2; "Ruth Holds Runless Record," *The Sporting News*, September 19, 1918, p. 6.

27. Lane, "The All Star Baseball Club of 1918," *Baseball Magazine* 22 (December 1918): 81, 85; Lane, "Striking Features of the 1918 Record," *Baseball Magazine* 22 (March 1919): 281–83; "The Spalding Base Ball Hall of Fame," in *Spalding's Official Base Ball Record: 1919*, ed. John B. Foster (New York: American Sports Publishing Company, 1919), pp. 24, 26.

28. Richter, "Review of the 1918 Season," p. 14; Seymour, *Baseball: The Golden Age*, p. 252; "No Great Issue in Jake Daubert Case," *The Sporting News*, November 28, 1918, p. 5.

29. "New Plan for Split of World's Series Purse," *The Sporting News*, January 10, 1918, p. 3.

30. J. G. Taylor Spink, "I Recall," pp. 1–3, Ban Johnson File 1, Sporting News Archives. A fine summary of the World Series squabble is presented in Robert W. Creamer, *Babe: The Legend Comes to Life* (New York: Simon & Schuster, 1992), pp. 174–82.

31. Thomas Rice, "Red Sox Were Good Four to Two Wager," *The Sporting News*, September 19, 1918, p. 5.

## 5. Jim Crow Baseball

1. A succinct analysis of Jim Crow baseball can be found in Charles Alexander, *Our Game: An American Baseball History* (New York: Henry Holt and Company, 1991), pp. 49–51. See also Robert Peterson, *Only the Ball Was White: A History of Legendary Black Players and All-Black Professional Teams* (New York: Oxford University Press, 1970), pp. 3–51; Mark Ribowsky, *A Complete History of the Negro Leagues: 1884 to 1955* (Secaucus, N.J.: Citadel Press, 1997), pp. 10–47; and Phil Dixon with Patrick J. Hannigan, *The Negro Baseball Leagues: A Photographic History* (Mattituck, NY: Amereon House, 1992), pp. 31–81.

2. Howard A. Phelps, "Andrew 'Rube' Foster," *The Half-Century Magazine* (March 1, 1919): 8; C. D. Marshall, "Taylor's Champs May Win from Foster," *The Indianapolis Freeman*, January 26, 1918, p. 7.

3. Ibid.; Peterson, *Only the Ball Was White*, pp. 104–05.

4. Phelps, "Andrew 'Rube' Foster," p. 8.

5. John L. Footslug, "In the World of Sports ..... ," *The Indianapolis Freeman*, December 18, 1905, p. 6.

6. Rube Foster Officials File, National Baseball Hall of Fame Library; John Holway, *Voices from the Great Black Baseball Leagues* (New York: Da Capo Press, 1992), p. 3.

7. Rube Foster, "How to Pitch," in *Sol White's History of Colored Base Ball, with Other Documents on the Early Black Game 1886–1936* (Lincoln: University of Nebraska Press, 1995), pp. 96, 99–100.

8. David Wyatt, "Baseball War for Chicago," *The Indianapolis Freeman*, December 4, 1909, p. 7; "Historically Speaking," *Black Sports* (November 1, 1977), p. 58; Billy Lewis, "The American Giants!," *The Indianapolis Freeman*, March 6, 1915, p. 7.

9. Foster, "Pitfalls of Baseball," *The Chicago Defender*, December 13, 1919, p. 11; "Base Hits of Chicago," *The Indianapolis Freeman*, July 25, 1908, p. 7; F. C. Leland, "Leland Giants Making a Record," *The Indianapolis Freeman*, p. 7.

10. "Champion Leland Giants to Go South for Spring Training," *The Indianapolis Freeman*, February 20, 1909, p. 7; "Leland

Giants Complete a Successful Southern Trip," *The Indianapolis Freeman*, May 15, 1909, p. 7.

11. "City Champs Win from Lelands, 4-1," *The Chicago Daily Tribune*, October 19, 1909, p. 8; "Foster Argues; Schulte Scores," *The Chicago Daily Tribune*, October 22, 1909, p. 12; "Cubs Trim Giants in Final Game, 1-0," *The Chicago Daily Tribune*, October 23, 1909, p. 14.

12. Foster, "Success of the Negro as a Ball Player," *The Freeman Supplement*, April 16, 1910, p. 9.

13. Lewis, "The American Giants!," p. 7; Young, "More about Foster's Baseball Team," *The Half-Century Magazine* (June 1, 1919): pp. 8, 13.

14. *The Negro Leagues Book*, ed. Dick Clark and Larry Lester (Cleveland: Society for American Baseball Research, 1994), p. 21.

15. "The Sporting World," *The Chicago Defender*, August 24, 1912, p. 6; Foster, "The American Giants, Champions — in Los Angeles, CAL.," *The Indianapolis Freeman*, November 9, 1912, p. 7; Julius N. Avendorph, "'Rube' Foster's Giants Hold Their Own in California," *The Chicago Defender*, December 14, 1912, p. 7; Frank Albert Young, "The Colored Men in Athletics," *The Indianapolis Freeman*, January 25, 1913, p. 7.

16. Billy Lewis, "Baseball Is Now the Subject," *The Indianapolis Freeman*, February 15, 1913, p. 7.

17. Carey B. Lewis, "American Giants Take Four out of Five in Series from Plutos — Foster Wins Two Games — Smart Set Here Sunday," *The Indianapolis Freeman*, June 7, 1913, p. 4; "Lincolns Win Best Seven out of Twelve Games," *The Indianapolis Freeman*, August 23, 1913, p. 4; Billy Lewis, "The American Giants!," p. 7; "Americans Win," *The Indianapolis Freeman*, August 30, 1913, p. 4; "The Foster Banquet," *The Indianapolis Freeman*, August 30, 1913, p. 4; "Base Ball Doings in the Windy City," *The Indianapolis Ledger*, October 18, 1913, p. 4.

18. Baxter, "Colored Demons Play Here Today," *The Seattle Post-Intelligencer*, April 3, 1914, p. 11; Baxter, "Seattle Loses a Great Game to a Great Team," *The Seattle Post-Intelligencer*, April 4, 1914, p. 11; Royal Brougham, "'Rube' Thinks Black Men Will Play in Big Leagues," *The Seattle Post-Intelligencer*, April 5, 1914, part 3, p. 11.

19. "Color Line Has Kept Many a Good Ball Player out of Majors," *The Indianapolis Freeman*, June 19, 1915, p. 7.

20. "Taylor Replies to Foster," p. 4.

21. "American Giants Win the Pennant," *The Chicago Defender*, January 8, 1916, p. 7; "A Big League of Negro Players," *The Indianapolis Freeman*, February 12, 1916, p. 7; "Rube Foster off for the Coast," *The Chicago Defender*, January 22, 1916, p. 5.

22. "A Big League of Negro Players," *The Indianapolis Freeman*, February 12, 1916, p. 7.

23. Billy Lewis, "Rube Foster Setting the Base Ball Pace," *The Indianapolis Freeman*, March 25, 1916, p. 7; "American Giants Trim Portland," *The Chicago Defender*, April 15, 1916, p. 8; Baxter, "Crack Chicago Giants Aggregation Trims Dug's Pets in Uneven Contest," *The Seattle Post-Intelligencer*, April 8, 1916, p. 12; Baxter, "Seattle Giants Drop Second to Colored Cracks," *The Seattle Post-Intelligencer*, April 9, 1916, p. 1; Baxter, "Colored Giants Win an Exciting Battle from Seattle in the Ninth," *The Seattle Post-Intelligencer*, April 10, 1916, p. 12; Billy Lewis, "Rube Foster on the Coast," *The Indianapolis Freeman*, April 22, 1916, p. 7; "Rube's Team Taking in Everything!," *The Indianapolis Freeman*, April 29, 1916, p. 7.

24. Carey B. Lewis, "Foster's Giants Capture a Title," *The Indianapolis Freeman*, August 26, 1916, p. 4; "Flag Day," *The Chicago Defender*, September 6, 1916, p. 6; "Andrew Rube Foster," *The Chicago Defender*, September 6, 1916, p. 6; Wyatt, "American Giants and All Nations Pull Largest Crowd of the Season," *The Indianapolis Freeman*, October 7, 1916, p. 7; "White Sox Stars See Giants Win," October 14, 1916, p. 8; "Foster's Giants to Play Series Here," *The Indianapolis Freeman*, October 21, 1916, p. 7.

25. Phil Dixon, *The Negro Baseball Leagues: A Photographic History* (Mattituck, New York: Amereon House, 1994), 113–14; Young Knox, "Rube Foster Takes First Game," *The Indianapolis Freeman*, October 28, 1916, p. 7; "Andrew 'Rube' Foster," *The Indianapolis Freeman*, October 21, 1916, p. 7. For the American Giants' manager's take on the contested 1916 series between his team and the Indianapolis ABCs, see Mr. Fan, "Rube Foster Tells a Few Things of Interest," *The Chicago Defender*, November 11, 1916, p. 10 and "Rube Foster Speaks," *The Chicago Defender*, November 18, 1916, p. 9.

26. Knox, "Rube Fosters Takes First Game," p. 7; "A.B.C.'s Win World Series," *The Indianapolis Freeman*, November 4, 1916, p. 7.

27. J. R. Warren cartoon, "An Attempted Hold-Up," *The Indianapolis Freeman*, December 2, 1916, p. 7.

28. F. A. Young, "Rube Foster Challenges the Cubs," *The Chicago Defender*, October 18, 1913, p. 8; "Rube Foster Challenges Tinker's Feds," *The Chicago Defender*, October 2, 1915, p. 7; "Desired City Series: Rube Foster vs. Cubs," *The Chicago Defender*, September 23, 1916, p. 6; "American Giants Arrive Safely in South; Turn Down Havana Trip," *The Chicago Defender*, February 2, 1918, p. 10.

29. Mr. Fan, "American Giants Begin Local Season Sunday," *The Chicago Defender*, April 21, 1917, p. 7; *The Chicago Defender*, October 27, 1917, p. 7; Wyatt, "Baseball!," *The Indianapolis Freeman*, October 13, 1917, p. 7; Wyatt, "Base Ball!," *The Indianapolis Freeman*, September 29, 1917, p. 7.

30. Foster, "The Season of 1917 Closes. Rube Foster Makes an Observation. The Status of the A.B.C.'s of Indianapolis," *The Indianapolis Freeman*, October 20, 1917, p. 7.

31. Wyatt, "Baseball!," *The Indianapolis Freeman*, June 9, 1917, p. 7; Wyatt, "Baseball!," *The Indianapolis Freeman*, September 29, 1917, p. 7.

32. Foster, "The Season of 1917 Closes," p. 7.

33. Mister Fan, "American Giants to Present New Line-Up for This Season," *The Chicago Defender*, March 30, 1918, p. 9; Mister Fan, "American Giants Open Baseball Season Sunday," *The Chicago Defender*, April 13, 1918, p. 9.

34. Dave Wyatt, "Penn Red Caps Are Beaten by Foster's Shipwrecked Crew," *The Chicago Defender*, August 10, 1918, p. 9; Wyatt, "American Giants' Draft-Wrecked Crew Returns from the East," *The Chicago Defender*, August 17, 1918, p. 9; "American Giants Face Hardest Test in History," *The Chicago Defender*, July 20, 1918, p. 9.

35. "American Giants — Championship Winners 1918," *The Chicago Defender*, August 31, 1918, p. 9; "Rube Foster's System Blinds Managers, Players and Critics," *The Chicago Defender*, November 2, 1918, p. 9, "Andrew 'Rube' Foster," *The Chicago Defender*, September 7, 1918, p. 9.

36. "Rube Foster's System Blind Managers, Players and Critics," p. 9.

37. "Penn Red Caps Are Beaten by Foster's Shipwrecked Crew," *The Chicago Defender*, August 10, 1918, p. 9; "Giants Lose Both Games to Beloit," *The Chicago Defender*,

July 27, 1918, p. 9; Wyatt, "Whitworth's Arm Wins Another Victory for American Giants," *The Chicago Defender*, September 21, 1918, p. 9; "Beloit Returns to Wrest Championship from American Giants," *The Chicago Defender*, September 21, 1918, p. 9; "Beloits Take Both Ends of Twin Bill; Giants' Batters Off Watch," *The Chicago Defender*, September 28, 1918, p. 9; "All-Stars Win First Game in Series against the Giants," *The Chicago Defender*, October 5, 1918, p. 9.

38. "Beloit Returns to Wrest Championship from American Giants," p. 9; "Beloit Take Both Ends of Twin Bill," p. 9; "All-Stars Win First Game in Series against the Giants," p. 9; "American Giants Take Series from All-Star Big Leaguers," *The Chicago Defender*, October 19, 1918, p. 9; "Am. Giants Win Series from All-Star Team," *The Chicago Defender*, October 19, 1918, p. 9.

39. "Influenza Epidemic Closes Baseball Season for American Giants," *The Chicago Defender*, November 2, 1918, p. 9.

## 6. Postwar America and the National Pastime

1. Lane, "Baseball's Future," *Baseball Magazine* 21 (September 1918): 407; Lane, "The Future Prospects of Major League Baseball," *Baseball Magazine* 22 (November 1918): 19–20; Charles W. Murphy, "Why I Believe Professional Baseball Should Continue during the War," *Baseball Magazine* 22 (November 1918): 21–22; Murphy, "Baseball a War Time Necessity," *Baseball Magazine* 22 (December 1918): 87–88.

2. Frederick E. Parmly, "Baseball Will Win the War," *Baseball Magazine* 22 (December 1918): 107–08.

3. Robbins, "Thoughts Turn to Baseball as Natural Corollary of Peace," *The Sporting News*, November 21, 1918, p. 1; "Editorial Comment," *Baseball Magazine* 22 (January 1919): 134; Phelon, "When the Baseball Stars Come Home," *Baseball Magazine* 22 (February 1919): 227.

4. Seymour, *Baseball: The Golden Age*, pp. 262–63.

5. G. W. Axelson, "For National Commission Chairman," *The Chicago Herald*, November 3, 1918, p. 18.

6. H. Andrew, "Contest Is on for Baseball Control," *The Sporting News*, November

28, 1918, p. 1; "Editorial Comment," *Baseball Magazine* 23 (January 1919): 136, 158. "Dictator Scheme Already a Fizzle," *The Sporting News*, November 28, 1918, p. 1; Ralph S. Davis, "Taft Considerate in Refusing to Ride," *The Sporting News*, December 5, 1918, p. 1; Richter, "Review of the 1918 Season," p. 15.

7. Thomas Rice, "One-Man Commission Not Possible Says Thomas Rice," *The Sporting News*, December 5, 1918, p. 1.

8. Lane, "Big Baseball Reforms in Immediate Prospect," *Baseball Magazine* 22 (January 1919): 137–38.

9. "Herrmann Is Ready to Relinquish Job," *The New York Times*, January 2, 1919, p. 12; "Heydler Will Vote Against Herrmann," *The New York Times*, January 3, 1919, p. 6; "Deadlock over Chairman," *The New York Times*, January 15, 1919, p. 12; *The New York Times*, January 17, 1919, p. 10.

10. "Editorial Comment," *Baseball Magazine* 22 (March 1919): 264.

11. "Suit Halts Naming of New Chairman," *The New York Times*, March 1, 1919, p. 10; "Verdict against Organized Ball," *The New York Times*, April 13, 1919, p. 21; "Baseball Moguls See Dire Changes," *The New York Times*, April 14, 1919, p. 10.

12. "In Restraint of the Baseball Trade," *The New York Times*, April 15, 1919, p. 10; "Editorial Comment," *Baseball Magazine* 23 (June 1919): 71.

13. Pietrusza, *Judge and Jury*, p. 143.

14. Ibid., pp. 145–48; "Bomb Plot to Kill 22 Leaders of Nation," *The Chicago Herald-Examiner*, May 1, 1919, p. 1; "Find Death Machine in Landis' Mail," *The Chicago Tribune*, May 1, 1919, p. 1.

15. "Landis, Ripsnorting, Wiry American, Fears No Bomb," Landis Scrapbook.

16. Robbins, "Chicago Fans Fret Because Commy Refuses to Speak up," *The Sporting News*, January 2, 1919, p. 1; "Comeback Joe Jackson," *The Sporting News*, January 2, 1919, p. 3.

17. "The Return of the Prodigals," *The Sporting News*, January 2, 1919, p. 4.

18. "Honor for Gleason Pleases Phil Fans," *The Sporting News*, January 9, 1919, p. 1; John J. Ward, "The New Leader of the White Sox," *Baseball Magazine* 22 (March 1919): 273; "Gleason in Rowland's Job," *The New York Times*, January 1, 1919, p. 14; George S. Robbins, "Big Controversy in Chicago over Change in Sox Managers," *The Sporting News*, January 9, 1919, p. 1.

19. "Though Joe Jackson may return … ," *The Sporting News*, January 9, 1919, p. 4; "Not a Happy Situation," *The Sporting News*, January 9, 1919, p. 5.

20. "Not a Happy Situation," p. 5.

21. Robbins, "Gleason Wants All Old Sox to Return," *The Sporting News*, January 23, 1919, p. 1; Phelon, "The Passing Month in Baseball," *Baseball Magazine* 22 (February 1919): 215.

22. Robbins, "Ship Yard Jumpers Plague to Commy," *The Sporting News*, February 20, 1919, p. 1.

23. Robbins, "They Still Debate over Joe Jackson," *The Sporting News*, February 27, 1919, p. 1.

24. Ibid.

25. Ibid.

26. Ibid.

27. Stein, *The Ginger Kid*, p. 129.

28. Robbins, "Gleason Has a Gift of Hypnotic Power," April 3, 1919, p. 1; Hugh Fullerton, "Buck Weaver and Heine Groh Top Leagues at Third Base," *The Chicago Tribune*, April 7, 1919, p. 19.

29. "Gotham Fans Don't Figure on Cobb Yet," *The Sporting News*, January 2, 1919, p. 1; "To the Credit of the Players," *The Sporting News*, January 2, 1919, p. 4.

30. James O'Leary, "Frazee Thinks He Has Ruth Held Safe," *The Sporting News*, January 30, 1919, p. 1; "Babe Ruth's Story in Figures as Compiled by Munro Elias," *The Sporting News*, January 30, 1919, p. 6.

31. O'Leary, "Looks like a Frame up against Frazee," *The Sporting News*, March 6, 1919, p. 1; "Three Big Stars Still Holdouts," *The New York Times*, March 18, 1919, p. 12; O'Leary, "Red Sox Stars Seem to Have Doubts as to Sticking Ability," *The Sporting News*, April 3, 1919, p. 1.

32. O'Leary, "Red Sox Stars Seem to Have Doubts as to Sticking Ability," p. 1; O'Leary, "Barrow and Ruth Coming to a Clinch Pretty Soon," *The Sporting News*, April 10, 1919, p. 1.

33. "Ruth, Long Distance Gun," *The New York Times*, April 19, 1919, p. 14.

34. "Real Struggle in American League," *The New York Times*, April 20, 1919, part 2, p. 6.

35. Ibid.

36. Ibid.

37. O'Leary, "Babe's Ambition a New Boston Worry," *The Sporting News*, May 1, 1919, p. 1.

38. "Babe Ruth Accepts Ultimatum of Club," *The Sporting News*, May 8, 1919, p. 1.

39. Grantland Rice, "The Spotlight," *The New York Tribune*, April 26, 1919, p. 20.

40. O'Leary, "Discussing What to Do with Babe Ruth," *The Sporting News*, June 19, 1919, p. 1.

41. "Editorial Comment," *Baseball Magazine* 23 (July 1919): 130; Phelon, "The First Lap of the Pennant Race," *Baseball Magazine* 23 (July 1919): 157–58; Phelon, "When the Big Clubs Strike Their Stride," *Baseball Magazine* 23 (August 1919): 205–06.

42. "Injunction Issued against Johnson," *The New York Times*, August 7, 1919, p. 16.

43. "Yankees Get Carl Mays," *The New York Times*, July 31, 1919, p. 6; "Mays's Suspension Shock to Yankees," *The New York Times*, August 1, 1919, p. 8; "Injunction Issued against Johnson," p. 16.

44. "War of Factions in American League," *The New York Times*, August 10, 1919, p. 18; "Mays Injunction Hearing Is Delayed," *The New York Times*, September 6, 1919, p. 12.

45. Murphy, "How Most Ball Clubs Lose Money," *Baseball Magazine* 23 (September 1919): 280.

46. Robbins, "White Sox Expect to Be Attraction on Eastern Trip," *The Sporting News*, June 5, 1919, p. 1.

47. Robbins, "White Sox Heavy Artillery Unlimbers and Saves Games for Wobbly Pitchers," *The Sporting News*, August 21, 1919, p. 1.

48. O'Leary, "Barrow's Life One Round of Problems to Be Settled," *The Sporting News*, July 10, 1919, p. 1; "Baseball Season Is Record Maker," *The New York Times*, July 27, 1919, p. 21; "Babe Ruth Aims Higher," *The New York Times*, July 31, 1919, p. 6; "Following Babe Ruth in His Quest for Home Run Record," *The New York Times*, August 25, 1919, p. 12.

49. "Ruth on His Way to Top Freeman's Mark," *The Sporting News*, August 28, 1919, p. 2; O'Leary, "Boston's Interest in Ruth's Swatting," *The Sporting News*, September 4, 1919, p. 1; "Babe Ruth Equals Home-Run Record," *The New York Times*, September 6, 1919, p. 12; "Ruth Wallops out his 28th Home Run," *The New York Times*, September 25, 1919, p. 10; "Ruth Gets 29th Homer," *The New York Times*, September 28, 1919, sect. 10, p. 3.

50. O'Leary, "It's Fitting to Give This Space to Babe," *The Sporting News*, October 2, 1919, p.1.

51. "Ruth Stands Alone as a Heavy Hitter," *The New York Times*, October 12, 1919, sect. 10, p. 6.

52. "The Spalding Base Ball Hall of Fame," *Spalding's Official Base Ball Record: 1920*, ed. by John B. Foster (New York: American Sports Publishing Company, 1920).

53. Lane, "The All American Baseball Club of 1920," *Baseball Magazine* 24 (December 1919): 481–86, 503–04.

54. Rice, "The Spotlight," *The New York Tribune*, December 19, 1919, p. 14.

55. Ibid.

## 7. In the Eye of the Storm

1. Robbins, "Can't Hold off any Longer in this Case," *The Sporting News*, June 21, 1917, p. 1.

2. Whitman, "New Uniforms on Boston Pastimer," *The Sporting News*, November 22, 1917, p. 1; "Drive to Be Made against Gamblers," *The Sporting News*, February 28, 1918, p. 2; Louis Bennett v. Carl Mays, Superior Court, Commonwealth of Massachusetts, November 15, 1917, copies of court transcripts at National Baseball Hall of Fame Library; Ban Johnson to D. T. Green, April 22, 1921, p. 1, National Baseball Hall of Fame Library.

3. "Editorial Comment," *Baseball Magazine* 22 (December 1918): 74; Vila, "Decision in Chase Case Is a Boost for Game Says Joe Vila," *The Sporting News*, February 13, 1919, p. 1.

4. Vila, "Decision in Chase Case," p. 1.

5. "Hal Chase Cleared by Verdict of Heydler," *The Sporting News*, February 13, 1919, p. 5; John E. Wray, "It's Third and Final Coat for Hal Chase," *The Sporting News*, February 13, 1919, p. 4; "Matty Due This Week," *The New York Times*, February 17, 1919, p. 10.

6. Arthur Irwin, "How the World's Series Has Hurt the Game," *Baseball Magazine* 22 (March 1919): 285–86.

7. "Editorial Comment," *Baseball Magazine* 22 (April 1919): 33–31; Lane, "What Are the Odds?," *Baseball Magazine* 22 (April 1919); 337–39.

8. "To Suppress Gamblers," *The New York Times*, July 13, 1919, p. 18.

9. Vila, "No Room in Giants' Park for Howlers," *The Sporting News*, July 17, 1919, p. 1.

10. Ibid.

11. William D. Miller, *Pretty Bubbles in The Air: America in 1919* (Urbana: University of Illinois Press, 1991), pp. 136–37.

12. "The Colored Clubs," *Baseball Magazine* 22 (December 1918): 117.

13. Phelps, "Andrew 'Rube' Foster," p. 8.

14. "Foster Asks Patience," *The Chicago Defender*, April 19, 1919, p. 11; "Giants's Seating Capacity Enlarged," *The Chicago Defender*, June 7, 1919, p. 11; Foster to W. T. Smith, July 2, 1919, Rube Foster Officials File, National Baseball Hall of Fame Library; "25,000 See Am. Giants Cop Doubleheader," *The Chicago Defender*, August 30, 1919, p. 11.

15. William M. Tuttle Jr., *Race Riot: Chicago in the Red Summer of 1919* (Urbana: University of Illinois Press, 1996).

16. Tuttle, *Race Riot.*

17. "A Report on the Chicago Riot by An Eye-Witness," *The Crisis* 18 (September 1919): 11–12.

18. Walter F. White, "Chicago and Its Eight Reasons," *The Crisis* 18 (October 1919): 293–97.

19. Carey B. Lewis, "Baseball Circuit for Next Season," *The Chicago Defender*, October 4, 1919, p. 11.

20. Foster, "Pitfalls of Baseball," *The Chicago Defender*, November 29, 1919, p. 11.

21. Foster, "Pitfalls of Baseball," December 13, 1919, p. 11.

22. Ibid.

23. Foster, "Pitfalls of Baseball," *The Chicago Defender*, December 27, 1919, p. 9.

24. G. W. Axelson, *"Commy": The Life Story of Charles A. Comiskey* (Chicago: The Reilly & Lee Co., 1919) pp. 281–82, 286–88.

25. Ibid., p. 318.

26. "Plenty Hitting in America," *The Sporting News*, October 30, 1919, p. 2.

27. "Chicago Waking up to Fact That It has Another World Series Coming," *The Sporting News*, September 11, 1919, p. 1.

28. "Nine Games and H.C.L. Prices Make World's Series Purse Fat," *The Sporting News*, September 18, 1919, p. 2.

29. "White Sox Strong in All Positions," *The New York Times*, September 14, 1919, sect. 9, p. 3; "Analysis of Strength of White Sox and Reds Leaves World Series Result in Doubt," *The New York Times*, September 21, 1919, sect. 10, p. 3.

30. "Delay of White Sox Doesn't Mean Slip," *The Sporting News*, September 25, 1919, p. 1.

31. Ibid.; Vila, "Vila Hopes against Hope for the Reds," *The Sporting News*, October 2, 1919, p. 1.

32. "Joy if Reds Win — But a Shock if They Do," *The Sporting News*, October 2, 1919, p. 3; Robbins, "White Sox to Win in Seven Games," *The Sporting News*, October 2, 1919, p. 3.

33. "Joy if Reds Win," p. 5.

34. Billy Evans, "Dope Goes Wrong in Both Leagues," *The New York Times*, September 22, 1919, p. 12; Evans, "Reds Stronger in Box, Thinks Evans," *The New York Times*, September 27, 1919, p. 14; Evans, "Both Clubs Have Batting Strength," *The New York Times*, September 28, 1919, sect. 10, p. 1 ; Christy Mathewson, "Christy Mathewson Says Batting Powers of Reds May Prove Too Much for White Sox," *The New York Times*, September 28, 1919, sect. 10, p. 1.

35. Evans, "Sox Have the Edge on the Defensive," *The New York Times*, September 29, 1919, p. 9.

36. Phelon, "How the Reds and White Sox Compare," *Baseball Magazine* 24 (November 1919): 392, 440.

37. W. O. McGeehan, "McGeehan Favors White Sox to Repeat 1917 Triumph," *The New York Tribune*, September 28, 1919, p. 22; W. J. Macbeth, "Gleason's Team Has Every Advantage over the Reds," *The New York Tribune*, September 28, 1919, p. 23; Ray McCarthy, "Year of Great Upsets May End with Moran Victory," *The New York Tribune*, September 28, 1919, p. 23.

38. Grantland Rice, "The Spotlight," *The New York Tribune*, September 23, 1919, p. 12; Rice, "The Spotlight," *The New York Tribune*, September 24, 1919, p. 12; Rice, "The Spotlight," *The New York Tribune*, September 25, 1919, p. 16; Rice, "The Spotlight," *The New York Tribune*, September 26, 1919, p. 11; Rice, "The Spotlight," *The New York Tribune*, September 27, 1919, p. 10; Rice, "The Spotlight," *The New York Tribune*, September 28, 1919, p. 20.

39. Lane, "The Star of American League Third Basemen," *Baseball Magazine* 24 (November 1919): 405.

40. Ibid.

41. Grantland Rice, "9-1 Rout of Sox Makes Reds Favorites in Series," *The New York Tribune*, October 2, 1919, pp. 1, 12; "Reds Rout White Sox in Opening Game of Series," *The New York Times*, October 2, 1919, pp. 1, 13; Eliot Asinof, *Eight Men Out: The Black*

*Sox and the 1919 World Series* (New York: Henry Holt and Company, 1987), pp. 46–47; Mathewson, "Sallee Beats Sox with Shine Ball," *The New York Times*, October 3, 1919, p. 12.

42. Asinof, *Eight Men Out*, p. 93–94.

43. "Cincinnati Takes Fourth Game of Series by 2 to 0," *The New York Times*, October 5, 1919, sect. 11, p. 1; "Cicotte Loses Again in Fourth but on Errors, Not Box Work," *The Sporting News*, October 9, 1919, p. 5; Grantland Rice, "Cicotte Loses His Own Game; Reds Win, 2-0," *The New York Tribune*, October 5, 1919, p. 1.

44. Rice, "Cicotte Loses His Own Game," p. 18.

45. "The Red Tide," *The New York Tribune*, October 3, 1919, p. 1; Mathewson, "Strategy Boards at Work on Series," *The New York Times*, October 6, 1919, p. 10; "Chance Remarks of Leading Players at the Big Games," *Baseball Magazine* 24 (December 1919): 466; Mathewson, "Eller Is Best of Series' Pitchers," *The New York Times*, October 7, 1919, p. 15; "Gossip of Fifth Game," *The Sporting News*, October 9, 1919, p. 5.

46. "Rich Series for Players," *The New York Times*, October 15, 1919, p. 15.

47. J. G. Taylor Spink, "Shock Absorber Needed to Handle This Year's Series," *The Sporting News*, October 9, 1919, p. 3.

48. "Concerning Bets and Bettings," *The Sporting News*, October 9, 1919, p. 4.

49. Harry P. Edwards, "White Sox Far from Playing Real Game," *The Sporting News*, October 16, 1919, p. 1; Rice, "Reds Capture World Title; Sox Lose 10-5," *The New York Tribune*, October 10, 1919, p. 14.

50. Edwards, "White Sox Far from Playing Real Game," p. 1.

51. "World's Series Hitting," *The Sporting News*, October 16, 1919, p. 4.

52. Veeck, *The Hustler's Handbook*, p. 259.

53. J. C. Kofoed, "The Hero of the World's Series," *Baseball Magazine* (November 1919): 467–68.

54. "Editorial Comment," *Baseball Magazine* 24 (December 1919): n.p.

55. Ibid.

56. Ibid.

57. "$2,000,000 Bet on Series," *The New York Times*, October 10, 1919, p. 13; "Get Gamblers Out — So Say All of Us," *The Sporting News*, November 27, 1919, p. 3.

58. Ginsburg, *The Fix Is In*, pp. 131–32.

59. "No Evidence Found against White Sox," *The Sporting News*, December 18, 1919, p. 1; "To War on Gambling," *The New York Times*, December 19, 1919, p. 18.

60. Fullerton, "Comiskey Has Been on Point of Dropping Several Men," *The New York Evening World*, December 18, 1919, p. 28.

61. Fullerton, "Judge Landis Asked to Take Charge of Investigation," *The New York Evening World*, December 20, 1919, p. 8.

62. W. J. Macbeth, "Commission Should Probe World's Series Scandal," *The New York Tribune*, December 21, 1919, p. 20.

63. Ibid.

64. Ibid.

65. Ibid.

66. "Judge Landis Ready to Act as Arbiter, but Plan Fails," *The New York Tribune*, December 30, 1919, p. 12; Vila, "Revival of Series Scandal Emphasizes Need of Inquiry," *The Sporting News*, December 25, 1919, p. 1.

67. "Out with What You Know," *The Sporting News*, December 25, 1919, p. 4.

68. "Comiskey Renews Offer," *The New York Times*, December 31, 1919, p. 9.

## 8. The National Commission

1. Vila, "Vila Hopes against Hope for the Reds," *The Sporting News*, October 2, 1919, p. 1; Vila, "Mad Bedlam Greets Returning Heroes," *The Sporting News*, October 9, 1919, p. 1.

2. "Ruppert-Johnson Breach Is Widened," *The New York Times*, November 6, 1919, p. 10; "No Third League in Sight," *The New York Times*, November 10, 1919, p. 14.

3. Henry P. Edwards, "Wanted, A Moses to Lead Them to Peace," *The Sporting News*, November 13, 1919, p. 1; Vila, "Vila Ridicules Talk of Bolt by Enemies of Ban Johnson," *The Sporting News*, November 13, 1919, p. 1.

4. Reichow, "Somebody Will Eat Humble Pie in American League," *The Sporting News*, November 27, 1919, p. 1.

5. "Johnson Cohorts Hold Whip Hand," *The New York Times*, December 11, 1919, p. 14.

6. "Herrmann to Quit Post as Chairman," *The New York Times*, December 11, 1919, p. 14; "Baseball Tangle Deeper than Ever," *The New York Times*, December 27, 1919, p. 10.

7. "Get Your Commission First," *The Sporting News*, December 25, 1919, p. 4.

8. Al Spink, "Landis Election as Chairman Is Way to End War," *The Chicago Evening Post*, January 7, 1920, Landis Scrapbook.

9. "Peace Proposal with Strings," *The Sporting News*, January 8, 1920, p. 4.

10. Henry P. Edwards, "National League Is Reported to Be Solid for Chicago Man," *The Cleveland Plain Dealer*, January 10, 1920, Landis Scrapbook; "Chicago Writer Says Judge Landis Is Willing," Landis Scrapbook; Frederick G. Lieb, "Judge Landis in Receptive Mood toward Baseball," *The Philadelphia Sun*, January 11, 1920, Landis Scrapbook; George Daley, "Judge Landis Is now in Receptive Mood," *The New York World*, January 11, 1920, Landis Scrapbook.

11. "August Herrmann Resigns as Chairman of the National Baseball Commission," *The New York Times*, January 9, 1920, p. 18; "Must Stamp out Gambling," *The New York Times*, January 11, 1920, sect. 10, p. 2; "Herrmann, Tired of Criticism, Chucks His Commission Job," *The Sporting News*, January 15, 1920, p. 13; "Many Mentioned for Chairmanship," *The New York Times*, January 10, 1920, p. 12; Rusty, "John Heydler Tells of Sort of Man National Game Needs," *The Sporting News*, January 15, 1920, p. 1.

12. Rusty, "John Heydler Tells," p. 1.

13. Ibid; "Yankee Owners Are for Judge Landis," *The Sporting News*, January 29, 1920, p. 1.

14. Spink, "Landis' Election To Help Baseball," *The Chicago Evening Post*, Landis Scrapbook.

15. "Players Ask Place on the Commission," *The New York Times*, January 27, 1920, p. 17.

16. "American League's Bitter Factional Fight Is Ended and Legal Actions Are Withdrawn," *The New York Times*, February 11, 1918, p. 18.

17. "Baseball Solons Raise Admissions," *The New York Times*, February 12, 1920, p. 13.

18. Ibid.; "Judge Landis Is Eliminated from Chairmanship Contest," *The New York Times*, February 15, 1920, p. 20.

19. "Edwards Favored for Chairmanship," *The New York Times*, February 26, 1920, p. 18.

20. Phelon, "Recent Echoes from the Big League Circuits," *Baseball Magazine* 24 (March 1920): 585–87.

21. "Curing a Cancer with Prayer," *The Sporting News*, January 1, 1920, p. 4.

22. Ibid.

23. Ibid.

24. Rusty, "Ray Schalk Never Hinted at Anything Wrong in Series," *The Sporting News*, January 8, 1920, p. 1.

25. "Must Stamp out Baseball Gambling," p. 2.

26. "The New Gambling Charges," *The Sporting News*, March 4, 1920, p. 4.

27. Grantland Rice, "The Spotlight," *The New York Tribune*, March 4, 1920, p. 12.

28. "Magee Says He'll Publish Charges," *The New York Times*, March 24, 1920, p. 10; "Editorial Comment," *Baseball Magazine* 25 (May 1920): 662; "Lee Magee's Charges," *The Sporting News*, April 1, 1920, p. 4.

29. W. O. McGeehan, "In All Fairness," *The New York Tribune*, April 12, 1920, p. 12.

30. Ibid.

31. Ibid.

## 9. The Sale of Babe

1 "Babe Ruth Follows Precedents," *The Sporting News*, October 30, 1919, p. 4.

2. O'Leary, "Babe May Make a Tour of World Yet," *The Sporting News*, November 27, 1919, p. 1.

3. "Ruth Wants to Be Boxer," *The New York Times*, December 3, 1919, p. 17.

4. "Ruth Demands $20,000," *The New York Times*, December 25, 1919, p. 18; "Ruth Talks of Retiring," *The New York Times*, December 27, 1919, p. 10.

5. Barrow, *My Fifty Years in Baseball*, pp. 107–08; "Yankees Get Mighty Ruth," *The Los Angeles Times*, January 6, 1920, p. 3, p. 1; "Records Give New View of Ruth Deal," *The New York Times*, November 27, 1920, p. 14.

6. "Uniform Agreement for Transfer of a Player to or by a Major League Club," December 26, 1919, Babe Ruth File, National Baseball Hall of Fame Library; "Something about 'Babe' Ruth, Price $125,000," *The Literary Digest* 64 (January 17, 1920), pp. 128, 130; "Yankees Get Mighty Ruth," p. 1; O'Leary, "Ruth's Liking for Boston Is Pathetic," *The Sporting News*, January 1, 1920, p. 1; "The Ruth Plot Thickens," *The Sporting News*, January 1, 1920, p. 4.

7. "Ruth Bought by New York Americans for $125,000, Highest Price in Baseball's

Annals," *The New York Times*, January 6, 1920, p. 16; "Yankees Get Mighty Ruth," *The Los Angeles Times*, January 6, 1920, sect. 4, p. 1; "Yankees Buy 'Babe' Ruth for $150,000," *The New York Tribune*, January 6, 1920, p. 1.

8. Ibid.

9. "'Ruth Delighted to Play with Yankees,'" *The New York Tribune*, January 7, 1920, p. 16; "Ruth Says He'll Try to Break His Home Run Record," *The New York Tribune*, January 7, 1920, p. 16.

10. "The High Cost of Home Runs," *The New York Times*, January 7, 1920, p. 18.

11. Abe Kemp, "Gigantic Deal for Babe Ruth Is Not Going to Aid Baseball, Wise Fans Cry," *The San Francisco Bulletin*, January 7, 1920, p. 14.

12. "Frazee Explains Sale; 'Injustice to Keep Slugger,'" *The New York Tribune*, January 6, 1920, p. 15; "Yankees' Terms Satisfy Babe Ruth Who Will Sign Later," *The New York Times*, January 7, 1920, p. 22; "Rumpus Caused by Ruth's Sale," *The Los Angeles Times*, January 8, 1920, part. 3, p. 1.

13. "Think of the Baseballs Frazee Will Save," *The Boston Herald*, January 6, 1920, Babe Ruth File.

14. *The Boston Post*, n.d., Babe Ruth File.

15. *The Boston Herald*, n.d., Babe Ruth File.

16. "New York Americans Decide to Return to Jacksonville for Spring Training This Year," *The New York Times*, January 8, 1920, p. 18.

17. Ibid.

18. O'Leary, "Frazee Finds Defender in His Release of Babe Ruth," *The Sporting News*, January 15, 1920, p. 1.

19. "Ruth Tells Tales of His Boston Days," *The New York Times*, January 16, 1920, p. 11.

20. Phelon, "Recent Echoes from the Big League Circuits," *Baseball Magazine* 24 (March 1920): 585.

21. Babe Ruth, "Things Which I Believe Have Been Responsible for My Successful Batting," *Baseball Magazine* 24 (April 1920): 618–21, 656; Harry Frazee, "The Reasons Which Led Me to Sell 'Babe' Ruth," *Baseball Magazine* 24 (April 1920): 626, 654; "Prominent Baseball Men and Their Opinions of Babe Ruth," *Baseball Magazine* 24 (April 1920): 654–55.

22. Lane, "How 'Babe' Ruth Became the Home Run King," *Baseball Magazine* 24 (April 1920): 611–14, 650–51, 659–60.

23. "New York Scolded for Its Moral and Other Shortcomings," *Current Opinion* 68 (April 1920): 524.

## 10. A Season of Courage: Rube Foster and a League of His Own

1. "Nine Ex-Soldiers Lynched in South," *The Chicago Defender*, January 3, 1920, p. 1.

2. "The Old and the New," *The Chicago Defender*, January 30, 1920, p. 14.

3. Ibid.

4. "Radicals and Raids," *The Chicago Whip*, January 10, 1920, p. 8.

5. Bruce Lenthall, "Covering More than the Game: Baseball and Racial Issues in an African American Newspaper, 1919–1920," in *Cooperstown Symposium on Baseball and the American Culture (1990)*, ed. Alvin L. Hall (Westport, CT: Meckler, 1990), p. 57.

6. Foster, "Pitfalls of Baseball," *The Chicago Defender*, January 3, 1920, p. 9.

7. Ibid.

8. Ibid.

9. Ibid.

10. Foster, "Pitfalls of Baseball," *The Chicago Defender*, January 10, 1920, p. 9.

11. Ibid.

12. Foster, "Pitfalls of Baseball," *The Chicago Defender*, January 17, 1920, p. 9.

13. Ibid.

14. Ibid.

15. Taylor, "The Future of Colored Baseball," p. 76.

16. Ibid., pp. 76–78.

17. Ira F. Lewis, "National Baseball League Formed," *The Competitor* 1 (March 1920): 66–67.

18. "Call for National League Issued," *The Chicago Defender*, February 7, 1920, p. 11; Mark Ribowsky, *A Complete History of the Negro Leagues 1884 to 1955* (Secaucus, N.J.: A Citadel Press Book, 1997), p. 100.

19. "Baseball Magnates Hold Conference," *The Chicago Defender*, February 14, 1920, p. 11.

20. "Baseball Men Write League Constitution," *The Chicago Defender*, February 21, 1920, p. 9.

21. Ibid; Al Monroe, "What Is the Matter with Base Ball?," p. 28.

22. "Baseball Men Write League Constitution," p. 9.

23. Ibid.

24. "Southern Baseball League Is Formed," *The Chicago Defender*, March 6, 1920, p. 12.

25. "'Rube' Assigns Players to Giants," *The Chicago Defender*, March 20, 1920, p. 9.

26. Ibid; Russell Streur, "Rube Foster: Father of Negro League Baseball," *Sports Collector's Digest*, February 8, 1991, p. 186.

27. Wyatt, "National League of Colored Clubs Prepare for Season's Opening," *The Competitor* 1 (April 1920): 74.

28. "Managers of Baseball Circuit Get Busy," *The Chicago Defender*, March 27, 1920, p. 11.

29. Wyatt, "Success of the League Is up to the Fans," *The Chicago Defender*, April 3, 1920, p. 9.

30. Ibid.

31. Ibid.

32. Wyatt, "A. B. C.'s Triumph in First Home Games," *The Chicago Defender*, May 8, 1920, p. 9.

33. "National Association for the Advancement of Colored People," *The Crisis* 20 (July 1920): 132, 134.

34. "League Standings," *The Chicago Whip*, July 3, 1920, p. 5.

35. "Big League Making Progress," *The Competitor* 2 (July 1920): 69.

36. Ibid.

37. "A Cry for Courage," *The Chicago Whip*, July 10, 1920, p. 8.

38. Wyatt, "American Giants Lead Pennant Drive," *The Chicago Whip*, August 28, 1920, p. 5.

39. "Giants Win 4th and lose 5th in Detroit," *The Chicago Whip*, September 18, 1920, p. 5; "A.B.C. Flayed," *The Chicago Whip*, September 25, 1920, p. 5.

40. Wyatt, "Foster Team Ends Chicago Season," *The Chicago Whip*, September 25, 1920, p. 5; "Knoxville Downed in Title Game by Chicago Aggregation," *The Chicago Whip*, October 2, 1920, p. 5.

41. Wyatt, "League Meeting Assures Success in Baseball," *The Chicago Whip*, December 11, 1920, p. 7; Ira F. Lewis, "Baseball Men Hold Successful Meeting," *The Competitor* 3 (January–February 1921): 51, 54; "Baseball Magnates in Big Harmony Meeting," *The Chicago Defender*, December 11, 1920, p. 6.

# 11. A Season of Grace: Babe in Pinstripes

1. Lane, "Should the Spit Ball Be Abolished?," *Baseball Magazine* 23 (June 1919): 67–70, 118; Murphy, "Why Freak Deliveries Must Go," *Baseball Magazine* 23 (August 1919): 219–20.

2. Vila, "Vila Adds His Denunciation to Chorus against Freaks," *The Sporting News*, November 6, 1919, p. 1.

3. "Sweeping Changes in Baseball Code," *The New York Times*, February 10, 1920, p. 19; "No Regrets and No Trouble," *The Sporting News*, March 4, 1920, p. 4; "Editorial Comment," *Baseball Magazine* 25 (May 1920): 662, 698; Ward, "Important Changes in the Baseball Rules," *Baseball Magazine* 25 (May 1920): 681–82.

4. "Meusel Will Play Third for Yankees," *The New York Times*, April 1, 1920, p. 12; "Yankees to Close Jacksonville Stay," *The New York Times*, April 3, 1920, p. 18; "Comment on Current Events in Sports," *The New York Times*, April 15, 1920, p. 19.

5. "Ruth on Way East to Demand Part of Big Purchase Price," *The New York Times*, February 5, 1920, p. 11; "Yankees' Owners to Take Out $150,000 Policy on Babe Ruth," *The New York Times*, February 17, 1920, p. 10; "Yankees to Close Jacksonville Stay," *The New York Times*, April 3, 1920, p. 18.

6. W. J. Macbeth, "Huggins Grooming Ruth for Center Field Position," *The New York Tribune*, March 4, 1920, p. 12.

7. Vila, "Shore Being Boosted as Man to Put Yankees in the Race," *The Sporting News*, March 18, 1920, p. 1; Macbeth, "Ruth Finally Recovers His Batting Eye and Pounds Ball out of Jacksonville Lot," *The New York Tribune*, March 20, 1920, p. 12.

8. "Superbas Topple Yankees for Third Time in Southern Series by Heavy Stick Work," *The New York Times*, March 21, 1920, p. 20; Macbeth, "Dodgers Take Third Straight Game from Yankees, 5 to 1," *The New York Tribune*, March 21, 1920, p. 20.

9. "Superbas Topple Yankees," p. 20.

10. "Comment on Current Events in Sports," *The New York Times*, March 22, 1920, p. 19.

11. Phelon, "Who Will Win the Big League Pennants?," pp. 664–65; Vila, "One Might Think Baker Real Big Noise of Yankee Team," *The Sporting News*, March 25, 1920, p. 1; "Meusel Will Play Third for Yankees," p. 12; Macbeth, "Home Run Baker in Letter to Huggins Says He Is Through with Baseball," *The New York Tribune*, April 1, 1920, p. 14.

12. "Ping Bodie Quits Yankees in Huff; Starts for North," *The New York Times*, March

26, 1920, p. 14; Macbeth, "Dodgers Humble Crippled Yankees for Fifth Time in Succession by a Score of 2 to 0," *The New York Times*, March 26, 1920, p. 14; Macbeth, "Home Run Baker in Letter to Huggins," p. 14.

13. Macbeth, "Ruth Drives out First Homer in Series with Dodgers," *The New York Tribune*, April 2, 1920, p. 14; "Ruth's Double Clinches Game in 6th Inning," *The New York Tribune*, April 9, 1920, p. 14; "Big League Teams of Greater City Play on Home Fields Today — Yankees Beat Dodgers," *The New York Tribune*, April 10, 1920, p. 12.

14. Ray McCarthy, "Giants and Yankees Picked as Likely Flag Winners," *The New York Tribune*, April 11, 1920, p. 19; Rice, "The Spotlight," *The New York Tribune*, April 16, 1920, p. 16.

15. "Babe Ruth's Muff Tosses Game Away," *The New York Times*, April 15, 1920, p. 12; "Muff by Ruth Beats Hugmen in Eighth, 3-1," *The New York Tribune*, April 15, 1920, p. 16.

16. "Ruth Strikes out Thrice, but Mates Win, 4-1," *The New York Tribune*, April 16, 1920, p. 14; McGeehan, "In All Fairness," *The New York Tribune*, April 19, 1920, p. 10; Isaminger, "Big Crows Pay to See Ruth Fall Down," *The Sporting News*, April 22, 1920, p. 1.

17. "Hub Sluggers Bat out Mays and Mogridge," *The New York Tribune*, April 20, 1920, p. 14; "Red Sox Rally in Ninth Inning for 3-2 Victory," *The New York Tribune*, April 21, 1920, p. 14.

18. Vila, "Big Town Fans Keeping Stiff Upper Lip as Heroes Falter," *The New York Times*, April 22, 1920, p. 1.

19. "Yankees Open with Victory but Pay Price in Injury to Babe Ruth," *The New York Times*, April 23, 1920, p. 9; McGeehan, "Yankees Open Home Stand with 8-6 Victory in Ragged Game," *The New York Tribune*, April 23, 1920, p. 14; Vila, "Ruth Finds a New Way to Keep Yankee Fans on Edge," *The Sporting News*, April 29, 1920, p. 1.

20. McGeehan, "Ping Bodie Returns to Yankees," *The New York Tribune*, April 24, 1920, p. 10.

21. McGeehan, "Yankees Beat out Senators in the Ninth, 3 to 2," *The New York Tribune*, April 27, 1920, p. 14; "Walter Johnson Mows down Yankees," *The New York Tribune*, April 30, 1920, p. 14.

22. "Ruth Drives Ball over Grand Stand," *The New York Times*, May 2, 1920, p. 20.

23. McGeehan, "Ruth's Homer in 6th Inning Decisive Blow," *The New York Tribune*, May 3, 1920, p. 10.

24. "Harry Sparrow Is Lost to Baseball," *The New York Times*, May 8, 1920, p. 20; Vila, "Death of Sparrow a Climax to Yank Woe," *The Sporting News*, May 13, 1920, p. 1.

25. McGeehan, "Goliath of Swat Defeats Gleason's Invaders, 6 to 5," *The New York Tribune*, May 12, 1920, p. 14; Macbeth, "Ruth Gets Another Homer; Williams' String Broken," *The New York Tribune*, May 13, 1920, p. 14.

26. Macbeth, "Cicotte Slated to Do Pitching for Sox To-Day," *The New York Tribune*, May 14, 1920, p. 14.

27. "Yanks Lose Home at Polo Grounds," *The New York Times*, May 15, 1920, p. 18.

28. Ibid.; "Stoneham Discusses Move," *The New York Times*, May 15, 1920, p. 18.

29. "Throng of 38,000 at Polo Grounds," *The New York Times*, May 17, 1920, p. 11; "Speaker's Indians Pound Mays While 38,600 Moan; 15,000 Fans Turned away," *The New York Tribune*, May 17, 1920, p. 12.

30. "Throng of 38,000 at Polo Grounds," p. 11; "Speaker's Indians Pound Mays," p. 12.

31. "Ruth Is Far Ahead of His 1919 Record," *The New York Times*, May 18, 1920, p. 12; "The Babe Finds Himself," *The New York Times*, May 20, 1920, p. 4.

32. "Hunt for Home Is Spared to Yanks," *The New York Times*, May 22, 1920, p. 19; Vila, "Gotham Glad Yanks Don't Have to Move," *The Sporting News*, May 27, 1920, p. 1; "Hunt for Home Is Spared to Yanks," *The New York Times*, May 22, 1920, p. 19.

33. McGeehan, "Substitute Vick's Double Clears Bases in the Third," *The New York Tribune*, May 19, 1920, p. 12; McGeehan, "Ban Johnson Comes to Aid of Two 'Orphan Colonels,'" *The New York Tribune*, May 22, 1920, p. 14; McGeehan, "Mighty Slugger Hits Ball over Grand Stand Flag Pole," *The New York Tribune*, May 24, 1920, p. 12; "Ruth Spurns Lower Stand in Hitting His Home Runs," *The New York Times*, May 24, 1920, p. 19; "Ruth Belts Ball out of the Park," *The New York Times*, May 24, 1920, p. 18.

34. McGeehan, "Mogridge Bags First Victory of Season, 4-1," *The New York Tribune*, May 27, 1920, p. 14.

35. "Bob Shawkey in Fist Fight with Umpire," *The New York Tribune*, May 28, 1920, p. 16; "Ruth's Record of Four Homers in 3 Days Only Once Equaled," *The New York Times*, May 28, 1920, p. 14; "Babe Ruth Bangs

out Two Homers," *The New York Times*, May 28, 1920, p. 14; "Yanks Once More Trounce Red Sox," *The New York Times*, May 29, 1920, p. 19.

36. "Comment on Current Events in Sports," *The New York Times*, May 31, 1920, p. 13.

37. McGeehan, "In All Fairness," *The New York Tribune*, May 31, 1920, p. 12.

38. Ibid.

39. Ibid.

40. Ibid.

41. McGeehan, "Eight in Row for Hugmen; Rallies Defeat Senators," *The New York Tribune*, June 1, 1920, p. 12.

42. McGeehan, "Ruth Turns to Pitching to Help out Teammates," *The New York Tribune*, June 2, p. 12.

43. McGeehan, "Huggins' Climbers Lose, 6-7, after Winning 10 Straight," *The New York Tribune*, June 3, 1920, p. 12; "Babe Ruth Hits 3 More Home Runs," *The New York Times*, June 3, 1920, p. 12.

44. "Yanks Show Great Power with Stick," *The New York Times*, June 6, 1920, sect. 8, p. 2; "Yankees Play before 108,200 Fans in 5 Consecutive Days," *The New York Times*, June 6, 1920, sect. 8, p. 2; "Babe Ruth Hits 3 More Home Runs," p. 12; "Speaker Leads in the American; Hornsby Sets Pace in National," *The New York Times*, June 6, 1920, sect. 8, p. 2.

45. "Yanks Reach Top of League Ladder," *The New York Times*, May 7, 1920, p. 18; "Major League Baseballs Not Changed One Iota, Says Shibe," *The New York Times*, June 6, 1920, sect. 8, p. 2; Isaminger, "Heavy Hitting Not Due to New Sphere," *The Sporting News*, June 10, 1920, p. 1.

46. Rice, "The Spotlight," *The New York Tribune*, June 10, 1920, p. 14; McGeehan, "Huggins' Clan Evens Series in a Heavy Slugging Match," *The New York Tribune*, June 14, 1920, p. 10; "Yanks Bury Indians under 14-0 Defeat," *The New York Times*, June 14, 1920, p. 14; McGeehan, "Coveleskie Again Checks Hugmen's Dash to Front," *The New York Tribune*, June 15, 1920, p. 12.

47. McGeehan, "Hugmen Pull out Victory in Last Two Innings, 7-4," *The New York Tribune*, June 17, 1920, p. 12; "Babe Ruth Slams Another of Them," *The New York Times*, June 18, 1920, p. 13; McGeehan, "Two on Bases When Slugger Clears Fence," *The New York Tribune*, June 18, 1920, p. 12.

48. McGeehan, "Ruth Docile, but Shawkey Pulls through for Victory," *The New York Tribune*, Jun 19, 1920, p. 10; "Yanks Again Turn Chicago into Camp," *The New York Times*. June 19, 1920, p. 16; McGeehan, "Ruth, Injured, Is Forced to Quit Game in Fourth," *The New York Tribune*, June 20, 1920, p. 16; "Yankees Downed in 10 Innings, 6-5," *The New York Times*, June 20, 1920, sect. 9, p. 2.

49. Rice, "The Spotlight," *The New York Tribune*, June 20, 1920, p. 16; McGeehan, "In All Fairness," *The New York Tribune*, June 21, 1920, p. 11.

50. Lane, "Secret of My Heavy Hitting: An Interview with the King of Sluggers," *Baseball Magazine* 25 (August 1920): 419.

51. Ibid, pp. 419–20.

52. Ibid., p. 420.

53. Ibid.

54. Ibid., pp. 422, 465.

55. Phelon, "A Close up Snap Shot of the Pennant Race," *Baseball Magazine* 25 (August 1920): 437; R. J. Kelly, "Red Sox Clinch Pastime with Three Runs in the Ninth," *The New York Tribune*, June 26, 1920, p. 10; "Ruth Makes Two, but Yankees Lose," *The New York Times*, June 26, 1920, p. 12.

56. McGeehan, "In All Fairness," *The New York Tribune*, June 28, 1920, p. 11.

57. Ibid.

58. "The Verdict is Clear Enough," *The Sporting News*, June 24, 1920, p. 4.

59. "Ruth Escapes when Auto Is Smashed," *The New York Times*, July 8, 1920, p. 12; "Yankees Battling Squarely with Old Jinx Still on Their Trail," *The Sporting News*, July 15, 1920, p. 1; "Ruth Makes 25th and Yankees Win," *The New York Times*, July 10, 1920, p. 8; "Ruth Has Hit 12 Homers off Left-Handers, 13 off Right," *The New York Times*, July 10, 1920, p. 8.

60. "Babe Whales out Another of Them," *The New York Times*, July 12, 1920, p. 10.

61. "Ruth's 29th Wins Overtime Battle," *The New York Times*, July 16, 1920, p. 13; Vila, "Fresh Tales of Woe Come from Camp of the Yankees," *The Sporting News*, July 22, 1920, p. 1; "Ruth Still Has 61 Games in which to Add to Record," *The New York Times*, July 16, 1920, p. 13.

62. "Babe Sets Record, then Adds Another," *The New York Times*, July 20, 1920, p. 8; "Yanks Break Even with White Sox," *The New York Times*, July 21, 1920, p. 14; "Yanks-White Sox Series Sets a New Record for Attendance," *The New York Times*, July 21, 1920, p. 14.

63. "Yanks Take Lead in Pennant Race," *The New York Times*, July 24, 1920, p. 10; "Indians Win Final Game from Yanks," *The New York Times*, July 25, 1920, p. 18.

64. "Yanks Give Browns Fearful Larruping," *The New York Times*, July 31, 1920, p. 8; "Yankee Twirlers Suffer a Mauling," *The New York Times*, August 1, 1920, p. 20.

65. "Huge Throng Sees Yankees Shut Out," *The New York Times*, August 2, 1920, p. 10; "Yankees Greatest Drawing Card in Baseball History," *The New York Times*, August 2, 1920, p. 10.

66. "25,000 Chicagoans Cheer Ruth's 38th," *The New York Times*, August 3, 1920, p. 11.

67. "Ruth Scores His Forty-First Homer," *The New York Times*, August 7, 1920, p. 6.

68. "Chapman Suffers Skull Fracture," *The New York Times*, August 17, 1920, p. 14.

69. Phelon, "The Checkered Current of 1920 Baseball History," *Baseball Magazine* 25 (October 1920): 535, 537.

70. An Interview with Ray Schalk, "Why Outguessing Ruth is Baseball's Toughest Problem," *Baseball Magazine* 25 (October 1920): 519–21, 557.

71. "Ruth's Blow Fails to Rescue Yanks," *The New York Times*, August 20, 1920, p. 10.

72. "Ruth Will Be out Ten Days with Infected Right Wrist," *The New York Times*, August 29, 1920, p. 17; "Babe's Two Homers Establish Record," *The New York Times*, September 5, 1920, p. 15.

73. An interview with Chet Thomas, "Babe Ruth the Super Player," *Baseball Magazine* 26 (November 1920): 586.

74. Ibid., p. 586, 611.

75. "Bodie out with a Broken Ankle," *The New York Times*, September 9, 1920, p. 12; "Ruths Gets No. 47 but Yankees Lose," *The New York Times*, September 10, 1920, p. 14.

76. "Ruth Injury Story a Gamblers' Canard," *The New York Times*, September 10, 1920, p. 17.

77. "Ruth Gets No. 47 but Yankees Lose," *The New York Times*, September 19, 1920, p. 14; "Another for Babe Helps Yanks Win," *The New York Times*, September 11, 1920, p. 9; "Ruth's 49th Brings Victory to Yanks," *The New York Times*, September 14, 1920, p. 13.

78. "Hugmen Drop Down Ladder and Kill Pennant Chances," *The New York Tribune*, September 19, 1920, p. 18; Vila, "Only Those Blind to Reason Can See Hope for Yankees," *The Sporting News*, September 23, 1920, p. 1.

79. McGeehan, "In All Fairness," *The New York Tribune*, September 20, 1920, p. 13; "Ruth in a New Role," *The Sporting News*, September 30, 1920, p. 4.

80. "Ruth Crashes out Homers 50 and 51," *The New York Times*, September 25, 1920, p. 9.

81. "Ruth Crashes out Two More Homers," *The New York Times*, September 28, 1920, p. 9; "Yankees Wind up by Winning Two," *The New York Times*, September 30, 1920, p. 10.

82. Phelon, "A Brief Review of the Year's Campaign," *Baseball Magazine* 26 (December 1920): 343.

83. Macbeth, "Ruth Features Great Season; Yanks Prosper," *The New York Tribune*, December 26, 1920, p. 19; John F. Foster, "Introduction," *Spalding's Official Base Ball Guide 1921*, ed. John B. Foster (New York: American Sports Publishing Company, 1921), p. 3; Irving B. Sanborn, "American League Season of 1920," in *Spalding's Official Base Ball Guide of 1921*, p. 133.

## 12. A Season of Fortitude: Tris's and Robbie's Men of Summer

1. Y. R. Young, "Ruth as Yank Does Not Scare Indians," *The Sporting News*, January 15, 1920, p. 1.

2. Young, "You Don't Hear of Indian Holdouts," *The Sporting News*, February 5, 1920, p. 1; Young, "Speaker Dopes out What He Must Beat," *The Sporting News*, March 18, 1920, p. 1.

3. "Too Much Flag Talk to Please Speaker," *The Sporting News*, March 25, 1920, p. 1.

4. Rice, "Ebbets Crowed Too Soon so It Seems," *The Sporting News*, March 11, 1920, p. 3; Phelon, "Recent Echoes from the Big League Circuits," p. 586.

5. Rice, "The Spotlight," *The New York Tribune*, April 11, 1920, p. 18.

6. McCarthy, "*Giants and Yanks Picked as Likely Flag Winners*," *The New York Tribune*, April 11, 1920, p. 19.

7. "Bats Win for Cleveland," *The New York Times*, April 15, 1920, p. 13.

8. "Dodgers Open with an Easy Victory," *The New York Times*, April 15, 1920, p. 12.

9. "Long Tie in Hub Sets New Record," *The New York Times*, May 2, 1920, p. 20; "Major League Record Broken; Score Is 1 to 1," *The New York Tribune*, May 2, 1920, p. 18.

10. Rice, "The Spotlight," *The New York Tribune*, May 6, 1920, p. 14.

11. Ibid.

12. Young, "Indians Doing All that Can Be Asked," *The Sporting News*, May 27, 1920, p. 1; Wilbur Wood, "Rookie Thinks It's Really Scandalous," *The Sporting News*, June 10, 1920, p. 1.

13. "Speaker Leads in the American; Hornsby Sets Pace in National," *The New York Times*, June 6, 1920, part 8, p. 2.

14. Phelon, "Flashlights on the Pennant Race," *Baseball Magazine* 25 (September 1920): 491, 493.

15. Wood, "Indians Chuckle with Glee as They Study the Schedule," *The Sporting News*, July 15, 1920, p. 1.

16. Ibid; "Leading Batsmen of the Major Baseball Leagues," *The New York Times*, July 31, 1920, p. 8.

17. Wood, "Speaker Sets Pace in Indians' Spurt," *The Sporting News*, July 22, 1920, p. 1.

18. "Chapman Suffers Skull Fracture," p. 14; "Ray Chapman Dies; Mays Exonerated," *The New York Times*, August 18, 1920, p. 15.

19. "The Red Sox Bean Ballers," *The Sporting News*, May 3, 1917, p. 4; Weart, "Weart Is Sarcastic at Bean Ball Alibis," *The Sporting News*, May 10, 1917, p. 1.

20. "Discuss Plan to Bar Mays," *The New York Times*, August 18, 1920, p. 15; "Chapman Dies; McGeehan, Mays Absolved of All Blame," *The New York Tribune*, August 18, 1920, p. 1; Vila, "Joe Vila as an Eye Witness Exonerates Mays from Blame," *The Sporting News*, August 28, 1920, p. 1.

21. "Chapman Dies; Mays Absolved of All Blame," p. 1.

22. "Umpires Criticise (sic) Mays," *The New York Times*, August 19, 1920, p. 10.

23. McGeehan, "In All Fairness," *The New York Tribune*, August 23, 1920, p. 11; "Mays May Not Pitch Again, Says Johnson," *The New York Times*, August 21, 1920, p. 8.

24. McGeehan, "A Square Deal for Carl Mays," *The New York Tribune*, August 19, 1920, p. 10; "The Pitch That Kills," *The Sporting News*, August 26, 1920, p. 4; "Talk of Baseball Strike Dies Away," *The New York Times*, August 28, 1920, p. 8.

25. McGeehan, "Star Infielder of Cleveland Hit in Head by Pitched Ball; Fate in Doubt at Midnight," *The New York Tribune*, August 17, 1920, p. 12.

26. Mike Sowell, *The Pitch that Killed: Carl Mays, Ray Chapman and the Pennant Race of 1920* (New York: Macmillan Publishing Company, 1989); McGeehan, "Chapman Dies; Mays Absolved of All Blame," *The New York Tribune*, August 18, 1920, p. 1; "Cleveland Team to Mourn at Chapman's Bier," *The New York Tribune*, August 19, 1920, p. 10; "Cleveland Mourns Favorite Player," *The New York Times*, August 19, 1920, p. 10.

27. "Chapman Services to Be Held Today," *The New York Times*, August 20, 1920, p. 10; "Thousands Attend Chapman Funeral," *The New York Times*, August 21, 1920, p. 8.

28. Phelon, "The Checkered Current of 1920 Baseball History," *Baseball Magazine* 25 (October 1920): 537.

29. Ibid., pp. 535–36.

30. "Speeding Giants Turn back Giants," *The New York Times*, September 27, 1920, p. 1.

31. McGeehan, "In All Fairness," *The New York Tribune*, September 27, 1920, p. 11.

32. Ibid.

33. Wood, "Two Recruits Keep Cleveland in Race," *The Sporting News*, September 23, 1920, p. 1.

34. Ibid.

# 13. A Season of Infamy: Gambling and the Chicago White Sox

1. Daniel E. Ginsburg, *The Fix Is In: A History of Baseball Gambling and Game Fixing Scandals* (Jefferson, North Carolina: McFarland & Company, Inc., 1995), pp. 208–210.

2. Bill Veeck with Ed Linn, *The Hustler's Handbook* (New York: G. P. Putnam's Sons, 1965), pp. 256–57.

3. "Editorial Comment," *Baseball Magazine* 24 (February 1920): 519.

4. Ibid.

5. Ibid.

6. Ibid.

7. Ibid.

8. Ibid., p. 530.

9. "Curing a Cancer with Prayer," *The Sporting News*, January 1, 1920, p. 1.

10. Ibid.

11. Rusty, "Ray Schalk Never Hinted at Anything Wrong in Series," *The Sporting News*, January 8, 1920, p. 1.

12. "Editorial Comment," *Baseball Magazine* 24 (March 1920): n.p.

13. Ibid.

14. Reichow, "Gandil Quite Positive, but He Can't Keep away from It," *The Sporting News*, March 11, 1920, p. 1.

15. Elbert Sanders, "White Sox Finally Get to Work for Another Season," *The Sporting News*, March 18, 1920, p. 1.

16. Veeck, *The Hustler's Handbook*, pp. 265–66; "American League Player's Contract" for Joe Jackson, Joseph Jefferson Jackson Papers, National Baseball Hall of Fame Library.

17. Stein, *The Ginger Kid*, pp. 200–01; "Threaten to Drop Stars," *The New York Times*, March 27, 1920, p. 16.

18. "The World of Sports," *The Chicago Whip*, March 27, 1920, p. 5.

19. Reichow, "Eagerness to Know how Commy Fixed It," *The Sporting News*, April 1, 1920, p. 1.

20. Ibid.

21. "Weaver Rejoins White Sox to Play out His Contract," *The New York Times*, April 3, 1920, p. 18; Reichow, "Gleason like Truth and Won't Stay Put," *The Sporting News*, April 15, 1920, p. 1.

22. Rice, "The Spotlight," *The New York Tribune*, April 10, 1920, p. 12.

23. Ray McCarthy, "Giants and Yanks Picked as Likely Flag Winners," *The New York Tribune*, April 11, 1920, p. 19; Phelon, "Who Will Win the Big League Pennants?," p. 663.

24. Reichow, "Mitch Has Reason Enough for Worry," *The Sporting News*, April 22, 1920, p. 1; Sanders, "Little Sunshine in Life of Chicago Fans," *The Sporting News*, April 29, 1920, p. 1.

25. Asinof, *Eight Men Out*, p. 145.

26. Reichow, "Why Do Honest Ball Players Stand for Crooks in Ranks?," *The Sporting News*, May 6, 1920, p. 1.

27. Reichow, "National Gets Results in Its Crusade against Gamblers," *The Sporting News*, May 13, 1920, p. 1.

28. Vila, "Death of Sparrow a Climax to Yank Woe," *The Sporting News*, May 13, 1920, p. 1.

29. Phelon, "The Season's First Month in Review," *Baseball Magazine* 25 ( July 1920): 383; Rice, "The Spotlight," *The New York Tribune*, May 13, 1920, p. 14.

30. Rice, "The Spotlight," *The New York Tribune*, May 16, 1920, p. 18.

31. "WORTH MOST ANY PRICE," *The Sporting News*, May 20, 1920, p. 1.

32. "Decide on Drastic Action against Baseball Betting," *The New York Times*, May 22, 1920, p. 19; "Launch Drive on Baseball Gamblers," *The New York Times*, May 25, 1920, p. 12; "47 Arrested in Chicago," *The New York Times*, May 25, 1920, p. 12; "More Ball Park Arrests," *The New York Times*, May 28, 1920, p. 14; "Six More Arrests Made," *The New York Times*, May 29, 1920, p. 19.

33. "Magee Loses Suit against the Cubs," *The New York Times*, June 10, 1920, p. 12; Editorial Comment," *Baseball Magazine* 25 (August 1920): 418.

34. Ibid.

35. Reichow, "First of July Finds White Sox Talking of a Pennant Drive," *The Sporting News*, July 1, 1920, p. 1.

36. Reichow, "Faith in Themselves Has Lot to Do with White Sox Success," *The Sporting News*, July 22, 1920, p. 1.

37. Asinof, *Eight Men Out*, pp. 145–47.

38. "25,000 Chicagoans Cheer Ruth's 38th," p. 11; Phelon, "The Checkered Current of 1920 Baseball History," *Baseball Magazine* 25 (October 1920): 537.

39. "A Lesson for Some People," *The Sporting News*, August 12, 1920, p. 4.

40. Reichow, "Charity Asked for in Carl Mays' Case," *The Sporting News*, August 26, 1920, p. 1; Asinof, *Eight Men Out*, p. 147.

41. Rice, "The Spotlight," *The New York Tribune*, August 25, 1920, p. 8.

42. Asinof, *Eight Men Out*, p. 148.

43. Ibid.; Ginsburg, *The Fix Is In*, pp. 132–33.

44. Rice, "The Spotlight," *The New York Tribune*, September 5, 1920, p. 14.

45. Seal Rock, "Players Tardy in Their Part toward Keeping Game Clean," *The Sporting News*, August 26, 1920, p. 3.

46. "Cubs Are Named in Gambling Charges," *The New York Times*, September 5, 1920, p. 16; "Baseball Writers to Probe Charges," *The New York Times*, September 6, 1920, p. 8.

47. McGeehan, "In All Fairness," *The New York Tribune*, September 6, 1920, p. 9.

48. Ibid.; Sanders, "Veeck Shows Vigor in Probing Charges," *The Sporting News*, September 9, 1920, p. 1; "Jury to Probe Charges," *The New York Times*, September 8, 1920,

p. 12; "A New Friend on High," *The Sporting News*, September 16, 1920, p. 4.

49. Sanders, "Veecks Shows Vigor in Probing Charges," p. 1.

50. Reichow, "Gleason Begins to Prod His White Sox," *The Sporting News*, September 16, 1920, p. 1.

51. Rice, "The Spotlight," *The New York Tribune*, September 14, 1920, p. 12.

52. Reichow, "Chicago Fans Held Breath for Awhile," *The Sporting News*, September 23, 1920, p. 1.

53. Ibid.

54. "Baseball Chiefs Called in Inquiry," *The New York Times*, September 21, 1920, p. 8.

55. Ibid.

## 14. The Scandal Unveiled and One Innocent Amid the Black Sox

1. "Seven Chicago Players Accused by Prosecutor," *The New York Tribune*, September 23, 1920, p. 14; "Says 1919 World's Series Was Fixed," *The New York Times*, September 23, 1920, p. 17.

2. "Giant Pitcher Chief Witness in Ball Probe," *The New York Tribune*, September 24, 1920, p. 10.

3. Stein, *The Ginger Kid*, p. 224.

4. "Scandal in Baseball," *The New York Times*, September 24, 1920, p. 14.

5. "Grand Jury Finds World Series 'Fixer,'" *The New York Tribune*, September 25, 1920, p. 1.

6. Ibid; "Grand Jury Hears World Series Plot," *The New York Times*, September 25, 1920, p. 9.

7. "Grand Jury Finds World Series 'Fixer,'" p. 10.

8. Ibid; "Grand Jury Hears World Series Plot," p. 9.

9. "Charges Series 'Fixing' Began in August, 1919," *The New York Tribune*, September 26, 1920, p. 1.

10. Ibid., p. 1.

11. "Heydler Gives out Facts on Ball Scandal," *The New York Tribune*, September 27, 1920, p. 1.

12. Ibid., pp. 1, 11.

13. Ibid, p. 11; Asinof, *Eight Men Out*, p. 167.

14. Asinof, *Eight Men Out*, pp. 63, 125, 166.

15. "White Sox Owner Convinced that Series Was Fixed," *The New York Times*, September 27, 1920, p. 1.

16. Ibid., p. 8.

17. Sanders, "Silver Linings for Game's Dark Cloud," *The Sporting News*, September 30, 1920, p. 1.

18. Isaminger, "Public in No Humor for Any More Baseball Whitewashes," *The Sporting News*, September 30, 1920, p. 1.

19. McGeehan, "In All Fairness," *The New York Tribune*, September 27, 1920, p. 11.

20. "Comment on Current Events in Sports," *The New York Times*, September 27, 1920, p. 11.

21. Ibid.

22. "Sox Players Sold Series, Says Maharg," *The New York Tribune*, September 28, 1920, p. 1.

23. "New Witness Tells of Baseball Plot," *The New York Times*, September 28, 1920, p. 1.

24. Ibid., p. 10.

25. Ibid.

26. "Eight White Sox Players Are Indicted on Charge of Fixing 1919 World Series; Cicotte Got $10,000 and Jackson $5,000," *The New York Times*, September 29, 1920, pp. 1, 2; "Eight White Sox Are Indicted; Cicotte and Jackson Confess Gamblers Paid Them $15,000," *The New York Tribune*, September 29, 1920, p. 2.

27. "Eight White Sox Players Are Indicted on Charge of Fixing 1919 World Series," p. 2.

28. "Two Gamblers Indicted; More Players Confess Plot to Throw Games," *The New York Tribune*, September 30, 1920, p. 2.

29. "Eight White Sox Players Are Indicted on Charge of Fixing 1919 World Series," p. 1; "Eight White Sox Are Indicted; Cicotte and Jackson Confess Gamblers Paid Them $15,000," p. 1; "Will Reinstate Innocent, Drive Guilty from Game, Says Comiskey," *The New York Tribune*, September 29, 1920, p. 1.

30. "Yankee Owners Give Praise to Comiskey and Offer Him Use of Their Whole Team," *The New York Times*, September 29, 1920, p. 1.

31. "Eight White Sox Are Indicted; Cicotte and Jackson Confess Gamblers Paid Them $15,000," p. 2; "Indicted Ball Players Include Famous Stars," *The New York Tribune*, September 29, 1920, p. 2.

32. Ibid.

33. "Two Gamblers Indicted; More Players Confess Plot to Throw Games," p. 1; "Innocent White Sox Meet," *The New York Times*, September 30, 1920, p. 2.

34. "Indict Two Gamblers in Baseball Plot; Men Named by Williams in Confession; Inquiry Here to Guard the 1920 Series," *The New York Times*, September 30, 1920, p. 1.

35. "Two Gamblers Indicted; More Players Confess Plot to Throw Games," p. 1.

36. Ibid., p. 2.

37. Ibid.

38. Ibid.

39. Ibid.

40. Ibid.

41. Ed R. Hughes, "Baseball Bigger than Crooks in It," *The San Francisco Chronicle*, September 29, 1920, p. 10.

42. Abe Kemp, "Get Rid of the Crooks," *The San Francisco Bulletin*, September 30, 1920, p. 14.

43. "The Baseball Scandal," *The Los Angeles Times*, September 30, 1920, part 2, p. 4.

44. Rice, "The Spotlight," *The New York Tribune*, September 30, 1920, p. 12.

45. Ibid.

46. "Baseball Inquiry Will Go through to End, Says Judge," *The New York Times*, October 1, 1920, p. 1.

47. Ibid; "Grand Jury to Push Baseball Quiz to Limit," *The New York Tribune*, October 1, 1920, p. 2.

48. "Herzog Slashed by Fan at Joliet Ball Park," *The New York Tribune*, October 1, 1920, p. 1; "Herzog Is Stabbed Three Times by Fan," *The New York Times*, October 1, 1920, p. 1: "'Benedict Arnolds' of White Sox Denounced by Boston Newsboys," *The New York Tribune*, October 1, 1920, p. 1.

49. "No Crime?," *The New York Times*, October 1, 1920, p. 10.

50. Asinof, *Eight Men Out*, p. 208.

51. "Jenkins Tells how White Sox Men Lost Games," *The Sacramento Bee*, October 2, 1920, p. 23.

52. "Hoyne Says 1920 Series Was about to Be Fixed," *The New York Times*, October 2, 1920, p. 3; "A Plain Duty Neglected," *The New York Times*, October 2, 1920, p. 14; "Converts Chicago Jury to Continue Inquiry," *The New York Times*, October 3, 1920, p. 2.

53. "Dodgers Cleared of Any Suspicion in Coming Series," *The New York Times*, October 3, 1920, p. 1.

54. William L. Chenery, "Why Gambling and Baseball Are Enemies," *The New York Times*, October 3, 1920, sect. 8, p. 1.

55. "White Sox Accuse Teammates," *The New York Times*, October 4, 1920, p. 8.

56. "When Baseball Gets before the Grand Jury," *The Sporting News*, October 7, 1920, p. 2.

57. Ibid.

58. "Comiskey Gives $1500 to Each Honest Player," *The New York Times*, October 5, 1920, p. 3; Charles Comiskey to Edward Murphy, October 2, 1920, Black Sox File, National Baseball Hall of Fame Library.

59. McGeehan, "In All Fairness," *The New York Tribune*, October 1920, p. 13.

60. "Now That Comiskey Knows," *The Sporting News*, October 7, 1920, p. 4.

61. "Lesson to Players They Won't Forget," *The Sporting News*, October 7, 1920, p. 5.

62. Reichow, "Chicago Fans Grieve Most for Weaver and Still Hope for Him," *The Sporting News*, October 7, 1920, p. 2.

63. Ibid.

64. Phelon, "A Stirring Month in Baseball," *Baseball Magazine* 26 (January 1921): 385–386.

65. Veeck, *The Hustler's Handbook*, pp. 283–284.

66. Frank G. Klein, "Collins Charges 1920 Games 'Fixed,'" *Collyer's Eye*, October 30, 1920, pp. 1, 5.

## *15. Savior of the Game: Baseball's Great Dictator*

1. Pietrusza, *Judge and Jury*, p. 149.

2. "Two Hundred Reds Taken in Chicago," *The New York Times*, January 2, 1920, p. 1.

3. "Second Raid Made on Chicago Reds," *The New York Times*, January 3, 1920, p. 1.

4. "Reds Raided in Scores of Cities; 2,600 Arrests, 700 in New York; Deportation Hearings Begin Today," *The New York Times*, January 3, 1920, p. 1; "Soviet Ark Moves Slowly," *The New York Times*, January 3, 1920, p. 2.

5. "Heydler Advocates New Baseball Body," *The New York Times*, October 1, 1920, p. 2.

6. "Four Clubs Move to Put Baseball in People's Hands," *The New York Times*, October 2, 1920, p. 1.

7. Rice, "In the Spotlight," *The New York Tribune*, October 5, 1920, p. 13; McGeehan, "In All Fairness," *The New York Tribune*, October 5, 1920, p. 13.

8. "Editorial Comment," *Baseball Magazine* 26 (December 1920): 315–16, 334.

9. "Tris Speaker, the Star of the 1920 Baseball Season," *Baseball Magazine* 26 (December 1920): 317.

10. "Owners of Five Clubs Talk over Lasker Plan," *The New York Times*, October 6, 1920, p. 3; "National League Favors a Change," *The New York Times*, October 8, 1920, p. 16.

11. McGeehan, "In All Fairness," *The New York Tribune*, October 11, 1920, p. 11.

12. Ibid.

13. "Johnson Opposes Baseball Meeting," *The New York Times*, October 15, 1920, p. 14; "Heydler Hurls the First Brick in Baseball War," *The New York Tribune*, October 15, 1920, p. 13.

14. "Magnates Would Reorganize, and Abolish Old Commission," *The New York Tribune*, October 19, 1920, p. 12: "Heydler Is Ready to Take Orders from New Chief," *The New York Tribune*, October 19, 1920, p. 12.

15. "Twelve-Club Circuit Threat of Ban's Foes," *The New York Tribune*, October 20, 1920, p. 10; "Anxious Only to Uplift Game, Says Ruppert," *The New York Tribune*, October 21, 1920, p. 12.

16. Vila, "Vila Gives Three Hoots for Lasker Plan and Its Boosters," *The Sporting News*, October 21, 1920, p. 1.

17. McGeehan, "Baseball Fans Want Action," *The New York Tribune*, October 22, 1920, p. 13.

18. "Wadsworth Is Ready to Help Rescue Baseball," *The New York Tribune*, October 23, 1920, p. 23.

19. "Judge Kenesaw M. Landis ...," *The New York Tribune*, October 23, 1920, p. 23.

20. "Indicts Three More in Baseball Fixing," *The New York Times*, October 23, 1920, p. 4; "Rothstein Cleared in Baseball Fixing," *The New York Times*, October 27, 1920, p. 17.

21. Frank G. Menke, "Blast for Magnates Who Would Make Johnson Goat," *The Sporting News*, October 28, 1920, p. 3.

22. "Grand Jury Inquiry Climaxed by Proof that Comiskey Was Told," *The Sporting News*, November 4, 1920, p. 3.

23. "Comiskey Denies He Withheld Plot Evidence," *The New York Tribune*, November 5, 1920, p. 15.

24. "Two Ball Players Give Up," *The New York Times*, November 6, 1920, p. 18.

25. "Finds Baseball Generally Honest," *The New York Times*, November 7, 1920, sect. 2, p. 1.

26. "Club Owners Vote for New League and Baseball War," *The New York Times*, November 8, 1920, p. 1.

27. "Baseball Conflict Shifts to Minors," *The New York Times*, November 10, 1920, pp. 1, 15.

28. Kemp, "Baseball War Means Large Salaries and Army of Ball Players Are Praying for It," *The San Francisco Bulletin*, November 11, 1920, p. 1; "Baseball Troubles Near Settlement," *The New York Times*, November 11, 1921, p. 1; Macbeth, "Bid to Landis Master Stroke by Reformers," *The New York Tribune*, November 13, 1920, p. 13.

29. "Landis Heads Baseball after Peace Is Made," *The New York Tribune*, November 13, 1920, p. 1; "Landis Baseball Chief," *The Chicago American*, November 12, 1920, p. 1; "Landis Heads Baseball," *The Chicago Herald Examiner*, November 13, 1920, p. 1.

30. "Landis Heads Baseball after Peace Is Made," p. 1; "Baseball Peace Declared; Landis Named Dictator," *The New York Times*, November 13, 1920, p 1; "Judge Landis was hearing ... ," *The New York Tribune*, November 13, 1920, p. 13; "Doing It for the Kiddies," *The St. Louis Globe-Democrat*, November 13, 1920, Landis Scrapbook.

31. Landis telegram, November 12, 1920, Kenesaw Mountain Landis Papers, National Baseball Hall of Fame Library; "Landis Heads Baseball after Peace Is Made," p. 13; "Baseball Peace Declared," p. 1.

32. Macbeth, "Federal Laws Urged to Stamp Out Baseball," *The New York Tribune*, November 16, 1920, p. 13.

33. "Comment on Current Events in Sports," *The New York Times*, November 15, 1920, p. 18; "Another Peace Treaty," *The New York Times*, November 15, 1920, p. 14; "Landis Has No Fears about Ability to Handle Two Jobs," *The New York Times*, November 17, 1920, p. 14.

34. "Landis Calls on Garry Herrmann," *The New York Times*, November 21, 1920, sect. 8, p. 2.

35. McGeehan, "In All Fairness," November 22, 1920, p. 12; Reichow, "Magnates Should Press Issue of Cleaning out the Crooks," *The Sporting News*, November 25, 1920, p. 1.

36. Dean Snyder, "A Walk and a Talk with Judge Landis," *The Sporting News*, November 25, 1920, p. 3.

37. Lane, "Baseball's Dictator," *Baseball Magazine* 24 (February 1920): 413–16, 448, 452.

38. "Landis Discusses Baseball Reform," *The New York Times*, November 29, 1920, p. 18; "New Head of National Game Says Gambling Must Stop," *The New York Tribune*, November 29, 1920, p. 12.

39. Reichow, "Landis only Waits Authority to Startle Baseball World," *The Sporting News*, December 2, 1920, p. 1.

40. Vila, "Landis Must Fight for His Principles," *The Sporting News*, December 2, 1920, p. 2.

41. Harry F. Pierce, "Judge Landis Here on Visit Seeks Fans' Aid in Gambling Crusade," *The St. Louis Star*, December 4, 1920, Landis Scrapbook.

42. McGeehan, "In All Fairness," *The New York Tribune*, December 13, 1920, p. 12; Macbeth, "New Agreements Indorsed (sic) by Committees Representing both Major and Minor Leagues," *The New York Tribune*, December 13, 1920, p. 12; Vila, "Landis Given All Powers Asked for to Keep Baseball Clean," *The Sporting News*, December 16, 1920, p. 1; Reichow, "Johnson Endorses Power Given Landis," *The Sporting News*, December 16, 1920, p. 1.

43. McGeehan, "In All Fairness," *The New York Tribune*, December 20, 1920, p. 13; "Huston Launches Attack on Johnson," *The New York Times*, December 21, 1920, p. 14; "Frazee Launches Attack on Johnson," *The New York Times*, December 23, 1920, p. 12; McGeehan, "In All Fairness," *The New York Tribune*, December 27, 1920, p. 10.

44. "Players' Fraternity Revived; Baseball Magnates to Be Asked for Big Salary Increases," *The New York Tribune*, December 1, 1920, p. 12.

45. Eaton, "Organized Baseball's Big Legal Battle," *Baseball Magazine* 26 (December 1920): 346, 355–356; "Judgment against Majors Reversed," *The New York Times*, December 7, 1920, p. 14; Macbeth, "Federal League Makes Legal Move Which Means Fight to Finish against Organized Baseball," *The New York Tribune*, December 24, 1920, p. 10; Eaton, "Baseball's Great Legal Victory," *Baseball Magazine* 24 (February 1920): 425.

46. "Let the Reserve Clause Rest," *The Sporting News*, December 16, 1920, p. 4.

47. "Players Plan Fight," *The New York Times*, December 19, 1920, p. 19; Macbeth, "Los Angeles Judge Quashes Indictment of Ball Players Accused of 'Throwing' Games," *The New York Tribune*, December 25, 1920, p. 8.

48. Lane, "The All America Baseball Club of 1920," *Baseball Magazine* 26 (December 1920): 339–42.

## 16. The Season After

1. "Majors and Minors Reach Agreement," *The New York Times*, January 13, 1921, p. 15; "Keeping Faith with Landis," *The Sporting News*, January 20, 1921, p. 4.

2. "Judge Landis Promises Hot Time for Crooks in Baseball," *The New York Times*, January 31, 1921, p. 16.

3. "Landis Impeached by Welty in House," *The New York Times*, February 15, 1921, pp. 1, 2.

4. Harvey Brougham, "America's Erratic Judge," *Overland Monthly* 77 (April 1921): 9–11.

5. Statement by Edward T. Collins to Commissioner Kenesaw M. Landis, February 19, 1921, Court Transcripts of Carl Mays and the Black Sox, the National Baseball Hall of Fame Library; Statement by George Dauss to Commissioner Kenesaw M. Landis, February 25, 1921, Court Transcripts of Carl Mays and the Black Sox, the National Baseball Hall of Fame Library; Statement by William James to Commissioner Kenesaw M. Landis, February 26, 1921, Court Transcripts of Carl Mays and the Black Sox, the National Baseball Hall of Fame Library.

6. "White Sox Players Banned by Landis," *The New York Times*, March 13, 1921, p. 16; "Indicted Players Win Point in Court," *The New York Times*, February 17, 1921, p. 2; "White Sox Trial to Be Postponed," *The New York Times*, March 14, 1921, p. 6; "Comiskey Ousts Indicted Players," *The New York Times*, March 17, 1921, p. 9.

7. "Baseball Cases Dropped in Court," *The New York Times*, March 18, 1921, p. 4; "Starts New Action against Ball Players," *The New York Times*, March 19, 1921, p. 1; "Eighteen Indicted in Baseball Fraud," *The New York Times*, March 27, 1921, p. 14.

8. "Landis Declares Kauff Ineligible," *The New York Times*, April 8, 1921, p. 14.

9. "Ousted White Sox Forming Team of Their Own," *The New York Times*, April 9, 1921, p. 12; "Playing up the Black Sox," *The Sporting News*, April 21, 1921, p. 4; Reichow, "Just like Nuts Go to See a Murderer," *The Sporting News*, May 19, 1921, p. 1.

10. McGeehan, "Miller Huggins Will Manage Yankees for Another Year," *The New York Tribune*, October 29, 1920, p. 10; "Yanks and Boston Close Big Trade," *The New York Times*, December 16, 1920, p. 22.

11. Vila, "Yankee Club Owners Pick Site for Their New Home in Bronx," *The Sporting News*, February 10, 1921, p. 1; Vila, "Yankees Need Be in No Hurry about Building New Stadium," *The Sporting News*, February 17, 1921, p. 1.

12. Lane, "Can Babe Ruth Repeat?," *Baseball Magazine* 26 (May 1921): 555–57.

13. Lane, "How Babe Ruth Wins for the New York Yankees," *Baseball Magazine* 27 (June 1921): 291.

14. "Gothams Great Opener Proof of Game's Hold on Public," *The Sporting News*, April 21, 1921, p. 1; Creamer, *Babe*, p. 238.

15. Lane, "The Home-Run Epidemic," *Baseball Magazine* 27 (July 1921): 339–40, 372–73; "Editorial Comment," *Baseball Magazine* 27 (August 1921): 386; Lane, "Has the 'Lively' Ball Revolutionized the Game?," *Baseball Magazine* 27 (September 1921): 435–39, 477–78.

16. "New Setback Halts Ball Players' Trial," *The New York Times*, July 28, 1921, p. 7.

17. "Accused Players Prosper," *The New York Times*, July 1, 1921, p. 16.

18. Johnson to Frank J. Navin, July 9, 1921, Court Transcripts of Carl Mays and the Black Sox, the National Baseball Hall of Fame Library; Frank J. Navin to Ban Johnson, July 10, 1921, Court Transcripts of Carl Mays and the Black Sox, the National Baseball Hall of Fame Library.

19. "Arguments to Quash Indictments Heard," *The Sporting News*, July 7, 1921, p. 1; Stein, *The Ginger Kid*, pp. 265–67; "White Sox Players Greet Indicted Men," *The New York Times*, July 12, 1921, p. 17; Rice, "Tom Rice Doesn't Like Way White Sox and Black Sox Mingle," *The Sporting News*, July 21, 1921, p. 3.

20. "Two Men Go Free in Baseball Case," *The New York Times*, July 28, 1921, p. 1.

21. "Asks 5-Year Term for the White Sox," *The New York Times*, July 31, 1921, p. 9.

22. Ibid.

23. Macbeth, "In All Fairness," *The New York Tribune*, August 1, 1921, p. 9.

24. "White Sox Players Are All Acquitted by Chicago Jury," *The New York Times*, August 3, 1921, p. 1.

25. "Baseball Leaders Won't Let White Sox Return to the Game," *The New York Times*, August 4, 1921, pp. 1–2.

26. Ibid., p. 1.

27. Ibid., pp. 1–2; "Gleason Bans 'Black Sox'," *The New York Times*, August 4, 1921, p. 2.

28. "Baseball Leaders Won't Let White Sox Return to the Game," p. 2; "Landis Bans Black Sox from Baseball Forever," *The New York Evening World*, August 3, 1921, p. 1; "Whitewashed White Sox Can Not Come Back," *The New York Tribune*, August 3, 1921, p. 4; "Weaver Sues White Sox Club, Claiming $20,000 in Salary," *The New York Times*, October 19, 1921, p. 15.

29. "Purified Baseball," *The New York Times*, August 4, 1921, p. 14.

30. "Jury's Decree Fails to Make Black White," *The Los Angeles Times*, August 4, 1921, sect. 3, p. 1.

31. "Editorial Comment," *Baseball Magazine* 27 (October 1921): 488; Lane, "Why Babe Ruth Has Become a National Idol," *Baseball Magazine* 27 (October 1921): 483.

32. Lane, "Why Babe Ruth Has Become a National Idol," p. 484.

33. "Yankees and Ruth Have a Gala Day," *The New York Times*, September 16, 1921, p. 13; "Ruth's 59th Homer Feature of Finale," *The New York Times*, October 3, 1921, p. 9.

34. "Players Threaten to Violate Rule," *The New York Times*, October 16, 1921, sect. 8, p. 2; "Ruth Defies K. M. Landis," *The San Francisco Bulletin*, October 17, 1921, p. 11.

35. "Ruth Defies K. M. Landis," p. 11.

36. "Fans Back of Landis," *The San Francisco Bulletin*, October 19, 1921, p. 16.

37. "Editorial Comment," *Baseball Magazine* 28 (December 1921): 578, 622.

38. Vila, "Not Conscience Alone that Caused Ruth to Change Tack," *The Sporting News*, October 27, 1921, p. 1; "Organized Revolt Behind Babe Ruth?," *The Sporting News*, October 27, 1921, p. 3; "Let the Players Get this Straight," *The Sporting News*, October 27, 1921, p. 4; "'Twill Help Game to Put Ruth in Place," *The Sporting News*, November 3, 1921, p. 4.

39. "Ruth Is Suspended; Fined Series Money," *The New York Times*, December 6,

1921, p. 22; "Ruth Eligible for Exhibition Games," *The New York Times*, December 7, 1921, p. 20.

40. Lewis, "Big Clubs Ready for Season," *The Competitor* 3 (April 1921): 37.

41. "Editorial Comment," *Baseball Magazine* 27 (June 1921): 291.

42. "National League Circuit Will Be Changed at January Meeting," *The Chicago Defender*, November 26, 1921, p. 10.

43. Foster, "Rube Foster Tells What Baseball Needs to Succeed," *The Chicago Defender*, December 10, 1921, p. 10; Foster, "Rube Foster Tells What Baseball Needs to Succeed," *The Chicago Defender*, December 17, 1921, p. 10.

44. Foster, "Players Prove Serious Drawback to Baseball," *The Chicago Defender*, December 24, 1921, p. 10; Foster, "Future of Race Umpires Depends on Men of Today," *The Chicago Defender*, December 31, 1917, p. 10.

# 17. Legacies

1. Asinof, *Eight Men Out*, pp. 279–80; "Weaver Applies to Landis for Reinstatement," *The Chicago Tribune*, January 14, 1922.

2. "Landis Turns Down Appeal of Weaver for Reinstatement," *The New York Herald Tribune*, March 14, 1927; Weaver to the Commissioner, January 29, 1953, Buck Weaver File, the National Baseball Hall of Fame Library.

3. Farrell, *My Baseball Diary*, pp. 181, 185–86; Al Wolf, "Sportraits," February 1956, Buck Weaver File, Sporting News Archives.

4. Sullivan, "The Low Down," February 1956.

5. Sec Taylor, "Sittin' In," Buck Weaver File, Sporting News Archives; Hugh Brown, "Sports Parade," *The Philadelphia Evening Bulletin*, February 2, 1956, Sporting News Archives.

6. Menke, "Landis Is Asked about Stoneham," *The Sporting News*, November 15, 1923; Menke, "Has Landis Spoiled Chance to Be of Service to Game?," *The Sporting News*, December 6, 1923.

7. "Landis' Retirement from Bench," *Sporting Life*, March 18, 1922, p. 6; "Judge Landis Dies; Baseball Czar, 78," *The New York Times*, November 26, 1944, p. 56.

8. "The Babe Ruth Papers," *Sports Illustrated* (December 21, 1959): 116; "What Is Babe Ruth Worth to the Yankees?," *The Literary Digest* 104 (March 29, 1930): p. 40.

9. Holway, *Blackball Stars: Negro League Pioneers* (New York: Carroll & Graf Publishers, 1992), p. 28; Donn Rogosin, *Invisible Men: Life in Baseball's Negro Leagues* (New York: Kodansha International, 1995), p. 184.

10. Streur, "Rube Foster," p. 186; Holway, *The Father of Black Baseball*; Normal "Tweed" Webb, "Tweed Reflects 60 Years of Records Black Greats," *The St. Louis Argus*.

11. John B. Holway, *The Father of Black Baseball*.

# Bibliography

## Primary Documents

National Baseball Hall of Fame Library, Player and Official Files:

| | | |
|---|---|---|
| Ed Barrow | Shoeless Joe Jackson | Dick Redding |
| Ray Chapman | Ban Johnson | Wilbert Robinson |
| Oscar Charleston | Judge Kenesaw Mountain | Joe Rogan |
| Charles Comiskey | Landis | Babe Ruth |
| Stanley Covelski | John Henry Lloyd | Tris Speaker |
| Jake Daubert | David Malarcher | Buck Weaver |
| Rube Foster | Carl Mays | Zach Wheat |
| William Foster | John McGraw | Smokey Joe Williams |
| Gary Herrmann | Jose Mendez | |

National Baseball Hall of Fame Library, Ashland Files:

| | | |
|---|---|---|
| Oscar Charleston | John Henry Lloyd | Joe Rogan |
| Martin Dihigo | David Malarcher | Smokey Joe Williams |
| Rube Foster | Jose Mendez | |
| William Foster | Dick Redding | |

National Baseball Hall of Fame Library, Subject Files:

| | | |
|---|---|---|
| Black Sox Papers | Gambling | Racism/Minorities |

National Baseball Hall of Fame Library, *Black Diamonds* (collection of tapes)

## Periodicals

Abbotts Monthly
The American Review of
  Reviews
Amsterdam News
The Atlantic Monthly
Baseball Digest
Baseball Monthly
Baseball Research Journal
The Baseball Blue Book
The Century Magazine
Chicago Defender
Chicago Tribune
Chicago Whip
Chico Daily-Enterprise
The Crisis

Harper's Monthly
  Magazine
Indianapolis Freeman
Kansas City Call
The Literary Digest
Los Angeles Times
The Messenger
The Nation
The National Geographic
  Magazine
New York Age
New York Herald-Tribune
New York Times
Oregonian
Outing

The Outlook
Overland Monthly
The People's Voice
Philadelphia Tribune
Pittsburgh Courier
Rising Sun
Sacramento Bee
St. Louis Argus
San Francisco Chronicle
Seattle Post-Intelligencer
Spalding's Official Base
  Ball Guide
Sporting Life
The Sporting News

## Books

Adomites, Paul, and Saul Wisnia. *Babe Ruth: His Life and Times.* Lincolnwood, Illinois: Publications International, Ltd., 1995.

Alexander, Charles. *John McGraw.* Lincoln: University of Nebraska Press, 1988.

_____. *Our Game: An American Baseball History.* New York: Henry Holt and Company, 1991.

_____. *Rogers Hornsby.* New York: Henry Holt & Co., 1995.

_____. *Ty Cobb.* New York: Oxford University Press, 1984.

Anderson, Dave, et al. *The Yankees: The Four Fabulous Eras of Baseball's Most Famous Team.* New York: Random House, 1979.

Asinof, Elliot. *America's Loss of Innocence.* New York: Donald I. Fine, Inc., 1990.

_____. *Eight Men Out: The Black Sox and the 1919 World Series.* New York: Henry Holt and Company, 1987.

Axelson, Gustav W. *"Commy": The Life Story of Charles A. Comiskey.* Chicago: The Reilly and Lee Co., 1919.

Barrow, Edward, and James M. Kahn. *My 50 Years in Baseball.* New York: Coward-McCann, 1951.

*The Baseball Encyclopedia: The Complete and Definitive Record of Major League Baseball.* Tenth Edition. New York: Macmillan, 1996.

Berrol, Selma. *The Empire City: New York and Its People, 1624–1996.* Westport, CN: Praeger, 1997.

Burk, Robert F. *Never Just a Game: Players, Owners, & American Baseball to 1920.* Chapel Hill: The University of North Carolina Press, 1994.

Chadwick, Bruce. *When the Game Was Black and White: The Illustrated History of Baseball's Negro Leagues.* New York: Abbeville Press, 1992.

Coben, Stanley. *Rebellion against Victorianism: The Impetus for Cultural Change in 1920s America.* New York: Oxford University Press, 1991.

Creamer, Robert. *Babe: The Legend Comes to Life.* New York: Simon & Schuster, 1992.

Curran, William. *Big Sticks: The Phenomenal Decade of Ruth, Gehrig, Cobb, and Hornsby.* New York: HarperPerennial, 1991.

De Valeria, Dennis, and Jeanne Burke De Valeria. *Honus Wagner: A Biography.* New York: Henry Holt, 1995.

Dixon, Phil, with Patrick J. Hannigan. *The Negro Baseball Leagues: A Photographic History.* Mattituck, NY: Amereon House, 1992.

Dumenil, Lynn. *The Modern Temper: American Culture and Society in the 1920s.* New York: Hill and Wang, 1995.

Farr, Finis. Chicago: *A Personal History of America's Most American City.* New Rochelle, New York: Arlington House, 1973.

Farrell, James T. *My Baseball Diary.* New York: A. S. Barnes, 1957.

Frommer, Harvey. *Shoeless Joe and Ragtime Baseball.* Dallas: Taylor Publishing Company, 1992.

Gershman, Michael. *Diamonds: The Evolution of the Ballpark.* Boston: Houghton Mifflin Company, 1993.

Ginsburg, Daniel E. *The Fix Is In: A History of Baseball Gambling and Game Fixing Scandals.* Jefferson, North Carolina: McFarland & Company, Inc., Publishers, 1995.

Greenberg, Eric Ralph. *The Celebrant.* New York: Everest House, 1983.

Gropman, Donald. *Say It Ain't So, Joe!: The True Story of Shoeless Joe Jackson.* New York: Carol Publishing Group, 1995.

Gutman, Dan. *Baseball Babylon: From the Black Sox to Pete Rose, the Real Stories behind The Scandals That Rocked the Game.* New York: Penguin Books, 1992.

Hall, Alvin L., ed. *Cooperstown Symposium on Baseball and the American Culture* (1989). Meckler.

Hawley, Ellis W. *The Great War and the Search for a Modern Order: A History of the American People and Their Institutions, 1917–1933.* Prospect Heights, Illinois: Waveland Press, Inc., 1997.

Holtzman, Jerome. *The Commissioners.* New York: Total Sports, 1998.

Holway, John B. *Blackball Stars: Negro League Pioneers.* New York: Carroll & Graf Publishers, 1992.

_____. *Black Diamonds: Life in the Negro Leagues from the Men Who Lived It.* Westport, CT: Meckler Books, 1989.

Honig, Donald. *Baseball America: The Heroes of the Game and the Times of Their Glory.* New York: Barnes and Noble Books, 1997.

James, Bill. *The Bill James Guide to Baseball Managers from 1870 to Today.* New York: Scribner, 1997.

_____. *The Bill James Historical Baseball Abstract.* New York: Villard Books, 1988.

Katcher, Leo. *The Big Bankroll: The Life and Times of Arnold Rothstein.* New York: Harper and Row, 1959.

Kavanagh, Jack. *Walter Johnson: A Life.* South Bend: Diamond Communications, Inc., 1996.

Keene, Kerry, et al. *The Babe in Red Stockings: An In-Depth Chronicle of Babe Ruth with the Boston Red Sox, 1914–1919.* Champaign, IL: Sagamore Publishing, 1997.

Koppett, Leonard. *Koppett's Concise History of Major League Baseball.* Philadelphia: Temple University Press, 1998.

Lieb, Fred. *Baseball as I Have Known It*. New York: A Tempo Star Book, 1977.

Lindberg, Richard Carl. *Stealing First in a Two-Team Town: The White Sox from Comiskey to Reinsdorf*. Champaign, IL: Sagamore Publishing, 1994.

Lowenfish, Lee. *The Imperfect Diamond: A History of Baseball's Labor Wars*, revised ed. New York: Da Capo Press, Inc., 1991.

Luhr, Victor. *The Great Baseball Mystery: The 1919 World Series*. South Brunswick, New York: A. S. Barnes and Co., Inc., 1966.

Malamud, Bernard. *The Natural*. New York: Harcourt Brace Jovanovich, 1952.

McCabe, Neil, and Constance McCabe. *Baseball's Golden Age: The Photographs of Charles M. Conlon*. New York: Harry N. Abrams, Inc., Publishers, 1993.

Miller, William D. *Pretty Bubbles in the Air: America in 1919*. Urbana: University of Illinois Press, 1991.

Murdock, Eugene C. *Ban Johnson: Czar of Baseball*. Westport: Greenwood Press, 1982.

_____. *Baseball Players and Their Times: Oral Histories of the Game, 1920–1940*.

_____. *Baseball between the Wars: Memories of the Game by the Men Who Played It*. Westport: Meckler, 1992.

Ottley, Roi. *The Lonely Warrior: The Life and Times of Robert S. Abbott*. Chicago: Henry Regnery & Company, 1955.

Peterson, Robert. *Only the Ball Was White: A History of Legendary Black Players and All-Black Professional Teams*. New York: Oxford University Press, 1992.

Pietrusza, David. *Judge and Jury: The Life and Times of Judge Kenesaw Mountain Landis*. South Bend: Diamond Communications, Inc., 1998.

Ribowsky, Mark. *A Complete History of the Negro Leagues 1884 to 1955*. New York: Carol Publishing Group, 1997.

Riess, Steven A. *Touching Base: Professional Baseball and American Culture in the Progressive Era*. Westport, Conn.: Greenwood Press, 1980.

Riley, James A. *The Biographical Encyclopedia of the Negro Baseball Leagues*. New York: Carroll & Graf Publishers, Inc., 1994.

Ritter, Lawrence. *The Glory of Their Times: The Story of the Early Days of Baseball Told by the Men Who Played It*. New York: William Morrow, 1986.

_____, and Donald Honig. *The Image of Their Greatness*. New York: Crown Publishers, 1979.

_____. *Lost Ballparks: A Celebration of Baseball's Legendary Fields*. New York: Penguin Studio Books, 1992.

_____ and Mark Rucker. *The Babe: The Game that Ruth Built*. New York: Total Sports, 1997.

Robinson, Ray. *Matty: An American Hero*. New York: Oxford University Press, 1993.

Rogosin, Donn. *Invisible Men: Life in Baseball's Negro Leagues*. New York: Kodansha International, 1995.

Santa Maria, Michael, and James Costello. *In the Shadows of the Diamond: Hard Times in the National Pastime*. : The Elysian Fields Press, 1992.

Seymour, Harold. *Baseball: The Early Years*. New York: Oxford University Press, 1989.

_____. *Baseball: The Golden Age*. New York: Oxford University Press, 1989.

_____. *Baseball: The People's Game*. New York: Oxford University Press, 1991.

Smelser, Marshall. *The Life That Ruth Built: A Biography*. Lincoln: University of Nebraska Press, 1993.

Sobol, Ken. *Babe Ruth and the American Dream*. New York: Ballantine Books, 1974.

Solomon, Burt. *The Baseball Timeline: The Day-by-Day History of Baseball, from Valley Forge to the Present Day.* New York: Avon Books, 1997.

Sowell, Mike. *The Pitch That Killed: Carl Mays, Ray Chapman and the Pennant Race of 1920.* New York: Macmillan Publishing Company, 1989.

Spink, J. G. Taylor. *Judge Landis and Twenty-five Years of Baseball.* New York: Thomas Y. Crowell Co., 1947.

Stein, Harry. *Hoopla.* New York: Dell Publishing, 1997.

Stein, Irving M. *The Ginger Kid: The Buck Weaver Story.* Dubuque, Iowa: The Elysian Fields Press, 1992.

Thorn, John, et al. *Total Baseball: The Official Encyclopedia of Major League Baseball.* Sixth Edition. New York: Total Sports, 1999.

Tuttle, William M. Jr. *Race Riot: Chicago in the Red Summer of 1919.* Urbana: University of Illinois Press, 1996.

Veeck, William, Jr., and Ed Linn. *The Hustler's Handbook.* New York: G. P. Putnam's Sons, 1965.

Wagenheim, Kal. *Babe Ruth: His Life and Legend.* New York: Henry Holt and Company, 1992.

White, G. Edward. *Creating the National Pastime: Baseball Transforms Itself 1903–1953.* Princeton: Princeton University Press, 1996.

White, Sol. *Sol White's History of Colored Base Ball, with Other Documents on the Early Black Game 1886–1936.* Lincoln: University of Nebraska Press, 1995.

Whitehead, Charles E. *A Man and His Diamonds.* Vantage Press, 1980.

# Index

# Index

 WEST END  10/02

BAKER & TAYLOR